Drawing
&
the Blind

JOHN M. KENNEDY

Drawing
&
the Blind

Pictures to Touch

YALE UNIVERSITY PRESS

NEW HAVEN AND LONDON

Set in Simoncini Garamond type by The Composing Room of Michigan. Printed in the United States of America by Vail-Ballou Press, Binghamton, New York.

Library of Congress Cataloging-in-Publication Data

Kennedy, John M. (John Miller), 1942–
    Drawing and the blind : pictures to touch / John M. Kennedy.
    p.   cm.
    Includes bibliographical references and index.
    ISBN 0-300-05490-4
    1. Blind—Education—Art.   2. Drawing.   I. Title.
HV1664.A75K45   1993
371.9'1452—dc20   92-40624
                                                       CIP

A catalogue record for this book is available from the British Library.

The paper in this book meets the guidelines for permanence and durability of the Committee on Production Guidelines for Book Longevity of the Council on Library Resources.

10   9   8   7   6   5   4   3   2   1

Contents

vii Preface

1 Chapter One/To Touch and to Picture the World

21 Chapter Two/Pictures, Lines, and Shape-from-Shadows

56 Chapter Three/Blind People and Outline Drawings

95 Chapter Four/Drawings by the Blind

127 Chapter Five/Drawing Development

180 Chapter Six/Perspective

216 Chapter Seven/Metaphor

252 Chapter Eight/Impressions and Universals

290 Chapter Nine/Drawing Conclusions

301 References

311 Index

Preface

Perception is successful at its job if it gives us accurate knowledge of the world and access to physical representations. Without these representations, perception is trapped in the here and now, the literal and the actual. Representation frees us from the present.

Representations take us far afield in many ways. It will be an important day in many disciplines, not just perception psychology, when we can confidently say that we understand physical representations—the pictures, images, reliefs, sculptures, charts, medical and technical displays that challenge us with scenes, some contemporary, some ancient, some plausible, some impossible.

Among the new avenues of perception and representation are "raised" pictures that can be perceived by touch and hence are accessible to blind people. The new can only be appreciated fully if its connection with the old is clear. In this case, the bridge from the old to the new is the fact that raised drawings by blind people sketching pictures for the first time are much like drawings made by sighted people who are also novices at drawing. And blind people can often identify a raised picture without any instruction in how to do so.

Trying to understand these basic abilities has led me into virtually every cranny of modern perceptual and cognitive psychology, philosophy of depiction, art history, communication theory, and rhetoric. Little wonder: perception is concerned with everything we can perceive, and pictures are concerned with what we can perceive not only in the world of material objects but also in that special world of matter governed by the intent to communicate.

I first began this work following a thesis I wrote for James J. Gibson, my mentor, a man whose life and work I treasure more each year. Eleanor J. Gibson was my adviser, too, and she provided me with more than I can put into words. I have tried to give my graduate students something of the Gibsonian heady mixture of freedom, stimulation, hard work, and straight thinking I found at Cornell. My experience at Ithaca with Mr. and Mrs. Gibson was possible because of the encouragement I got in Belfast, at Queen's University, with Peter McEwan, a warm, careful observer of psychology and students. After Cornell, I went to Harvard and fell in with a vigorous group gathered by Nelson Goodman. I taught in the Department of Social Relations at Harvard, alongside Roger Brown, Jerome Kagan, and Marshall Haith. Dr. Brown may especially appreciate the analysis here of the claim that metaphors in pictures are intelligible without explanations; Dr. Kagan may respect the large-scale investigation of drawing development leading toward consistent use of a vantage point; and Dr. Haith may value the finding that outline cannot portray black-white contours of a scene with natural illumination. Brown, Kagan, and Haith set me examples in each of these directions. The Goodman group—"Project Zero"—included David Perkins, who taught me about cubic corners and caricature, and Howard Gardner, who vitalized my interests in the arts and human development. At Project Zero I also learned a good deal from Barbara Leondar (literature), Jeanne Bamberger (music), and Diana Korzenik (depiction).

At Harvard I got to know Rudolf Arnheim personally. His work and his presence are extraordinary. He is able to teach people to see what is in a picture by way of value and meaning as well as shape. His example has given me courage to speak up for "figures of depiction" on a par with "figures of speech." I know too that he is a premier critic of the account I give of axes and outlines, vantage points and perspective, and touch and depiction.

Most of the colleagues who influenced the work presented here are acknowledged by mentioning their publications. But not everyone who deserves to be acknowledged has pertinent work to be cited. I would like to take the opportunity, then, to single them out here.

In chapter 1, the claim that touch is spatial developed in part through discussions with the tactile research group of the Psychonomics Society fostered by Carl Sherrick and James Craig. The International Society for Ecological Psychology, of which I served as a director, has many members who warmly endorsed this direction of my research.

In chapter 2, I argue that outline stands for relief edges, not brightness differences or related borders found in the optic array. Steen Folke Larsen, Albert Yonas, and Susan Petry have asked me keenly about this idea.

Preface

In chapters 3 and 4, I show that blind people can understand and produce raised pictures. The Blind Organization of Ontario with Self-help Tactics (BOOST), the National Federation of the Blind, the Canadian National Institute for the Blind, and Art Education for the Blind (especially Elizabeth Saltzhauer-Axel and Lou Giansante) have offered encouragement and opportunities to pursue these ideas. The North York Board of Education (particularly Frances Paling), the Holywood School (Scarborough), and the Scarborough Board of Education have been helpful.

Chapter 5 lays out the developmental progression in drawing. The Ontario Science Centre provided facilities for a great deal of the testing in studies on drawing development I undertook with Andrea Nicholls, ably aided by Carol Flynn. Studies on the blind were conducted at the St. Vincent School for the Handicapped, Port-au-Prince, Haiti. The Haitian research was made possible by assistance from Diane Girard and Vanessa Tourangeau, both of whom gave extraordinary aid at critical times. The Foundation for Blind Children, Tucson and Phoenix, and the Brentwood School, Calgary, have also been extremely helpful. I must thank especially Margaret Healey and the Parents Group in Calgary for their aid. The Helen Keller Institute of New York provided further opportunities to work with blind teenagers and adults.

In chapter 6, I contend that pictures can be metaphoric. The Toronto Semiotic Circle (especially Paul Bouissac, Marcel Danesi, Paul Perron, and David Savan) provided an important forum for discussions of this idea. During my term as president of the Circle I was fortunate to have spirited discussions of the role of metaphor in meaning change and in Renaissance emblematica, and I learned a great deal from Pat Vicari.

In chapter 7, I propose that perspective is pervasive in tactile perception. Fragile pictures conform to the performance of objects with a large angular subtense. John Willats explained Brunelleschi's demonstration to me. Helen Rosenthal and my son Robert helped with some of the calculations. Kim Veltman kept me informed about this history of perspective.

In chapter 8, I consider how there may be music in touch. I am grateful to the American Psychological Association, Division 10, Psychology and the Arts, for the opportunities it has given me as an invited speaker and as president of the organization to explore ideas about pictures and music with a deeply interested audience. I thank particularly Charlotte Doyle, Stephanie Dudek, Margery Franklin, Howard Gruber, Nathan Kogan, Lawrence Marks, Colin Martindale, and Ellen Winner.

Funding for this work was provided by the National Science and Engineering Research Council, Canada. I especially thank M. P. Bryden for his evaluation of my program of research and study during his time with the psychology panel of the Council. Through generous grants the Canada Council made it possible for me to take leaves of absence from the University of Toronto so that I could conduct research in Haiti and consult with European colleagues. More recently, the Danish Research Academy kindly supported another semester in Europe, at the Institute of Psychology at Aarhus University.

The Department of Psychology at the University of Toronto, through the Division of Life Sciences, Scarborough College, provided essential services and general support throughout the preparation of this work. I thank particularly Judith Smith and Laurel Wheeler, and in the graphics department, Diane Gradowski, David Harford, and Tony Westbrook.

The work I describe here has only been possible through the dedicated, steady efforts (as collaborators and critics) of many enthusiastic and gifted students. I can only mention a few. Graduate students who spent long hours with me included Sally Bailes, Jay Campbell, Lisa Chalifoux, Jane Conway, Ramona Domander, Nathan Fox, Paul Gabias, Christopher Green, Chang Hong Liu, Richard MacLaren, Lochlan Magee, Andrea Nicholls, Terri Richard, William Simpson, John Vervaeke, and Colin Ware. I also benefited from several research associates—Maryanne Heywood, Ruggero Pierantoni, Barry Richardson, and Joanne Rovet.

Susan Hillerby gave me excellent detailed notes on my manuscript. At Yale University Press, Jeanne Ferris, Otto Bohlmann, and Richard Miller offered me a warm reception, patience, and insightful criticism in a balanced mixture I have appreciated.

I will never forget the encouragement of family and friends at important times during the writing of this book. Jeanne Brown, Kate Hamilton, and Robin and Michael Kennedy—thank you. To Robert, Brian, Patrick, and Mathew, thank you for trying out and commenting on my perceptual materials many times. In Canada, the Thompson family and the Burtons have been a source of strength, much as the Fausts and Grossmans have been during my time in the United States. In Ireland, good friends now for many years have included Betty Mills and Brian Scott, as well as the Millers, Burnses, and Kirkpatricks, a good crew. Friends at Unicamp (such as Valerie Colgan), the Don Heights Fellowship (like Doug and Peggy Sloan, Janet Vickers, and Brian and Toni Norman), and the First Unitarian Congregation have been important in many ways. They remind me of institutions in Belfast that nurtured values and ideas expressed here—the First Non-Subscribing Presbyterian Church and the Royal Belfast Academical Institution.

Permission to reproduce figures 2.2, 2.15, and 2.16, from J. M. Kennedy and A. S. Ross, 1975, *Perception* 4:391–406, was given by *Perception*. Permission to reproduce the solid-black part of figure 2.13 was given by C. M. Mooney and the *Canadian Journal of Psychology*; the figure is adapted from Mooney, 1975, *Canadian Journal of Psychology* 11:219–226. Permission to reproduce figures 5.3 and 5.4, adapted from A. L. Nicholls and J. M. Kennedy, 1992, *Child Development* 63:227–241, was given by *Child Development*. I am pleased to acknowledge these courtesies.

Drawing
&
the Blind

CHAPTER ONE

To Touch and to Picture the World

This book is about pictures and touch, a combination that may sound paradoxical. We usually think of touch as the sense of immediate contact. As Loomis and Lederman (1986) note, this supposition has led theorists to call touch a "proximal" sense—one concerned with sensing objects that are in contact with the body. In contrast, vision and audition are "distal" senses: they deal with impressions of objects far removed from the sense organ. How can a sense that is proximal use pictures, which represent distant objects? My focus is on the perception and production of pictures by blind people, which may seem to be an extraordinary pouring of one paradox onto another.

The possibility that pictures made in a raised form could be readily deciphered by the blind is a source of deep curiosity to a wide variety of scholars, scientists, and teachers. As a psychologist of perception, I was astonished when I first tested blind people, with no known vision since birth and no known experience with pictures, and found that they could often recognize raised-line sketches with their questing fingertips. What ability was being used—what faculty was allowing the pictures to be recognized by touch? An educator of blind children would want to know, the better to judge how to communicate ideas about objects, places, spaces, and shapes in school lessons.

In philosophy, psychology, mathematics, and art, questions have been asked for centuries about the role of the senses in stimulating a basic under-standing of form. Evidently, there is a pressing practical and theoretical need to explain what underlies the successful identification of tactile pictures. If the ability could be understood, ways might be found to aid blind and visually impaired people to gain access to the information generally found in figures and pictures. Important clues to the nature of perception and representation might be obtained. The search for an understanding of a pictorial facility that is relevant to touch as well as vision will succeed splendidly if it contributes to the most aerial debates on the philosophy of representation and, simul-taneously, provides some sensible guidelines and practical procedures for rehabilitation workers and human-factors psychologists who work with hand-icapped people.

Work on aids for blind people has often raised profound questions about perception, representation, and knowledge. Inescapably, both the conclusive and the partial answers I present here are significant for any attempt to understand the nature of awareness of space and form. Indeed, the major questions I ask arose initially from the ideas of the perception theorist James J. Gibson, my mentor, who set out to show how perception serves cognition. His guiding hypothesis was that perceptual systems like vision and touch evolved as detectors of useful properties of our surroundings. He believed that even in a complex technological culture, with every year bringing new kinds of imag-ery to the senses, the stamp of evolution is evident in the detailed workings of perception. Any readily understood graphic methods of representation and any swiftly adopted new kinds of imagery capitalize on what evolution has required of observers for eons.

Following Gibson, I shall argue that much of our perception arises because we are successful at using the geometry of flat and curved surfaces. We are able to perceive because objects have distinct surfaces, both visibly and tangibly (the surfaces also affect taste and audition). Our perceptual systems extract information about surfaces from our sensory arrays, and more than one sense detects the relief formed by arrangements of flat and curved surfaces, their corners, vertices, edges, and boundaries.

Pictures involve a geometry of surfaces that can be known by vision and touch. I shall emphasize research on outline pictures, demonstrating that outlines show edges of flat surfaces and boundaries of rounded surfaces, which are perceptible to both vision and touch. The reason for my emphasis on outline drawings is that they have been the main stimuli for research on pictures because of their many advantages. They are easy to create. They are easier for blind people to make than almost any other form of graphic representation—certainly easier than three-dimensional models and bas-reliefs. Moreover, there are convenient, inexpensive kits for making raised-line drawings. (Occasionally, I will mention studies from Japan and Norway on bas-reliefs. Their conclusions are in keeping with those of the bulk of the research on outline drawings.)

A vital point—on which a good deal of this book hangs—is that spatial properties of surfaces are accessible by touch as well as by vision. The hand can feel corners and edges that the eye can see. If many properties are perceived by both touch and vision, then it is reasonable to conjecture that the tactile and visual perceptual systems share many of the same operating principles for perceiving the shape of our surroundings. Both the sighted and the blind person's environments are furnished in similar ways. A table is both a visual table and a tactile table. And, if we share the same domain and are interested in the same properties—if touch and vision often use the same tactics in analyzing the world—then is it not possible that sighted and blind people can process depictions the same way?

These are important claims, which can be investigated by demonstrations of the similarity of picture perception and production by hand and by eye. Philosophers, cognitive scientists, and neuroscientists ought to take these tests and results seriously. The similarities in visual and tactile processes need to be systematically evaluated. In this book, I shall attempt to lay out broad principles of perception, communication, and representation. I will provide a coherent overview of how pictorial representation works, starting with elements like outlines, moving on to general geometries like the shapes made by combinations of surfaces, and then proceeding to major principles underlying communication with pictures. I cannot supply a detailed working model of the physiological machinery that makes depiction possible, for the present state of neurophysiological knowledge is inadequate for that task. But delineating some of the phenomena that need to be explained may be of help to the neuroscientist searching for the underlying mechanisms.

At each stage of this analysis, it will be necessary to overturn some well-entrenched conceptions. Ideas about touch, pictures, line drawings, perspective, blindness, communication, and the development of drawing will need to be revised. Ripples from any unexpected finding jostle established truths. If it seems startling that blind people may be able to understand pictures, the startle reflex is a symptom that deep-seated ideas may have to change, as Arnheim (1990) noted.

In this chapter I begin with the first of many misconceptions—the idea that pictures, which often portray distant objects, cannot possibly be appreciated by touch. In keeping with the notion that touch is proximal, theorists have emphasized what might be called a patchy quality of touch: we feel only a few parts of some objects at any one time (Berla, 1982, p. 375; Ostad, 1989, p. 60). The implication for some theorists is that touchers have trouble unifying a set of touches (Dunlea, 1989). Therefore, they cannot easily gain an overall impression of a complex shape, or the spatial layout of a set of objects, or the arrangement of rooms in a house (Katz, 1989, sect. 46). Touch needs guidance from vision, it is claimed. Touch is inadequate for organizing, and it provides a poor basis for attempts to remember spatial patterns. It is inherently less efficient than vision. (Bailes and Lambert, 1986, criticize this view.)

Given these putative limitations of touch, some theorists have believed that pictures cannot be useful to touch, although they admit that pictures can be made of raised lines or varied areas on an otherwise flat surface. Indeed, pictures with some relief have been made for centuries, but typically they show features of objects varying in depth from the observer. Because touch deals with direct contact, how can it appreciate something representing variation in depth?

The thesis that touch is proximal (Revesz, 1950), that it uses vision as its basis for organization (Attneave and Benson, 1969), and that it cannot use depiction (Gibson, 1962) has been strongly asserted throughout this century. It has been vigorously challenged, however (Krueger, 1982; Landau and Gleitman, 1985, pp. 14–17; Fraiberg, 1977). Katz (1925, 1936) pointed out that we can detect objects somewhat beyond the region of skin contact. In palpation, for example, medical practitioners feel through tissues to detect the presence of lumpy tumors beneath, although the searching fingers do not contact the foreign bodies directly. Impatient children similarly try to feel through the packaging of Christmas presents to find out what lies within.

Furthermore, Gibson (1962) noted that touch uses a succession of contacts across time to discover the shapes of objects. At any instant, only a few contacts are made, but across time touch can discern the layout of widely distributed objects (Arnheim, 1990). It is when touch is not given time or opportunity to explore that it yields a patchy disorganized percept. Magee and Kennedy (1980) found that a fingertip moving over a stationary pattern can lead to much better identification of the pattern than if parts of the pattern are traced on an immobile fingertip. The crucial factor is that the hand is moving; it is not a stationary recipient of information on a single patch of skin. Indeed, passive motion of the hand guided by the experimenter can lead to even better identification than active motion of one's own hand, as Magee and Kennedy found. (Similar findings have come from Heller, Nesbitt, and Scrofano, 1991).

If touch can palpate to discover something distal, if, in motion, it can discover arrangements of objects, and if it can identify patterns that take time to explore, then it is not restricted to discerning only a few impressions of immediate contacts. But can it also use depiction? And if so, what kinds of things could be represented in pictures for touch?

Touch deals with the shapes of individual objects and the arrangements of objects in the environment in many of the same ways that vision does. It incorporates principles governing how features can be arranged in an object and how objects can be arrayed around an observer. Thus, blind people can depict the same features in a line drawing as sighted people can—the same features, the same object shapes in many instances, and the same arrangements of objects.

Consider some drawings. Each was produced by a blind person using a flat plastic sheet that makes a raised line when a ballpoint pen is run over it. The volunteers were asked to draw an object. Figure 1.1 shows a car and a dog drawn by a blind adult, Cal, from Toronto, who became totally blind at age two. He has no recollection of ever seeing a picture. The car is being chased by a dog. Smoke is emerging from the car's exhaust. Note that the raised-line drawing is much like a sighted person's drawing. The outline depicts the same edges of the object that a sighted person would choose to show. Note too that a blind person's outline drawing of an object—say, a snowman (fig. 1.2)— may have the same overall shape as a sighted person's drawing.

Some perspective principles governing the arrangement of parts of an object, including convergence, make sense to the blind. Figure 1.3 uses two interesting kinds of perspectives to depict a jar. First, the jar is shown from the side and from above. Second, there are thick lines for parts that are near and thin lines for parts that are distant. The lines across the glass are thick when the glass is represented as near to the observer and thin where the glass

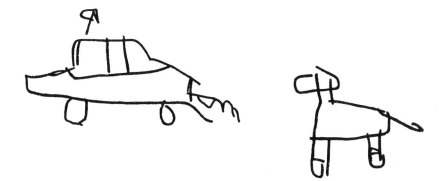

Fig. 1.1. Picture of a car being chased by a dog. It is a copy of
a raised-line drawing by Cal, blind since age two.

Fig. 1.2. A picture of a snowman. It is a copy of a raised-line
drawing made by Pat, totally blind since age two.

recedes from the observer. In the view from above, lines indicate the base of
the jar, which is apparent through the open top.

In addition to outline and perspective, I suggest that a blind person can
understand metaphor in pictures. If an object's edges appear in touch as they
do in vision, making the same overall shape in both tactile and visual perception, then blind people should notice when there is an error in the drawing.
This idea reveals a fascinating aspect of representation. In any medium of
representation, the referent can intentionally be shown incorrectly. For example, we can say, "He had the heart of a lion." This is a deliberate error; the
purpose is to convey courage dramatically. Similarly, we can paint troops
being led into battle by a general whose head is a grinning skull. This is
erroneous, but it shows the general's indifference to the deaths of followers. If
lion-hearted is a metaphor, the general's skull is, too.

Sighted people come across a wide range of pictorial metaphors daily.
Political caricatures often portray politicians and celebrities in odd guises—
the president as a sloth, for example, or the duplicitous prime minister's head
spinning like a top. Sighted observers understand sly references in pictorial
metaphors, but could a tactile picture use a metaphor? And would it be

Fig. 1.3. Pictures of a glass bottle, from the side and above, by Cal. In the drawing
from the side, parallel lines crossing the interior of the bottle are thick in the
center and thinner to the outside, suggesting that the rounded surfaces of
the bottle recede toward the side boundaries of the glass. The device
uses convergence, an aspect of perspective.

readily understood by the blind person without laborious explanation? I shall
offer evidence that the answer is yes on both counts.

My chief concern here is people who have been blind from very early in life
and hence cannot rely on memory of visual experiences with objects and
pictures of objects. When a blind person who has previously had a long period
of sight recognizes the contents of a picture by touch, it is hard to disentangle
the effects of visual experience, including tuition with pictures, from any
contributions derived from native abilities in touch. Therefore I have emphasized the abilities of early-blind people.

The studies I shall report involved as many congenitally blind individuals
unfamiliar with depiction as could be mustered—not an easy task, for not
many individuals fall into this category while remaining within a normal range
cognitively, that is, able to join in an experiment. I shall also include some late-
blind and normally sighted individuals (usually tested blindfolded) to assess
how proficient the congenitally blind volunteers were in comparison. Of

course, at an early age some blind volunteers may have had some pictorial experience with raised displays that they did not recall. No single study can ever eliminate all reasonable alternatives to the conclusion that blind subjects are recognizing displays without any visual experience or unremembered coaching about pictures. It is the weight of the evidence, across many individuals and many studies, from many experimenters and many countries, that is convincing.

Tactile pictures are possible only if touch can discern representations of objects. Logically, to understand how pictures might function in touch, a theory of the world encountered by touch is needed (Jansson, 1988; Arnheim, 1990). All perceptual systems use variations in the receptor organs of the body to obtain information about the world. These variations were described classically as the proximal stimulus. In this terminology, the world is the distal stimulus. If we understand what conditions allow distal perception to occur for any perceptual system, then we can describe the conditions that allow distal touch. Gibson defined *haptics* as "the sensibility of the individual to the world adjacent to his body, by the use of the body" (1966, p. 97). Here I seek to show how haptics is about distal matters besides the spaces adjacent to the body.

PERCEIVING THE WORLD

Perception occurs only when a chain of events is complete. The chain starts with an object in an environment and runs through to the actions of an observer in the environment. For vision, the object provides light—typically, light reflected from a few luminous sources in the environment. For touch, the object provides resistance—typically, resistance at a surface to compression. The actions of the observer, in the case of vision, include adjustments of the eye and changes in vantage point to gain more information about the object. The actions of the observer, in the case of touch, include adjustments of the hand, the chief tactile organ. Theorists of touch often overlook other movements, which take touch from one vantage point to many others, all the while gaining more information about the object.

Between the object and the observer's actions come many links. The complete chain is as follows: object; medium; receptor system; the nerves; brain reception, cognition, and motor areas (none easily distinguished from the others); and the adjustment and exploratory actions that change the vantage point.

To show that touch is distal, two links of the chain need special discussion: the object and the medium.

To Touch and to Picture the World

The parts of the environment controlling perception of an object are chiefly the surfaces. Our surroundings are composed of materials in solid, liquid, or gaseous state whose surfaces are their boundaries. The task of perception is finding out about our surroundings. It is accomplished by discovering the properties of the materials—their layout and their type. The surfaces govern the information available for perception. What happens there is the major factor enabling perception to complete its task. The surfaces of the environment reflect light, used by vision. They yield vibrations, used by audition. They render particles, used by smell. They dissolve into parts, used by taste. They resist pressure, used by touch. Thus, each sensory mode is affected by what is occurring at surfaces.

The perception of shapes and the perception of distance are alike in requiring the discovery of the arrangement of surfaces. Their only difference is that shape perception customarily discerns the shape of a single object, and distance perception involves lengths from the observer. But shape is the proportion of lengths of parts, and length is a ratio of one fixed object to another. A big object, like a tall building, is perceived by methods no different in principle from the perception of the distance between an observer and, say, the end of a garden pathway. Any differences in definitions of shape and distance are matters more of convenience and habit than of geometrical principle. When the core common to shape and distance is evident, it is easier to understand how touch can achieve distal perception. It does so by means of shape perception across distances, as we clamber over objects and walk along pathways.

Because perception relies on surfaces, all the modes of perception can be described concisely. Our receptor organs, of whatever kind, tell us how, when, and where surface properties vary. If we walk around a dark room, we discover when the smell of the rose is strongest, and this indicates where the rose is. The location of our two ears allows sensitivity to tiny time differences, which are perceived in terms of the direction of the sound source: the source must be closer to the ear that heard the sound first. Likewise, we discover by touch when resistance is suddenly evident, and this tells us where the wall is. Gibson (1966) noted that if a violin bow is drawn across a spot on our skin, the length of time taken by the directional friction tells us how long the bowstring is.

Surfaces can face toward a vantage point or face away from it. The surface of a coin facing toward the vantage point is the front surface. The surface facing away is the rear surface. There is also a rim joining the front and rear, and it can be called the side surface.

All the surfaces of the environment are flat or curved. To be flat is merely to have zero curvature. All the objects of the perceptible world are made of combinations of flat and curved surfaces. Two flat surfaces can meet at a corner, and three or more flat surfaces can meet at a vertex. As the nineteenth-century mathematician W. K. Clifford wrote, a corner is nature's real, perceptible equivalent of a Euclidean ideal imaginary line. And a vertex in surface geometry is the visual equivalent of an imaginary point in Euclidean plane geometry. A cube in surface geometry has six flat surfaces, all perceptible, not imaginary; twelve corners, all perceptible; and eight vertices, again all perceptible. To see a cube we can rotate it or walk around it, and it will reveal its shape across time. Its shape exists all at once, at any moment, but our perception of it may take time. At a single instant the eye can see only three surfaces, nine corners, and seven vertices. As the cube turns, the full set of surfaces, corners, and vertices is revealed.

Corners can be concave or convex. The corners of a solid cube are all convex to vantage points, outside the cube's boundaries. The interior of a cubic room has concave corners, enclosing the vantage point within the room. A convex corner measures more than 180° from one of its flat surfaces through a vantage point the surface faces to the other flat surface. A concave corner measures less than 180°.

A convex corner can be arranged so that only one of its surfaces faces the vantage point and its other surface faces away. If so, the corner has a front and a rear surface from this vantage point, and the corner itself is an occluding edge. The rear surface is hidden behind the front surface, which is foreground, and if a line drawn from the vantage point grazes the occluding edge without touching the front surface, the line can be extended into the background. In the background there may be other surfaces or empty "sky." In the terrestrial environment there is always a background surface except when the edge is arranged against an empty sky. From a vantage point there is an increase in depth on either side of an occluding edge.

Occlusion is also possible with rounded objects. A ball has a front surface and a rear surface from any vantage point. A rounded surface like a ball or a hill or the limb of a tree gradually changes its inclination from place to place. When the tangent to the surface passes through the vantage point, to one side there is front surface, facing toward the vantage point but with a strong incline, and to the other side there is rear surface. The division between front and rear is, let us say, an occluding boundary of a rounded object. Although a rounded object has no edges, it has occluding boundaries between front and rear surfaces. An occluding bound, like an occluding edge, can have empty sky or a surface for background.

If a line is drawn connecting the vantage point to a concave or convex corner, it meets the two surfaces forming the corner at two different inclinations, or slants. There is an abrupt change in slant on either side of a corner.

Similarly, there is an abrupt change in depth from front surface to background surface on either side of an occluding edge or boundary.

Two rounded surfaces can also meet like a corner; the prow of a ship, the cutting edge of an axe and the business end of a person's teeth are examples. For present purposes these can be treated as corners, and when they occlude they can be called occluding edges. An occluding bound, by definition, is present only when the surface's inclination changes gradually.

The perceptible environment is composed of surfaces, flat and curved, in various combinations. If a picture shows part of the environment, it shows surfaces and their products: corners, occluding edges of flat surfaces, and occluding bounds of rounded objects. To the extent that touch and other perceptual systems encounter these features of surface layout, they have much in common with vision. They share the geometry of surface layout. To the extent that an element in a picture can depict a feature of surface layout, it can depict the perceptible features of the environment.

The second link in the chain of events that creates perception is the medium, which can be defined as the set of possible vantage points. The vantage points for a set of surfaces lie in the spaces between the surfaces. The medium comprises the space between the surfaces of the environment.

Vantage points are places that we can look from or reach from; they are places light or objects can come to. For vision, the vantage points lie in any transparent region. Chiefly, they lie in air, but they also lie in water and, in modern times especially, in the vacuum of space. Vision can take advantage of any transparent medium, like glass or plastic.

Vision is not restricted to a static observer glancing at the part of the world that happens to confront him at the moment from a fixed vantage point. Vision, J. J. Gibson (1979) wrote, is ambulatory, as well as ambient; it involves a moving observer, as well as one who sits and looks at what surrounds his vantage point. The mobile observer sees as he travels through the environment. A cube is seen by means of the visual changes that occur as the observer—as the vantage point—courses around it. We see while we steer. We identify shapes and safe passageways as we move. Vision finds the changes during motion helpful. With a few shifts from side to side, a nearby tree stands out from a more distant copse. So long as the observer is in motion, the tree will be distinct. Three views of a rigid plane surface specify its shape, whereas a single view is ambiguous.

The medium for vision has two key properties. One is the property of optical transparency: it allows informative light to pass to the receptor. The other is the property of object and observer mobility: it allows the object and the observer to move to gain a better view and to gain information that is available only across multiple views or a sequence of views. This latter property was much neglected by vision science until J. J. Gibson broke new ground by pointing it out, emphasizing what he called the information in visual events, and the flowing optic array taken in by the observer who walks from one vista to another. Comparable ideas must now be developed concerning touch.

Touch, like vision, has media, and relies on a mobile observer and events that unfold across time. The parallels with vision are close largely because touch encounters precisely the same surface features as vision and often uses the same media. Informative events, for all the senses, frequently require motion through a medium. The observer has to move, or the object has to move. The medium that permits light to be transmitted usually allows objects and observers to move. The observer moves his eyes to collect transmissions from a surface, picking them up at some distance from the surface. The observer moves his body to detect variation in the resistance of surfaces. As objects move, we see around them, or we feel around them. We look around an object to *see* its solid shape. We reach around it to *feel* its solid shape. We stroll around a maze to learn its layout. We could look at it while we stroll, but equally we could be feeling around the maze blindfolded.

Touch can use many of the same vantage points as vision. The property of object and observer mobility is present for haptics as it is for vision. Touch also has an equivalent for transparency in its media. Just as we can see through a transparent surface—looking through a window at a tree in the garden—so we can feel through a nearby surface to detect a more distant object. We can feel through blankets to detect the child playing peek-a-boo. Although touch chiefly requires contact, skin encountering a surface, we can also feel the onrush and passage of a train as we stand on the station platform. Standing in a pool, we can feel a swimmer stroke past us. Thus, touch makes use of effects transmitted through a medium. Pressures generated by the wind of passage of the train or the turbulence from the swimmer activate touch. We learn thereby about distal objects.

The tactile medium can be air (gas) or water (liquid), but it can also be solid. A bicycle rider, for example, uses her hands to steer. The hands contact only rubber grips on the handlebars. What comes to the hands via the medium of the grips, however, is not just information about rubber. The rider can feel the hardness of the steel handlebars. She can feel whether the grips are tight on the bars or are slipping slightly, whether the bars are secure in the bicycle frame or are twisting occasionally, whether the front forks of the frame are holding the wheel loosely or tautly, whether the tire is well inflated or flat, whether the tire travels over mud or loose gravel. Through her hands, she can perceive several different sources of vibrations, each one farther removed from the hands, as she attends to contributions from the grips, the bars, the frame, the forks, the wheel, the tire and the roadway. Each component acts as its own source of vibration and as a medium transmitting vibrations from more distal sources.

Touch takes in a medley and separates one component from another. In vision, in a single prolonged gaze, we might look through a smoky room, through a window, past drifting snow, through water to see a shiny coin at the bottom of a fountain. We call "looking through" a matter of transparency. We should call "feeling through" a surface a matter of transparency. Distal perception occurs in either case.

Recall the example of vibrations from a train coming to a station platform, and consider now the walls of the station and the seat that the observer may be sitting on. The impending arrival of the train creates vibrations that the solid environment transmits through the walls, platform, and seat as tellingly as the wind of passage is transmitted through the air. Similarly, touch detects the vibratory events caused by a truck passing the house or by a door slamming in the wind. The observer can even detect the train before it comes over the horizon: a faint pulsing of the rails will give the train away. When riding, we can feel a winter storm buffeting a car, or waves slapping against a boat. These examples show that it is nonsense to think of touch as solely proximal or as insensitive to information acquired passively. Touch is proximal and distal, active and passive. Its media are the spaces we reach through, stroll around, and explore—the air and water that permit us to move around and that permit objects to rush past us, sending us information that caresses us or buffets us. The media are the surfaces that create pressures and, in their turn, pass on vibrations from more distant sources. Touch takes time, as vision does. It collects a set of variations across time and assesses it for sources, proximal or distal.

Two further examples provide simple instances of touch as a useful space-and-shape sense working across time, involving motion, and being both active and passive, often simultaneously.

Imagine examining a table. A few touches reveal that the table is smooth, rectangular, partly covered by a thin oval tablecloth, and set with knives and forks, with thick round platters between the knives and forks. The knives are sharp, and the forks have four tines. Beside each knife is a wineglass. The glasses are full, and the surface of the liquid is fizzy. There are rough rectangular mats with hot covered serving dishes on them. We can locate the dishes simply by moving our hands near them, in a circle, not touching them but noting the center of the radiant heat.

To Touch and to Picture the World

A few seconds of touching has revealed that the table is set for four, and the shape of each object has revealed its likely function. The shape and arrangement of parts have been discovered rapidly, but if we had taken ten times as long, the same basic facts would have been discovered. Perception of shape takes place in time, but in principle, it is independent of time taken.

Now imagine sneaking through a strange house at night; you do not turn on a light, because you do not wish to wake anyone. You get out of bed and move stealthily to the door, walking alongside the bed and then sidestepping to avoid a chair, running your hand along its back. You may realize the bed is larger than your own and that the chair is high-backed and rectangular. You can feel a slight draft from an open window as you pass it, and when you open the door, the draft increases considerably. You step out into the corridor. Right away, your feet discover a step, and then your side brushes against a thin door. It is the closet you are seeking for an extra blanket. You reach for the handle, and the door opens with a shudder, telling you the hinges are in poor condition. You feel one of the shelves. It rocks, indicating that it is warped. You pull on one of the blankets, and when it takes a few seconds to come free, you detect that it is caught on its right side. Another tug frees it, and you realize that a hook on the wall has come loose. You push the hook back on its screws and feel that the wallboard is soft at first and then more solid. You return to your bed. In this brief excursion, touch has revealed shape, size, distance, corners, and things located behind things.

In one assessment of manual skill, Klatzky, Lederman, and Metzger (1985) found that adult subjects could identify 100 common objects with very few errors in a mean response time of less than two seconds. Lederman and Klatzky (1987) argue that typically we have specific procedures to detect specific properties of objects. Characteristically, texture is found by rubbing a surface; hardness, by pressing it; temperature, by static contact; weight, by lifting or holding the object; and volume or size, by manually enclosing it. We get a general idea of shape by enclosing the object; more precise ideas of shape depend exclusively on following the edges with the fingers. Lederman and Klatzky are surely correct in saying that touch can use these procedures and find the specified properties thereby. But touch is not restricted to an invariant procedure for finding a tactile property. We can rub along an extended surface to detect its temperature, or we can avoid contact altogether, picking up a strong temperature disparity by holding a hand at a slight distance from the surface. We also press through coverings to discover shapes (such as the small bony body of a lapdog covered by masses of fur). We enclose an object to keep it warm or feel its warmth. We run our hands along an object to find its length. We enclose an object and tap it on another one (using unsupported holding) to determine its hardness. Static contact with a moving object reveals how hard it is, depending on how much it jolts our passive hand.

Lederman and Klatzky do well to emphasize that a variety of procedures serve touch. But several of their definitions do not involve active motion, a point they miss. Pressure can be active or passive. Static contact is not active, nor is holding. It is correct to expect all these to serve accurate perception. Touch uses the skin (the cutaneous system) and deeper regions of the body (the kinesthetic system of joints, tendons, and muscles). The skin reacts equally to actively and passively obtained stimulation. In either case, the proximal mechanical event specifies the external source. (Gibson, 1966). The joints and tendons, too, react no differently to actively or passively obtained information (Gordon, 1978). The muscles are innervated in two ways—getting input from the brain and giving output once they have engaged in the action directed by the input.

It is the output from the muscles, not the input to the muscles, that is the crucial information about the influence of the object being touched (McCloskey and Gandevia, 1978). Logically, observers should not depend closely on their intentions, reflected in the input to their muscles. Rather, skillful input from the brain arranges the receptors so that they give rise to the most useful output to the brain. It is this informative pattern in the output that indicates the shape of the object being touched. The same information could in principle be present in the output from the muscle even if there were no particular input to the muscle from the brain. A skillful guide can lead another person's exploration. The guide might even save the explorer a lot of effort wasted in searching in the wrong place or, by removing some of the need to plan and execute movements, give the observer more opportunity to monitor the effects of his or her movements. Indeed, Magee and Kennedy (1980) reported that passive subjects, whose hands were guided by the experimenter, recognized more tactile pictures than active, self-guided subjects.

Lederman and Klatzky present a conception of manual exploration. My aim here has been to put this kind of exploration into context. The more general notion of haptics that I am offering is ambulatory as well as manual. Touch gives us access to spiral staircases, arrangements of furniture in hallways, the plans of cathedrals, the form of piazzas, the drumlins of a countryside, and the long steep slopes of mountains. The hands form part of one grand tactile perceptual system with the feet, the legs, the torso, the arms, and even the head, the hair, the teeth, and the tongue. We adjust our hands, arms, legs, feet, etc., and make movements lasting seconds, minutes, or hours that change the vantage point and garner information about the environment. The observer perambulates in time (Arnheim, 1990).

In principle haptics could provide information about spatial arrays, but in practice does it serve blind people well? It might be that the human perceiver requires a visual scaffold to organize tactile input. A fundamental question about our apprehension of space has been debated for centuries: whether apprehension is due to a particular sensory channel (Appelle, 1991; Hollins, 1989; Strelow, 1985; Morgan, 1977). Some theorists argue that vision is a necessary faculty for a sense of spatial layout (von Senden, 1960). Berkeley (1709) thought that touch is essential. Alternatively, spatial vision and spatial touch may be able to develop independently, though each one is superior in some respects (Heller, 1991; Kennedy, Gabias, and Heller, 1992). It may also be that both vision and touch can stimulate amodal apprehension, a kind of apprehension that is not primarily rooted in one sensory modality—a theory advocated by Descartes (1637) and Gibson (1966).

It is not possible at the moment, given the current state of knowledge, to decide among all these competing theories. But we can ascertain whether spatial abilities are reflected in the problem-solving skills of the blind. Of the many studies I have reviewed elsewhere (Kennedy, Gabias, and Heller, 1992), I shall select a recent convincing one for mention. (Later, I shall describe some others in connection with perspective.)

Klatzky, Loomis, Golledge, Fujita, and Pellegrino (1990) studied navigation in the absence of landmarks by three groups of subjects. One group of volunteers comprised sighted blindfolded adults; another, adventitiously blind adults; and the third, congenitally blind adults. The paths that the investigators asked their subjects to traverse involved turns with different angles and variations in total distance. The volunteers proceeded along the routes at different speeds on different trials. The tasks were of two sorts. In simple walking tasks, the subject made one turn or walked along one straight path. In complex walking tasks, subjects took a path with several turns and had several straight stretches. After the simple walking task, subjects had to estimate or reproduce the turn or the straight journey. After the complex walking task, subjects either reproduced the journey or tried to make a shortcut from the terminus of the journey straight to its origin.

Klatzky and her coworkers found no consistent differences in the levels of performance of the three kinds of subjects. In this test of spatial skill, the blind equaled the sighted.

An important finding was that the sighted and blind groups performed at the same level when the scale of the task changed. Changes from room size to tabletop size did not affect the blind more than the sighted.

Millar (1991) makes the important point that blind people usually have to engage in actions to discover shapes. Visual inspection is more able to garner shape information with less motion by the observer. Millar points out that a fixed set of actions may play a large role in attempts by blind people to reproduce the shape of a route. She writes that "haptic recognition is indirect and has its basis in movement or output plans" (p. 323). Exploratory procedures (Klatzky and Lederman) and movement or output plans (Millar) have much in common. A kind of specific code (one of action) underlies spatial apprehension in this theory, which has precursors in the writings of Diderot, Lotze, and Katz (Morgan, 1977; Kennedy, Gabias, and Heller, 1992).

The theory of encoding specificity (Tulving, 1983) has compelling advantages and serious flaws. We cannot recall the words of a familiar song in reverse order without a great deal of effort; it is encoded in memory in a specific order. Often, our spatial knowledge may be encrypted in a specific order, too. But human beings are semantic engines, not automatons. We all know how to paraphrase the text of a song if a child asks, "What does that mean?" And, as Klatzky and her fellow researchers showed, we can extract a shortcut from a route involving several turns. We can repeat the route, as encoding specificity requires, or we can retrace our steps, or we can take shortcuts. All these are vital to tactile apprehension of space and to a fair extent are independent of the order of the actions taken in the space in the first place. The conclusion must be that actions may be necessary to discover spatial layout, but spatial understanding is governed by an ability to paraphrase the actions while keeping the spatial information intact.

Tactile pictures change the scale of a form and would usually be explored by actions different from the motions used to explore the depicted object. If haptics was ruled entirely by encoding specificity, tactile pictures would be ineffective for most purposes. But matters are more flexible than encoding specificity requires. The blind have a sense of spatial arrangement comparable to that achieved by blindfolded sighted subjects, as the evidence from Klatzky et al. indicates, and they are capable of using this spatial perception at various scales. The potential of haptic pictures, then, is not in principle capped by any limit in the haptic abilities of the blind.

One final clarification is in order. I am not denying that encoding specificity can arise. Indeed, it must arise. In any situation in which we find ourselves, we can notice only some aspects of our surroundings and think about the meanings of only some of what is available for our attention. And only what we have noticed or considered has much likelihood of being recalled. Similarly, we can discover only some of the actions that we can undertake in a given situation, and those actions must have some impact on our knowledge of the situation. All that I am questioning is the idea that our knowledge is a carbon copy of what we have noticed, thought about, and done. All our knowledge is open to paraphrase and expression in at least some new format. Encoding specificity does not lead to response specificity. Rather, it leads to some kind of general knowledge. In the case of movements that explore space, it leads to a kind of awareness of shape that can be shown by entirely new actions, including changes of scale, changes in the order of actions, and changes in the directions used to get from place to place. Because that awareness can be reached and expressed in visual and tactile tasks, it could indeed be amodal.

TYPES OF STIMULATION

Since my purpose here is to describe touch, a perceptual system, and then to examine a particular form of stimulation, tactile pictures, major kinds of stimulation available to perception must be distinguished. What kinds of events move along the chain of stimuli underlying perception? How are they to be studied?

There are three distinctions to bear in mind: events at different energy levels, events making different kinds of patterns, and events that are or are not guided by an intention to communicate. Mixing them up can cause havoc in a theory of perception.

All events involve energy. Physics describes the kinds of energies, and physiology describes the operations of the energies in the human body. Events occur at different energy levels. Each kind of energy is measurable on a dimension of intensity. The discipline of psychophysics studies how perceivers respond to changes in energy levels along intensity dimensions. Further, each kind of energy can vary on temporal dimensions, such as the number of cycles per second. Changes in frequency can occur independently of overall energy level. Psychophysics also studies how perceivers respond to changes in frequency, tells us how much change is needed for a perceiver to detect a change, and measures how much change the perceiver estimates has occurred when easily detected energy or frequency changes are presented.

The energy in events can change leaving their patterns invariant. A white square on a black table is brighter than its background in dim illumination just as it is in bright illumination. Whether I press hard or lightly, the brass model of an airplane made by my father and given to me as a boy retains its pattern to my hand. Pattern perception aims to detect invariant shape despite changes in energy levels—to see the roadway in blinding sun or twilight, to feel whether the wheel is solid or loose in the forks whether we grip or barely hold the rubber on the handlebars. Roughly speaking, it detects what is there, eliminating any irrelevant changes in energy levels.

Many different kinds of patterns can be present in perception, and many different kinds of principles can govern it: the principles of geometry, botany, perspective, geology, astronomy, and so on. The list involves major categories of existing things, each having its rules for form—rules that allow certain kinds of shapes to exist, to continue, to be stable, and to change. Perception involves getting to know these rules. They allow us to say, "That's a lizard. That's a bird. That's a rock. That's a crystal. That's a tree. That's a coastline. That's a planetary body." We can distinguish these types even if we have never seen the particular example in front of us. We are probably genetically endowed to invent and use some of these types-of-form rules on the basis of sparse and inadequate evidence. A few rough examples, with no clear set of counterexamples (Kennedy and Ross, 1975), probably suffice for the infant to decipher many types of form (for example, human and botanical forms and the shapes of enclosure). Vision and touch probably both access these types of form. That is, congenitally blind people and sighted people not only have particular forms in common (like scissors, telephones, roses, dogs) but also have general principles of form in common.

Besides "how much" and "what" events, there are events that inherently involve a mind. In "A Child's Christmas in Wales," Dylan Thomas describes a child who has received a book about wasps that lists everything known about them except "why." Some events do have a message, an intent, or purpose. It makes little sense to ask "why" about a tree in the woods, unless one has a botanist's or theologian's bent. But it makes complete sense to ask "why" when someone calls. What message do they want to convey?

Besides events at different energy levels and patterned events, there are communicating events—events made to communicate ideas. At a meeting, someone might sketch the speaker as a man with a little rabbit inside his head peering out. The picture uses a metaphor to convey the idea that the man is timid. Unless we ask why a rabbit is drawn inside the head, we fail to appreciate the intent of the picture. What tells us that intent matters here is the anomaly—the rabbit inside the head. Not all pictures are so blatant. Similarly, by saying "Party time?" we might be ironically encouraging others to go back to work (Olson, 1988). But pictures are artificial objects. They do not exist until they are made by people. They invite their user to ask what purpose they serve. They are not like waves on the sea, which only exceptionally invite us to ask "why," because pictures are invariably products of intention. They might allude to something more than they show by being deliberately incomplete, or anticipate a turn of events, or flaunt something normally taboo. They can give a clue (an associate or effect of something). They can expose something in a matter-of-fact, seemingly unprovocative way. They can portray an object or a person to insinuate but not declare something unpleasant.

Vision allows exposure to pictures and gives the observer an opportunity to ask and answer questions about intention. One wonders just how much of the observer's readiness to answer "why" questions about pictures depends on being able to see and on being enmeshed in a visual culture. I shall argue that at times it is not necessary to be sighted to detect the intent of a picture, and that congenitally blind people can readily appreciate the problem of intent raised by pictorial metaphor.

CHAPTER TWO

Pictures,
Lines, and
Shape-from-Shadows

 In this chapter I describe how outline drawings function in vision. The essential properties of outline drawings that are useful in vision could be quite effective in touch as well. Indeed, some of the visible features of the environment that are difficult to access in touch prove extremely difficult to show in outline drawings for vision. To explain this decidedly curious combination of powers and limits of outline drawings, I suggest a theory of stages in visual perception. Vision relies on brightness differences in its early stages; whereas in later stages it can operate just as well on black lines on white paper as on white lines on a black board. This everyday fact has important implications for a theory of outline drawing. It also points to a possible use of outline by the blind since what outline drawings do, even in vision, is show the features of the environment that can be touched. Vision uses optic properties like brightness and shadow to perceive properties of the environment that are tactile as well as visual, such as edges of surfaces.

 I am not arguing that depiction rests on the observer's finding contours in common between the object and the picture. Far from it. It is clear in the case of outline drawing that something extra occurs, something that cannot be explained by contending that the line shares with its referent the capacity to present a brightness contour to the observer. I suggest instead that outlines are perceived in terms of axes, not contours. Vision and touch may operate with outline in the same way. Both may extract the axes of lines, then use the axes to generate percepts of features of relief. The features of relief that are selected may be governed by laws of shape and surface geometry. These laws may be amodal, equally available to vision and touch. To begin an exposition of this theory, the first step is to establish how vision extracts axes from outlines.

Figure 2.1 is an outline drawing of a house and hills. It uses the length and direction of lines to depict arrangements of surfaces. The drawing shows occluding edges and bounds, sometimes with the background being another surface and sometimes with the background being empty sky. It shows corners such as the concave corner of a walled-in garden and the convex exterior corner of the house. Also shown are wires and cracks (where the door fits into the wall) formed by corners and features of occlusion close together, elongated, and parallel. The drawing employs the geometry of surfaces to show how flat and curved surfaces can meet to form corners and provide occluding boundaries like the tip of the roof and the brow of a hill.

In sum, figure 2.1 shows changes of relief. The lines instigate visual effects that are quite unlike those given by a description of a scene in printed words on a page. To vision, the lines demarcate apparent changes of depth (at features of occlusion) and apparent changes of slant (at corners). Vision readily follows the laws of surface geometry, spontaneously applying them to the outline sketch. Drawings like this one, where lines stand for changes in relief, can be recognized by children less than 20 months old without training in a convention (Hochberg and Brooks, 1962; DeLoache, Strauss and Maynard, 1979). Hochberg and Brooks noted that a child observer with no training in labeling drawings could name a key, a shoe, and a box, for example, drawn in outline. Kennedy and Silvers (1974) found that cave art from opposite

Fig. 2.1. The features of relief can be shown by outline. In this scene outline stands for change of slant at concave and convex corners, as well as for occluding edges of flat-surfaced objects. The lines also stand for cracks and wires formed by relief features that are parallel, close together, and elongated. Some of the line endings show cusps, and the line junctions provide L, Y, and X shapes.

ends of the globe used outlines to stand for the same features as in figure 2.1—changes of depth and slant. Kennedy and Ross (1975) found that the Songe, a small tribe of people of Papua New Guinea who have no pictures in their culture, could recognize outline drawings showing depth, such as a drawing of a boy standing in front of a man and partly obscuring the man, with the man being in front of a house and partly occluding the house (fig. 2.2).

The house-and-hills drawing contains line endings where the line simply terminates to show hill slopes ending (or "cusps" in the terms of Whitney, 1955, and Malik, 1987). Sometimes lines end on other lines, forming junctions. Two lines can meet at an L, as in the lower corner of the house. Other junctions involve three lines meeting like a Y, where two of the angles formed by the lines are greater than 90°. A Y can suggest three surfaces meeting to form a vertex. A Y junction shows the nearest vertex of the house where all three surfaces composing the vertex—two walls and a roof—are visible. Alternatively, the three can meet to form an arrowhead, where two of the angles are less than 90°. This suggests a feature where only two surfaces of the vertex are visible, like the far vertex of the house where only the roof and one wall can be seen; the third surface is to the rear, out of sight. Three lines can

Fig. 2.2. Picture of a scene in outline. The depths indicated in this
scene were identified correctly by the Songe of Papua New Guinea.
The Songe have no pictures in their culture.

also meet to form a **T**, where two of the lines join with no change in curvature and look like a single unbroken line. A **T** can easily be seen as depicting one surface overlapping or "occluding" another one, for example, where a foreground hill occludes a rear surface edge or corner. Four lines can meet at an **X**, where pairs of lines join with no change of curvature in each pair, and look like a wire crossing a background feature. Four lines can also meet in a **T** with one extra line at an acute oblique angle to show, for example, two vertices of a cube one alongside the other. They can also meet like an arrowhead with an extra line to show, for example, the vertex of a diamond, where three surfaces are visible. If the arrowhead points vertically and the extra line is horizontal, this could show two front flaps and the top of a pup tent.

Outline drawings are flat patterns of lines of various lengths and shapes which often meet at junctions. To understand outline drawings we have to describe what a line is, what impressions a line can stimulate in perception, and what line terminations or junctions can show. But it is just as important to discover what lines cannot do. The mixture of functions and limits of outline drawings in vision could have implications for outline drawings in touch. Much of what I describe has been of deep concern to computer vision scientists for two decades (from Guzman, 1968, Huffman, 1971, and Clowes, 1971, to Malik, 1987, and Nalwa, 1988). Their chief concern has been to establish the circumstances under which a line drawing with junctions has enough detail to specify an arrangement of surfaces. I shall argue that specificity is not necessary for vision to use an outline drawing as a picture of surfaces.

I should like, first, to make a distinction between the success of outline in generating visual impressions of relief and the failure of outline drawings to show some purely visual matters to do with shadow or chiaroscuro and, second, to analyze the ways junctions may operate.

CHIAROSCURO AND TYPES OF SHAPES

Outline drawings enable vision to have an impression of arrangements of surfaces. The layout of surfaces is, however, as much the concern of touch as it is of vision. Accordingly, it is possible that the principle allowing vision to use outline as changes of surface relief would operate readily for touch. But it is also possible that outline drawings call on features that are purely visual and hence unknowable by touch, such as shadows. If so, they are doomed to be incomprehensible to touch. I shall entertain these concerns and attempt to dispel them. For outline actually fails in vision when it acts to copy patterns formed by shadows.

The inherently visual components of perception include shadows, highlights, and changes of color and reflectance on a surface. A *set* of these components, with some geometrical or probabilistic regularity to the set, can cover a region of surface as a *texture*. We may call these inherently visual variations the *chiaroscuro* on a surface, borrowing Leonardo da Vinci's term (Veltman, 1986). A smooth, uniform surface with no corners or edges can have many regions varying in chiaroscuro.

Differences in chiaroscuro can be abrupt or gradual. A shadow can provide a gradual penumbra or an abrupt, well-defined border between the illuminated region and the shadowed region. A stain can have a sharp margin or be blurred at its borders. Let us call an abrupt change in chiaroscuro on a surface a *contour*. Marr called the optical projection of this kind of change a zero-crossing, meaning a crossing-over from black to white (Marr, 1982). In figure 2.1, all the lines are printed ribbons of pigment on the page. They have two contours, and optically they project two zero-crossings: there is an abrupt change from the white page to the black line on each side of the line, and hence two contours per line. It is important to know what role the contours of a line play in the perception of outline drawings because lines are defined by their contours.

Contours and gradual chiaroscuro changes on a surface give rise to patterns in the light that comes from the surface. These patterns contain a great deal of visual information about the surface's relief. The shape of the shadow cast by a the gnomon of a sundial can tell us not only about the direction of the sun but also about the flatness of the face of the dial and about the shape of the gnomon.

A contour of a shadow divides a region of uniform surface into two adjacent parts. One part is brightly illuminated and one is dark, so the light coming to a vantage point above the surface from the two parts has a corresponding division in intensity—a luminance division or zero-crossing—which I shall call a *contrast*. A set of contrasts at a vantage point I shall call the structure of the optic array at the point (following Gibson, 1979). Optic array structure can also be given by changes in wavelength (hue) or changes across time. Contrasts in light often correspond to contours on surfaces. The contrasts are in the optic array at a point, and they originate from contours on surfaces projecting light to the point.

Contrasts sometimes correspond to changes of relief, but not always. For example, a foreground surface darker or lighter than its background produces a contrast in the optic array. A corner with different colors, reflectances, or illumination on its two surfaces also gives rise to a contrast. Evidently, a contrast can arise either from pure chiaroscuro change on a uniform surface or from chiaroscuro change accompanied by modulation in relief. The origin of the contrast is ambiguous. Several factors can, however, dispel the contrast's ambiguity, notably change of vantage point and the shape of the contour.

Multiple vantage points provide information about the status of contours by changing the relation between foreground and background surfaces. Parts of a background surface become hidden behind the foreground surface when the vantage point moves. The change is especially clear when the surfaces have definite textures. Background texture projecting to one vantage point can be gradually concealed behind a foreground surface if the vantage point moves. This gradual deletion of optic texture on one side of a contrast indicates that a background surface is moving behind a foreground *occluding edge* (Gibson, 1979). If the vantage point reverses its direction of motion, the texture of the background is uncovered. The optical events at the contour specify which side of the contour is the foreground surface. The information is given by the optic array differences between one vantage point and the next. At an *occluding bound* of a rounded surface not only is the rear surface's texture covered and uncovered as the vantage point shifts, but also the foreground surface undergoes a telltale transformation in the optic array. In the light projected to a vantage point from an occluding bound, the optic texture compresses steadily as it approaches the contrast corresponding to the bound, and then after being compressed to a line it is deleted. The gradual compression during approach to the contrast, followed by deletion, reveals that the surface projecting the light is rounded and offers an occluding bound. If the optic texture is the same on both sides of the contrast and there is no accretion or deletion during any shift of the vantage point, then it is likely that the contrast is purely chiaroscuro—a shadow on a flat surface, perhaps.

In addition to optic events at contrasts, the shapes of contrasts can also help dispel ambiguity about their origins. Shapes of contrasts can be complex and of many kinds. The familiar silhouettes of the Eiffel Tower, Winnie-the-Pooh, and playthings from toy lambs to Lamborghinis can influence vision of a contrast. The shape of the contrast could arise from the edges of actual objects or from contours of a line on a page. General knowledge of the shape of the actual object can help dispel indecision in inspecting the line form and in trying to decide which features of the line's shape are pertinent.

Familiar forms are by no means the sole principles of shape that govern perception. Indeed, they can often be overridden by principles that govern types of forms. A set of objects can have some general features influencing vision even if no particular object is familiar. The shapes can look rectangular or ovoid or can display an intricate combination of Euclidean shapes. Biederman (1987) pointed out that most objects can be considered combinations of parallelipipeds (bricks), cylinders (straight and curved), and pyramids. Vision also uses perspective, topological geometry, and fractal geometry to some degree. That is, we can cope with some changes in a shape that are *projective* and see them as due to rotations of the object and not changes in the object's shape. Some modifications in a shape are topological, keeping all the borders intact, and are due to the object stretching and changing the distances between parts. Moreover, some variations in a form leave it fractal; for example, weathering or tidal action may produce natural landforms with details nested inside details of the same type. (A fractal shape is one where the small details resemble larger parts of the shape, which in turn resemble still larger parts of the shape, and so on.)

Vision is only approximately and informally geometrical. An equilateral triangle is no more a triangle than is a form with two sides 50 cm long and one side 2 mm long, but vision tends to see one as a triangle and the other as a stick with parallel sides. Some changes in perspective do produce apparent change in shape so far as vision is concerned. Although an ellipse may be a perfectly valid perspective projection of a ball (that is, the ball may cast an elliptical shadow), an ellipse in a photograph often suggests to the viewer an egg, not a sphere (Pirenne, 1970). Cubes in a wide-angle picture can look like city blocks (Kennedy, 1988c; Kubovy, 1986; Olmer, 1943). Vision also accepts some pictures made with parallel projections, though parallel projections are only truly correct for objects subtending very small angles, close to 0°. Further, we cannot tell apart single spirals from double spirals (one spiraling line from two spiraling ribbons) at a glance, though topology defines them as different.

Vision, it seems, has rather inexact general rules of form of many kinds. Figure 2.1 calls on vision's use of surface geometry to determine whether a form is a hill or a cloud. Similarly, we have general if imperfect rules for telling whether a pattern looks crystalline or clockwork, astronomic or electronic. Furthermore, we have rules for recognizing types of buildings and styles of architecture, clothing, painting, furniture—the list is long.

Vision uses perspective geometry, shape-from-shadow analysis, surface geometry, and laws about types of objects. Both particular forms we know well and general principles of form influence vision as it deals with an optic contrast and ascertains its origin. Gaining perception of the world is, by definition, discerning those origins. Since optic contrasts and gradual changes in the optic array are the basis for vision, and since the contours of lines provide optic contrasts, it is tempting to leap to a conclusion. Don't outlines show the parts of the world that give rise to optic contrasts? Hochberg's (1962) explanation for outline representation was based on contrasts. Edges usually produce contrasts in the optic array, as do the contours of outlines.

27

Hence outlines can produce the same effects as edges, Hochberg argued. The conjecture is that outline depiction occurs when a flat surface is printed with marks that repeat the structure of contrasts arising in the natural world. For every contour there is a contrast, and for every contrast a corresponding outline in the drawing. Ratliff (1971) argued that outlines represent local changes in brightness and color; Jennison (1972), Hayes and Ross (1988), and Halverson (1992) agree.

Alas, outline drawing is not that simple. Outline, I shall argue, shows only some of the origins of contrasts, not all, and therefore the contrasts per se are not the basis of outline drawing. The reason could be that some origins of contrasts are assessed early in vision, before the system can make use of outline as depiction.

REPEATING THE STRUCTURE OF CONTRASTS IN OUTLINE

In Figure 2.1, the lines succeed in representing surface relief, that is, changes in depth and slant. The foreground-background arrangements of surfaces can be seen. But figure 2.1 could be supplemented by adding the inherently visual components of perception: the shading or chiaroscuro of shadows, highlights, and changes of reflectance or color on a surface. Let us now incorporate chiaroscuro into a scene and then check the appearance of the scene when chiaroscuro is drawn in outline.

Figures 2.3 and 2.4 are sets of three pictures. The first is a high-contrast picture of an object in strong directional illumination. The white shows regions that are illuminated, and the black shows regions in shadow. This kind of picture is called a positive. The second is its negative: black stands for illuminated regions and white stands for shadow. The third is a line drawing, in

Fig. 2.3. Two-tone or high contrast images of an object in directional illumination, including a positive, a negative, and an outline version of the pattern.

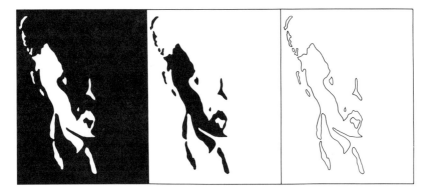

Fig. 2.4. Positive, negative, and outline versions of a chiaroscuro pattern.

which the line replaces the contours between black and white in the negative and the original positive.

The positive creates a vivid impression. The shape of the relief molding of the object is clear. The object provides shading based on the direction of illumination. The visual system engages in "shape-from-shadow" analysis (Cavanagh and Leclerc, 1989; Berbaum, Bever, and Chung, 1984; Todd and Mingolla, 1983).

The negative chiaroscuro figures 2.3 and 2.4 are less successfully analyzed by vision; that is, vision has difficulty recovering the shape of the original object from them. The poorer performance is to be expected. Negatives usually give false information about the location of surfaces when they involve shadow. Moving a lamp will shift a column's shadow on the ground from right to left, but it will not make the shadow bright, as a negative does. In a negative, a bright patch on the ground beside the column would look like an open trapdoor through which light from a cellar was visible. Cavanagh and Leclerc (1989) noted that shape-from-shadow analysis requires the contour of a shadow to be dark on the correct side.

The line drawing faithfully follows the contour of the other images, tracing exactly the same pattern. Indeed, it contains the contours of both the positive and the negative since the line has two sides. One side of the line is a change from white to black, the other a corresponding change from black to white. Yet the line drawing is the least successful of the three images in showing the original object. The negative in figure 2.5 was correctly identified as a portly gentleman by 15 out of 20 undergraduates shown it for 20 seconds (Kennedy, 1988a). The line drawing based on the negative was identified by only one of the 20 ($p < 0.01$, binomial test). Kennedy, Gabias, and Nicholls (1991) tested

Fig. 2.5. Positive, negative, and outline versions of a chiaroscuro pattern.

the ability to identify moving images. They reported that negatives in motion are more identifiable than outline images in motion. In the Kennedy, Gabias, and Nicholls study, the negative and the outline were based on precisely the same positive moving picture of objects in directional illumination. The objects included a face, a baby's bootie, a spider, and a cube made of thick wires. (The positive and the outline versions were prepared by P. Cavanagh and S. Anstis.)

Compare the debilitating effects of transforming chiaroscuro figures to outline drawings with the minor effects incurred by outlining a nonchiaroscuro figure. Figures 2.3, 2.4, and 2.5 have outlines paired with figures made of black and white patches governed by principles of directional illumination. Figure 2.6 offers another set of patchwork figures, but the black and white patches are independent of illumination. These patches include as parts of their contour occluding edges and bounds of the objects they depict. The patchwork figures of figure 2.6 are based on images of a rabbit, a horse and rider, and an airplane made by Street (1935), and turning Street's images into outline produces hardly any loss of recognition. The ones that are hard to identify stay hard, and the easy ones stay easy.

Figure 2.7 is a version of figure 2.1 with some lines added to show shadows falling on the ground. With figures showing such cast shadows, I once argued (Kennedy, 1974a) that subjects could recognize that the lines stand for shadow boundaries. Gibson (1979) noted that a line could specify an abrupt discontinuity of shading. My earlier formula was that lines stand for abrupt discontinuities in the light to the eye, that is, optic contrasts. The figures here do physically copy shadow boundaries and specify abrupt discontinuities of shading. But what are their visual effects? Recognition of outlined shadows is slow and the results are quite inferior to perception of outlined surface edges, as figures 2.3, 2.4, and 2.5 reveal. Also, in figure 2.7 the lines standing for

Fig. 2.6. Patchwork figures, based on images devised by Street (1935).

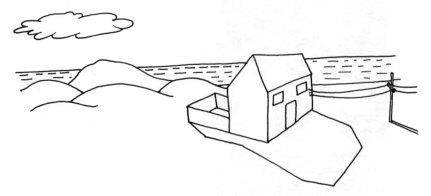

Fig. 2.7. Outline scene with outlines of shadows added. Apparent depth
and slant can be induced by outline drawings, but apparent
shadows, a form of chiaroscuro, cannot.

surface edges create appropriate depth and slant impressions in vision. We *see*
the referents that the lines stand for, in the case of surface edges. The lines in
figure 2.7 standing for shadow borders, on the other hand, do not create the
relevant bright and dark impressions in vision: we do not *see* the referents that
these lines stand for. In line drawings the line can represent a change of color,
but there is no appearance of color in the percept of the picture. When lines
stand for a change of relief, however, there is an appearance of depth in the
picture.

Thus, although lines in outline drawings can depict surface features involving change of depth and slant, they cannot depict chiaroscuro (Kennedy,
1983). This lesson is reinforced by evidence from cave art and studies on
nonpictorial cultures. Kennedy and Silvers (1974) studied cave art from opposite parts of the globe. The art includes many outline sketches where line
stands for surface edges, but it almost never uses line for chiaroscuro margins.
A rare instance may involve line standing for a color marking on the hide of an
animal. Kennedy and Ross (1975) found that nonpictorial peoples in Papua
New Guinea readily identify lines in outline drawings standing for surface
edges but usually do not identify lines standing for color boundaries like
contours of plumage markings on birds or half-moons on fingernails. Fussell
and Haaland (1976) found that a drawing of a silhouette of a mountain was
recognized by 48 percent of the Nepalese villagers they tested, and when
chiaroscuro cross-hatching was added 56 percent still identified it correctly.
But when the internal detail shown via cross-hatching was simply outlined, the
recognition rate fell to 28 percent.

Vision fails to use a line to see shading differences the way it uses a line to see apparent slant or depth differences.

CONTOURS, IMPRESSIONS, AND PATTERN

Outline's failure to depict chiaroscuro in vision can be explained in two ways, one involving local impressions alongside a line compared to impressions induced by ends of lines, and one concerning the perception arising from the pattern formed by the line compared to patterns formed by patches.

First, lines are successful at generating impressions of change of slant and depth alongside a line, but differences in brightness are not generated on either side of a line. In figure 2.8, striking effects of brightness are generated, however, at the ends of the lines, in the interior of each region surrounded by radiating lines. In addition, subjective contours link the ends of the inducing lines. They provide boundaries for the subjective brightness effects. Slight differences in the terminations of the lines markedly change the subjective

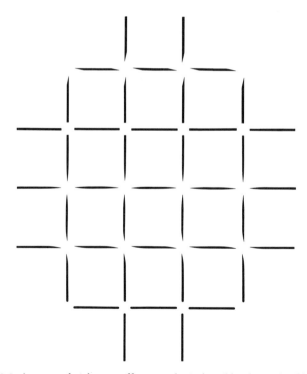

Fig. 2.8. Apparent brightness effects can be induced by the ends of lines.

contour and associated brightness effects (Kennedy, 1988b). Any sharp subjective contour is an extension of stretches of real contour at the line terminations (figure 2.9). Ergo, line terminations have visual capacities not shared by line segments. What happens visually at line endings is not the same as what happens alongside lines. There is in principle no reason why vision could not have the capacity to generate vivid differences in brightness on either side of a line. But in reality that is not how vision operates.

Second, outline forms do not function in vision in the same way as patches of solid color do. Whereas the patches can be analyzed by vision as a picture of a three-dimensional object following the rules for the production of shadows, the outline copies of the patches cannot, though the shape of a patch and the version in outline are geometrically congruent. Relief is well shown by both outline and solid-color patches, whereas chiaroscuro analysis can only be engaged by the contours of solid-color patches. Part of the reason is that a visual difference between outline and solid-color figures is evident even in simple forms (Kanizsa, 1968; Koffka, 1935, p. 141; Johansen, 1954, 1959). It is easy to see two overlapping forms in the solid-color version of figure 2.10. This "scission"—the breaking of one shape into two shapes with apparent occlusion—is harder to discern in the outline version, which suggests a single shape with handles or ears rather than the overlap of two unattached forms. Scission, however, is not the whole story. The form of a solid-color patch can depict a surface gradually varying in orientation with no overlap, such as a brow, nose, and cheek viewed frontally. On visual inspection the patch will appear as a molded, gradually varying relief. The same patch in outline will often only allow vision to produce a percept of a flat form like a map of an island.

This demonstration shows that chiaroscuro analysis in vision takes the outlines to be flat marks on a surface. These lines can be passed on to a later visual processing stage, where the rules of surface relief, independent of illumination, can be applied to the lines. Vision undertakes two analyses of lines—first as flat marks with contours, and second as features that can trigger perception of surface relief. An important result of the first analysis is that lines and borders of patches are treated differently. Even though borders of patches and outlines can share a common contour, the presence of the second contour of the line seems to make it impossible for the line and the contour of the patch to be treated identically in the first analysis. This first analysis by vision is responsive to the presence of black-white borders and is unable to treat two borders as equivalent to one. It is also affected by the "polarity" or black-white orientation of the border: it cannot treat a negative as equivalent to a positive.

The two analyses that vision applies to lines could proceed in at least two ways. They could be entirely independent, always undertaken by separate and distinct visual pathways, which in turn are engaged by separate and distinct displays. Or, one kind of analysis could precede the other, the polarity version before the depiction of relief, or vice versa. If one analysis precedes the other, then both kinds of analysis are engaged by the displays, albeit in a fixed order.

The separate-and-distinct alternative can be ruled out. The outline drawings here provide contrasts. Contrasts are differences in luminance. Therefore, the drawings stimulate polarity analysis, in addition to generating impressions of surface relief. Further, outline drawings that succeed in representing relief simultaneously stimulate the appearance of flat marks on a surface. That is, they offer two impressions at the same time—the flatness of marks on a surface and the depicted relief. Polarity analysis in vision could provide the flatness impression. It would be triggered regardless of whether vision also tries to use a display as a picture.

If one analysis precedes the other, it is more likely that the polarity version precedes the relief-depiction version. The polarity analysis is affected both by the location of the contours in the display and by the polarity of the contours. It incorporates the rules of chiaroscuro. The relief-depiction version, on the other hand, is only concerned with the locations. It does not care whether it is receiving white chalk on a black board or black ink on a white sheet. It does not incorporate the rules of chiaroscuro. It is more abstract and has cast aside some information. Hence, it is likely to come later than the polarity version in the sequence of visual processes.

FROM BORDERS OF BRIGHTNESS TO AXES

Let us see how the visual system can use different layers of cells to eliminate polarity while keeping alive some visual information about a line—its axis.

In the eye, in the initial visual processes, luminance is crucial simply to stimulate the receptors. At the later level of visual processing, where outline drawings are effective, brightness polarities are not important. The bridge between the two levels could go something like this. The receptor cells in the initial levels are stimulated by the intensity of incoming light. A cell at a higher level can be connected to the lower level so it fires if there is a luminance border with a particular orientation, say from black on the left to white on the right. We know that these kinds of brightness polarities deeply influence chiaroscuro processing. Let us call these cells polarity cells. Cells at a still higher level can be set to fire when there is any change present. That is, they fire when either of two lower-order polarity cells fires, either black to the left and white to the right or the reverse. Let us call these change cells. We know that Street figures can be recognized equally well as black patches or white patches, so they are more pertinent to change cells than to polarity cells. However, change cells may also feed to still higher levels. Outline analysis occurs when two contours are present, and outline Street figures function as well as figures made of black patches and white patches. Hence, there may be a level of cells—let us call them axis cells—that are set to fire when fed either by a single change or by two changes close together. Cells that fire to one change correspond closely to the single contour in the display and indicate its location. Cells that fire to two changes close together do not indicate the locations of the two changes. They do not correspond exactly to either of the two changes. Rather, they take the two changes to act as a single one and to stand for a single feature. Let us call the single feature the axis of the lines or contour. The axis is a location. It shows the location of the feature depicted by the line. Stripping away information about polarity of contours as visual analysis reaches higher and higher levels of abstraction produces a visual axis of a contour or line, supported by cells firing to one or two contours in the stimulus display. The axis cells enable the outline to depict features of relief. These axis cells could serve outline or contour depiction of edges and corners.

As described, these layers of interconnecting cells would be fired by a few spots scattered on a surface, dark spots on white paper or white spots on a dark sheet. It is necessary to connect the upper-level axis cells to *rows* of lower-level cells to be sure they are dealing with extended lines and contours. The axis cells that allow relief depiction independent of polarity would need to be connected not only to two changes very close together, since they fire to fine lines, but also to two changes a variety of widths apart, since they can fire to lines of medium thickness as well as to rather fat lines. Or, to put this in angular terms, a line drawing can be brought closer to the eye, thereby in-creasing the angular subtense of each line's body, and the line depiction will be equally effective over a wide range of angles. The fact that a variety of angular widths are equally effective means that either the cellular networks going from change cells to relief depiction cells would be incredibly dense or the job is done in several steps.

Another important problem here is that a visual line can be made of a very large number of different things. This is a matter of the *constancy* of outline. Outline input to vision can be in the form of a line of dots, or a line of Xs, or a mixture of dots, Xs, and other characters with various lengths. The change cells need to have quite sophisticated connections to enable this set of ele-ments to be accepted as one kind of group. This cannot be done just by blurring the set, since the elements can be extremely fine dots and blurring would simply eliminate fine dots visually. Evidently, the layers of cells that lead to axis perception are more sophisticated than the elementary model I have described.

It is also necessary to arrange the lower-level cellular networks dealing with polarity so that they reflect the laws of chiaroscuro. Cells dealing with polarity produce percepts of relief features in directional illumination. Each feature that is noted has an effect on a few adjoining or neighboring features, helping to set impressions of the direction of illumination, the orientation and coloration of a surface, and the kind of shadow margin, cast or attached. This means the polarity cells must be connected to each other so that a group in a row can all agree that a contrast is a particular kind of shadow margin all along its length. It also means that the polarity cells must be relevant to surface orientations and to some laws of relief. That is, the polarity cells do more than just form groups; they also *mean* things in depth so far as perception is concerned.

The same story pertains to the relief depiction cells, which need to incorporate geometrical laws of surface arrangements. Each feature of relief that is depicted can influence neighboring features. Each relief depiction cell has to be capable of *meaning* perceptible features in depth.

No one as yet knows how to devise cellular networks that embody laws of chiaroscuro or laws of relief and mean things, though the challenge is being taken up by neural-network theorists, such as Stephen Grossberg and Ennio Mingolla, of Boston University, and artificial-vision researchers. Rather than showing how geometrical principles can be embodied in cell networks, at present theory of outline depiction modestly has to take two forms. First, it must describe a physical or physiological method which in principle can extract location information from brightness, especially brightness differences, using cell layers. The principle involved is that one cell layer, late in visual processing, accepts input from several cells having opposite brightness polarities, earlier in vision. Second, it must sketch in the abstract the functions served by visual analyses, and the order in which various meanings are obtained during visual processing.

The consequence of the discussion so far is that the likely order of business should be described as follows:

In the world there are lines on surfaces, projecting light patterns made of contrasts. These engage *transduction,* the transformation of optic energy to receptor firings.

Receptor cells feed to higher-order cells that group receptor cell messages, finding contours with orientations and occasionally producing subjective contours. I shall call this phase of perception *early grouping.*

Once grouped, the contour-indicating cells can analyze following laws of *chiaroscuro,* which govern matters of directional illumination and surfaces with various reflectances and orientations. Here lines are treated as two contours on a continuous surface. The chiaroscuro analysis likely can influence the grouping and apparent surfaces in a kind of feedback, and change (often considerably) the subjective contours and scissions we see in the figure.

The next phase involves the extraction of *axes* and information about their *location* independent of brightness polarities. Single contours and two contours close together can be treated as equivalent at this stage.

Once treated as locations of axes, lines and contours can stimulate impressions of surface relief features in a succeeding phase of visual processing. The relief features being generated can influence the extraction of axes and location information in a kind of feedback, since they can change whether we use a line as two contours or as one. Further, the location of the axis must be governed by the pattern around it, as I shall demonstrate shortly in discussing line junctions. But since they have gone without brightness polarity, axes cannot affect chiaroscuro percepts.

Figures 2.8, 2.9, and 2.10 use line endings and L-shaped bends in lines or contours. These are some of the possible junctions that can be present in an outline drawing. Having studied some of the powers and limits of the line, let us now turn to the line junctions.

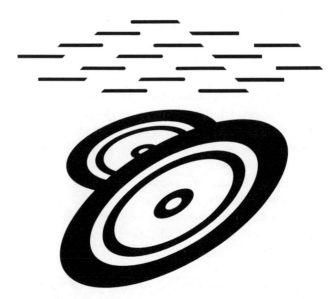

Fig. 2.9. Apparent borders can follow the directions of real contours.

Fig. 2.10. Apparent scission of a region can be caused by contour. The scission is comparatively ineffective in the outline version.

LINE JUNCTIONS

Figure 2.1, for example, has line endings and L, T, and Y junctions. These endings and junctions can show all possible surface combinations, depicting overlap and coplanar surfaces, wires and cracks, flat and curved surfaces.

In figure 2.1 line endings depict the initial swell that commences an occluding bound at the base of a hill. Thus, a line termination can show a *cusp,* that is, a fold ending where a feature of occlusion joins a continuous surface. It can also show the end of a wire or crack.

Figure 2.10 reveals that an L junction in a line form operates visually unlike an L made of a contour. Scission occurs only for the contour L. This is curious, since the outline L is made of two contours close together. There is an inner contour to the outline form as well as an outer contour. The outer contour is physically identical in shape to the contour of the solid-color form. But that does not ensure that scission occurs equally readily in both forms. The inner contour parallel to the outer one seems to prevent scission, partly because it cuts across the region where scission would occur in the early grouping phase. In that stage of vision it may not be possible to engage in scission across the inner contour.

The image in figure 2.11 contains T junctions. The outline form appears to be two equal-sized squares, one overlapping the other. When the front form becomes solid black, the figure still appears to be two equal-size squares, one overlapping the other. Now consider the result when the rear form becomes

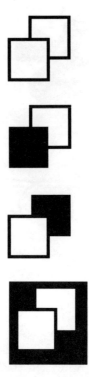

Fig. 2.11. Two squares in outline, and solid-color versions with
the contours of the outline figure preserved.

solid black. The solid rear square seems to expand to the inner contour of the
front square. Finally, let the background become solid black. Both forms
shrink; they also become detached, and the front may appear to cast a shadow
on the rear.

In the outline form, the visual system makes the scission between the front
form and the rear form following the outer contour of the front form. Changing the front form from outline to solid does not change the scission between
front and back. But changing the rear form from outline to solid moves the
perceived boundary of the rear form to the inner contour of the front square.
Hence, the rear form increases in size. Changing the background shrinks both
forms to their inner contours. The line becomes a bar separating them and
suggests a shadow cast by the near surface on the rear one.

A T junction is a three-line vertex. It readily allows scission, unlike an L
junction made of lines. Some three-line T vertices may be perceived entirely in
terms of axes. This is best shown using Y junctions. When a Y appears as the
front vertex of a cube, the percept is based on the three axes of the lines, which

meet in the center of the vertex. If we define the vertex by the contours of the lines, the cube looks oddly distorted (figure 2.12). The vertex looks flat, and the sides of the depicted object no longer look like squares. Vision finds it difficult to extend the three collinear contours to meet at a point and is much happier using the axes of the lines as indicators of the vertex.

In short, scission can follow and extend stretches of contour. The presence of a parallel contour can make a single contour into an outline and prevent scission. Outline Ys are seen in terms of axes of lines.

There is an important connection between scission at junctions and chiaroscuro. Patchwork figures can use shape-from-shading rules to dictate which patches group together and which scissions are relevant.

The lesson is clear in figure 2.13: a distinctive, solid patchwork image (from Mooney, 1957) showing an elderly person, and an outline copy. Vision can see the person in the solid-color version, though not in the outline twin. In the outline version, vision fails to subdivide the eye region on the right to see the eyelid fold. Neither does it make the relevant scissions to see the end of the nose against the background cheek and to see the chin against the shoulder.

The grouping analysis in vision fails to disconnect the parts within each outline patch of figure 2.10. That is, it fails to use scission to sever the L junctions in the outline. Likewise, it cannot connect the outline patches distributed around the image in figure 2.13 into one object—a face—in three dimensions. Vision also fails to generate impressions of differences in shadow and illumination alongside each individual line. Observers comment that the figure seems like a contour map of an unfamiliar coastline with scattered islands and lakes. The chiaroscuro analysis by their vision merely notes the flatness of the lines on the paper surface (quite correctly).

Faces are a kind of form we know well. A study of the elderly person in Mooney's picture may tell the observer what to look for in the outline twin

Fig. 2.12. Cube in outline, with the central vertex
indicated by three collinear contours.

41

Fig. 2.13. Face in illumination in outline version and
patchwork version (Mooney, 1957).

alongside it, but the benefits are slight. Even once we are familiar with the person via the patchwork image, the outline version looks like flat-surfaced lakes and low islands in a silhouette. Therefore, neither familiarity with a kind of form (faces) nor familiarity with a particular form (the elderly person) can make the outline engage many of the functions that a contour patch readily serves in vision. The line and its junctions do not comply with knowledge of an object in shadow.

Compare figures 2.13 and 2.14. Figure 2.13 is a structure that specifies a human face, in detail. It is quite precise about eyes, mouth, brow lines, nose, cheeks, and chin. Figure 2.14 is much more schematic. Very few details are present, but the drop in specificity does not lead to a corresponding loss in successful depiction. Rather, the more schematic drawing of a face is the one that is more readily seen as a face. The schematic drawing entails lines depicting occluding bounds, and a crack-like division between the lips. Notice that in the lips there is a Y junction where the stem of the Y shows a foreground crack, not a background corner or edge. In this instance, the Y junction once again uses axis-of-line perception in all of its segments. Schematic drawings, with minimal specificity, function as effective depictions so long as the lines

Fig. 2.14. Schematic outline drawing of a face.

stand for relief features. They allow junctions to act in distinctive ways. But detailed drawings, even if they have sufficient detail to be specific to a recognizable individual of a familiar species of common objects, fail if the lines are providing purely chiaroscuro structure.

Kennedy and Ross (1975) found that schematic outline drawings were recognized by Songe people from Papua New Guinea with no pictures in their indigenous culture. Figure 2.15 shows a person in outline. The lines stand for occluding bounds. No limb is outlined in its entirety. No internal detail is

Fig. 2.15. Highly schematic drawing of a person in
outline, recognized by the Songe.

present. Without question there is not enough information to specify a familiar individual. Nonetheless, the drawing was recognized as a man by all twelve of the 10–19-year-olds and all twelve of the 20–39-year-old Songe volunteers tested. Evidently, schematic outline, too brief to single out an individual, works efficiently for people comparatively unfamiliar with pictures when the lines stand for relief changes.

In stark contrast, Kennedy and Ross found that the Songe had great difficulty with lines standing for chiaroscuro change even if the lines provide a highly specific pattern characteristic of a member of a species. Figure 2.16 was identified as a bird by all twenty-four Songe 10–39-year-olds tested. But only two described the plumage markings as "designs" or the like. They more often remarked that there were lines on the bird's chest that were puzzling and that perhaps the bird had been cut. Other interior lines, for the edge of the wing or the beak, provided no difficulty. It seems that lines stand readily for edges involving relief (such as borders of wings), and the Songe took the lines standing for color changes to be extra edges, not chiaroscuro boundaries, in the body. It was easier for the Songe to see the lines as indicating the body to be altered from its customary natural shape, and hence to be damaged, than to fit the lines with chiaroscuro designs inherent in the intact familiar object.

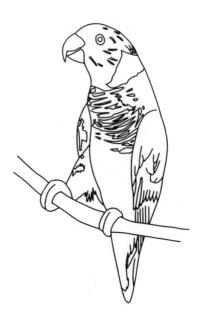

Fig. 2.16. Outline drawing of bird, recognized by the Songe. The lines standing for divisions between regions of different color were not recognized.

Pictures, Lines, and Shape-from-Shadow

OUTLINE RELIEF AND TOUCH

Having examined many characteristics of outline drawings in vision, it is time to return to the question that began this chapter. Do any of the characteristics suggest outline drawings would work in touch?

The most striking aspect of outline is its success in showing relief and its failure with chiaroscuro. There is a direct link here for touch. Relief is tangible, chiaroscuro purely visual. If outline shows relief for vision, it could well do so for touch. But if outline is based on chiaroscuro, it is unlikely to work in touch.

A second aspect of line in outline drawings is its use of the contour on one side of the line. A tangible line offers a tangible ridge falling off on either side. The tangible falling-off could, hypothetically, function in touch much like a contour on one side of a visible line.

A third aspect of outline is its use of junctions and ends of lines to show vertices and cusps without relying on brightness differences. In many cases, these aspects of outline may depend on axes of lines, not the brightness contours of the line. To the extent that outline depiction uses the length and direction of axes of lines, it is based on a characteristic that is not inherently a matter of brightness. Axes are locations, not brightness changes. It is feasible that axes could be deciphered by touch. If axes are determined by processes that are quite late in visual analysis, they may be influenced by pathways that can be accessed by touch as pathways common to more than one perceptual system.

A fourth useful characteristic is outline's relative independence from detailed specificity. Highly schematic outlines much too sketchy to single out an individual member of a species can stand for relief boundaries. Touch may be less acute than vision and slower to examine a complex layout. It might be vital in outline drawings for touch to omit many finer details of a scene and, if it is to be understood relatively quickly, to be rather sketchy. If outline only worked when drawings were highly specific, so detailed that they were unambiguous about each line segment, this might not rule out haptic pictures entirely, but it would be a burdensome handicap. Often, touch is slower than vision at deciphering details. Any drawing might require many minutes or even hours of painstaking haptic exploration to discover specifying details. If a schematic haptic picture can function well, that would make haptic pictures practical for daily use. Indeed, the addition of detail can be confusing, as figure 2.7 showed by adding outline shadows to an otherwise clear figure. The additional outline was standing for the wrong kind of element, and providing the wrong kind of structure.

Fifth, outline drawings standing for relief change function in perception without need of training in a convention. Children in the United States and people from a nonpictorial culture in Papua New Guinea do not need to have the meaning of lines in outline drawings explained to them. If outline drawing functions in touch as it does in vision, then it should not be necessary to explain how to use outline in a haptic picture. Blind people with no visual experience should recognize when a haptic line stands for a feature of relief.

POSSIBLE MECHANISMS

Why do outline drawings work as they do? One possibility is that lines in outline drawings stand for what can be termed the high-frequency components of the visual input. Hayes (1988), for example, examined line images and spatial-frequency components of visual arrays. Hayes and Ross (1988) argued that outline is closely related to certain high-frequency components.

Gradual changes (in intensity or color) across an array can be described as having low spatial frequencies. To have a low spatial frequency is to have a low number of changes per unit angle. Rapid changes can be described as having high spatial frequencies. To have high spatial frequencies is to have many changes per unit angle. Technically, contrasts and gradients in intensity, the changes involved in an array, can be described as a composite of many sine waves. Sine waves are a kind of gradual change. Fourier analysis is a method for determining which sine waves are parts of the composite. In Fourier analysis, a contour on a surface and its associated optic contrasts are a set of high spatial frequencies, since they are abrupt changes. An area of uniform intensity alongside the contour gives rise in the optic array to a set of lower spatial frequencies than the set that is produced by a contour.

Hayes's stimuli included high-contrast versions of photographs of faces with chiaroscuro, like figure 2.13. He called these *bilevel* pictures, since a picture with many gray levels has been reduced to two levels, in this case highly contrasting black and white. Hayes noted that the bilevel images preserve the low spatial frequencies of the original photographs, which had many gray levels. Just as the high-contrast images in this chapter have revealed, the low frequency components allow vision to interpret the image.

By definition, bilevel images retain the low spatial frequencies of a multi-level image. Bilevel images have large stretches of uniform color and hence low rates of change, that is, low spatial frequencies. Hayes noted that it is the low-frequency components of negative images that present difficulties for vision. This is not actually a result; it is a matter of definition. What differs, when a negative is compared to a positive, is the location of expanses of black and white. These are the uniform expanses that are low spatial frequency by definition. Whereas it is an empirical finding that some negatives are much harder to recognize than positives, it is a matter of definition to say that this resides in the low spatial frequency components of the displays. The high spatial frequencies or contours are identical in the positives and negatives, by definition.

Hayes asserted that visual subjects would be as easy to identify in negative as in positive if they were readily identified by their high spatial frequencies. Of course, a white chalk drawing on a blackboard is as identifiable as a black pencil drawing on a white page; both have the same high spatial frequencies, and their brightness differences are irrelevant. Hayes was not speaking only about black and white lines, however. He meant that a patchwork figure can as readily be seen in black patches or in white patches if its contour, with its high spatial frequencies, is sufficient to produce ready recognition. Hayes's claim is the reciprocal to that of Kennedy (1988a), who argued that if a form could as readily be seen with black patches as white patches, then it could readily be identified in outline. But Hayes's claim, like Kennedy's, is a description that requires explanation. Hayes substitutes the terms *high spatial frequencies* for contour and *low spatial frequencies* for patchwork expanses of black or white. The change of description moves the theory no further ahead. An additional line of discussion is required.

A contour by definition comprises higher spatial frequencies than a region of shadow, since one is abrupt and the other is a region. The question is why the boundaries of shadows, which can be contours in a high-contrast display, cannot be shown by outlines. Such outlines will not produce impressions of shading differences akin to impressions of relief, and will not allow vision to engage in a shape-from-shading analysis on their overall form in the display. The spatial-frequency description merely rephrases this problem.

Hayes used a particular set of spatial frequencies when comparing shadow expanses to contour. This may be misleading. One cannot expect a shadow to be always a fixed proportion of the width of the object that casts it. The shadows may be smaller or larger than the object, like our shadows on the ground at high noon or sunset. Similarly, the shadows on a face from the nose can be smaller or larger than the nose. The eye-socket can be deep in shadow or contain very little shadow. A mere sliver of the side of the face may be illuminated, and the rest of the face may be in shadow. The shadow of the profile may fall outside the head—on a background wall, for instance—and be enormously elongated compared to the illuminated sliver. The laws of projection of light allow shadows to be tiny or vast compared to the illuminated object. Likewise vision, in analyzing chiaroscuro, can be influenced by tiny shapes, turns of contour that occupy fractions of a degree, or by large sweeping curves.

In short, spatial-frequency descriptions are alternatives to the ones using the terms *contours* and *patchworks,* and there is no set of spatial frequencies in terms of an object's size that define the size of shadows. Spatial-frequency analysis does not seem helpful as an explanation of outline's failure with chiaroscuro. An analysis of the details of contours of lines and axes of lines may be more productive.

Often, the axis of a line corresponds closely to the median between the two contours defining the line, though the visual system may have to smooth over some bumps and irregularities in the contours. In this case, the operation of finding the axis line can follow tightly defined and simple mathematics, putting the axis midway between the contours. One way to proceed is to locate midpoints between points on boundaries. More circuitously, to find the midpoint between contours one might first construct a line joining tangents to the contours and then divide the line in half. As Rubin (1915) pointed out, the two contours of a ribbon of pigment forming a line are not identical. So the location of a midpoint or the choice of places along the contour to draw tangents and then to join with a line is not entirely obvious. But in many cases, such as straight-line figures, this is not an issue. A procedure for finding the "middle" of a straight line can be uncomplicated; but whatever procedure is favored, it needs to be applicable to physically separated elements so as to cope with dotted lines.

Even if finding the axis is often easy, deciding which geometry to use in analyzing the figure is not solved by locating axes. A sketchy undulating line figure may be depicting a profile, the crack between clam shells, the silhouette of mountains, the border of an island, paint dripping from a can, or water streaming on the far side of a windshield. It may as well be a line on a graph. The rules governing the type of form that an observer perceives are many and varied. For an observer examining a sketchy line form, what shape in the form is relevant will change drastically each time the classification of the form is changed. Alternatively, the form may be sufficiently detailed to make a classification unambiguous. Each detail reinforces the lesson of its neighbor. There is sufficient detail in a painstaking drawing of a horse to distinguish it as a type of object from any other botanical or geological form. Where there is not much detail, finding the axis often follows finding the general type of form. It is "top-down." But finding the abstract type of form to apply depends on characteristics of the line shape, and its axes, in the first place. So the top-down process is like an echo in the system returning to influence the axis-finding on which it is based.

Hence, while at one stage in vision the system determines the axes of lines, and the product of this analysis is offered to rather more abstract analysis, the influence is not all one-way. The abstract analysis likely can influence in a feedback or top-down fashion how the axis-finding stage uses contours to find axes or, at a still earlier stage, whether the visual system engages in scission. T junctions, for example, can function in various ways depending on their context or the perceiver's consideration of different types of forms that the display might show. In essence, the visual system accesses general principles of form, using outlines, but the general principles can then reach back to dictate what is done to the contours that allow outlines to be perceived.

Von der Heydt and Peterhans (1989) argue that some of the production of subjective contours related to scission occurs in area V2 of the cerebral cortex, and they find V1, the first visual reception area in the cortex, unresponsive to patterns that induce subjective contours. I would guess—and I stress this is little more than a reasonable expectation—that V2 must have an intimate connection with an area dealing with shape-from-shading, so that some subjective contours can be scissions dictated by chiaroscuro laws. Lines presumably stimulate V1, then V2, then the shape-from-shading area (where they are diagnosed as flat marks) and then proceed to become axes. Axes then eventually stimulate a kind of general shape processing that is not inherently visual. It is a set of principles governing understanding of shape and accessible through any sensory channel. It may lie in a parietal brain area, a region that can be accessed via vision and touch (Stein, 1978). There the set of principles about shape-in-general, rather than inherently visual shape, could be readily accessed by touch and to some extent by audition, pain, smell and taste as these attempt to discover the spatial arrangement of sensory sources in the environment and the body.

It makes good sense for shape-in-general to be accessed by a perceptual system and to be an influence on the system, in turn. The knowledge of shape should be jointly accessed by vision and touch, for example, in looking at the front of an object while holding and turning the object by its back. Each perceptual system is obtaining a part of the object in motion, and the shape-in-general system can deal with the object shape indicated by the two parts. Knowledge of the back may help vision decide between two possible interpretations of the layout of the front. Therefore the general principles, accessed by both touch and vision in this case, should then reach back to influence vision and touch, in top-down fashion.

Since the information obtained by one perceptual system may be quite schematic compared to the information obtained by another, it makes good sense for each perceptual modality to be free of the need for specificity when interpreting a line segment or a contour. This explains why we are so good at using sketchy outline drawings. Vision of a fence may be impoverished in the dark or in a fog and may need top-down input from another sense, such as touch, to help dispel an ambiguity. As a result, vision is free of a need for visual specificity.

I have concentrated on brightness differences in my analysis here and neglected color differences. Both are purely visual percepts, of course, and thus color is akin to pure chiaroscuro. My argument that outlines cannot stimulate shape-from-shadow processing even if we know they are standing for shadow margins applies with equal force to color differences. No matter how familiar the color markings, lines showing them will not produce the appearance of reds and blues, lights and darks, that we know belong in our flags (fig. 2.17).

In our current state of knowledge of the visual system, comprehension of shape-in-general can only be identified speculatively with some largely unknown process separate from chiaroscuro processing. Can anything more precise be said about lines and junctions?

There is considerable interest at present in visual channels or pathways, and various physiological streams of neurons have been defined as the bases for these channels (De Yoe and Van Essen, 1985; Hubel and Livingstone, 1987; Ramachandran, 1987; Cavanagh, 1987; Von der Heydt and Peterhans, 1989). Some of the streams are sensitive to color differences, others to brightness differences or motion. The distinctions are still quite controversial. Some claim that outline drawings are impaired in perception if they are solely defined by color boundaries (Livingstone and Hubel, 1987). Others claim that a display based solely on color boundaries will impair subjective contour perception but not outline perception (Cavanagh, 1987). All agree that shape-from-shadow requires correctly oriented black-white contours.

The examination of junctions and the ideas about axes here make plain what kind of physiological pathways are to be sought, even if the loci of the cells making up the pathways are open to debate. The pathways must be fairly acute, since outline uses minute twists and turns of line. They must not deal with shape-from-shading structure after dealing with outline. They must be capable of using two adjacent contours to determine an axis. They must also be capable at times of using contour at T and X junctions made of wide stripes for scission.

There appear to be two abilities of physiological pathways with respect to contours—the ability to produce scission, and the ability to produce an axis. The scission process is likely to be rather low-order, at the early grouping-analysis level of vision, and axis interpolation is enacted higher in vision. Being

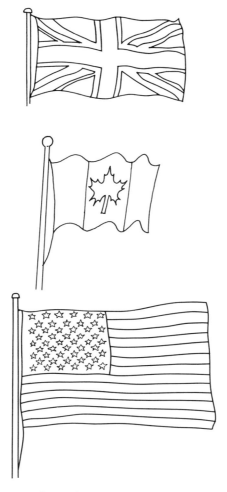

Fig. 2.17. Flags in outline induce apparent depth but not apparent color.

so separate it is unclear how they cooperate to form a coherent figure, but it may help if these functions belong to one pathway. Since there are many kinds of contours (such as shadow margins and borders seen binocularly), other pathways may be able to perceive contour and some kind of figure-ground without scission and axes. If so, the distinction between the two kinds of pathways could help resolve the conflict between Cavanagh (1987) on the one hand and Livingstone and Hubel (1987) on the other.

Livingstone and Hubel report that a channel sensitive to color differences cannot use outline drawings. Such a channel cannot create subjective contours (Ramachandran, 1987) and most likely cannot create scission. It would fail utterly at any T and X junctions made of wide stripes requiring scissions that continue or extend contours. It might do reasonably well, however, at creating apparent occluding edges at contours between junctions. Livingstone and Hubel do not distinguish reports on outline drawings emphasizing junctions from reports based on the lines between the junctions. Nor does Cavanagh (1987; cf. Cavanagh and Leclerc, 1989), who asserts that the channel sensitive to color differences can use outline depiction. The channel could fail to create scission at T and X junctions but still succeed in using lines as representations of occluding edges and borders. It could use a single contour of the line to produce impressions of occlusion while ignoring the other contour. It would only have difficulty at junctions and at any feature that required axis perception.

The color-difference borders stimulate a channel called the Parvocellular Interblob Pale stripes (PIP) channel. It is possible that the PIP channel uses an outline's contour in some respects but fails to create scission at outline junctions. Ramachandran (1987) notes that so-called shadow-lettering shapes that succeed in defining letters in black-white and white-black versions fail if the borders are only color differences. I take this to mean that the color-difference borders fail to extrapolate and interpolate shapes between them. If so, they would fail to produce scission, subjective contour, and axis-of-line phenomena. Shadow-lettering shapes only show the attached shadows of block letters. They do not use cast shadows or terminators of shadows on rounded surfaces. They are not a full test of chiaroscuro processing. Ramachandran's observation, however, is in keeping with the general consensus that shape-from-shadow processing cannot be stimulated by contours that are based purely on color differences. All the indications are that the PIP channel is not the home of vision's rules for chiaroscuro.

In addition to the PIP channel, two others are being closely examined by contemporary visual physiologists. One is the Magnocellular-Thickstripe– Medial Temporal system. This system is especially concerned with motion and binocular disparity, and in some regions it involves cells with large receptive fields. The large receptive fields may mean that the system has comparatively low acuity. If so, it is unlikely to be the dominant channel for outline drawings. It may, however, help generate subjective brightness around subjective contours. Often, the brightness effects vary in strength while the contours are invariant in clarity. The two effects—brightness and subjective contour— must be somewhat independent, though the subjective contours can often corral the brightness effects.

Another channel is the Interlaminar–Thin Stripes (ITS) channel (Van Essen, 1985). This channel may have high acuity, and it is excited by line endings. It operates on brightness differences. It could be involved in subjective-contour and scission production. I speculate that it can be the instrument for scission at L, T, and X junctions. It may also be capable of interpolating between contours to find axes. If so, it would facilitate the use of Y junctions as vertices. Since both outline and chiaroscuro processing sometimes require attention to fine details, they would fit within the characteristics of the ITS channel. The channel may have a primary stage where chiaroscuro analysis is undertaken and a secondary, later stage where outline evokes percepts of features of relief. The later stage may work in concert with areas accessible by other sensory systems concerned with relief, such as touch.

There are still many unresolved issues in the study of the visual physiology of contours. Little direct attention has been paid to the physiology underlying outline drawing. The reports by Hubel and Livingstone, on the one hand, and Cavanagh and Leclerc, on the other, are contradictory, perhaps because they rest on different aspects of outline drawings. Figure 2.18 shows the need for careful distinctions. It presents shapes where the L and X junctions are some-times contours and sometimes lines. Where an X junction is drawn as thick stripes depicting solid bars, all of its four contours are L shapes. There is no difficulty in seeing one solid bar behind the other. Where the X junction is

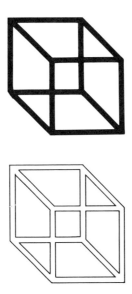

Fig. 2.18. Unlike outline, thick stripes at X junctions, with L-shaped contours, allow overlap.

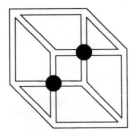

Fig. 2.19. Covers are placed on the **X** junctions of
figure 2.18, aiding overlap perception.

made of four **L**-shaped lines, it is very difficult to see one solid bar behind the other. The **L**-shaped lines prevent scission at the **X**, although each **L** can depict an edge of a surface.

Notice that the difficulty in seeing the depicted bars in depth entirely resides in the **X** junction. There is no problem seeing the diagonal outlines as occluding surfaces slanting back in depth, like bars viewed on the oblique. Notice too that the **Y** junctions allow three-dimensional perception in both versions of the figure. Both the solid-stripe **Y** and the outline **Y** are easy to see as a vertex of a cube. There are three **L** junctions in every **Y**, and each **L** allows perception of edges, arrayed in apparent depth, forming 90° corners in three dimensions visually.

Consider the effect of covering the **X** junctions in the outline figure. As a result (fig. 2.19) the outline form stands out in depth as vividly as the solid-stripe form does. It reverses in depth, changing the front-back orientation of the cube in both versions. Unlike the **X** junctions, the **Y** junctions evidently work equally well in solid and outline versions. Presumably the **Y** junctions can produce a percept of a three-dimensional vertex of a cube either by creating axes for each of their three limbs or by using the three **L** shapes of their borders.

SUMMARY

Are there any characteristics of outline drawings for vision that suggest that outline drawings would work in touch? The answer is a guarded yes. Shape-in-general should be available to both systems, meaning shape that is not purely following the rules of chiaroscuro. The form dealt with after chiaroscuro analysis is a relief form that is tangible as well as visual. The line element in an outline drawing operates at this higher level in perceptual processing since it can only depict features of relief. Indeed, the line element fails to produce an appearance of chiaroscuro differences alongside the line. In striking and emphatic fashion, line patterns that copy chiaroscuro patterns fail in vision to engage shape-from-shading analysis.

Detailed, unequivocal specificity of form is not a sine qua non. Sketches can be effective at producing impressions of relief, a practical advantage since touch is often considerably slower than vision. If it were necessary to have detailed specificity, haptic pictures might be cumbrous—eminently possible but thoroughly impractical, a matter for patient computers but not people.

An inspection of line junctions finds that some T and X junctions made of wide stripes create impressions of scission along subjective contours that follow real contours. Scissions rely on brightness borders. But just like a border produced as a pure color difference, an outline L will not allow scission. Locations of brightness borders and axes of lines interpolated between borders may be vital at times, rather than the brightness borders themselves.

It is conceivable that no axis can be perceived by human observers without a mechanism that is triggered by brightness borders. But it is also possible that some of the perceptual systems that do not use brightness can find axes between perceptual borders. They may be able to use these axes as means to instigate perception of features of relief.

Rose, Gottfried, and Bridger (1983) found that infants can recognize visually outline drawings of objects they have touched. Can they recognize by touch outline drawings of objects that they have only seen or, if they have never had sight, that they have only touched? Many reasons can be given to expect outline drawings to make the same kind of sense in touch as they do in vision. There are respectable caveats as well. What is required in addition to a theory, however, is empirical investigation. Let us now turn to the evidence.

CHAPTER THREE

Blind People
and Outline
Drawings

The wife of William Molyneux of Dublin, author of *A Treatise on Dioptricks* (1692), was blind. Molyneux was moved to ask a question that has become celebrated in the history of thought on the senses and the transfer of information between the senses. His wife was quite familiar with cubes tactually. Molyneux wondered whether she would be able to recognize a cube visually on its first presentation to her eyes if by some miracle she was given sight. Rather like William Molyneux, let us ask what a blind person would make of a raised-line drawing of a solid object on its first presentation. Would it seem like a haphazard collection of lines, flat on a piece of paper?

In this chapter, I shall review a fairly extensive body of research on blind people's ability to identify raised pictures by touch. Some of the volunteers for these studies were congenitally blind; in other cases they had been blinded quite early in life, and in still others later in life. Their scores are compared to those of blindfolded sighted volunteers. The results of these studies are like weights in a scale. One pan of the scale holds evidence that blind people cannot recognize pictures without training in a convention. The other is for evidence that to some extent they can. If the scale tips in favor of the view that they can, then a vigorous theoretical debate on the processes involved is worth the time and trouble. This chapter, however, is not the arena for that debate. Rather, the goal here is to gather enough weight of evidence to motivate it.

Outline Drawings

A study on the question of recognition of pictures by the blind which I conducted with Nathan Fox and Kathy O'Grady (Kennedy, Fox, and O'Grady, 1972; Kennedy and Fox, 1977) used eight line drawings (fig. 3.1). Four of the drawings were "imprints," shapes one would get by pressing objects into a flat tablet of soft clay. The objects were a hand, a fork, a flag, and a man with one arm upraised. The other four drawings were "projections," involving overlapping parts and perspective effects. The objects were a face, a cup, a table, and a man with arms crossed. Half of the imprints and projections were of objects that are normally about hand-sized. Half were of objects normally larger than hand-sized. The drawings were about 10 cm by 7 cm. They were presented in a cardboard window 13 cm by 9 cm.

Before they were shown to blind people, the pictures were tested by 34 undergraduate students from Harvard, who tried to identify the drawings first by touch while blindfolded and then, immediately afterward, visually. The drawings were presented in random order. In the pretest (table 3.1), the mean number of drawings identified per blindfolded person was 2.4. One subject identified no drawings. The most identified drawing was the hand (28 out of

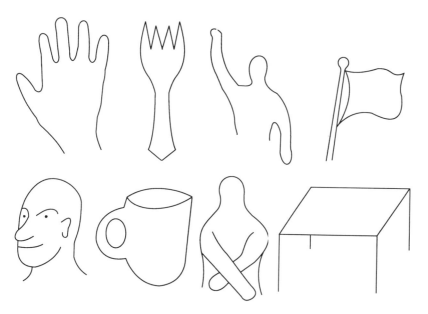

Fig. 3.1. Copies of raised-line drawings: four imprints and four projections.

TABLE 3.1

Identifications of raised-line drawings by 34 sighted
blindfolded Harvard undergraduates.

	Displays	Number of Identifications
Imprints	Hand	28
	Fork	8
	Man with arm raised	1
	Flag	9
	Subtotal	46
Projections	Face	10
	Cup	11
	Man with arms crossed	1
	Table	14
	Subtotal	36
	Total	82
	Range per person	0–7
	Rate correct: 30 percent	

34 subjects) and the least identified drawings were the man with arms crossed (one identification) and man with arm up (one identification).

But when the subjects took off the blindfolds and tried to identify the drawings by sight, the task became much easier. All of the drawings were recognized by all the subjects. Furthermore, they were often quite surprised at the fact that they had failed in their tactile attempts shortly before. Quite often subjects made a remark such as, "Why didn't I think of that?" The fact that all of the drawings were identified by sight by all of the subjects provides a benchmark. Other testing conditions can be compared to the standard given by vision. It is apparent that tactile exploration is much harder for the sighted than visual examination is, even if the subjects are highly familiar with pictures and highly educated.

What results would be obtained from blind subjects who have no experience with tactile pictures? To find out, we tested the imprints and projections with a group of blind students at Harvard and a group of blind teenagers and college students in Toronto.

Outline Drawings

There were eight Harvard students (table 3.2). They ranged in age from 18 to 23. Five were blind since birth, one since age six years, one since age three years, and one since age three months. They were totally blind with the exception of the man who went blind at six, who can visually detect large objects. They were all able to identify simple line drawings of a circle, a square, a triangle, a V, and a line. But they reported no experience or training with pictures, though plastic sheets for drawing letters or maps were familiar.

They were individually tested and given the set of imprints as a group and projections as a group, in random order. They were assigned the same task as the sighted volunteers: to identify correctly each imprint and projection. By this standard, the blind students successfully identified a total of five imprints and five projections, or 1.25 per person. However, four of the blind students identified none of the drawings, and two identified only one drawing each. Two contributed eight of the identifications. The drawings successfully identified were the hand (three times), the fork (twice), the cup (twice), the table (twice), and the face (once).

Clearly, the blind volunteers identified fewer drawings per person than the blindfolded sighted subjects did. Two of the blind, however, scored higher than most of the blindfolded. Moreover, there were many near-misses; for example, subjects described the fork as the clawed paw of an animal, a bell on a chain, a leaf, and a candle with flames. These suggestions might be counted as acceptable since they make sense of the display as a picture in ways that

TABLE 3.2

Identifications of haptic displays by Harvard blind volunteers.

Age at Testing (Years)	Age at Onset of Blindness	Imprints	Projections	Displays
20	3 years	0	0	—
21	3 months	1	0	hand
23	birth	0	0	—
20	birth	2	2	hand, fork, cup, table
22	6 years	1	3	hand, face, cup, table
19	birth	0	0	—
20	birth	1	0	fork
18	birth	0	0	—

vision finds allowable. If so, the fork picture could be said to have been identified six times. But the range of the criterion is now becoming unsettled. If the criterion is vague, clear comparisons cannot be drawn between different pictures or different groups of people. What should one do, for example, with the response of the blind subject who identified the display as a fork and then retracted that identification? And what of the suggestions that the blind volunteers later made for modifying the pictures to make them more recognizable? The modifications were in keeping with how sighted people might draw or conceive the shape of objects. It was pointed out that a line might show the corner where the handle meets the body of the cup. Another comment was that a straight-on view of the face would be easier to identify. One person said that the man's shoulders were too rounded. The fork was said to be unusual, "like a garden fork", with a handle "like an ice scraper." Another comment was that the fork handle is too rounded. Furthermore, in many cases blind volunteers, like their blindfolded sighted counterparts, said that they "should have gotten it." Errors were often attributed to pictorial matters, such as taking the hole in the handle of the cup as a surface instead of background.

The eight Toronto volunteers were more heterogeneous than the Boston group. They ranged in age from 13 to 22 years (mean age 17). Three had sufficient vision to make out large objects with strong contrast between the object and the background. Three had had some sensitivity to light since birth. Two are now totally blind, one since 10 months of age and one since nine years of age; the latter had the visual ability to detect large objects until the age of nine. All were attending school except the oldest, who had just finished college.

The Toronto blind volunteers began by examining the raised line drawings of geometrical shapes. They were able to identify these. Then they were asked to identify the imprint and projection drawings (the set of imprints first or the projections first, in random order). They were given two minutes per drawing. As table 3.3 shows, they recognized 14 of the drawings (1.75 per person). The most commonly recognized pictures were the hand, fork, and face (three identifications each), and the least identified pictures were the man with arms crossed and the cup (no identifications). Only one subject failed to identify any of the drawings, and six identified two or more. As in the Harvard study, the volunteers committed errors that do not appear to be random but make visual sense. The table was called a house (twice); the fork was called a brush, bagpipes, a foot, a tree (twice), a flower, a candlestick, and an ice-cream cone; the flag was called a sign. The man with one hand upraised was called a camel.

At this point, 16 blind people had been tested and seven of the eight drawings had been identified. Only the "man with his arms crossed" had not

TABLE 3.3

Identification of haptic pictures by Toronto blind volunteers.

Age at Testing (Years)	Age at Onset and Status of Blindness	Imprints	Projections	Displays
13	2 years, large object detection	2	1	hand, fork, face
14	1–1½ years, large object detection	1	1	hand, face
17	Birth, large object detection to 9 years, now totally blind	1	1	hand, table
17	Birth, light perception	1	0	fork
18	10 months, totally blind	0	0	—
18	Birth, light perception	1	1	fork, table
18	Birth, light perception	0	2	man with arm up, table
22	Birth, large object detection	1	1	flag, face

been identified. It seemed clear from comments made by the blind volunteers that outline pictures made sense. No one had asked, "How can lines stand for anything?" or "How can a line be like someone's mouth, legs of tables, corners of objects or parts of rounded objects?" Admittedly, no one volunteer had identified many drawings. But neither were the volunteers entirely baffled, as they would have been if confronted with a foreign language.

These results are encouraging to those who expect a similarity between visual and tactile recognition of images, but they are not decisive. They indicate that some pictorial ability is present in the blind volunteers that allows some kinds of tactile outline drawings to be identified. A 10–20 percent success rate, however, seems somewhat impractical. On the other hand, it is reasonable to expect improvement if a suitable context is provided.

The youngest of the Toronto volunteers, Betty, surprised me after the test by saying, "I'm not a very good drawer, but I like drawing." She told me about drawing faces. "I tell my brother to sit still," she said, "then I feel his face, his nose and then I draw his nose and one eye and so on." She added, "I was taught how to make lines and circles. I put them all together myself to make drawings." When she was asked who taught her to draw faces, she answered,

"Taught myself." She said she drew with a geometry set and had drawn things for science: "flask, tree, leaves, people's faces, brain." She used to draw with a raised-line drawing system (cards on rubber pads), but now she draws with crayon as well. Betty said that her vision had improved marginally within the past year, but she drew long before then. (Betty now has large-object detection visually but cannot read large print.) Betty's intriguing comments indicate a spontaneous and sustained interest in pictures and show that drawing can arise in the blind. She was the first blind person I heard making such comments, but not the last.

STORIES WITH ILLUSTRATIONS

In the next study, pictures were given in context. The question was: If simple pictures are given in a context such as a story, will they be readily identified, or will the blind have to be told outright what they are? I sought assistance from BOOST, the Blind Organization of Ontario with Self-Help Tactics. Members volunteered to test some simple stories with illustrations. Maryanne Heywood and I wrote and illustrated four stories for children. With the cooperation of the Canadian National Institute for the Blind, we had the stories printed in Braille. The illustrations were lines or raised dots on stiff Braille-style paper.

I shall refer to the four stories as Guitar, Elephant, Tricycle, and Duckling. The full titles are "A Night in the Life of a Mouse," "Something Very Curious Indeed," "What's All the Noise About?" and "It Has Little Wings" (see pp. 91–94). In each story we followed a principle. An object was gradually introduced one part at a time. Finally, the whole complex object was presented in a composite picture, each part in its proper position. The picture of a complex object might be difficult to understand. Our expectation, however, was that if each component was examined separately, knowing something about the referent of the illustration, it would be understood. Then, when the composite was encountered, the only problem would be to check the relationship between each piece. We also expected that this manner of introducing the illustrations would motivate the readers to apply themselves to identifying the picture. There is an element of mystery in the stories, since the whole object is named only in the last pages of the story.

To assess how difficult the illustrations were to understand, we presented the test to BOOST members this way. We told them that the stories were intended for blind children and asked whether the illustrations seemed suitable. If they are unlikely to be understood easily by blind children, we said, tell us what the problems are likely to be and how we might remedy them. Last, we asked each volunteer to tell us whether the marriage between story and illustrations would be satisfactory for blind children.

The BOOST members took to the task. In previous studies we often had problems obtaining "guesses" or "comments" from shyer subjects when we asked them to try their own skills at identifying pictures. But when one is asked to say whether a display would create some difficulties for children, the focus on the self is removed and shyness seems to recede. Accordingly, we received a lot of comments. It should be noted that although we requested the participants to attempt to decipher the stories and illustrations unaided, we also offered assistance if asked. This gave a clear response category. Were we asked to assist in comprehension of any illustration on any story?

Seventeen BOOST members participated (table 3.4). Ten of the participants are totally blind, four (Lys, May, Dee, Jay) having congenital total blindness and two (Pat and Pau) having lost sight at or before age two. The remaining four went blind after age 5 and can be called *late blind*. I shall compare their abilities here since, as Warren (1984) and Bailes and Lambert (1986) noted, it is often argued that there are considerable differences between those who lose sight before 2–3 years of age and those who go blind at three years and older. In Warren's terms, the early blind are said to lack a spatial reference system as a means of unifying the perceptual experiences.

Four of the volunteers can be called *light perceivers,* in that they can sense light and dark. Two of these have congenital conditions (Nip and Joan) and two are late blind.

Three are capable of *low vision:* they can make out headlines on newspapers held very close but are unable to tell whether someone has an arm upraised from a distance of one meter in normal room illumination. Two have congenital conditions; one is late blind.

TABLE 3.4
Adult participants from BOOST in picture recognition tests.

Onset of Blindness and Degree of Loss	Participants
Early (0–2 years), totally blind	Dee, Jay, Lys, May, Pat, Pau
Early, light perception	Joan, Nip
Early, low vision	Dot, Val
Late, totally blind	Ann, Ely, Mik, Ray
Late, light perception	Gord, Nyb
Late, low vision	Jon

The ages range from 17 to 47 years, including one at 47 (late, totally blind), one at 37 (late, light perceiver), one at 33 (late, totally blind), and the others 30 or less. All have had some secondary schooling and three have attended university.

I shall describe the condition of those who lost sight before 36 months and who are totally blind as *early, totally blind.* Similarly, those who lost sight after 36 months and who are sensitive to light I shall call *late, light perception.*

Every participant tried at least two stories, with the order of stories assigned at random. Often, two stories and comments on the stories took up all the available interview time. We found it difficult to take volunteers through all the procedures we had planned during the allotted time. Five participants, however, were able to undertake further testing, and stories were tested seven times . The list of stories tested is presented in table 3.5. In toto, there were 41 occasions on which a story was tested.

The key result of this testing is that *on only two occasions out of 41 was*

TABLE 3.5
Illustrated stories tested by BOOST participants.

	Duckling	Guitar	Elephant	Tricycle
Ann		x	x	x
Dee	x	x		
Dot	x			x
Ely		x	x	
Gord		x	x	x
Jay		x		x
Joan			x	x
Jon	x			x
Lys		x	x	
May	x		x	
Mik		x	x	
Nip		x		x
Nyb			x	x
Pau	x	x	x	x
Pat	x			x
Ray	x	x	x	x
Val		x	x	x
Total	7	11	11	12

assistance required. We received requests from Lys and May, both of whom have been totally blind since birth and were coded as early, totally blind.

Lys attempted two stories, Guitar and Elephant. In the Elephant story, the first she attempted, she asked for assistance on two pictures. The rectangle standing for a cylinder (a tree trunk) was mysterious initially, though once it was explained the picture was deemed understandable and acceptable. Second, that the elephant's head projects more forward than up from the body was unexpected and made it difficult to identify. Lys identified the trunk, tail, and legs, however, while saying "the head should be at the top." Lys also was troubled that only one eye and one ear of the elephant were shown. "Ears should be on two sides of the head," she said.

May (early, totally blind) attempted two stories, Duckling and Elephant. In the Duckling story, her first, she asked for assistance on two illustrations. She was troubled that the "wings" were centered in the oval for the body; she thought that "they should be sticking out from the sides." In the picture where the head of the duckling was added, she felt that the picture needed a second eye. She was told it was a side view. After the Elephant story, she noted that she was "ready to accept the side view of the elephant, because I'd already seen the duckling from the side."

On 39 occasions the illustrations were interpreted by the participant without aid. There were moments of difficulty, doubt, and indecision, but each overcame them on his or her own. Lys, for instance, said of the mouse in Guitar, "The eyes are a little close together. Doesn't a mouse have ears? If you're going to show the whole animal, you should show all the parts." And May said of the piece of clay shaped like a snake in Elephant, "It doesn't have any face! Oh, it's not a snake. It's clay like a snake!" As in these two examples, reasons for an initial query were often clearly enunciated, together with an explanation once the difficulty was overcome or settled.

Many specific comments indicated concerns about the figures like Lys's about the mouse's ears. But overall it was said that the stories were interesting and the illustrations appropriate to them and suitable for blind children. Generally the pictures were deemed to be clear, though they might be improved with some additions, and some illustrations were easier to follow than others.

Pointed comments about specific illustrations include the following:

Guitar: Joan (early, totally blind) and Gord (late, light perception) were confused at first by the top view of the mouse and said that a side view would be better. Ann (late, totally blind) thought that the best depiction would include both top and side views on one page. Jay (early, totally blind) initially took the sound hole of the guitar to be a detached, foreground object lying on top of the guitar.

Elephant: Pat (early, totally blind) said she had no previous experience of a rectangle depicting a cylinder but found it understandable, and she explained the depiction in detail. Joan (early, light perception) found the omission of lines in the whole or composite figure confusing at first.

Tricycle: Jay (early, totally blind) thought the handlebars should be drawn at the top of the page, running left to right, and the seat should be directly below "as if you were sitting on it." When she was told that the picture was a side view she said, "Then it's perfect."

Duckling: Dot (early, low vision) said the angle of the duck's legs indicated that it was running. Ray (late, totally blind) had difficulty with the duck's feet, which are a top view, whereas the rest is a side view. Pat (early, totally blind) said that the duck's feet seemed rounded and ought to be flat. She volunteered to draw examples of feet (fig. 3.2) that she said would convey flatness. These were the first raised-line drawings I ever obtained from a blind person, and I believe these to be the first raised-line drawings Pat had ever made. They are astonishingly good for a beginner.

That the illustrations in the stories were interpretable by the subjects can be attributed in part to the skill of the participants and in part to aid from the context. To continue the assessment of pictures without any context, we invited the BOOST members to try a second kind of test. We prepared a set of 14 pictures to be examined with no story context. The pictures were of a coat hanger, a door, a pair of scissors, a button (with two holes), a spool, a belt, a shoe (top view, with no laces), an apple, a pear, a banana, a bunch of grapes, a telephone, a chest of drawers, and a branch with leaves.

The five of the BOOST members with the least visual experience partici-

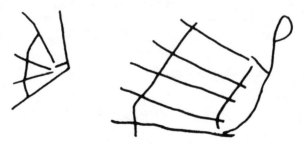

Fig. 3.2. Pat (early, totally blind) drew a duck's foot twice.

pated—Lys (early, totally blind), May (early, totally blind), Jay (early, totally blind), Nip (early, light perception) and Ray (late, totally blind). They were told that each picture showed an object, which the volunteers were to try to identify initially without clues. We supplied clues or hints—general categories like food or furniture—if the first guesses were wrong, and then the actual identity of the object if the participant asked. I shall describe the first guesses in detail. Hints improved the success rate considerably: May, totally blind since birth, recognized all but three objects after she was given general hints.

Unaided, the subjects managed 24 correct identifications (34 percent): Lys, one; May, two; Jay, five; Nip, six; and Ray, 10. The coat hanger was identified once, the door once, the scissors three times, the belt once, the telephone twice, the chest of drawers twice, and the branch twice. Three people—Jay, Nip, and Ray—identified all four fruits, which were always presented as a group on one page; hence their scores may be inflated. Counting the fruit as one rather than four, their scores should be revised: Jay, two; Nip, three; and Ray, seven. The success rate for the five participants then falls to 25 percent.

The success of the illustrations in the stories and the limitations on recognition when text is removed suggest that the BOOST members were strongly aided by context. Of course, the context could be a picture, not text. Once one of the fruit was identified, the other three were soon identified. Morton Heller pointed out to me that the individual objects in a pictorial scene might be easier to recognize than the same objects out of context would be. With Heller's advice I drew figure 3.3.

Three blind volunteers were told that the figure was a picture of a single place containing several objects. The volunteers were Ray (late, totally blind), Kathy R. (early, totally blind), and Kathy N. (early, totally blind at 34 months as a result of operations for congenital cataracts; prior to the operation she was diagnosed as having only light sensitivity). Ray identified every object in the scene, beginning with the flower in the vase. Kathy R. was unable to identify any object until I told her the identity of the table. Then she identified every object except the flower. Beginning with a chair, Kathy N. identified every object. She noted there was no "tie" to pull back the curtains but they "hang just below your window sill, as all good curtains do." Heller's point is vindicated: A scene can produce high rates of object identification.

How do various categories of blind volunteers fare? Heller (1989) gave raised-line pictures of individual objects to early blind, late blind, and blindfolded sighted subjects to identify. The eleven early blind subjects included five totally blind and six with light perception. They ranged in age from 22 to 51. The early blind were blind from birth, with the exception of two, who

Fig. 3.3. A scene presented to blind adults as a raised-line drawing.

suffered from glaucoma and had had sight up to three months of age. The early blind subjects had no known disorders other than blindness, and they had all performed well on tactual tasks or nonpictorial displays such as textures. Heller also tested eleven late blind adults ranging in age from 25 to 54. Two of the late blind had light perception and the remainder were totally blind. Loss of sight was a result of an accident (in five cases) or medical conditions (optic neuritis, optic glaucoma, diabetes, glaucoma, and, in two cases, retinitis pigmentosa). The sighted controls (mean age 33 years, range 21–57 years) were recruited at an undergraduate college and included two recent graduates.

The pictures Heller used were a face, a man, a battery, a key, a bottle, a rubber stamp, a telephone, a hanger, a watch, a pair of scissors, a cane, and an umbrella. The subjects first attempted to identify the pictures unaided and then after the list of possible objects was given. The mean percentage correct on first attempt was 13 percent for the sighted, 9 percent for the early blind, and 36 percent for the late blind. After a list of the names of the objects was given the scores were much higher—60 percent, 49 percent, and 82 percent. The late blind were superior at identifying the pictures both before and after the list of names was given. Heller points out that the late blind have the advantage, like the sighted, of familiarity with pictures and, like the blind, of good tactual exploratory skills. He also notes that the tactile pictures varied considerably in their identifiability. The face was identified unaided by 10 of the 33 volunteers (four sighted, two early blind, and four late blind) and the body by 15 (two sighted, five early blind, and eight late blind). The watch was not identified unaided. After the list of 12 objects was given, the face was identified by 22 subjects (ten sighted, three early blind, and nine late blind) and the body by 27 (seven sighted, nine early blind, and eleven late blind). The watch was identified by 17 people (five sighted, four early blind, and eight late blind) after the list was given. The lowest score after the list was given was for the picture of a bottle, identified by only 14 (three sighted, three early blind, and eight late blind).

Heller asserts that it is inappropriate to argue that all raised-line pictures fail in touch. Some are easy, others hard to identify. The face, he notes, was harder to identify on its own than in the context of the body, so it is not always the simplest pictures that are easiest to identify. He also observes that the elimination of details, to simplify the picture, can mislead subjects. One blind person commented that Heller's picture of a telephone could not be a telephone because Heller had omitted the cord. Many of the "errors" made by the blind make sense of the pictures visually, as Kennedy and Fox (1977) found. One said that the phone was shaped like a mushroom. Another said that the rubber stamp, presented in the shape of a T, was like a table, and that the watch, with a central round dial and short bands on either side, resembled a tray. Heller's volunteers often seemed to know the gross shape of the picture, but since lines can stand for any of several kinds of edges and corners, that knowledge is not enough for identification. It is necessary to run through several possibilities, and to move on to new possibilities if the first one does not make complete sense of the picture.

Heller's conclusion is that visual experience is probably not necessary for tactile perception of pattern and picture perception. His picture of an umbrella involved a half circle for the canopy, shown from the side, and a J for the handle and the shaft, meeting the base of the half circle and showing in depth the shaft of the handle going into the open canopy. The near edge of the canopy occludes the shaft. Understanding this (by eight sighted, six early blind, and eleven late blind) after the list of possible objects was given indicates appreciation of matters of depth, foreground, and background, an edge of a surface overlapping a stick at a T junction. Furthermore, the key picture shows occluding edges. The body and the bottle are defined by occluding bounds. Heller's hanger is a wire shape. Interior detail is sometimes a hole (in the handle of the scissors) and sometimes a raised area (like the buttons of a telephone pad). Heller also notes that few of the pictures were life-sized. Most were reduced in scale, like the umbrella, the walking cane, the man, and, less so, the face, the coat hanger, the telephone, and the bottle. He points out that there was no obvious relation between the absence or presence of change of scale and picture identifiability. "The sighted," he concludes, "did not hold any advantage over the congenitally blind" (p. 387). He argues that if the sighted hold an advantage in some circumstances, the likely reason will involve familiarity. The sighted, he points out, are probably more familiar than the blind with light bulbs and candles, for example (Heller, 1991). Conversely, the blind would have an advantage if the pictures showed devices meant for the blind such as a braille typewriter, a watch dial with braille numbers, a folding long cane, an Optacon scanner (a hand-held device for turning ink print into tactile patterns), or a harness for a guide dog.

Lederman, Klatzky, Chataway, and Summers (1990) and Loomis, Klatzky, and Lederman (1988) present evidence on recognition rates for tactile raised-line pictures from the sighted and the blind. In both studies the pictures included images of a sweater, a pencil, a sock, a light bulb, a comb, an envelope, a screw, a carrot, and a key—objects whose portrayal Lederman et al. described as two-dimensional—and, in addition, a bowl, a candle, a screwdriver, a cup, a hammer, a lock, a whistle, and an ashtray—objects whose portrayal Lederman et al. described as three-dimensional. Lederman et al. also used pictures of a tennis racquet, a baseball bat, a plug, a tie, and a book, and Loomis et al. included pictures of spectacles, scissors, a coat hanger, a glove, a spoon, and a knife.

The Loomis et al. pictures were identified by blindfolded sighted people at rates of 40–50 percent through touch, using one finger or two fingers pressed together. Similar rates were obtained when the pictures were viewed through a narrow aperture, simulating the effect of scanning without input from the perceptual periphery. All of the Loomis et al. pictures except one (the spoon) involved T and X junctions and therefore required decisions about possible edges occluding other features.

The Lederman et al. study found recognition rates of 33 percent among blindfolded sighted participants, slightly lower than Loomis et al., perhaps reflecting the absence of relatively easy images like a spoon, a coat hanger, and a glove, and the presence of the tie and baseball bat images (both of which also had curiously low rates of agreement as drawings examined visually as printed images, perhaps because the pictures had some anomalies or distracting ambiguities).

Lederman et al. asked seven congenitally blind subjects to identify their 22 raised-line drawings. The recognition rate was 10 percent. Like Kennedy and Fox (1977), they found identical recognition rates for their two-dimensional and three-dimensional items. The absolute rates of identification, unaided, were comparable to Kennedy and Fox (12 percent) and to Heller (9 percent, in the part of his study on the congenitally blind).

Lederman et al.'s classification of some pictures as two-dimensional and some as three-dimensional according to the presence of perspective cues or internal lines depicting edges allows room for misgivings. The hammer, classified as three-dimensional, is close to a silhouette, which Kennedy and Fox would have called an imprint. The light bulb, classified as two-dimensional, has internal detail and T junctions indicating occlusion (three-dimensional). The envelope, classified as two-dimensional, has occlusion of one flap by another (three-dimensional). The screwdriver (supposedly three-dimensional) could be an imprint (two-dimensional).

Following the attempt to identify the pictures without any aids, Lederman et al. listed the 22 objects for the subjects and asked them to try again, but this was of no avail. The evidence from other studies, however, is that context and a list of possible objects boosts recognition rates by as much as four or five times the original unaided rates. In Lederman et al., however, the subjects were not encouraged to make their best guess, and they were allowed simply to give up without continuing to the end of the time period.

Pring (in press), of Goldsmith's College, University of London, tested a young girl, Sally, at age 11 years. Sally had lost all her vision at age 16 months. Sally identified only two raised-line pictures (a gun and a comb) out of 15 she attempted. But Sally did not guess at all of the pictures; had she done so, her scores likely would have been somewhat higher. Her errors when she did guess sometimes made good sense: for example, she guessed that a picture of a flower showed a toothbrush because it had a stalk and a head. Pring went on to present another set of drawings together with general hints. A frying pan was described as an object that belongs in a kitchen. Pring writes that Sally's performance then improved dramatically and became almost completely accurate. Pring (1987) found the same result with other congenitally blind children. In a series of studies Pring and her colleagues have found that congenitally blind children succeed at recognizing pictures in texts (Pring and Rusted, 1985) and at using pictures in a variety of memory tasks (Pring and Rusted, 1985; Pring, 1987).

Katz (1946) devised an interesting twist to picture recognition. He obtained drawings from a variety of blind teenagers in Sweden, and after several weeks a sample of the drawings was shown to the people who had made them. More than twenty drawings were tested, and over 75 percent were recognized. Katz went on to determine whether the blind children could understand drawings that were produced by their companions. He gave 12 drawings to 10 volunteers. The teenagers recognized the drawings in 80 of the 120 trials. The best scores were from two who recognized more than 10 pictures each. The two lowest scores were five out of 12 pictures identified. In general, these scores are comparable to those obtained when the subjects tried to identify their own drawings. Katz's subjects were identifying drawings of a man (six examples), a house (four examples), and other objects.

Despite initial appearances, Katz's results are not out of the ordinary. His testing conditions no doubt raised identification rates considerably. It is unusual to ask people to identify the same object drawn by several different people. Also, the subjects had participated earlier in drawing the same objects. I should add that the Katz drawings were in many cases remarkably similar to drawings I have collected from blind teenagers. Unfortunately, Katz gave few details about his volunteers. He described them as 30 pupils aged 12 to 18 years old, but did not make clear how many were congenitally blind. The extent of their blindness was described as very restricted, and he commented that their residual sight could not have had any influence on their drawings. He also mentioned that none of the pupils had any opportunity to practice and develop their drawing ability. For all of his volunteers it was the first time they produced an imaginative drawing. (I shall discuss the drawings further in the next chapter.)

Katz's study of drawings by blind teenagers was largely unknown for many years, until Dankert Vedeler and Alan Costall translated it in 1991 and added valuable commentary (Costall and Vedeler, 1992). It is a unique anticipation of findings that only began to emerge again in the 1970s. Katz himself pointed out the striking similarity of many of the drawings he obtained to drawings by young sighted children. He drew few theoretical lessons from his observations save one: that the three-dimensional spatial imagination of the blind is impressive. Blind people, he asserted, should be considered as having genuine representations of space.

Lederman, Klatzky, Chataway, and Summers (1990) conclude their discussion of low identification rates cautiously. They suggest that "the blind can understand the medium of depiction in principle" and note that the blind "are able to use it to produce their own drawings." But they go on to point out that the blind encounter difficulty in interpretation when unaided by suitable context. They stress the need for displays that feel appropriate, that is, have the relevant texture, thermal properties, and hardness. In terms used by Spelke (1987), they contend that the blind have a sensation-centered version of representation. In addition, Lederman et al. argue that exploring pictures by fingertips is not like grasping and lifting the solid object shown in the picture. In Spelke's terms, they point out action-centered differences.

Of course, sighted people use pictures such as outline drawings that omit color, texture, and changes of occlusion as the vantage point moves. Representation is not literally re-presentation. Sighted people also scan more efficiently and faster with experience. As Heller (1991) argues, so far as tactile pictures for the blind are concerned, "it is not known . . . how much improvement could be expected with practice and training." Shape information, too, does not inevitably depend on the action taken to discover it. We can walk over a curved hill, grasp a curved ball, run a finger over a curved racquet, or be driven around a curve in the road. The different actions discover the same curve at different scales. I think one can share Lederman et al.'s basic conclusion that the blind have a capacity to understand pictures, but there is still much to explore that may improve recognition rates and indicate the basis for the capacity.

CHILDREN IN NORWAY WITH BAS-RELIEFS

Ostad (1989) undertook an important, practical training study with blind school-age children in Norway to investigate ideas raised by Merry in the 1930s (Merry, 1930; Merry, 1932; Merry and Merry, 1933). The Merry experiments attempted to train blind children to identify two-dimensional pictures of three-dimensional objects, with mixed results, perhaps because a sizable proportion of the children had handicaps other than blindness. Some commentators, however, interpreted the results rather one-sidedly as indicating that blind people could not understand perspective "via the tactual modality" (Berla, 1982, p. 365).

Ostad used bas-reliefs and haut-reliefs rather than raised-line drawings. Bas-reliefs use raised areas, not lines. They indicate the foreground surface by a raised plateau (1 mm or 0.4 mm in height in Ostad's study). Unlike raised-line drawings, there is no ambiguity about the location of foreground and background in bas-reliefs. The ambiguity that remains is whether the raised margin stands for an occluding edge or an occluding bound. Further, raised lines can depict convex or concave corners, and bas-reliefs omit these features. A bas-relief in principle could show a wire, track, or crack. Typically, however, fine internal details such as cracks between adjoining surfaces are omitted. In this way bas-reliefs are comparable to silhouettes. All the bas-reliefs used by Ostad show objects in profile, their main axes parallel to the picture surface, like the imprints used by Kennedy and Fox (1977).

The haut-reliefs were representations made by a thermoforming process. Thermoforms are plastic moldings of objects. A plastic sheet is heated and allowed to mold itself to an object, with some assistance by vacuum suction to ensure a close fit. The sheet is then allowed to cool and solidify and the object is removed from beneath it. The result is a stiff plastic mold that provides the same pattern of protrusions and hollows as the original object had. The object to be copied is usually left flat on a supporting surface, with the plastic sheet to be thermoformed resting on the object. In effect, the object forms an imprint with internal detail. Objects like a hammer, which is elongated chiefly in two dimensions, make a clear haut-relief. A rounded object like a ball or pear, which is elongated equally in three dimensions, is usually sliced in half before the process is begun, and only the side facing the observer is copied. Four of Ostad's haut-reliefs were based on models, such as of a ladder and a walking stick. Others were natural-sized.

The objects made as bas-reliefs and haut-reliefs by Ostad were a pear, an apple, a banana, a spoon, a fork, a knife, a boot, a shoe, a cap, a mitten, a jug, a cup, a bottle, an egg cup, pliers, a hammer, scissors, a bottle opener, a modern key, an old-fashioned key, a weight (a cylinder with a knob on top), a hand, a horseshoe, a ruler, a walking stick, a spade, a saw, and a ladder. (Only some of Ostad's pictures are easily identified by vision, it should be noted. Some are fairly ambiguous as silhouettes in visual inspection—for example, a cap in the form of a toque or skier's cap with a tassel). The egg cup and the weight are easily confused with each other, the ruler is merely a rectangle, and Ostad's mitten resembles a face with a prominent upturned nose. I tested Ostad's ink print versions of his figures on three sighted colleagues. One failed to identify three figures, another four figures, and the third six figures.)

The subjects in Ostad's study were 40 pupils from schools in Norway. Total blindness or light perception was the key criterion for inclusion. In the case of three pupils, the amount of vision may have been slightly more than light perception, but their vision was not enough to be used functionally in a school setting. The students were blind from birth (33) or went blind during the first year of life (six), except for one pupil who lost vision gradually during the first year of life, reaching total blindness around one year of age. No student had a disability that prevented the use of language in the interview, or tactual exploration of the displays, or participation in ordinary education in standard Norwegian curricula. Most (26) were in an institution for the blind, and 14 were integrated into regular classrooms. There were 16 girls and 24 boys, ranging in age from seven to 18. The numbers are close to the maximum that could have been tested in Norway at the period of the study. (Norwegian records indicate a further seven blind students; some were not involved in Ostad's study because of illness at the time.)

Ostad pretested half of the materials, gave some training on the same materials, and posttested both the training set and the nontrained materials.

Ostad began by asking the students to identify real objects or solid models of objects. The identification rate was 91 percent. The pretest also included bas-reliefs, in a mixture of sizes ranging from 10 cm to 1.5 cm, and haut-reliefs. Overall the children identified 25 percent of the bas-reliefs and 32 percent of the haut-reliefs.

Evidently the change from real objects to plastic molds of the objects introduces difficulty, in part by making the material of the stimuli uniform and different from that of the original object. Deregowski (1989) notes that sighted people in Ethiopia unfamiliar with pictures also find that unfamiliar material forming a picture's surface interferes with their perceiving the picture as a representation. From first principles one would predict that as regards recognizability bas-reliefs should be intermediate between haut-reliefs and outline drawings, since they use edges with more ambiguity than haut-reliefs and less ambiguity than outline. At 25 percent the results are indeed intermediate between the 32 percent for Ostad's haut-reliefs and the 10–12 percent recognition rate for individual outline pictures without context obtained by other investigators.

In the pretest Ostad investigated size differences. Pictures between 10 cm and 6 cm in height were identified at comparable rates (the 6 cm pictures at a slightly higher rate than the 10 cm ones). Natural-size pictures scored somewhat higher (24 percent higher) and 1.5 cm pictures noticeably lower (about 50 percent lower). The results suggest that natural size is a good clue to an object's identity; but once that size is changed, the scale can vary without effect on recognition rates until the image becomes too small for the shape on the picture surface to be easily discriminated.

Ostad divided his pupils into three age groups, mean eight years old (13 students), mean 11 years old (14 students) and mean 15 years old (13 students). He found no statistically reliable difference in their identification rates; indeed the youngest group scored marginally higher than the older two. Ostad also studied the relation between identification rates and various measures of the students' abilities. As one might expect, pupils scored better if they had good fine motor skills, were attentive, showed a higher level of motivation, were better at following instructions, had good vocabularies, had good memory for tactile patterns, and scored higher in a measure of attention span plus, oddly enough, an arithmetic test. Apart from fine motor skills, these sound like measures of alertness and test-taking skills rather than anything specific to a pictorial task.

An important part of Ostad's study was an assessment of the effects of a brief training period. Pupils were tested for the recognition task one day, then were given brief training and retested the next weekday. The retest involved new items. The items used in the first test and training for half the pupils were used in the retest for the other pupils. In total, the amount of time for all the tests and training was no more than two hours.

The training procedure involved showing the objects themselves and then pictures, proceeding from the natural-size picture down to the smallest picture of each object. Initially, one picture was examined at a time. The experimenter pointed out the important features that characterized particular objects. Once five items had been examined individually, the five pictures were given as a group for the student to identify all five. A further five items were then explained, and the student was asked to identify the ten items practiced thus far. Then the remainder of the objects were examined. Finally, pictures of practiced objects were selected at random, one at a time, for the student to identify.

The result of this training was that students improved on both practiced items and new, untested items. Among the haut-reliefs 82 percent of the practiced items were identified on the posttraining test with more than 40 percent of the students identifying all the practiced haut-reliefs. On the unpracticed items 50 percent were identified, a significant increase from the original 32 percent found on the pretest. (It is not possible to find out from Ostad's procedure how much of the improvement on practiced items was due to getting the list of possibilities during the training period, but it is probably quite sizable.) On the bas-reliefs 80 percent of the practiced items were identified. On the unpracticed items 37 percent of the pictures were identified, again a significant increase from the original 25 percent on the pretest. All three age groups improved by comparable amounts. Ostad also found that the amount of gain on practiced items and the degree of transference of training to unpracticed items were not related to any of a battery of items on which the children were rated by their teachers, including such matters as ability to follow instructions. Further, Ostad reports that the amount of improvement was not dependent on the size of the picture being tested. Recognition of small pictures improved about as much as that of larger pictures. Similarly, amount of improvement was not related to the student's fine motor skills. In Ostad's words, "the correlations between the age of the pupils and the results for pretest, posttest–practiced and posttest–unpracticed and as regards gain and transference of learning were in no case statistically significant" (p. 179).

Ostad summarizes the results thus: "after a fairly short period of training (about 1½ hours) . . . gain was statistically significant. . . . [O]ur results are rather better than we had reason to expect" (p. 223). Ostad is concerned that not enough transfer to the unpracticed items occurred to ensure their recognition. He notes, however, that sizable improvements were found for the un-practiced items. I wonder if merely presenting the list of possible objects in the unpracticed set would achieve a sizable boost, as happened in the studies of several investigators using outline drawings. It may not be necessary to give the test subjects much more assistance in identifying unpracticed items to bring the identification rate close to that for practiced items. To be certain of achieving identification, explicit training may be necessary, but the thorough procedure Ostad used may lay most of the ground on which new items could be identified with little additional help.

In sum, this study on the majority of early-blind school-age students in Norway, using pictorial bas-reliefs, finds initial rates of identification of picto-rial displays that are reasonable in light of previous investigations with outline drawings. Major gains on a group of practiced items result from a short training session, even for the youngest children in the study. Unpracticed bas-relief items in the final test were identified at a rate of almost 40 percent, a practical level of performance and an encouraging indication of what can be achieved with minimal training. With a modest extended training program, who knows what level would be attained?

Ostad's study produced one especially curious and unsettling finding. Some of the students who were youngest and scored highest in the pretest (over 35 percent of the bas-reliefs originally) slipped on posttesting with the unpracticed bas-reliefs (to just over 25 percent). With the practiced bas-reliefs, this group scored well (close to 85 percent). It is not clear why they performed less well on the unpracticed items than other students. There may have been a shift in criterion. Students who had done well originally and were almost always correct on the practiced items may have been increasingly unwilling to reveal their ideas and "guess" on unfamiliar items. This kind of problem can be avoided by forced-choice procedures.

Ostad's work reveals, I think, a basic ability among the blind to decipher pictures, probably without being taught, and it reiterates something we should take for granted: namely, that blind people can be taught. There is no major scientific lesson in the fact that Ostad's students improved. But for some readers—parents and educators especially—it may be vitally important to know just how brief the training period can be and still produce noticeable results. There is nothing in Ostad's report, I hasten to add, to say that the full 1–2 hour period was necessary, or how much was achieved in the first or last minutes, or which part of the training procedure was most valuable, and for whom. These are all open questions. I expect that a boost was given by instruction on the first few pictures, which confirmed intuitions the children had about what outlines can stand for. I also anticipate that a large part of the improvement during the test resulted from learning the list of options. For some students a good deal of improvement may have come from the realization that the contour of the referent was a key factor. For others, the realization that they could decipher pictures unaided may have been quite motivating. For still others, the test-taking situation may have been something they gradually came to enjoy and feel relaxed about (though for a few an initial interest may have been followed by increasing boredom!). Training studies like Ostad's fall short in that they do not reveal what underlies the ability to identify pictures. Ostad's work should now be supplemented by careful investigation of the abilities shown by the children in the pretest and of the manner in which training procedures spread their effects from trained items—which gain, in Ostad's terms—to specific kinds of untrained items—which get transfer of training, in Ostad's words.

ORIENTATION AND THE PICTURE SURFACE

Pictures, as Lederman et al. point out, are a medium. Like all media, they have their own physical properties, which can be treated independently of the physical properties of the referent. If we raise a picture on the wall, we do not raise the apparent height of a child shown in the picture. If one places on one's lap a newspaper with a photograph of a man standing up, one is not fooled by the medium's orientation into thinking that he is lying down.

With BOOST adults Maryanne Heywood and I tested this understanding of orientation of the medium. We cut two circles of Braille paper. One circle was impressed with a raised-line drawing of a man facing sideways (see fig. 3.4). The other bore a picture of a man in front view. We presented these pictures vertically (as if on a wall) and horizontally (as if lying on a table). The man's axis was medial (parallel to the volunteer's body midline) or transverse (parallel to the volunteer's waistline). The volunteers were asked whether the man was portrayed in the picture as standing or lying down. Seventeen blind adults participated (see table 3.4): six early totally blind, four late totally blind, two with light perception since birth, two with light perception conditions arising later in life, and three with low vision, two congenitally and one with the condition arising later in life.

We sampled the possible array of stimulus conditions (Kennedy, 1980). We gave 45 medial presentations and 33 transverse. In every medial presentation (22 profile, 23 frontal) the depicted man was described as standing. Interestingly, in 16 of the 45 presentations the blind person mentioned as a secondary option that with an effort of will one can imagine the person as lying in bed and being observed from above. We gave 33 transverse placements (16 frontal

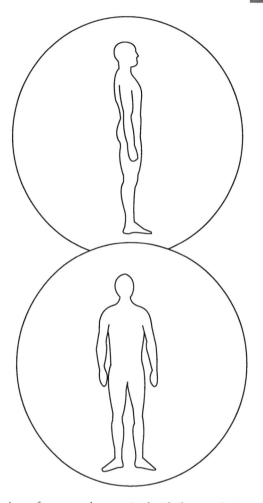

Fig. 3.4. Drawings of a man, to be examined with the page horizontal or vertical.

and 17 profile figures). In all but one the depicted man was deemed to be lying down. No volunteer mentioned a secondary option in this case. Sighted readers may care to try this demonstration for themselves, using figure 3.4. Sighted people typically find that the 90° change from horizontal to vertical makes no difference to the apparent orientation of the man portrayed. But the 90° change from medial to transverse makes it seem as though the man changes from standing to lying down. This is what the blind are reporting too. In the real world of solid objects, a person who is medial vis-à-vis another person is most likely standing up, except in the one exceptional case where the observer is standing at the foot of the person's bed. A person who is transverse vis-à-vis an upright observer is generally lying down. This freedom of the medium's orientation (horizontal versus vertical) is responded to similarly by the blind and the sighted.

A number of the participants in picture identification studies referred to the pictures as having a top and a bottom. They indicated, for instance, that it was natural to show an object such as an elephant or coat hanger with its head or hook at the top of the page and its feet or base to the bottom. Since the page is actually flat on the table in front of the subjects it is horizontal. What viewers call the top of the page is the part of the page farthest from the subject, and the bottom is the part nearest the subject. Whether one is reading Braille or reading printed text, the top of the page is the same part of the page. Conceivably, some of the similarity between visual and haptic orientation of a picture could be a spillover from reading. But I conjecture that the phenomenon has been with us since before reading was possible, in early childhood, and also in the days of cave art. I think that it is a product of our understanding of space, not print.

TESTS OF BLIND CHILDREN IN ARIZONA

The BOOST members we tested were adults and, being involved in self-help strategies for political and vocational assistance to the handicapped, are active, vociferous adults at that. One wonders whether blind children would show the same abilities that the BOOST adults revealed. To answer this question, Heywood and I took up an opportunity kindly offered to us by educators in Arizona (Foundation for Blind Children) and Haiti (St. Vincent School) to try some pictorial materials in schools for the handicapped in Phoenix, Tucson, and Port-au-Prince. Our United States study was conducted first in Phoenix and later in Tucson.

All the children we worked with in Arizona were blind early in life. Some were totally blind and some had a degree of sensitivity to light. Again I shall describe them, for example, as "early blind with light perception" or "early, light perception" for short. The Phoenix children included seven who were early, totally blind, and four who were early, light perception (table 3.6). The early, totally blind ranged in age from six to 13 (mean age 8.4) and the early, light perception children were ages 12–14. Apart from Hal, who went totally blind at age two as a result of a chemical accident, all were blind from birth. The Tucson children were three early, totally blind children and four early, light perception children. All were blind from birth.

The pictorial experience of some of the Arizona children included a few

TABLE 3.6
Blind children tested in Phoenix, Arizona. All are blind since birth except Hal, who is blind since age 2½.

Totally Blind		Light Perception	
Name	Age (Years)	Name	Age (Years)
Di	6	Li	12
Sean	6	Noel	12
Kit	8	Gale	14
Ray	8	Ted	14
Roy	8		
Eve	13		
Hal	10		

picture books. Notably, they had used the Expectation series from California. Generally the illustrations in these books are in a cartoon or caricature style, which is somewhat unrealistic. They are easy to recognize visually but complex and difficult to interpret in touch. One difficulty for touch is that the objects are often shown in unusual poses. An instance is a picture of a dragon resting on a walking stick with his tail curled under him. Another difficulty is the relative size of features. Small features are exaggerated. In one picture of a lion seated on his haunches, the teeth, the curls of the mane, the tail, the toes, and the claws are all the same size. No features are distinct. Teachers of the blind children and the librarians in schools for the blind, in conversation with me, indicated that they do not use these illustrations for the totally blind. They seem to be too complicated, the educators reported, or to be a mass of small features with no overall prominent shape. The children were not encouraged to decipher them. After a few failures, teachers and students gave up. Blind children, however, were often not expected by their teachers or librarians to understand any kind of depiction until our research with pictures and the blind came to the attention of the school staff. Perhaps with more suitable pictures, some persistence and modest expectations, renewed efforts would be rewarded.

The Phoenix children were asked to identify raised-line drawings (fig. 3.5) of a hand, a mitten, a place setting (plate with knife, spoon, and fork—scored all as one item), a cup, a teapot, a face, and a set of four pieces of fruit (scored as one item). The total possible score was 77 (11 children trying seven items). The children identified 37 of the items. The six younger children (aged 6–10)

Fig. 3.5. Drawings identified by blind children.

identified 15 items and the five older children (aged 12–14) identified 22 items.

The picture of a hand was identified by nine of the Phoenix children. The mitten was only identified by two—not surprising since mittens are not commonly worn by children in Arizona. The place setting was identified four times and all the other items in the first set of pictures were identified by five or six of the 11 children who attempted them.

Encouraged by this success, we arranged extended interviews. We were able to meet further with six of the children. Sean (age six), Ray (age eight), Kit (age eight), Hal (age 10), Noel (age 12), and Gale (age 14) were given an extra four pictures—a boot, a car, a telephone, and a hammer (figure 3.6). The total possible score was 24 (six children attempting four items). The children identified 13 of the pictures. This was the first study we conducted in which more than half of the pictures presented without context were identified. It was an occasion for celebration!

The boot was identified by three of the six children who attempted it, the car by five, the telephone by two, and the hammer by three. Rather than simply giving out a list of possibilities we tried prompting the children with hints once we judged that they were unable to identify a particular picture spontaneously. The hints were superordinate categories, for example, "It's a kind of fruit." These prompts were highly successful. Prompts after the 40 unsuccessful trials for the first set of 11 objects led to a further 30 identifications; after the 11 unsuccessful trials for the second set of four objects prompts produced a further eight identifications. Thus the success rate (al-

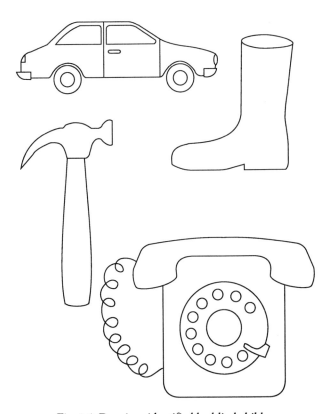

Fig. 3.6. Drawings identified by blind children.

most 75 percent) is extremely high after the target has been narrowed down by a superordinate category, just as in our earlier study illustrations made sense readily in the context of some story.

Following the first set of 11 pictures and their prompts, we invited all the children to try an illustrated story. We gave the Duckling story to 10 children. Nine went through the story unaided, to their own satisfaction. The child who needed assistance, Noel, said he didn't know why only one eye and one wing were shown. When it was explained that this was "from the side," he said "You drew only one side of it—the left side." We asked the children who did not request assistance about the presence of only one wing and one eye. Kit was asked where the second wing should be, as she tried the first picture, which presents a wing. On this picture she pointed to a place to one side of the first wing. But she corrected herself when she had the final picture, and indicated that the "other" eye and the "other" wing would have to be on the other side of the picture. Roy and Sean identified all the parts of the bird, but when asked where the second wing or eye would be, they said they didn't know. They did not, however, ask for aid; they seemed to accept each picture and identify its parts even if they could not answer our question about parts not shown. Clear answers to our question about missing parts were given by Li (age 12), Ray (age eight), Kit (age eight), and Gale (age 14). We noted with interest Li's comment on our composite picture: "This isn't like the ones in Expectations. You can't tell what they are. This one looks like a bird." I think the reason for the answer is that the cartoon-style caricature in the Expectations series appears less realistic than our plainer drawing with more realistic proportions and fewer, more pronounced major features.

In Tucson, we tested seven children (see table 3.7). Three (ages five, six, and seven) were totally blind from birth. Four (three age 12, one age 14) were capable of light perception—again all with congenital conditions. We attempted to test one child age seven who had attention difficulties, but had to give up. One of the 12-year-olds also had major attention and educational difficulties, but we persevered as long as we could in a single interview, and I shall report a tiny signal of ability from him.

The pictures we gave the children to identify were the hand, the place setting, the cup, the teapot, and the face. Lu (age five) identified one picture—the place setting. Tip (age six) identified the face. Amy identified the hand, the cup, the teapot, and the face—four out of five successful recognitions from a seven-year-old! We were quite impressed. Raf (age 12) also identified four pictures, all except the hand. Then Jef (age 12) identified all five. He was the first person in our interviews to identify every picture. It was a special occa-

TABLE 3.7

Blind children tested in Tucson, Arizona. All are blind since birth.

Totally Blind		Light Perception	
Name	Age (Years)	Name	Age (Years)
Lu	5	Jef	12
Tip	6	Lar	12
Amy	7	Raf	12
		Ole	14

sion. Lar (age 12), however, identified only one picture, the place setting. (He was regarded as two or three grades behind his peers, but I fear that was an optimistic assessment.) Ole (age 14) identified four pictures, all except the place setting.

The Duckling story was attempted by all of the children. Lu (age five) needed prompting. Tip (age six) identified all the parts, but when asked said she didn't know why only one eye was shown. Amy (age seven) identified the parts, but took the line representing the left part of the wing to be one wing and the line representing the right of the wing to be another wing. We corrected her about this wing. Then when we asked where the other wing is, she said, "On the other side."

Lar had the parts named for him, beginning with those he had already identified. He finally identified all the parts. Prompting for Lar had to be quite directive, with questions like, "What comes out of the *top* of a body?," to which he replied, "A head." He then went on, however, to point out the relevant parts. Lar showed a mixture of inability and competence. He had trouble figuring things out, but if questions were made progressively easier he could pick out the correct answer without it being told to him and then use that answer to proceed. Although he had extremely limited problem-solving abilities, once he had identified a part he could readily reidentify it. Much the same pattern was evident in his identification of individual pictures without context. We have credited him with identifying the place setting.

That instance of identification should be described, since we have some misgivings. Lar attempted to decipher the hand picture but failed. Then he was reminded that the picture had five things sticking out, and he was asked what part of his body had five parts sticking out. He guessed fingers. Lar was next given the place setting, and while checking the plate he said "circle," "apple," "ball." In examining the fork he guessed "my fingers," "a plastic hand." Lar may have been persevering with the previous information about the hand picture, so he was given what we consider to be a very nondirective nudge. He was told it was not a part of his body. He immediately guessed "fork." Then he guessed that the circle was a bowl, and identified the knife and spoon. Despite the nondirective hint, Lar is credited as having identified the place setting unaided.

In sum, the Tucson children identified many of the pictures (20 out of 35) and fared well with the Duckling story. Three 5–7-year-olds identified a total of six pictures, and the four older children (12–14 years old) identified 14 pictures.

The Phoenix and Tucson children were quite impressive in their abilities. The evidence they provide supplements Ostad's. It indicates that school-age blind children in Arizona, as in Norway, like the adult students tested in the Boston and Toronto studies, can use haptic pictures with little or no previous experience with pictures, and little or no tuition.

Studies with sighted children (Kennedy, 1974a, p. 57) indicate that pictures are readily identified across the whole range of intellectual ability. Experience with Lar gives us caution. Touch is a slower, more painstaking sense for shape and space than vision is. Perhaps the success with the Arizona children and the adults would not be easy to duplicate with a disadvantaged group. The Arizona children, for example, were quite skillful in tactual exploration. They had been taught by their teachers to be patient, and we noticed that they explored the displays thoroughly, checking every line. They often repeated their initial investigation of some parts. These are all skills that the Arizona schools emphasize. Sighted children, too, must build up attention skills and visual inspection skills in the first few years of life. As part of their perceptual education at home and at school they are exposed to hidden-figure puzzles or reversible displays, what's-different pairs of pictures, count-the-shapes patterns, and the like. Similarly, blind children need to improve their tactual inspection processes. If one does not inspect the bulk of the display, how can one be expected to identify it? If one does not have good test-taking skills, how can one show identification skills? All these questions loomed large in our next study. As shall become evident, we found, rather unexpectedly, that picture-identification skills can be minimal even if there are respectable picture-drawing skills. In this chapter difficulties with picture identification are described. In chapter 5, the same group of subjects are shown to be able to draw.

Outline Drawings

CHILDREN IN HAITI

Haiti is the least-developed country in the Western Hemisphere. If blind children in Haiti, who receive little or no schooling, could decipher raised-line pictures, then it could be claimed that haptic pictures would be useful to the blind anywhere in the world. But it is not so. The evidence leads me to think that general exploratory skills must be taught before exposure to haptic pictures can be helpful, although one should not conclude that pictorial skills per se need to be taught as a convention.

The Haitian children we interviewed were attending a residential school for the visually handicapped in Port-au-Prince. They were tested by Diane Girard and myself. There were 15 children, ranging in age from six to 18, with a mean age of 12.5 years. Their mean level of educational attainment was first grade (eight children were at kindergarten level, two at first grade, one at second grade, one at third grade, and three at fifth grade; see table 3.8). Their

TABLE 3.8

Blind children tested in Port-au-Prince, Haiti. All of the children except Jan, who has light perception, are totally blind.

Name	Age at Testing (Years)	Education	Status and Etiology*
Cel	6	Kindergarten	Blind before age 3 years, malnutrition
Mim	9	Kindergarten	Blind before 5, malnutrition
All	10	Kindergarten	Blind before 4, malnutrition
Ber	10	Kindergarten	Blind before 10, etiology unknown
Ron	11	Third grade	Blind before 2, glaucoma
Yvr	11	Kindergarten	Blind before 11, etiology unknown
Man	12	Kindergarten	Blind before 5, malnutrition
Ild	13	First grade	Blind before 3, malnutrition
Mit	13	Second grade	Blind before 9, etiology unknown
Jag	14	Kindergarten	Blind before 13, etiology unknown
Sol	14	Kindergarten	Blind before 14, etiology unknown
Phi	15	Fifth grade	Blind before 1½, blastosis and surgery
Ren	15	Fifth grade	Blind before 7, etiology unknown
Jan	18	Fifth grade	Light perception at 15, keratitis

*Age at onset of blindness often cannot be determined; instead the age at admission to the school for the visually impaired is given.

age at the onset of blindness was frequently unclear (medical records in Haiti are scanty). The reasons for their blindness were unknown in six cases, and the reason was malnutrition in five cases. All except Jan (light perception) are totally blind.

Many of the children come from regions beyond Port-au-Prince, but all are from poor quarters of the country. Health and educational resources are scarce in Haiti, and those few resources, as I discovered firsthand when I visited hospitals and schools there, are severely restricted for the poor. A technical high school I visited in Port-au-Prince was all but devoid of books, charts, and diagrams. Instruction seemed to be largely by demonstration, with a few machines for the boys and sewing equipment for the girls. A large part of education in Haiti consisted of learning texts by rote. The resources for the blind include a collection of Braille books without illustrations. My surveys of the school for the handicapped and discussions with the staff indicated that pictorial materials have not been used.

The children at the school for the handicapped are in many ways fortunate to have been enrolled there. The staff are warm and caring. The principal of the school is a saint. The volunteers give a great deal of themselves. The grounds of the school are a friendly place. The children learn a great deal about music and acquire basic literacy and numerical skills. It is a good guess that they are being educated better than most of their fellow Haitians. In addition, they are no longer malnourished.

For some of the children the records indicate blindness before age three. Since for five of them the reason was malnutrition at an early age, blindness is likely to be compounded by cognitive and attention difficulties.

Bearing in mind the setting for the test, we pared down the set of pictures to include only objects with which we could be confident the Haitian children were familiar: a face, a hand, and a hammer. All of the children had probably used one or had had the chance to explore a hammer tactually, since manual skills are emphasized. Also, there was construction under way at the school as we were testing, and noisy hammering rang through the rooms where we were interviewing.

In recognition tests of the three pictures, the Haitian children did not fare well. Only one child, Yvr (age 11, kindergarten-level attainments, totally blind, etiology of blindness unknown, age of onset unknown) identified any picture (the face).

As we watched the Haitian children exploring the pictures it was evident why they were not succeeding. They did not explore efficiently. They did not make contact with all of the picture. They often used a flat hand, involving a lot of palm and length-of-finger skin as though deciphering textures, with the fingers spread out to contact the display. Often very little hand motion was used. Rarely was any part of the display explored with the fingertips. This technique may be fine if one is going to pick up an object or is rubbing with a cloth, but to discover a pattern made of lines it is inadequate. The lines should be touched with the fingertips. The fingers should move over the display systematically and thoroughly. These are the kinds of exploratory moves used by the Arizona children and Boston and Toronto adults when they are given line displays.

If we had only undertaken picture-identification tasks in Haiti, we would have come away empty-handed. Certainly before going to Haiti we had a simplistic idea about the relation between identification and other pictorial tasks. For the sighted child it is much easier to identify a complex picture than to draw it. Identification tasks are much better for showing pictorial skills in the sighted than most other tasks, like estimating size or distance or mass or roughness. Drawing is especially difficult. This may not be so, however, in touch.

A complex pictorial shape that takes a blind adult several minutes to decipher may be beyond the spontaneous tactual skills of some blind children. But this is not to say that the referent's shape is unknown to the child. Over the years, a fairly good understanding of the complex shape of the real object may have been acquired. If we ask the child to draw, and to explain the drawing as she goes, the results may be revealing. The first few lines of the drawing may correspond clearly to the features of the referent. Perhaps only a few lines will be completed by the child, and the picture may never become sufficiently detailed to specify the particular referent. But her explanation of each of these few lines may fit exactly with the use that the sighted consider appropriate in outline drawings. Perhaps, too, the geometrical principles used to make the distribution of lines on paper fit with the arrangement of features on the object can be evident in those first few lines and their explanation. The geometrical system might even be one the sighted child uses.

In short, a complex picture may be too challenging a task to reveal much of the blind child's knowledge. But his own drawings may sometimes display what the complex pictures cannot bring out for lack of skills in exploration (see chapter 5).

All of the studies reviewed here revealed some success among the blind at identifying pictures. These limited levels of success are important. They give a practical base on which to proceed. The practical psychologist will want to know how to improve the rates of identification. The theorist will want to know what underpins the limited attainments.

The genuine, modest performances shown in the results do not immediately translate into a coherent theory of touch and depiction. But some interpretations flow fairly readily from the studies. One rather sour possibility is that outline pictures do not actually make much sense to the blind. Instead, the blind subject makes out a flat pattern, much like a meaningless flat map of the coastline of an unknown country. If a few suggestions are given verbally, then the blind person can decide that something is a fork and not a ball, since the drawing has some sharp points. But the drawing never falls into place; it never constitutes a coherent schema, where every line has a clear significance.

On some occasions, blind subjects may have identified a picture in this rather cramped way. Sometimes I have done the same when exploring a picture blindfold. But this cannot be the whole story. When asked to go over a picture piecemeal and identify the parts of an object or to comment on aspects that were difficult to decipher, blind people were found to be adept at detail. They gave a stream of comments about what was missing, what was present, and what was misleading. In short, there is a clear difference between a mass of indecipherable details with a few lines that permit some guesswork and a picture.

An alternative thesis is that haptic pictures feel like the objects they depict. Taken baldly, this thesis implies that blind people feel the roundedness of a cylinder when exploring a rectangle standing for an elephant's leg. Taken to extremes, the "feel-like" theory holds that a person can mistake a picture for the real thing (in miniature, perhaps). The picture, then, becomes a kind of illusion. There is no evidence to support the extreme feel-like theory. No blind person ever mistakes a flat surface for a three-dimensional scene or takes a depicted object to be a detached object lying on the flat surface of the picture.

The truth lies somewhere between the two extremes. The blind are not noticing an occasional feature and then guessing at the identity of the whole object, and they are not taking the depicted object to feel like the real thing. Rather, the lines in the drawings are understood as standing for a variety of features of relief. The configuration of the lines allows the observer to determine what individual lines stand for. A straight line stands for the occluding bound of a cylinder if it is part of a drawing of a limb. It can also indicate the occluding edge of a flat surface, or the leg of a table, or a corner. The observer is able to take an outline—a raised ridge on a flat page—and use it to stand for a feature of relief where depth and slant change. Even though the ridge has two sides, the observer can accept it as a depiction of a feature of relief formed by one change of depth or slant.

My supposition, following the discussion in chapter 2, is that touch extracts the axis of the ridge. It is not primarily concerned with matching one of the ridge's sides where depth falls off with a depth change in the depicted object. If that were the case, then a line might stand for an occluding edge or boundary. The line might also stand for a wire, using both of its sides to stand for the depth change on either side of a wire. But it would not be possible for a line to stand for a concave corner, where the slant changes on either side of the corner to bring the two surfaces from the corner closer to the observer. The depths on either side of the ridge are drop-offs, and the slants on either side of a concave corner are the opposite.

Presumably, haptics extracts the axis of lines in outline drawings and then dispenses with the information about depth on either side of the ridge forming the line. The axes are locations, not depth differences. The axis could be based on grooves rather than ridges. That is, they could be based on recessed lines formed by depth changes that are the opposite of raised lines.

Once haptics extracts the axes of raised lines, it is in the same situation as vision after vision has extracted the axes of lines formed by two brightness contours. It is in the position of noting that there is a feature of relief in a particular location. It must use the information around the line to determine which feature of relief is relevant. It will rely on rules of surface geometry and types of objects to establish the relevant feature. These rules are in common to vision and haptics since sight and touch both deal with surfaces and their arrangements. Hence, there is every likelihood that the processes affecting haptic use of outline drawings are the same processes that control vision when it employs outline drawings.

Blind people do recognize the same kinds of outline drawings of objects as sighted people. But it is not certain that touch extracts axes or uses them to stimulate amodal processes containing surface geometry. It will take much more inquiry to test and confirm some of the speculations about axes in touch. Some support for the basic observations here is still needed, and I shall now turn to a basic question stemming from the studies on recognition: If the blind can recognize some drawings made by sighted people, can they spontaneously produce drawings that follow the same principles?

TWO ILLUSTRATED STORIES USING RAISED-LINE DRAWINGS

Guitar: A Night in the Life of a Mouse

Once upon a time there was a little mouse with a long tail and little skinny legs. And the mouse had long whiskers so that at night he could tell the shape of things (1).

One night the mouse came across a big object lying on the floor. There were six things sticking out of the end of it like little doorknobs, and when he jumped on them they turned (2).

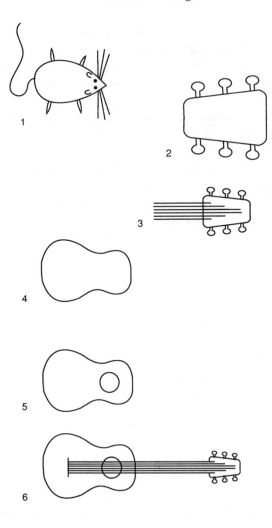

But they turned just a tiny bit, because each one was held very tightly by a string. As the mouse ran along the strings, they made a sound, "zing, zing" (3).

When he got to the other end of the strings, the mouse jumped off, and landed on some flat smooth wood. He ran all around the edge of it and found it was shaped like a big circle squeezed together near the middle (4).

When he ran across the wood, it was so smooth and slippery that he slipped and slid and fell right down into a hole! (5).

So he discovered that this object was hollow, and it echoed every little sound he made, as he sniffed all around the inside. Suddenly, he heard footsteps, and he jumped out of the hole, ran across the smooth wood, hopped up on the strings and ran along them, jumped onto the knobbly end, and ran away.

In a far corner of the room, the little mouse listened to the footsteps coming closer, and with each footstep, the object on the floor went "zing, zing" very very quietly but he heard it just the same, because mice as you know have very good ears. Then a boy came into the room and walked toward the object. The boy picked up his guitar and began to play it (6).

Tricycle: What's All the Noise About?

Bang! Bang! Clunk!

John came rushing out to see what all the noise was about. Someone was hammering and clanging in the garage. John ran over to the door, and there was his brother,

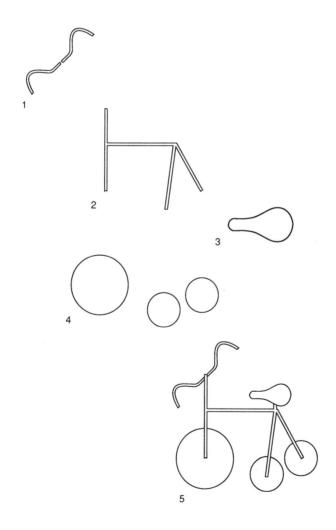

Mark, building something. But John couldn't tell what, because scattered all over the floor there were pieces of rubber and metal pipe.

John shouted over all the noise, "Hey, what are you making?"

Mark stopped for a minute, smiled, and said mysteriously, "Guess."

John tiptoed all around the odd-shaped bits and pieces. He noticed a curved metal tube (1). What could it be? A cow's horns? Would Mark be building a cow? It didn't seem very likely! There was another piece that looked more like part of a chair (2). But John thought, "My brother must be a strange carpenter—unless he's making a three-legged chair!"

John picked up a smaller piece. It was made of hard rubber, and shaped something like a squished pear (3). "Hmm," thought John, "Now I think I know what it is."

When he came across a big wheel and two smaller wheels (4), he was certain he knew.

"I've got it!" he shouted. "It's a tricycle!"

"You're right," smiled Mark.

And so the two brothers worked together, and later that day, John had a brand new tricycle (5).

CHAPTER FOUR

Drawings
by the
Blind

To ask blind people to draw is to ask people unfamiliar with pictures to show solid objects by means of flat paper and marks on the paper produced by a stylus. The task is one that young sighted children happily take on themselves. Like sighted children, blind people can be novices at drawing, but if they are articulate adults they can put into words some of the difficulties they meet in trying to draw. In this chapter, I shall examine the outcome of drawing tasks given to blind volunteers (adults and children) and discuss some of the issues raised by the participants.

My chief aim is to show that blind people draw using the same outline system that governs their recognition of haptic pictures. I shall provide examples of blind people using lines to stand for occluding edges of flat surfaces, occluding bounds of rounded surfaces, and single lines standing for features like wires. A secondary aim is to show that the patterns of lines produced by the blind are appropriate rough copies of the shapes of objects, demonstrating how the parts of objects are laid out with respect to each other and the observer's vantage point.

The axis theory of outline that I have presented in the previous chapters predicts that lines will be used by the blind to stand for features of surface relief. The amodal theory of spatial apprehension anticipates that blind people should try to depict the same spatial arrangements as the sighted. But depiction is a skillful act. It is not easy to step from what we know to what we can represent. Blind people might scout around attempting to use lines for a variety of features other than the ones that might capitalize on their abilities with axes before realizing the effectiveness of using lines to represent relief features. Spatial arrangements in three dimensions cannot be replicated on a sheet that only has two. Precisely how the novice might attempt this rendering of three via two is not something the amodal theory can predict. There are many ways three can be approached via two and many ways that the amodal sense of solid shape could influence sketches on a flat surface. I use the cautious term *influence* advisedly, because the intuitive understanding of amodal shape that allows us to recognize an object is only one of the factors governing drawing. Other players in the story will make themselves known as we proceed.

BLIND ADULTS DRAWING A HAND

The first drawing studies I undertook (Kennedy, 1980) were with adult volunteers from BOOST in Toronto, and the tests were conducted with the assistance of Maryanne Heywood. The studies were undertaken in response to two incidents in picture-recognition studies and a ground-breaking report from Susanna Millar (1975). Betty (age 14, who has large object detection visually) mentioned a long-term interest in drawing: "I was taught how to make lines and circles. I put them all together myself to make drawings." Pat (early, totally blind adult) on her own initiative made a drawing of duck's feet that was surprisingly good for a first drawing. These incidents suggested that there was both spontaneous interest to pursue and untutored ability to plumb. Millar (1975) reported that some blind children of elementary-school age could make raised-line drawings of people similar to drawings by sighted children. Millar recommended training blind children to draw. The recognition studies suggest, however, that there may be substantial untutored pictorial abilities present in the blind before any explicit training in depiction. How might these abilities manifest themselves in drawing tasks? A number of BOOST adults who had participated in picture recognition studies agreed to participate in drawing studies aimed at answering this question.

To begin with a subject that is universal, we asked some of the BOOST adults to draw a hand. The fingers of a hand can be drawn in outline sketches in either of two ways. Each finger can be shown by a single straight line, in which case the line is being used in stick-figure style. Alternatively, each finger can be drawn with a line showing the occluding boundary of the finger. Both kinds of drawings were produced by the volunteers. Thirteen adults were tested (see table 4.1). Of the thirteen, four drew stick-figure fingers (see fig. 4.1a and c) and nine drew occluding bounds (see fig. 4.1b).

We continued the hand-drawing task by requesting a drawing with overlap. The topic was one finger crossing over the other. The four adults who drew stick figures made one stick cross the other like an X. Their drawings gave no indication of which finger was on top and which one below. Hence, it is not certain how the X functions. There were no spontaneous comments on ambiguity or alternative impressions. All that can be said for certain is that the X is taken by the blind to suggest one elongated thing on top of the other. The nine who used lines for the occluding bounds of fingers responded to the overlap task by drawing the occluding bounds of both fingers in their entirety (fig. 4.1b). The result includes four X junctions. To the eye it looks like a drawing where one finger is transparent. This kind of drawing has been called "X-ray style." It is found for example in Australian aboriginal art.

A third task was given to the nine volunteers who had produced the transparency drawings. The aim of the task was to invite use of T junctions where the stem stands for a background surface occluded by the foreground surface delimited by the crossbar of the T. The volunteers were asked to show in their drawings which finger was on top. Five said that they did not know how. Four engaged the interviewer in discussion, seemingly in search of a solution, indicating they did not know it immediately. They asked, for instance, how a sighted person would solve the problem and what was meant by "one finger on top of the other." In responding, the interviewer attempted to leave the subject to his or her own devices and to be as nondirective as possible. But to avoid all guidance was impossible. To describe what was meant by "on top" we said that the top one was visible, the one underneath not. This was enough for Dee (early, totally blind) and May (early, totally blind) to realize that one could omit lines from X junctions to indicate by T

TABLE 4.1

Volunteers from BOOST who drew hands.

Onset of Blindness and Degree of Loss	Participants
Early (0–2 years), totally blind	Dee, Jay, Lys, May, Pat, Pau
Early, light perception	Joan, Nip
Early, low vision	Dot
Late, totally blind	Ann, Ely, Mik, Ray

Drawings by the Blind

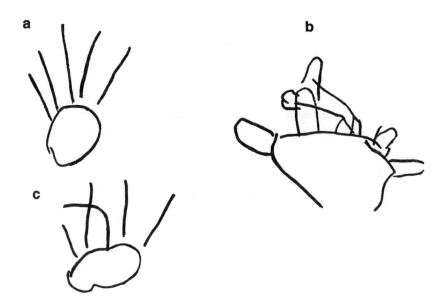

Fig. 4.1. Drawings of hands by blind adults in Toronto.

junctions which surface was on top. Ray (late, totally blind) reached the same solution without hearing a definition of "on top." The drawings by Dee, May, and Ray are shown in figure 4.2. Ann (late, totally blind) would have had considerable experience with overlap drawings before age 11. It was no surprise that in her drawing she indicated overlap by omitting lines. She was likely relying on memory, not displaying original problem solving. More originality can be claimed for Dee and May. Ray's drawing was reached by the most independent route.

Fig. 4.2. Drawings showing one finger on top of another, by Dee (early, totally blind), May (early, totally blind), and Ray (late, totally blind).

Drawings by the Blind

DRAWINGS OF A GLASS

The second drawing task for BOOST volunteers was a container, the obverse of a solid object. Containers are about as universal as hands, and any powerful drawing system must cope with them. Yet containers create several difficulties for depiction and raise questions about haptic perception of occluding bounds. How can one show an exterior surface with occluding bounds and an interior hollow? In the case of a cylinder, how can a flat picture show a form that is round in one cross-section and rectangular in another at right angles? Do the blind acknowledge these difficulties spontaneously?

We gave our volunteers (see table 4.2) a flat-bottomed glass and asked them to draw it. Presumably most if not all cultures have perfected the knack of putting a flat bottom on containers so they can stand without support. If so, the universal container has edges at the top (the lip of the glass) and probably corners at the bottom (where the sides meet the flat bottom). It has occluding boundaries given by the sides, marking the distinction between the visible front and hidden back from any vantage point to one side of the container. When we grasp a cylindrical container there is no sharp boundary between the front and the back. Hence, one might expect that the blind would find the occluding bounds of a cylinder unsuitable for outline drawing. Alternatively they might use the notion of a vantage point and occluding bounds of a container readily, as they did in drawing the occluding bounds of a solid object, namely fingers.

Three of our volunteers began thoughtfully by explicitly noting that there was more than one way to draw a tumbler. Five others drew more than one glass when asked to do so after their first attempts and their comments. Three

TABLE 4.2

Volunteers from BOOST who drew a flat-bottomed tumbler.

Onset of Blindness and Degree of Loss	Participants
Early (0–2 years), totally blind	Dee (2 drawings, after comment), Lys (2, upon request), May (2, req), Pal (2, req), Pau (2, req)
Early, light perception	Joan (2, spontaneous), Nip (1)
Early, low vision	Dot (1)
Late, totally blind	Mik (1), Ray (2, spont)
Late, low vision	Jon (3, spont)

drew only one glass. The three who indicated initially that they would make more than one drawing were Ray (late, totally blind), Joan (early, light perception), and Jon (late, low vision). Ray and Joan are of special interest since neither had had enough vision to use pictures.

Ray began by saying, "I'll do it this way first, then I'll draw it another way." He drew a rectangle and remarked, "This could be a glass from a certain angle but [it] doesn't show roundness." He noted further, "Could add lines." He proceeded to draw two lines across the rectangle—lines that were thick in the middle and thin at the side (fig. 4.3). In his comments Ray's grasp of the vantage point was clear and explicit. Furthermore, his device of varying line thickness has aspects of perspective about it. He went on to draw the glass "from the top," as he put it, which involved drawing two concentric circles. The inner line is the "inside perimeter," he noted, and the outer line is the "outside perimeter." The perimeter presumably is the inner and outer surface of the wall of the glass "from the top," as Ray said. He added intriguingly, "Be interesting to draw some pictures from different perspectives and see if people can figure out what it is!"

Ray's grasp of aspects of vantage points is lucid, and he explains his ideas well. One interesting possibility is that although Ray is unusually precise and clear in his explanations, his ideas about perspective are shared by many blind people. Alternatively, Ray's fine logical mind may allow him to arrive at ideas during our interview, ideas he was not using prior to the test and ideas very few blind people would use ordinarily. Moreover, Ray, despite his severely limited visual experience, may be basing his ideas on visual memories. To test these alternatives requires research with blind people of various ages, at a range of educational attainments. Ray's drawings and comments raise profound questions about perspective which cannot be settled on the basis of a single case. Shortly I will describe several experiments, with several groups of early and

Fig. 4.3. Drawing by Ray (late, totally blind) of a glass, with lines becoming thinner to indicate the roundness.

late blind volunteers, and compare different ways matters of perspective can arise in the tactile domain.

Joan also remarked that more than one drawing would be appropriate. She was given a glass, and as she held it and explored it manually she began to speak haltingly, "If the glass is open . . ." After a pause she went on, "I'll demonstrate my question by drawing two glasses, in different ways." Her first drawing was a single line, a rough U shape with a flat bottom. She said, "I've left the top open because a glass is open at the top." Her second drawing showed each side and the bottom by two lines parallel and close together. Then she added a single line across the top and said, "The single line on top shows it's still open" (figure 4.4).

We might call Joan's first glass a stick-figure glass in cross-section. One line, substituting for the thick wall of the glass, shows a referent with two surfaces. In the second, one line is used for each surface of the glass. Hence, a line can be used for the top surface—the lip or edge—of the glass. In the first drawing, though, the lip can be omitted since it does not have two surfaces. Notice that Joan, unlike Ray, never mentioned a vantage point. Her discussion was restricted to the parts of the glass. She never said, for example, that the inner surface would only be facing a vantage point if the glass were cut open or cross-sectioned. There is an important contrast between Ray's explicit use of "perspectives" or vantage points and Joan's way of drawing most shapes. Joan's glass can be described almost entirely as matching parts of the drawing to features of the glass in a geometry of similarities, treating the glass as an object independent of anyone's vantage point. The shapes of each part of the glass are repeated, in Joan's style, as shapes made of lines. One exception is the

Fig. 4.4. Drawings by Joan (early, light perception) of a glass. The one on the left leaves the top open. The one on the right uses a single line to indicate the lip of the glass and double lines for the walls and base of the glass.

single line for the lip of the glass. This is a straight line, though it is only straight as a projection to the side.

We encouraged four of the early, totally blind informants to try showing the roundness of the glass. The fifth early, totally blind subject (Dee) brought up the matter herself. Dee's drawings are in figure 4.5.

Dee began with a U shape with a flat base. Her comment was, "But it doesn't show the roundness of it, only how the sides come down and the bottom. It could be a number of things." For her second version she drew a U shape with a flat base but added an ellipse to the top. She commented, "But this would be confusing to someone else—the flatness of it. It's only in two dimensions. I don't think someone would think of it as a glass." Dee's ellipse likely is meant very generally as a rounded form, with no perspective effect intended.

Consider now drawings by Lys (fig. 4.6). Lys's glasses are like Dee's in many ways, though the process leading to her drawings was different. Lys began with the rounded shapes for the top and bottom. Then she added a single line, from top to bottom, linking the rounded shapes and running through the middle of the drawing. We asked her to explain. A glass "has a rounded top and bottom and comes straight down," she said. Lys's single line for "straight down" is not a line standing for an occluding edge or corner. It is not in outline style. It shows that the top and bottom of the glass are connected by a surface extending from one to the other. It does not show the left and right boundaries of the connecting surface; rather, it shows the surface's nearest part. One might jump to the conclusion that the straight-down line, and the absence of lines representing the sides of the glass, can be taken to indicate that Lys does not readily understand that lines can stand for rounded bounds of objects. Fortunately, in the interview she was asked if there was any way to show the sides of the glass. Right away she drew two parallel lines joining the extreme

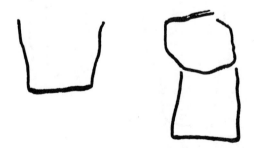

Fig. 4.5. Drawings of a glass by Dee (early, totally blind).

Fig. 4.6. Drawing of a glass by Lys (early, totally blind).

left and right portions of her rounded shapes. Evidently, she understood that lines could stand for rounded boundaries of objects without difficulty.

Next, Lys spontaneously drew the glass as a rectangle, saying that this was like the tree trunk in the elephant story which she had explored some minutes before. We asked her about the roundness at the top and bottom of a glass. Promptly she drew two circles (fig. 4.7).

Josiane Caron-Pargue (1985) studied sighted children drawing cylinders. She describes the children as "disintegrating" a cylinder into a rectangle and circles (p. 239). Their drawings comprise combinations of these two forms—"core" shapes, as Goodnow (1977, p. 143) puts it. Sometimes the drawing contains a full rectangle but only half-circles at top and bottom. Caron-Pargue considers this as emphasizing the rectangle. Sometimes the drawing includes two full circles but only two parallel lines join them. Caron-Pargue describes this as emphasizing the circles and correspondingly deemphasizing the rectangle. Both the rectangle and the circles are present in the cylinder as shapes of parts of the object. The artist, then, selects from among these features in making a drawing of the object. The selection process need not involve a vantage point. For the flat surfaces of the object, volunteers may have envisaged partial imprints. For rounded surfaces, they may have considered cross-

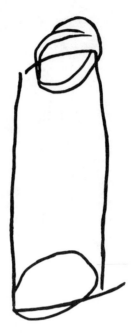

Fig. 4.7. Drawing of a glass by Lys (early, totally blind).

sections or the shapes of some of the outer surfaces of the object, following a similarity geometry.

In the terms used by Caron-Pargue, Dee emphasized the rectangle present in a glass, by drawing three sides of the rectangle at the outset, and secondarily copied the curved shape of the top of the glass. Lys in her first drawing emphasized the circles, adding only parts of a rectangle and making the addition only after being asked a pointed question. It is instructive that Lys and Dee made drawings on their first attempt that are similar to drawings by sighted children ages 7–9 studied by Caron-Pargue, although the sighted children have had much prior experience interpreting and drawing pictures.

Joan, Dee, and Lys failed to make explicit mention of a vantage point. In this they were unlike Ray. When Ray selected parts, he was guided by a vantage point both in the selection itself and in arranging the parts on the page. Ray considered the *direction* of parts from the vantage point. He did not draw both circles and a rectangle, only one or the other, since the circular parts of the cup face one vantage point and the rectangular parts face others. Ray never drew a line like Lys's single line for "straight down"; he only drew boundaries of the object from a vantage point. His lines denote corners and occlusions whereas Lys's straight-down line denotes how the object is ex-

tended, a very general aspect of surface layout since it belittles the shapes of
the margins of a surface. It is too general to distinguish corners from edges, or
either of these from curves or cracks. It indicates the orientation of the most
extended dimension of the object (Willats, 1989). Lys's straight-down line is
probably less sophisticated than lines for surface relief change.

May (early, totally blind) and Pau (early, totally blind) introduced a third
method of solving the drawing problems set by a cylindrical container. May
and Pau transformed the shapes used to show parts of the glass. May drew the
glass initially with a U shape, including a rounded base, and added a handle.
Then, after she was asked to think of another way to draw the glass, she drew a
flat base instead of a rounded base but made the sides curve instead of being
straight (fig. 4.8). Pau first drew a rectangle; then, when we asked him if he
could show that the glass was round, he drew a more circular shape, saying, "I
tried to make the lines rounder. The first one looks more like a door. It's
square" (fig. 4.9).

May and Pau modified the shapes they had used to show certain parts of
the object in order to show shapes of other parts. There is an instructive
difference between the explanations for shape modifications from May or Pau
and comments, for example, on change of shape from Pat (early, totally blind).
Pat drew a rectangle for the glass initially. When she was asked if she could
show the roundness, she drew a wide, shallow, rounded U; she said that the
top was deliberately wide and that "this is a different kind of tumbler." When
Pat changed the shape on the page to show a rounded container, she acknowledged that it suggested a differently shaped container from a glass with
parallel sides. May and Pau achieved both of the conflicting aims by allowing
their shapes to change, thereby producing a compromise image. Within the
limits that they acknowledge of the medium (Arnheim, 1974), they try to

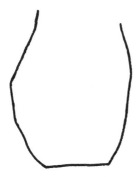

Fig. 4.8. Drawing of a glass by May (early, totally blind).

Fig. 4.9. Drawing of a glass by Pau (early, totally blind).

depict two contradictory functions with one representational unit. This is double entendre in language, and in depiction the equivalent might be called a pictorial pun.

The tumbler drawings reveal several ways to achieve pictorial ends. They show that the blind have no difficulty accepting a line as a boundary for a rounded object. Straight lines are used frequently to depict occluding bounds of cylindrical shapes. Junctions with L shapes may represent, for example, the rounded sides of the glass meeting the flat base. An explicit vantage point is occasionally used to select the shape for depicting a solid object, and the limits of the depiction are noted. Attempts to overcome the limits lead to some devices incorporating perspective (thickness of line) or context (such as a handle of the glass) or a compromise like a pun (depicting straight sides by round lines relevant to a neighboring feature).

DRAWINGS OF A TABLE

A third task we set for BOOST volunteers was to draw a table. A table consists of a surface that is horizontal and legs that are vertical, meeting the surface at its corners. It requires the solution of pictorial problems of the most profound kind. Surfaces that are at right angles have to be shown. I chose a table as an object exemplifying three dimensions, because it is comparatively familiar to people of all ages and likely to be found immediately in most cultures. A picture of a table can aim to show shapes of the supporting surface, as well as its edges, thickness, and orientation. It can show some or all of the legs, their connection to the horizontal surface, their shape, and their orientation. But not all the features of a table can be drawn in a single picture. Some have to be sacrificed. What guides the selection of some features and the elimination of others? What role do similarity geometry and vantage points play?

Though a picture is flat, it has many dimensions one can vary. That is, a picture, unlike a scale model, cannot replicate a three-dimensional scene, but it can include many kinds of arrangements. In mastering depiction the artist may select as relevant more and more aspects of the arrangements of lines on a surface. A novel, like a picture, is printed on flat paper, but it can be rich in dimensions of variation in style, elements, characterization, and arrangement or plot. It behooves the interpreter of novels or drawings to determine which modifications of the elements (Goodnow, 1977, p. 123) are being selected to stand for features of the world.

Pictures can be flat and thus two-dimensional in spatial extent but still multidimensional in other respects. A case in point is a video game that exploits relationships within the flat video screen to create the impression of depth. An airplane shape appears fixed in the center of the screen, pointing upward. The pattern on the screen around the airplane scrolls downward to suggest that the airplane is in motion. The terrain the airplane flies over is sometimes mountainous and sometimes level. The airplane has to rise high above the plain to be sure to avoid crashing into the first mountains it encounters. To indicate height, a black copy of the airplane simulates its shadow, moving close to the airplane when it is hugging the ground and receding from the airplane when it rises high into the sky. The distance between the airplane and its shadow on the screen is a dimension of variation within a two-dimensional surface that is information for depth.

In principle, flat surfaces can have many informative dimensions of variation. The top of the page can mean something different from the bottom. The diagonal can mean something different from the horizontal or vertical. The picture can involve special informative features such as parallels, space between lines, connections, angles between lines, straightness, curvature, and closed or open shapes (circles versus C shapes), and the features indicated by elements such as lines can change over time. An outline drawing from a vantage point employs many of these features. It incorporates many dimensions of variation. Indeed, a picture offers as many possible dimensions of variation as a section of the optic array. In depiction, as in nature, there are many informative variables. Optic arrays vary in ways related to arrangements of objects in depth. Perceptual systems, in turn, become sensitive to the variations and, in some cases, take them as the basis for perception of depth. Likewise, people making pictures employ some of the possible dimensions of variation in the picture surface to represent other variations in the real object. Which dimensions, one wonders, will seem pertinent to the blind person? What will show the shapes given by a table, an object that extends horizontally and vertically?

Nine volunteers from BOOST (table 4.3) attempted tasks involving depiction of a table. The volunteers devised quite diverse drawing systems.

Two of the volunteers, Ray (late, totally blind) and Dot (early, low vision), began with the comment that there is more than one way to draw a table. Dot

TABLE 4.3

Volunteers from BOOST who drew tables. A star table is a rectangle with four lines radiating one from each corner.

Onset of Blindness and Degree of Loss	Participants
Early (0–2 years), totally blind	Dee (star), Lys, May (star), Pal, Pat
Early, light perception	Nip
Early, low vision	Dot
Late, totally blind	Ray (star), Ely

had had many years of useful though very limited vision, and so Ray is the most important informant regarding the effects of blindness. Since Ray never had sufficient form perception to see a picture, his performance was impressive (fig. 4.10).

Ray said, "If you're looking straight down, you'd draw a rectangle without legs, because you won't see them." He proceeded to draw a rectangle. Next, he said "If you drew it directly from the side, you'd only see two legs—a rectangle with two legs." He then drew a rectangle with two straight appendages coming down the page. His third drawing was ingenious. He drew a rectangle with four appendages, each one radiating from a corner of the rectangle. He said, "But to see it this way, you'd have to be under the table."

Ray's three drawings of a table are an intellectual feat of some note. In brief sentences and apt drawings he summarized and applied lessons of perspective that were mastered by visual artists only in the Renaissance. His examples are chosen well and produced more adequately than I would have dared believe possible before this research was undertaken. His skill is admirable, not only for someone drawing without sight but also for anyone inexperienced in drawing, and with little experience of pictures. Indeed, each of his drawings is an excellent fit to the different vantage points he wished to demonstrate. His third table drawing, with legs radiating like a star, is a remarkable application of a vantage point. His choice of an unusual vantage point allows all of the parts of the table to be displayed, as well as the shape of the tabletop, the symmetrical placement of the legs, the straightness of the legs, and their connections with the tabletop corners. No part of the table obscures any other part.

Ray's drawings are particularly clever. But each of the features that his drawings display is present in drawings by other blind informants, including

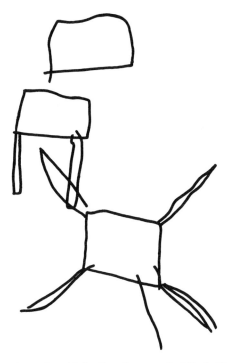

Fig. 4.10. Drawings of a table by Ray (late, totally blind). The top form is
a table from above, the middle form is a table from the side, and the
lower star-like form is a table from underneath.

his use of vantage points. Pat initially drew a rectangle with two appendages
and said, "It has four legs but just two are showing" (fig. 4.11). Later she
added the two "inner" legs. Shortly after, she made a similar drawing and said
about the two legs not drawn, "They would be behind these two, obscured."
Lys, Pau, Nip, and Dot each drew a table in an inverted U shape, like a
rectangle without the bottom line. This can be described as a table from the
side, with the horizontal line indicating the near edge or side surface of the
tabletop.

The most common table drawing from the blind volunteers was a rectangle
with four appendages. Everyone produced this pattern at least once. But it
was the product of two different drawing systems. Ray used vantage point to
produce the drawing. None of the others who drew this pattern mentioned a
vantage point. Both Dee (early, totally blind) and May (early, totally blind)
drew a table with its legs radiating in a star, like Ray's, but neither mention a
vantage point. Nip (early, light perception) had the four appendages to the

Fig. 4.11. Drawing of a table by Pat (early, totally blind).
Initially, only two legs were drawn.

central rectangle emerge two to one side and two to the opposite side. He said "I can't put the four legs down, so two have to go up." Two legs go down, matching the direction of table legs by a direction on the picture surface, but the other legs are drawn in ways that avoid putting the table legs and the table surface in one region in the picture surface. Goodnow (1977, p. 34) notes that sighted children ages 7–10 use the same rule. Lys (early, totally blind) draws two legs "coming down" and then two back legs, one going to the left and one going to the right. All the legs are at right angles to the table sides. Dee drew a second table where the rear legs meet the sides of the rectangle at about 30°, to show that all the legs come "down"; her choice of an acute angle allowed her to draw the legs without their running into the sides of the rectangle.

Evidently, two kinds of drawing systems need to be described. In one, the deployment of parts shows their directions from a vantage point. In the other, the deployment of parts is to match the features of the table, but not their direction from a vantage point. Legs "come down" or are "at right angles" to the table surface or radiate symmetrically "from the corners." Placement can be modified to avoid juxtapositions on the picture surface that are deemed to be unfortunate or prohibited, a principle that sighted children use (Goodnow, 1977, pp. 43–44).

The seven BOOST volunteers who had never had appreciable form perception were asked to complete two perspective drawings of a tabletop. One drawing was a trapezoid and the other was a rhomboid. The task was to add the legs. The rhomboid (fig. 4.12) could be taken to be a picture of a rectangu-

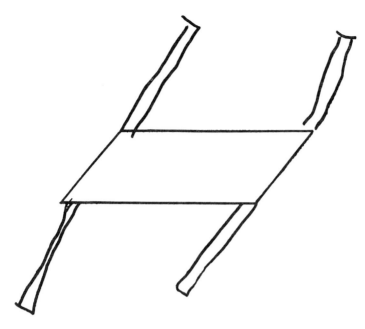

Fig. 4.12. Using a rhomboid to make a drawing of a table,
by Ray (late, totally blind).

lar surface in oblique projection, with oblique parallels indicating parallel
sides of the table receding into depth. The trapezoid could be taken to be a
rectangle shown in convergent perspective.

All but one of the volunteers considered the rhomboid and the trapezoid to
show the shapes of unusual tabletops, such as corner tables or some kind of
stacking tables that fit together. That is, the shape on the picture surface
generally was taken to be the shape of the table surface. Only one person, Ray,
made a comment that might indicate an understanding that a tabletop's
rectangular shape taken together with directions from a vantage point could
produce a nonrectangular shape on the picture surface. Ray commented when
examining the rhomboid, "I don't know if it's actually this shape or it's
perceived in this shape." We told Ray the table top was not actually this shape.
He then said, "So its seen from an angle." He went on, "In keeping with the
shape of it, you have to put legs on this way," and he proceeded to draw legs
that continue the direction of the short, parallel sides (fig. 4.12). Presumably
he thought that viewing on an angle produces a shape for the top of the table
that will also be produced for the legs of the table. He was unable to anticipate

that the legs, in one plane, can be affected differently from the tabletop, in a different plane, by the choice of vantage point and projection from it. He failed to intuit how oblique projection works.

Important limits to drawing skills in the blind may be inferred from the table study. Notions of vantage points were used by a number of the volunteers. But in every case where a vantage point was made explicit, the shape drawn on the page was similar to a shape in the referent. The tabletop, for example, was shown as a rectangle. None of the informants ever drew a shape different from that of the referent, as would result from considering the shape from a certain vantage point. They did not describe how the set of directions from a vantage point is preserved while the shape departs from similarity. Oblique projection does not come readily to the blind.

The table drawings corroborate the finding that lines can stand for occluding edges of flat-surfaced objects for the blind. Furthermore, sometimes two lines were used for a table leg, sometimes one, as occurred in drawings of fingers on a hand. The drawings often involve T vertices to show table legs meeting the edges of the table, and Y vertices showing the legs meeting the corners of the table. The arrangement of lines and vertices is governed at times by a vantage point system that maintains rectangular shapes. Frequently the system respects the connections between parts but treats the angles at vertices as a matter of convenience, as though the legs were folded out in whatever manner—up, down, sideways—was convenient to show all the legs without crossing into the space representing the tabletop. Shapes of distinct parts such as the legs and the tabletop are respected, and the connections are almost always preserved intact, but the angles formed by the parts at the connections are highly variable.

DRAWINGS OF THE VOLUNTEER'S CHOICE

In an attempt to broaden the inquiry and to loosen the rein on the volunteers' skills, we asked the BOOST adults to make drawings of their own choice. We suggested that they include drawings of things they had not had as miniature models, like toy houses and cars. We mentioned that they had probably not had model bathtubs or filing cabinets.

Eight BOOST members volunteered drawings (see table 4.4). Some of the volunteers adopted our suggestions. A bathtub from Lys (early, totally blind) shows the rectangular shape of the bathtub, the depth by means of arcs from the corners of the rectangle, which presumably suggest a kind of concave corner, and, in Lys's terms, "two little circles at the top end to put things on"

TABLE 4.4
Volunteers from BOOST who drew objects they themselves selected.

Onset of Blindness and Degree of Loss	Participants
Early (0–2 years), totally blind	Dee (filing cabinet, chair)
	Lys (bathtub)
	May (filing cabinet, bathtub)
	Pat (duck's foot, bathtub, gothic door, illustrations for a fairy story)
	Pau (sun, airplane wing, smoking chimney, drawbridge)
Late, totally blind	Joan (dog standing, dog lying down)
	Mik (filing cabinet)
Late, low vision	Jon (filing cabinet)

(fig. 4.13a). May (early, totally blind) showed the shape of the bathtub (fig. 4.13b), with a faucet (one end open) and two taps with ridges with which to grip the taps. She also drew a filing cabinet with two small drawer fronts and one large drawer front. Dee (early, totally blind) drew a filing cabinet and a chair with slats in the backrest (fig. 4.14). These drawings involve outlines showing occlusions and corners.

Joan (early, light perception) drew her guide dog twice, once depicting it standing up and once lying down. She said of the standing dog, "Do I draw two legs or four legs? Two legs, because I'm only drawing the side." She was frustrated with her drawing of the dog's head: "I don't know where the ears and nose and mouth go!" She left her first drawing of a dog unfinished, as she put it. Joan's difficulty depicting the dog's head is deeply instructive. She is perfectly familiar, in many respects, with the dog, and she can produce drawings of glasses and hands that she finds satisfactory and that appear competent to the eye. Her difficulties with the dog's head appear similar to ones reported by Critchley (1953) and others in studies of the blind. The root of the trouble, however, is probably not a matter of blindness, for the sighted encounter it as well. Most sighted people cannot draw a dog's head so that it can be distinguished from a horse's head or a squirrel's head. My own drawings of parts of an animal such as a dog's head or a horse's leg are, frankly, appallingly nondescript. My horse's legs make the horse look like it is wearing pajamas. By contrast, there is something about tables, hands, and glasses that makes

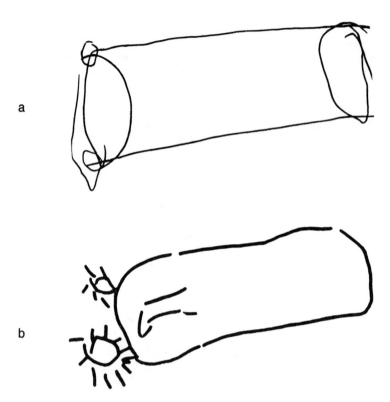

Fig. 4.13. Drawings of a bathtub, by Lys (early, totally blind)
and May (early, totally blind).

drawing them distinctively rather facile. That gap in depictability is likely determined by the number of features, the need for correct proportions (especially of curves), and the failure in most observers to have explicit knowledge of key relations, such as the shape of a dog's brow and a horse's fetlock, that distinguish these from analogous features in other animals or rag doll animals. If we try to draw a dog's nose-to-mouth line as prominently curved, like that of a human face, and a horse's rear leg as bending forward, like a human knee, we fail to draw the shapes of these features correctly. We know each of them tacitly, but not explicitly, until we attend to them. That failure to know familiar shapes explicitly is shared by blind and sighted observers, it seems. Although we may be able to call to our minds a tolerable image of a horse, that does not mean we can access the knowledge in the image to correct our drawing. Usually all we can say is that there is something wrong with the drawing of the rear leg or the head.

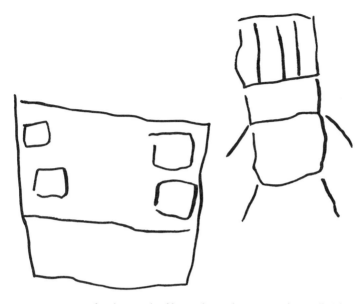

Fig. 4.14. Drawings of a chair and a filing cabinet, by Dee (early, totally blind).

Pat (early, totally blind) produced some revealing drawings. They include a bathtub and two illustrations for a fairy story (fig. 4.15). The bathtub is shown with a person standing outside it. Between two taps at the end of the bathtub is a faucet with a stream of water coming from it. Pat also drew a picture of a princess outside a castle, showing the door of the castle, a turret with a pole, and "a little spiky tree." To contrast with the spiky tree Pat also drew a bush, showing its overall configuration rather than individual branches. Another drawing shows the princess, in stick-figure style, sitting on a chair (shown from the side) by a spinning wheel. Inside the spinning wheel there is a "line of motion," and the wheel's perimeter is doubled. Both the stick-figure version of the person on the chair and the devices indicating motion are economical and intriguing uses of line. The stick figure uses lines as axes of bodies. The spinning wheel uses a line for something that is not an edge or occlusion. (I shall discuss its status later.) For a novice, Pat makes very competent use of line drawing. These drawings would do credit to sighted children of early school age. They indicate that a blind adult can draw competently using raised-line drawing materials after only a few moments' practice with the materials, and without having to experience stages like making scribbles or unrecognizable patterns.

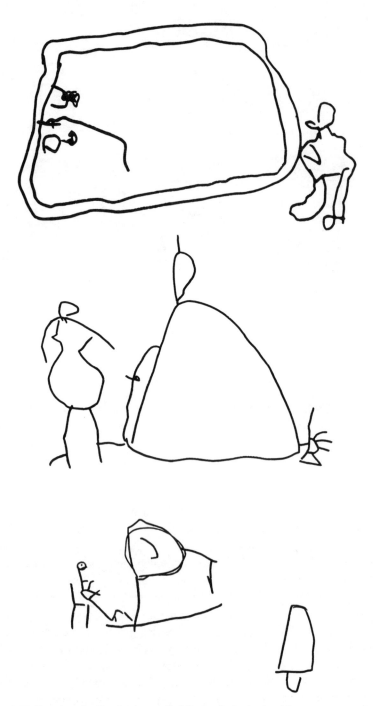

Fig. 4.15. Drawings by Pat (early, totally blind) of a bathtub with a person standing beside it, a princess beside a castle, a princess working a spinning wheel, and a bush. A curved line shows the movement of the wheel.

Drawings by the Blind

Tracy

I asked Tracy, an adult blind woman, to make a wide variety of drawings. Tracy lost her sight at age two (close to 24 months) as a result of an operation for retinal blastoma. At age 28, when she drew for me, she was totally blind. Tracy comes from a family with strong arts interests. Her parents are involved with dance, and both parents have training in graphic design. Tracy herself has taken an interest in drawing with raised materials. Her family has encouraged her, praising her drawings, but has not taught her. She has also tried to "figure out" printed outline drawings using an Optacon scanner. The scanner makes a pattern on the fingertip pad by means of small vibrating rods, copying the pattern under a small window (about fingertip size) in the scanner's wand. Tracy says she can "figure out" simple print pictures such as a silhouette of a seagull. She describes her drawing as largely self-taught. She notes that she makes raised pictures of such objects as her dog or a plastic model of an animal, then checks her picture against the original and corrects her picture, repeating the process until she is satisfied. In her deliberate use of this cyclical procedure Tracy shows a clearer appreciation of methods for improving one's drawing than most sighted people have, who often draw once, then simply confess failure to achieve the ends they had in mind.

Figure 4.16 reproduces some of Tracy's drawings. Included are a glass, a cat, a mouse, a head, a man standing, and a man lying down. The drawing of a glass repeats the pattern used by BOOST adults. I asked Tracy what the lines stood for and she ran her finger along the left occluding bound of the glass itself, across the bottom, and up the right side. When I asked her whether the lines could stand for another aspect of the glass, namely, the front, bottom, and rear, she said no. She reasoned that her drawing resembles the drawing one would get by laying the glass on the drawing surface, then running a pencil along the sides of the glass with its point resting on the drawing surface. Her words were, "If you laid this glass down [*she did so*] and drew around it [*she gestured so*] you'd get this [*her drawing of a glass as a U-shape*] but not across the top and not down the insides." This is a mechanical procedure that produces parallel projection. It reproduces a shape on a surface because it projects from a direction. Tracy was demonstrating by her procedure the kind of manipulation of space that resulted in Ray's tables and Joan's and Ray's glasses. Of her cat drawing she said, "That's my cat. He is a seated cat with his tail wrapped around his back feet. A pretty fat cat. He is looking at whoever is looking at him." I asked her where she got the idea from—a stuffed cat? "No, we have a real cat who sits around like this."

I asked Tracy to draw a man in profile. The head came too close to the top of the page so she redrew it, enlarging it. The main axis of the standing figure

Fig. 4.16. Drawings by Tracy (totally blind, sight lost at age two) of a glass, a cat, a mouse, a man lying down, a man standing, and a head.

is vertical on the page, that is, the feet are close to the person drawing when the page is flat on the supporting desk surface, and the head is farther away. This is taken to mean "standing," although the page is actually parallel to the floor. In these terms, the axis of the picture surface at right angles to the page vertical is to be described as horizontal. I asked her to draw a man lying down. Her drawing began with the legs, which she showed bent at the knee to indicate by his posture that he was reclining. The arms are shown over "the belly," she said. The use of the bent knees is astute as a way of showing that the man is lying down, as an addition to the horizontal main axis of the figure. Tracy's drawings recapitulate the lesson learned from picture-identification studies with BOOST subjects of a man standing or lying down (see chapter 3).

Tracy mentioned that she had once heard someone on radio discussing Walt Disney. Mickey Mouse, it was said, had been drawn economically using circles for the ears, head, and other body parts. Tracy had devised a drawing of a mouse based on these principles and wanted to show it. Her mouse sketch includes circles for the ears, the head, and the paws. The body is an oval, and other features are added to these simple forms. Tracy called this her Mickey Mouse drawing.

Tracy showed skill in visually depicting stereotypes. Stereotypes are a set of forms that can be readily repeated so that successive drawings have only minor variations. Wilson and Wilson (1982a, 1982b) report that many sighted children's drawings have this character. Tracy appears to have invented many of her own stereotypes based on experience with model figures, as well as real objects, and hearsay about simple bases for analyzing forms into parts. In principle, all forms can be analyzed into circles or cubes. They can be made of flat planes or building blocks or strips—hence the success of Meccano and Lego. Tracy seems to have heard about analysis into circles and applied the idea. Her man figures appear to be based on a conception of a posture and on knowledge of details of joints, shapes of the calf, the chin, and other small components of the profile. She shows how practice in drawing and a knowledge of form can be applied by blind people to produce a sketch specific to a narrowly defined referent and its posture. It is comparatively easy in looking at Tracy's drawings to make out the object, its species, its posture, and the vantage point adopted.

Heller (1989), after a study of picture identification by early and late blind volunteers, responded to interest expressed by the participants in drawing with the kit he had used to make his raised-line drawings. Several of his adult subjects produced chairs in profile and tables with only two legs shown. Some produced what Heller terms an "aerial" vantage point on the chair. The back and two legs were drawn in profile, and the seat was drawn as a rectangle. An early blind person drew a dog with all four legs shown. The posture was that of a dog rearing up on its hind legs. Heller mentions that many blind subjects spontaneously think of shapes in profile while attempting to decipher drawings. He notes that the blind subjects in his study were not familiar with picture perception or production. In Heller's report there are clear demonstrations of objects drawn from the side, as profiles, and from the front like a smile-face button. Lines are used as axes of extended bodies like a leg of a chair, for occluding bounds of a rounded object like a dog, and for occluding edges of the seat of a chair.

Sally

Pring (in press) reproduces drawings by Sally, an 11-year-old girl, totally blind since age 16 months. Sally was tested for intelligence, and both her verbal and performance scores rank within the top 2 percent for her age. She is successful in school. Pring tested her shortly after Sally had begun drawing using a raised-line drawing kit. Sally drew a cat, a woman, a train, a mountain, the sun, a telephone, a spider, and a tree. With the possible exception of the mountain, all of the drawings are immediately recognizable.

Sally was asked to describe her drawings as if for a visitor from outer space. She described a tree as "a shortish round cylinder [for the trunk, apparent at the bottom] with triangles, getting shorter as it goes up, like a pyramid." A wine glass, she said, was a flat round base with a cylindrical stick going up from it and curving out, ending in a slightly rounded box. Pring points out that these responses show Sally to be skillful at describing the spatial structure of objects. She does not describe parts in terms of their function, for example, the part the glass (or tree) stands on, the part you hold (or the part that holds the branches), and the part that contains liquid (or the part that takes the Christmas star).

Katz's Pupils

David Katz's (1946) long-overlooked study of drawings by blind adolescents (ages 12–18) contains several drawings that are instantly recognizable on sight. They include seven drawings of people, some as stick figures and some as filled-out spaces with such details as eyes, nose, and mouth. One pupil produced a detailed drawing of a bird from the side, showing a tail, a wing, two stick-figure legs and feet, a neck, an oval head, and a beak. Katz refers disparagingly to this drawing, saying he has never seen a drawing of a bird so hopelessly unskilled. He writes that the so-called body scheme that these adolescents drew is an utterly primitive representation of a man, and that even the best result of a 13-year-old blind child is not at the level one would expect from a six-year-old with intact vision. He notices grotesque proportions, and he suggests that when the children used individual lines for limbs the parts of the body are being reduced to stroke-like symbols without the least regard for their real form or their relative position. He demotes drawings by the blind to a lesser status, it seems, when he writes that the blind always draw animals from the side. They show a "highly abstract attitude" that never occurs in the sighted, he says (translation by Costall and Vedeler, 1992).

Katz is perplexingly indifferent at some junctures to the skill his charges showed. The bird drawing has excellent proportions for a goose. The fact that a 13-year-old blind girl who is a novice at drawing is perhaps at the level of a five- or six-year-old sighted child in her first few attempts at drawing is astonishing, not an indication of a fault. No one should expect mastery to be acquired and demonstrated instantly. While some of the drawings by Katz's blind subjects show odd proportions, so too do drawings by sighted children. Katz also reproduces well-proportioned pictures of large objects, for example, a house (with such details as front-door steps). He reproduces several creditable drawings of small objects: a stick-figure drawing of a dog is unmistakably an animal and not to be confused with the stick-figure drawings of people. Katz is quite off the mark when he regards stick-figures as symbols without form or relative position. Drawing animals from the side is entirely appropriate, as many authors have pointed out, for from the side they reveal most of the features of proportion that distinguish one animal from another. To achieve the same end with insects, the common practice is to draw them from above. Indeed, that is precisely what Linda Pring's student Sally did. Sally and Katz's pupils use stick-figure lines to show limbs of creatures. This is one of the appropriate uses of line, as much in keeping with the axis theory as lines standing for occluding bounds of the head or body. It is not a use that disregards the form of the object or the canons of outline drawing.

Katz's belittling comments may stem from his conception that drawing should not reveal an abstract attitude. What Katz means by this is unclear. He is certainly wrong in implying that sighted people do not draw in an abstract way. It is perfectly normal for a sighted person to sketch a room and squiggle something to show a plant of some kind in the corner. A squiggle can be an animal of some kind in a cage at a zoo, or a car of some kind in the driveway, or a tree of some kind at the end of a garden. I can make nothing of Katz's claim that blind children may draw "an animal of some kind" and sighted people never do. Fortunately, Katz did not halt there.

Katz invited his pupils to draw tables, cylinders, pyramids, and cubes. This is a remarkable anticipation of the choices of later experimenters! The selection reflects, I think, the attempts by independent investigators to present objects that are simple and well known but capture some of the key difficulties in moving from solid objects to pictorial surfaces. His findings were just as I have described here, following studies in North America and France. They are often drawn "folded-out," he notes, reporting that his pupils used phrases like "fold the sides upwards" about their drawings of cubes and pyramids. Katz then relents, it seems, and comments that the similarity with sighted children's drawings is striking. Alas, he fails to reach the conclusion that the principles sighted children employ as they advance will, with practice or suitable problems, be the principles the blind children will discover as *they* advance. Perspective drawing, he contends, will always have a flavor of artificiality as it must follow the laws and conditions of vision. Katz stresses that foldout principles are the principles the children will probably come to systematize. This is odd, since among the examples Katz reproduces are two finely executed clever cases. In one, a cube is drawn as two squares one atop the other. Presumably the top and front are shown, and presumably the sides are not shown because they are behind the top and front from the vantage point of the observer. This is a perspective drawing of sorts. Another shows a cube by a square with a rectangle on top. Presumably the rectangle shows the top surface of the cube foreshortened, because it slants away from the observer. This is indeed perspective drawing.

Katz, I conclude, found a great deal that is closely in keeping with later discoveries. But his interpretation was blinkered; he did not realize how good his charges were. It fell to later studies to repeat his findings and to realize their significance. On two points Katz was correct, though on one he hedged. Blind people can draw in outline (and quite well, on first attempt, with much more in common with the sighted than Katz surmised), and they have a good sense of three-dimensional shape and space.

TEACHING DRAWING AND CONSTRUCTING HUMAN FIGURES

George B. Wally pioneered the teaching of drawing to blind students in 1932. He has been tutoring students in reproducing particular shapes, varying the relative sizes of shapes to show depth, having lines converge to a vanishing point to show perspective, and applying color to suggest distant objects. His pupils master his system and learn to depict prototypical scenes— for example, landscapes. His great success is evident in the catalog of his collection (Wally, 1976), on the cover of which is a remarkable copy of Leonardo da Vinci's *Last Supper* by Maynard, a totally blind man 48 years old. The catalog includes exercises by Wally's blind pupils in two-point perspective, drawings of globes shown with latitude and longitude, drawings of candle flames, architecture, comets, the aurora borealis, bacteria, and portraits of Mao Tse-tung. Wally's results demonstrate that methods of technical drawing can be taught to the blind to good effect. Wally concludes, however, that the blind students derived their understanding of space and perspective from his methods. It is more likely that students had considerable awareness of spatial layout before undertaking his classes and that his methods built on this foundation.

Susanna Millar (1991) of Oxford, one of the most influential investigators of tactile skills and pictures for the blind, examined the abilities of blind children (ages 5 to 15 years) to draw human figures and make flat models of human figures by arranging discs, ovals, and sticks. She compared the drawing task to the assembly task in order to test the role of skills in executing drawing motions. The assembly task requires much less skill than is required in drawing arcs, complete figures, and straight lines. Millar added a recognition task, since recognition is often thought to be easier than either drawing or assembling. It does not require placing the lines and arcs in carefully judged orientations or juxtapositions.

Millar divided the children into three groups of seven according to age (the middle group ranged from age 8 years 7 months to 11 years 3 months). She established a scoring system for the drawing and assembly tasks. Whereas oldest children as expected made more successful assemblies than drawings, the middle group scored equally well on the drawing task and the assembly task. The youngest group fared marginally poorer on assembly than on drawing.

Millar's observations on the children's procedures help to explain her results. She points out that drawing is not a task on which one succeeds or fails solely as a result of motor skills or executive plans that indicate where to start and where to finish. Instead, it involves a conception of what needs to be done. The youngest children Millar tested did not succeed in drawing the human figure particularly well because they set out with goals that have fairly little to do with drawing recognizable shapes. Rather, they would make a mark and assert that it stood for, say, an ear. Another mark they might announce as the tummy. A further squiggle might be said to be two legs. Revealingly, as Millar carefully points out, a mark might even be described as skin. The child seems make a list of features and represent them graphically by means of marks that have no significant shape.

Millar's observations of the production of drawings by the children in her study make sense of the results with assemblies. The assemblies are also used by the children to list properties of the referent. An arc can be a head, a circle can be a leg, and a square can be the other leg if shape is irrelevant. Millar reproduces one such display made by a seven-year-old boy totally blind since birth.

When the children were tested on two raised-line drawings of people and a drawing of a house made by Millar, the results were emphatic. No child recognized Millar's drawing as a house. Only one child recognized a stick-figure drawing of a person, and only one child recognized a drawing of a person with lines standing for occluding bounds of an oval body and with stick-figure arms and legs. If the typical child brought the attitude to the display that shape was unimportant, little wonder the displays were not spontaneously recognized.

Millar conjectures that at times it may be necessary to point out explicitly that shape is relevant. She asked a congenitally, totally blind eight-year-old to draw an arrangement of four toys set on the corners of a large square and joined by a rope. The blind child walked around the square, guided by the rope, and felt and identified each toy. Young blind children typically draw this arrangement in the same manner as young sighted children—as a long straight line with four marks on it, each indicating a toy. The blind eight-year-old, while drawing a long line, said, "The rope is a long shape. It's got some turns." Millar told her to draw the turns. This very minimal addition to the instructions on the task was sufficient to get the child to draw a four-sided figure with some creditable right angles. Millar's point is that the child's conception of the task, including decisions about the irrelevance of matters of shape, can result in assemblies or drawings or recognition performance that fails to reveal much of the child's understanding of shape.

Millar concludes that initially children, whether blind or sighted, probably do not use simple flat forms to represent three-dimensional objects on the flat page. Subsequently, she suggests, both the blind and the sighted do come to such uses of flat shapes. Millar's point helps to make intelligible the observation that a hint or a question about the referent, or the set of possible referents, can increase identification rates for displays considerably. Her case in point shows that the same argument holds for drawing. There is, however, an enormous gap between knowing that shape is relevant and knowing what to check in a figure one is trying to recognize, or what to put on paper to draw a particular figure. The more options open in the task, the more opportunity there may be to find out what the novice brings to its definition.

Millar contends that drawings are chiefly versions of hand movements which the blind child is using to map or symbolize body movements. The resemblances between "body movements, or movements exploring a solid object, and movements describing an outline on a page, are not always immediate or direct in blind conditions" (p. 320). The match to be made is between a body movement and a tracing on the page. Recognizing familiar shapes, Millar believes, depends on systematic movement. The movements should be "active" in the sense of being selected, organized, and physically made by the subject without intervention by the experimenter. This, Millar expects, will lead to better recall and recognition and more efficient familiarization with stimuli. Also, better memory and organization will allow the person involved to spot "similarities between what are otherwise quite different forms of active movement (e.g. arm movement and locomotion)" (p. 321). Millar stresses that the efficient organization of movement often depends on obtaining clues from the context about what kind of object to expect, and the clues can bring out cognitive and inferential skills.

Much of what Millar proposes seems to be entirely appropriate. Information about relevance is often helpful. I suggest, however, that shape perception is in many ways independent of particular movements. The chief function of a movement is to gain information about shapes, and the layout of surfaces and lines can become known through a variety of movements. Just as sighted people can scan a visual scene with many different patterns of eye movements and yet always see a cube, so too we can feel the cube with one hand or two, one finger or many, with small or large arm movements, as we walk around the cube or turn it in our hands. The shape is invariant, but the movements are usually quite variable.

CONCLUSION

The drawing skills shown by blind adults attempting drawing for the first time are midway between the unrecognizable marks of the sighted child making drawings for the first time and the unmistakable accurate renderings of an adult draftsman aiming to be unambiguous and precise. Mostly the line elements are used by the blind in the universal outline style in which lines stand for edges and corners of various kinds. This use of the line seems accessible to blind adults even without tuition. Occasionally, however, there are other uses of line, such as for motion, that deserve some analysis. There are also matters of form and projection that call for attention. Sometimes forms are drawn from the side—"in profile," as Heller has it. Or the shapes of objects can be described as copied using a similarity geometry. At other times, rounded lips of glasses are drawn by straight lines. The blind person often realizes that the form drawn on the page as a rectangle, which appears to be a slab and not a cylinder, may nevertheless represent a glass, which is rectangular from the side. Likewise, a table can be drawn "from underneath." Hence projection of some kind, from certain directions, is often used. Tracy even went so far as to give a procedure, using a pencil, that models parallel projection. The mechanical procedure produces the same outcome as the drawing she made while thinking about projection without any mechanical aid.

The forms that the blind produce in drawing follow several principles for working with space and form and relating flat surfaces and lines to three-dimensional objects with continuous surfaces. The skills shown by the blind, and the spatial principles they understand, are likely to have a considerable history before our tasks tapped them in adult volunteers. But the evidence here indicates that this history is not a matter of rote learning. The blind volunteers have not been taught the possible meanings of lines or prototypical pictorial patterns for a set of referents, and they have not been taught how to use a particular principle to produce a picture in two dimensions of an object in three dimensions. The skills they show are products of understandings they possess as a result of abilities with line elements and general spatial principles that arise from the constitution of the perceptual systems and a general appreciation of the space around them available to several senses.

The levels of skills shown by blind adults are intermediate: they are several steps up from those of a beginner in early childhood, and yet they leave room for considerable improvement. Sophistication with principles, however, is not the same as accuracy with details. Blind adults often use what seem to be sophisticated principles although the drawing is not well executed, like a novice tennis player who has an understanding of good form but nonetheless keeps mis-hitting. I think that what previous researchers and, possibly, many educators of the blind have neglected is this distinction between understanding principles of varying degrees of sophistication, some developmentally early and some quite advanced, and executing them. The drawings by blind adults at times indicate a fair measure of skill in execution but, more important, they reveal principles, like projection from a vantage point, that are advanced even for many sighted adults. The principles and their level of sophistication in drawing development from child to adult, in the sighted as well as the blind, need careful assessment. I surmise that when that assessment is completed it will be evident that blind adults who have not been taught how to draw or use pictures are several steps above sighted children beginning to draw, that blind children are on a par with sighted children at the outset, and that much of what underlies drawing development can be understood to be a broad advance in mastery of space common to the blind and the sighted, and accessed by touch as well as by vision.

CHAPTER FIVE

Drawing
Development

During two interviews with me in New York, Tracy, age 28, totally blind since 24 months, produced several drawings of a cube, folded cards, and familiar objects. Her first drawing of a cube at my request was a square with four arcs, one in each of the corners. Figure 5.1 includes that drawing as well as one of Tracy's later drawings of a cube, made in her second interview with me and showing two well-executed rectangles joined along one side. These stand for the two sides of the cube that face the observer. They are joined by a decidedly puzzling line that curves across the top. It is not immediately obvious what Tracy means by this line or by the arcs in her first drawing.

A study of drawings of cubes by sighted children and adults, however, might reveal that Tracy's drawings fit into the kind of drawing development we see in many sighted children. Perhaps sighted children produce the same kind of drawings as Tracy's at certain ages. Warren (1984) and Hollins (1989) remark that drawings by the blind are extraordinarily varied. Arnheim (1974) notes a good deal of variation in the sighted. It is important to check whether the range of variation of the blind is within the bounds of variation found in drawings by the sighted. I shall delve into comparisons of drawing ability in sighted and blind children, attending especially to Tracy's cubes and other drawings to see where they might fit.

The general supposition behind this examination of Tracy's work is that there may be a close correspondence between drawing development in the blind and the sighted. Given a system of drawing used by a blind person, it

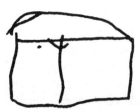

Fig. 5.1. Drawings by Tracy (early, totally blind) of a dog,
a horse, a cat, a man, and cubes.

may be possible to identify an age at which a sighted child would use that same
system.

DRAWING DEVELOPMENT THEORY

The first drawings of a sighted child 2–3 years of age bear fairly little
resemblance to their referent. The same can surely be said for those of many

blind children. It is generally expected that as they mature sighted children will come to show more advanced drawing skills, slowly acquiring principles of increasing sophistication. Perhaps the same is true for blind children even though they have had very little exposure to pictures. Indeed, it may be that much the same course is followed by blind and sighted children, though most of the blind children may not progress at the same rate as most of the sighted. In this chapter I shall consider how drawing skill develops in sighted and unsighted children. I shall present the results of one extensive study of sighted children, ages 4–15, and hazard a few guesses about what stages of development preceded those evident in four-year-olds. My plan is to consider the development of drawing in the sighted child and then to look for the main principles in drawings by blind children.

There are many factors influencing drawing and its development. The crucial ones here are those that apply most widely to the representation of objects, and I shall try to avoid factors with too narrow a range. Sketches can, of course, be made for restricted purposes, for example, with the esthetic aim of decoration rather than the aim of representing particular objects. Kellogg (1969, p. 26) argues that a great deal of child art has little to do with communication from artist to viewer but is a matter of esthetics and pleasure. As a result, some of the principles being brought to bear on drawing are at times applicable only to certain subjects; they follow from the desire to achieve a certain effect. Likewise, in drawings by adults some devices are restricted to a certain art style, convention of symbolic communication, or type of object. In many cases, children learn to copy rigidly invariant prototypes of objects. A prototype is a drawing with a fixed pattern repeatable at will. One prototype that was widespread for a time (in the late nineteenth and early twentieth centuries) but has now almost vanished was a two-eyed profile (a profile inside a circle, with two eyes) for the human face, and another was a mouth drawn like a ladder (Wilson and Wilson, 1982a, 1982b). Prototypes are common in sighted children's drawings, even though particular prototypes such as Snoopy are only widespread for a time. The medium in which the representation is made may also influence the child, as in making faces on a plate at dinner time with sausages for a mouth, a bacon-strip nose, and potatoes for eyes or—a more demanding task—making a snake from irregular straight strips in basket weaving (Arnheim, 1974; Golomb, 1990). Many of these influences on drawing development create skills that are comparatively isolated from each other and from the rest of psychological functioning. The result is a vocabulary of independent schemas alongside a general procedure for picking up the schemas (Wilson, 1985; van Sommers, 1984, p. 161–64).

Learning the ladder-mouth schema probably has little effect on drawing other subjects, such as an elephant's body. The fact that the schemas are independent of each other is reflected in such children's comments as "I don't know how to draw a giraffe" or such requests as "How do you draw an ear?" Each object is treated as a referent requiring its own pictorial formula. If the influences on a child's growth are like tributaries joining a river, these schema are like oxbow lakes thrown out by the main course of development without contributing much to the general flow. Psychological development is likely full of oxbows, directions useful for a time but cut off once a more direct and powerful route is found. It is a common observation that cognition allows room for remembering isolated items of trivial knowledge, although it is the general principles in each of the major domains of knowledge that are the engine of intellectual growth. It is these intellectual principles that I wish to identify in drawing development in the child.

Drawings made by the sighted seem to be governed by general principles as well as a mammoth dictionary of schemas. The general principles concern the nature of representation, restrictions on the use of an element, and configuration rules for arranging elements.

The nature of representation is that one item can stand for another in the sense that A represents B because A is intended to make someone think of B without there being any other intrinsic connection to B. The intention is known to the user of A and the receiver of A, if the intention succeeds. Propositions using A are about B. Showing A can be done to show B.

The restrictions on the use of an element in outline drawing are concerned with using the line to stand for features of objects, primarily features that the line evokes in perception and not just in cognition. In a picture the line does not stand for items chosen solely because a person has designated the line as a representation, establishing a convention. Nor has the line been allowed to represent items chosen on the basis of convenience or rules that are invented anew for each drawing. Rather, the line creates an impression of the designated feature. Presumably it does so chiefly because of functions in the perceptual pathways that treat lines as surrogates for features of relief.

Configuration rules are matters of projection. They relate the locations of lines in the picture to locations of parts of the object. They indicate how two lines can be adjoined as well as how they are shaped individually, and how long they may be in relation to other lines. These rules can include matters of perspective convergence and how to set the picture surface between the object and the vantage point. If one line in a picture representing a certain kind of scene is short and straight and represents something long and straight in the referent, this sets restrictions on the locations and lengths of the other lines in accordance with the configuration rules.

It should be immediately apparent that there is a direct conflict among the major principles defining pictorial representation. In its most general form, representation involves A standing for B and is achieved because of an intention to affect another person's thought, but without any intrinsic connections between A and B. Pictorial representation, by contrast, requires that A allow perceptual impressions of B in key respects. The conflict between these requirements results in the bipolar development of drawing in the child, one pole emphasizing representation without perceptual fidelity to the referent and the other insisting on representational criteria that adhere to perceptual impressions.

The fact that representation can rest on what is meant rather than on forms that unmistakably specify or resemble their referent is vital to many kinds of pictures—for example, rough sketches. It enables pictures to be understood while showing only a few aspects of the referent. That is, for a depiction to give appropriate perceptual impressions, it is not necessary for it to represent so many aspects that the species of the object, or the individual object, is unambiguous. The picture may show only a few relevant features and the object can be asserted to be represented. Even in the absence of specificity the few relevant features can give rise to the appropriate impressions in perception provided the features fit with the lines (or other elements) making up the picture. The assertion helps the perceiver decide what is relevant, and if the proper elements are present, aspects of the referent can be seen. On the other hand, the fact that perceptual impressions are used in pictures means that a detailed, unambiguous picture is likely to be seen as a faithful rendition of the referent by any observer, with no hints or training, provided the observer can recognize the real referent in the first place.

Developmental theories of outline drawing have to address the role of the line element stimulating perception, the configuration in which the element is placed, and the person designating the element as a representation. At one extreme, a theory could entail a combination of inadvertent actions and accidental specificity. It is conceivable, for example, that the child makes marks as an accidental accompaniment to motor activity. At some point the marks could become sufficiently complex that inadvertently they have a form specifying a category of objects in the environment known to the child, with enough distinctive features to single out that category rather than any of the others known to the child. The child might then be so impressed by the discovery of a recognizable, specified object that he or she sets out to repeat the form. After several attempts, the form becomes a pattern the child can execute reliably. Accidental discoveries are made repeatedly by the child, and in time mastery of a dictionary of schemas develops. Some of the schemas are copied deliberately from the pictures made by other people, especially other children. With time, the child invents more abstract principles, including aspects of perspective such as convergence. The child eventually becomes free of the need for recognizable objects and can draw unfamiliar arrangements of features of surface layout. Later the child's drawings may eventually become free of the need for specificity and become more abstract. The child can then draw a few lines and allow them to stand for a feature of layout in isolation without needing to rely on a great deal of context in the picture. At this juncture the intent to depict is finally enough support for the few lines to work well in perception. In this theory, drawing a picture is initially inadvertent. Children need a great deal of detail in the early stages of development of drawing; only later can they work with displays that are mere hints.

There is considerable merit to this account of drawing development. Children do enjoy motor activity, make accidental discoveries, learn schemas, and in some respects gradually become more abstract. It is not the whole story, however. In many cases, children begin with abstractions and gradually find concrete matter to which the abstractions can apply. An opposite, alternative theory is probably closer to the truth. The infant can intend to make a representational display, selecting what is relevant from the referent and putting marks on the display that stand only for the aspects that were selected. Specificity is not an issue for the young child who is drawing, since it is achieved by the will to represent and not by detail in the display. Only some aspects of the marks are relevant, and the child selects the aspects that matter (such as the number of objects or the length or form of a single object). Resemblance of shape is initially very general or highly abstract; only later is it a matter of proportions of curved and straight components of the line matching relief features and evoking impressions of relief. The ability to accept that a mark represents a referent even though it does not copy its form in detail, accurately, or evoke impressions of relief is never lost to the normal perceiver, and it surfaces in various different guises in development.

Let us consider some evidence about these rival theories of drawing development, one stressing unintended actions, the other stressing intentional representations. Lowenfeld and Brittain (1970) argued that the initial interest of the child in making displays was motoric. The child's motivation is in the movements, not in the graphic effects on the display surface, they suggested. Any marks that could be perceived as representations were thought to be inadvertent. Two studies undermine this suggestion.

Edward Mueller and I observed five 14–16-month-old sighted infants engaged in finger painting. The children were part of a play group that had met one morning previously. The finger-painting activity was a new option for these children. A coffee table was covered with white paper, and black paint was added in patches to the paper by an adult supervisor. The children approached the table slowly, inspecting the surface. For all five children, contact with the paint was initially limited—for example, they might examine it with fingertips, touching it only lightly, while looking at the paint. Motion of the hand was slight at first; only later were there lengthy pulling motions of the fingertips through the paint, toward the body, or pushing motions away from the body. Fingertip contact generally preceded palm contact. One hand was generally used before both hands, and a part of the hand before any other part of the limbs. Single motions (one push or pull) preceded combinations of motions (push-pull cycles). Vision was an important part of the infant's initial contacts, which were made while gazing in the direction of the contact, and only later would motions be made with the gaze off to the side. Here is a record of the initial 19 contacts of one of the children. The record is based on a slow-motion videotape of the events. "Gaze on" means the child was looking in the direction of the paint being contacted.

Robert finger painting
1. Two fingers, right hand, 1 pull. Gaze on.
2. Heel of left hand, 1 touch. Gaze off.
3. One finger, right hand, 1 pull. Gaze on.
4. Several fingertips (number unclear), right hand, 1 touch. Gaze on.
5. Four fingers, left hand, 1 slap. Gaze on.
6. Right knee, 1 touch. Gaze off.
7. Heel of left hand, 1 touch. Gaze on.
8. One finger, right hand, 1 pull. Gaze on.
9. Four fingers, right hand, 1 pull. Gaze on.
10. Four fingers, left hand, 2 push-pulls. Gaze on for the initial action, and off for the remainder.
11. Heel of right hand, 1 touch. Gaze off.
12. Whole left hand, 4 push-pulls. Gaze on.
13. Several fingers, right hand, 1 slap-pull. Gaze on.
14. Whole right hand, 4 push-pulls. Gaze on.
15. Whole right hand, 1 push-pull. Gaze on.
16. One finger, right hand, 1 pull, then 1 push-pull, then, in a continuous action, whole right hand 1 pull, then 1 push-pull. Gaze on. (Robert leaves the table briefly.)
17. Both hands fingertips, 1 touch. Gaze on. (Robert leaves the table briefly.)
18. Both hands, 1 slap-pull. Gaze on.
19. Both hands: left hand 1 finger 2 push-pulls, right hand all fingers 1 touch. Gaze off. (Robert leaves the table.)

Robert's record reveals delicate contacts preceding larger contacts, rather than precise restricted contacts emerging from undifferentiated global activity. The number of actions in a continuous sequence increases over time. The units of behavior expand to include more actions, larger motions, greater involvement of large muscles of the body. Gaze on precedes gaze off. The motions are not initially random gross actions eventually leading to refined brief touches. Gaze off likely indicates lack of interest—or interest caught elsewhere—rather than initially unfocused attention, which only later becomes precise. The child likely was engaged in exploration that included perception in the form of careful observation of the effects of motion. The initial actions were probably not undertaken primarily to enjoy bodily motion, as Lowenfeld and Brittain conjectured. The record suggests that the initial explorations by the child involved intense attention to each judicious, brief, tentative contact, and possibly to any effects of the manipulation.

The need for the effects of drawing actions to be observed by 14–16-month-olds is underscored in a study by Gibson and Yonas (1968), with slightly older children (ages eighteen months to three years). The children were given two kinds of markers. One left no clearly visible traces; the other did leave a visible track. Both contained fluid, and they were similar in all respects except for the visible stains left by one. If the children's scribbling behavior was largely motivated by motor consequences, then both markers should have been equally satisfactory. The result, however, was that the children quickly stopped using any marker that left no visible traces and sought the other. Scribbling was more prolonged with the markers that made visible tracks.

Lowenfeld and Brittain are no doubt in error in stressing the motor action to the exclusion of the close visual monitoring accompanying the action, and in implying that the body motions are the basis of finger painting or scribbling rather than the perceptible effects left on the display. Children understand full well that they can make marks. These are not accidents on the periphery of attention: they are deliberate. If so, they can be given an explicit role in communication. They are available to intention and can be subject to the will to represent. Since children see marks as deliberate, they have a basis on which to use a mark as an object intended to make a person think of another object, making the intention known to the other person.

A relation between picturing, announcing, and action is noted by Golomb (1990) and Wolf (1983). Wolf found that children at age two frequently announce that they are making marks concerned with some object that is related to their action. The children mention a rabbit while making their marker jump from one part of the page to another, leaving prints at each impact. Or the marker may circle around the page and the child may say something about a car while creating suitable sound effects. The marker leaves circles on the page, it should be noted, and does not just move leaving the page undisturbed. I have observed children making one mark for one person, with a few features of a person, another mark with fewer features for another person, and many more quite nondescript marks for a crowd of people, with an announcement of the person or the crowd being made as the action is undertaken (Kennedy, 1974b). My own observations and Wolf's suggest that children accept that a mark can mean something without having a shape that is related to the referent's shape. If so, the mark refers because it is subject to the desire to represent something. It may not be necessary that there be an action related intrinsically to the referent. In this case the mark is beholden to an act of will; that is, the child draws by fiat.

Drawings discussed by Wolf are a useful case in point. Wolf (1983), like Golomb (1981), studied two-year-olds making drawings under two conditions of supervision. In one, the children drew freely without suggestions, and in the other the children drew while items were suggested to them. Children ages two years four months and two years six months drew shapes that bore no obvious similarity to the object being drawn: houses were elongated squiggles, legs were large dots, and arms were large circles or spirals. Eyes were squiggles placed one above the other. One child drew the head as a small mark between the eyes. Thus each item being shown had its own representational mark, but the mark bore no affinity of form to the referent. In Golomb's words, "forms are utilized, but they are subordinated to the demands of the task i.e. to the meaning of the figure" (Golomb, 1981, p. 39). The marks refer by act of will. Golomb and Wolf, however, also noted that if two-year-old children drew parts of the body following suggestions, they could distribute marks along a spatial dimension with representational intent. When parts were explicitly suggested by a tester, children placed the mark standing for the head above the body, the body above the legs, and the legs above the feet. Thus the extendedness of an object could be shown implicitly, even where no mark bore the shape of the referent (Golomb, 1990).

As Strommen (1988) points out in a review of drawing development research, several recent theorists, notably Freeman (1980) and van Sommers (1984), closely examine specific devices children use. Freeman gives an account of a young child thinking of the features to show in a drawing and the order in which to show them. He suggests that much of drawing development can be explained as the ability to produce, first, pairs of right angles, later a pair of oblique angles, and finally one oblique and one obtuse angle. What encourages children to select these solutions to drawing problems? Some theorists give accounts of the amount of information the child can attend to and use to guide drawing, but I wish to stress the basic perceptual and cognitive spatial principles children apply rather than the number of principles or devices they use. Freeman points out that children may think of a "first" feature or main feature like a head and a "last" or ending feature like a leg and omit the rest. Often, the form is oriented on the page vertically, and the legs are connected to the head as parallel lines, producing a "tadpole" man with an appropriate spatial dimension (the feet away from the head). Wolf and Golomb found that when an adult supplies the list of features and thus frees the child of the need to think them up, the child supplies an appropriate spatial dimension for a large set of body features. The marks were distributed spatially, even though none of the marks was spatially similar to its referent. The key principle is the child's use of a basic spatial dimension, although the number of features depicted by the child may depend on the amount of support and instruction that is given.

It is a short step to the stage when children make spatial properties of many features of the object evident in the drawing on their own initiative. This stage may be typical of three-year-old sighted children. Golomb (1981) found that 80 percent of three-year-olds make "pictorials" (Kellogg, 1969) of this kind. John Willats (1989) has observed, "In drawings by very young children extendedness may be the only property to be represented: typically, lumps are represented by round regions, sticks by long regions or lines and heads by dots." Such preschool children, Willats asserts, attend to three basic shapes: "lumps" for objects like balls, heads, or houses which extend fairly equally in three dimensions; "slabs" for objects like books which extend more in two dimensions than in three; and "sticks" for objects that extend mostly in one dimension. If extended in one dimension, a region on the page looks like a stick; if extended in two dimensions, it looks like a lump. It is hard to invoke a slab perceptually using a system that only controls extension on the page as lines (one dimension) or rounded forms (two dimensions) and not as contour. A cube drawn in this system, as by 3–4-year-olds, becomes a round region. Of course, regions standing for whole objects could use some shape features of the regions. Moore (1986) noted that when children ages 5–7 draw a cube with colored faces, they may draw a roughly square region and then put all the colors in separate patches within the region. Thus, the square region stands for the whole cube and all of its faces. Similarly, Willats noted that children ages 5–7 drawing dice would draw an enclosed region and then put all the dots from all the faces inside the region. In employing extendedness, children use the shapes of the marks they make, with some similarity between the mark's shape and the referent's shape. Extendedness may be just one part of a geometry of similarity employed by the child. Some other notions of similarity of shape must be important, I think, even to very young children, because a child of three is surely able to draw a crescent moon as a C shape and a wiggly snake with S shapes. If extendedness were the only salient feature, the child could only draw a crescent as a circle and a snake as a straight line. My informal observations are that drawings by children ages three and four who draw cubes as circular regions often display a mixture of shape dissimilarity and shape similarity. Not only do wriggly lines show snakes with many curves; the lines are often oriented vertically or horizontally on the page to show the orientation of the object. I suggest that children do not draw just the main extension of many highly curved objects. If a gently curved horn is depicted as an arc, not a straight line, clearly children notice the axis of the form. If three-year-old children are attending to axes of forms, then extendedness is part of an articulate geometry of shape including straightness and curvature in some of the earliest pictures made by children.

If the child emphasizes shape properties such as extendedness, then the outline form on the page can match the silhouette of the object, as a square can depict a cube, without actually referring to the silhouette. The outline form often stands for the whole object. Willats points out that the line on the page marks the boundary of the region on the page, and the region on the page may be what is relevant to the child. Initially the child may not treat the line as a device for showing occluding boundaries or convex corners of the referent. That is, the notion of relief perceived from a vantage point is not being used. Since occlusion and corners are not singled out as the basis for outline, the child is free to think that the line and what it encloses may be able to depict a number of aspects of the form being pictured. The line can indicate length, for example. Or the width of the region between lines may stand for the width of an object without the child realizing that the lines betoken the edges of the object. In children's sketches I have noticed drawings with two lines crossing (forming an X) to show a quadrilateral face (by diagonals) or a cone (by parts leading up to the apex) as illustrated in Heller and Kennedy (1990). A telling comment from Willats is that to show a sharp edge or corner, the child may need to add a line alongside the outline form. Willats observed one child who drew three lines where one would be sufficient: one was a boundary of the region showing the left face of a corner, a second was for the boundary of the right face, and a third was for the corner itself. Let us call this a three-line corner. Katz (1946, fig. 14g) made a similar observation.

When shapes of the parts of an object are first being drawn, the child may show each part by a separate mark on the page, neglecting the overall shape of the object itself. In Wolf's study, sighted two-year-olds drew individual parts without an overall silhouette, and each one was often distributed without regard to the others. The parts were "listed" in the order they come to mind, one might say. Often a part was repeated. Caron-Pargue (1979, p. 156; 1985, p. 56) discovered that sighted 4–6-year-olds would draw a cube with closed quadrilateral or roughly circular forms. Though each form might stand for a side of the cube, the number of forms varied from one to more than a dozen. (I have never observed a case like this among the blind, but I have never tested blind four-year-olds.) The forms were often distributed quite widely and irregularly over the page, sometimes with them overlapping and sometimes with each form distinct. Sometimes two forms shared a side or several sides. In all these cases the distribution of forms ignored the extendedness of the object, and in all cases the connections between some of the sides were disregarded. What mattered to the child was that square shapes were relevant to faces of the object, and the number was unspecified.

An important step in drawing development is when the child insists on making the connections between parts evident. To show the connections correctly, their number has to be correct, and that helps keep the number of facets correct. It also means that the lines mark the occlusions and edges where connections between facets occur. An important ambiguity becomes resolved when children first begin to use lines as edges rather than as boundaries of regions on the page. A three-dimensional "slab," in Willats's terms, cannot be shown perceptually by a two-dimensional region on the picture surface: the region tends to look like a lump extending fairly evenly in three dimensions. To show a slab, such as a book or a chocolate bar, the boundary of the region has to be depicted. The details of the boundary can be used reliably by vision to obtain a vivid percept of a slab, as shown in figure 5.2.

Concentrating on edges of objects and the line around a region on the page involves drawing initially one facet of the object, with each line depicting its edges. The shape on the page is geometrically similar to the facet's shape. This initial step may be sufficient to draw the object for many children (say, for five-year-olds). Other children, however, may try to add more facets, one after another, to the drawing. Various strategies for adding facets may dominate the drawing development of school-age children. The first facet chosen is likely to be drawn completely, and others may be less complete if to draw them completely would make them cross the lines of the first. Goodnow (1977) notes that children ages 5–9 often avoid such crossings even when they are appropriate. The effect is noticeable in drawing curved objects, such as a cylinder, where a rectangle can show the cylinder's extendedness in two dimensions but circles are needed for the third. Drawing complete circles at the top and bottom would involve lines cutting into the interior of the rectangle. Often the

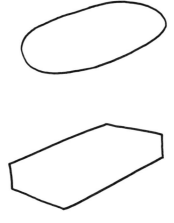

Fig. 5.2. A rounded region looks bulbous. Corners show a slab.

rectangle is drawn completely, but the child may merely draw half-circles for the top and bottom to avoid lines crossing each other. Caron-Pargue describes the part shown completely as "emphasized." Conversely, one side of a straight-sided figure may be drawn curved to show how it connects to another part. Katz (1946, figs. 14i, 14k, and 16d) reproduces drawings of cylinders by blind students with one or another part emphasized and no crossing lines.

Arnheim (1974) described the selection of a square for a cube and a rectangle for a cylinder as a "logical" analysis of the referent. These forms copy a basic distinctive part of the shape of the object. Arnheim noted that the added facets help to distinguish the referent, singling it out from the growing number of alternatives the child bears in mind as development proceeds. The circles added to a rectangle, in drawing a cylinder, show that the rectangle is part of a rounded form, not a slab. The progressive addition of facets can be described as drawing the object as though it were "folded out," a procedure that retains connections between parts but fails to maintain the angles between connecting parts. Katz (figs. 15c, 15d, 15e, and 17e) noted fold-out versions of a pyramid, a cylinder, a cube, and a prism.

Various fold-out drawings seem to occupy the sighted child asked to draw cubes and cylinders from the ages of six to about nine. Although the child draws facets with appropriate connections, it appears likely that connections are part of a more general class of features the child aims to depict (Golomb, 1990). Other features include enclosure as opposed to being alongside or behind. Goodnow's observations suggest that any lines meeting or crossing on the page are taken by the child to denote parts of the referent that are physically connected. In this vein, Piaget and Inhelder (1956) described the child as using topology, the geometry of connections. Topology, often called "rubber-sheet" mathematics, is the study of places that join other places, like knots, and barriers between places, like mazes. In topology, a flat ribbon is one connected surface, as is a circular plate or a crescent moon. These shapes, however, are surely treated as quite distinct by 6–9-year-olds (and probably so by 3–4-year-olds). Antlers are one connecting surface, but they will be drawn by branching lines, not circles. Thus pure topology is too general to describe the child's foldout drawings. Topological relations are important, but surely they are an addition to the earlier geometries using extension and similarity of shapes.

The foldout style of drawing has definite disadvantages. If an object has a large number of facets, drawing them leads to a confusing arrangement of a large number of forms on the page. The silhouette of the object is quickly obscured so that it is unclear what is a corner and what is an occlusion. The drawing is ambiguous about what is to the front and what recedes in depth to the side. It is impossible to draw all the connections without repeating a facet. While the meeting of the front with the top and the sides can be shown, it is impossible to show how the top and sides meet without distorting the shapes of the facets or drawing lines whose sole function is to link the facets. Children using the foldout style frequently comment that they had to add a line just for the purpose of connecting otherwise isolated parts of the drawing. Without the connecting lines there would be nothing to show that the parts adjoin in the referent.

There is no solution to the contradictory demands set by the foldout style. Probably as a result of this, at about 7–10 years of age children shift their aims, adopting a new criterion. They devise rules that derive from a geometry involving obliques and perspective, Willats and Caron-Pargue argue, corroborating Luquet (1927). These can, I think, be described as arising as ideas about the effects of a vantage point. The rules governing vantage points are a considerable source of debate in drawing development theory (Golomb, 1990). Among the possible rules a child might devise is that only the front and top should be shown, or oblique lines should indicate a side receding into depth (Arnheim, 1974), or convergence should indicate parallel sides receding into depth. For vantage point geometry, the key idea is that only those aspects of the object simultaneously facing in a single direction need to be drawn. Whereas the foldout system uses the shapes of facets copied by similar forms on the picture surface as its basis, the vantage point systems are concerned with the direction of the facets of the object from a point. In its simplest form the parts of the object facing a given direction are shown, with each facet being copied as in the foldout style, but in its sophisticated form the vantage point can be chosen at a well-defined spot at a given distance from the object. To use the sophisticated version one must recognize that the picture surface intervenes between the vantage point and the referent. Further, the surface can be placed at a particular slant between the object and the vantage point. Slight changes in the surface slant can produce all the effects sometimes attributed (as by Lee and Bremner, 1987) to change in the height of the vantage point. In the initial, developmentally earliest form, if the picture surface is ever considered explicitly, it is taken to be parallel to a major facet or axis of the object, and usually the orientation of the picture surface is vertical. In its sophisticated form, the picture surface can be placed at any convenient slant along the range from horizontal to vertical, whatever the orientation of the object may be. Given a sophisticated geometry, the direction of any point on the object from the vantage point can be established. Where the direction intersects the picture surface, the picture has a point representing the point on the object. Important theorems apparently first discovered by Filippo Brunelleschi in Renaissance Florence apply (Kubovy, 1986, p. 31), such as that the distance from the vantage point to the foot of the normal from the vantage point to the picture plane is the same as the distance from the foot to the vanishing points of parallel edges at 45° to the picture plane.

Sighted children generally do not offer formal theorems about their vantage point geometries, and there is controversy about the rules they follow. Certainly, most sighted children do not have sophisticated procedures for calculating exact angles at junctions and sizes of lines when they make drawings. Rather, they have an informal sense of proportion and general rules such as "Things in the distance are represented by progressively smaller angles" and "The picture surface is parallel to the main body of the object." As a result, the typical vantage point geometry evident in many children's drawings is intermediate between the simple and the sophisticated versions, and it is not clear how children progress beyond foldout principles through simple perspective toward the sophisticated version. The most general principle that researchers are likely to agree on is rather vague. It is the claim that sighted children at ages 8–12 draw following informal rules, checking their product by eye. If they correct their drawings, they do so by visual estimation of the correct proportions and angles, not by calculation.

Children who know that an object subtends a smaller and smaller angle as it moves away usually do not know how much smaller exactly. Often the more advanced children, say 11–13-year-olds, make some use of a horizon as a locus for vanishing points, but they do not calculate the correct vanishing points (Lee and Bremner, 1987). Except in rare cases they certainly do not know

Brunelleschi's formal rules for checking their drawings. Many children with an informal geometry of perspective will draw the side faces of cubes with parallel or converging lines without a clear understanding of when to use parallels and when to use converging lines. They will make the front face square, and the side face will almost invariably be given lines that are shorter than those of the front (about two-thirds the size of the front, Nicholls and Kennedy [1991] find). Notice that virtually no child will deliberately make the side face's lines much longer than those for the front. Their informal geometry fails to predict when the side face projects a much larger area than the front face on the picture surface. They make visual checks with both eyes and a moving head rather than monocularly from a fixed distance and at a fixed angle to the display. If they look at a drawing with a side face larger than the front face from a point directly in front of the drawing, their vision will reject it as a possible drawing of a cube (erroneously, as Pirenne's [1970] pinhole camera photographs show). The result is a geometry that departs wildly from proper single vantage point perspective.

I think it is reasonable to propose that 8–12-year-olds have a set of procedures or ordered actions present in their rules for making a drawing of an object (Freeman, 1980; van Sommers, 1984) as well as, somewhat independently, a procedure for checking the drawing at various stages of completion. A child may know that some drawings in perspective look erroneous at first, then fall into place as more details are added, the projection system becomes unambiguous, and the vantage point becomes evident. Perhaps from 8 to 12 years of age more and more drawing procedures using perspective become incorporated, and more and more projection principles become engaged in the inspections. But I think it is safe to say the criteria being used in the inspections are initially lax.

Even in adult observers familiar with perspective pictures, vision is not a perfect judge of polar perspective, in at least three respects. First, drawings of a cube or a landscape in parallel perspective are acceptable to vision. Freeman (1980) and others note that this tolerance of parallels is common in children and adults despite the fact that light converges to the visual vantage point. Parallel projection is incorrect, strictly speaking. It is probably tolerated by vision so long as its results approximate polar perspective effects. Second, drawings of a scene subtending less than a wide-angle view (less than about 30°) look appropriate even when viewed from the wrong vantage point (Kubovy, 1986; Johannson and Borjesson, 1989). The tolerance for an incorrect vantage point is much greater for flat-surfaced or cubic objects (up to 30–35°) than for rounded objects such as spheres (where the limits are often under 2°). The tolerance for an incorrect vantage point has well-defined limits even for cubic objects. In photographs taken of a scene subtending beyond 30–35°, cubic objects appear distorted in angle or proportion, or in both when viewed subtending a smaller angle (20° or less). Third, a scene can be drawn using different vantage points for different parts of the scene without vision recognizing that more than one was used (Kubovy, 1986, p. 117). All three findings indicate that vision uses lax criteria. (There is a fourth finding about perspective that may be explained by this laxity, but no one is yet sure. Spheres viewed off in the margins of a large picture such as a mural can be drawn as circles when strictly they should be drawn as ellipses.)

The vantage point geometry used by children to evaluate a picture contains profound principles, but likely it embraces only a few rules at first. Vision probably never follows all the rules of exact perspective without formal training. The rules vision follows could be matters of angle and proportion. Perkins (1972), for example, demonstrated that vision accepts projections of corners of cubes in drawings when they are in keeping with the angles projected by real cubes. The Perkins angle law probably has a sibling proportion law. I suspect that vision rejects side faces of cubes in drawings if vision can detect that the quadrilateral in the drawing representing the side face is larger than a square representing the front face. Vision prefers a proportion of about 0.6 for the side face if the front face is a unit square. These rules are imperfect versions of accurate perspective. Nevertheless, this is a geometry that lends itself to visual inspection of a drawing.

The more inspection comes to the fore, the more drawing becomes subject to an intuitive set of criteria whose profound central principle is direction from a vantage point. The criteria are in perception, not will. Vantage point criteria are in keeping with perception from a fixed point, so they apply perfectly to perception of a static picture. Essentially for the first time in development of drawing this makes it possible for the typical child to find drawing a difficult task in which to meet criteria for acceptability. The child is able to sense that his own drawing fails in adequately representing the object, and rejects it according to criteria that, being perceptual, lie outside of the act of drawing and the will to represent. Luquet (1927) called this stage "visual realism," and observed that it required the representation of all the characteristics evident from a vantage point (Costall, 1991). But it would be better to note that the child is satisfying a vantage point geometry of vision that can become a taskmaster without being entirely accurate or realistic; one might call it "vision's perspective."

Vantage point geometry stresses what can be perceived at a given moment lying in certain directions from a point in space; hence it can establish some clear criteria about what cannot be shown. That which is occluded in the referent cannot be shown in the picture. That which does not occur in a moment cannot be shown. These two criteria become allied with a sense of the limits of elements such as lines. That which is not evoked as an impression by the elements in the picture cannot be shown.

In a vantage point geometry emphasizing perceptual criteria, one of the novelties in the development of drawing is that for the first time many referents are deemed impossible to show. The child becomes aware of many parts of drawings that are violations of the rules given by the informal vantage point geometry and perception. Lines evoke spatial features—not sounds of cars, for example. Similarly, junctions become subject to perceptual matters. Y-shaped line junctions that are acute or obtuse on the page but look rectangular when seen in depth are preferred over T junctions that are rectangular on the page but look flat, when cubic corners are to be shown.

EVIDENCE FOR DRAWING DEVELOPMENT

How do children acquire vantage point criteria for drawings? Willats argues that there are six necessary stages. Caron-Pargue offers a much greater variety of routes than Willats. She even finds children drawing the sides of cubes as triangles or rounded forms and depicting internal detail by X, Y, or T junctions. Lee and Bremner (1987) identify an early phase when children draw using similarity geometry and a later phase, covering a wide swathe of ages, when perspective is represented by means of parallel obliques to show parallels receding into depth. Lee and Bremner suggest that drawing development is the acquisition of a series of local solutions, like parallel obliques, rather than a forced march through an invariant set of stages.

Are some stages much more important than others? To check on drawing development in the sighted and the emergence of vantage point criteria, Andrea Nicholls and I (Nicholls and Kennedy, 1992) examined drawings produced by children and adults. We based our analysis on types distinguished by Willats but also included some additional types, notably one taken from Caron-Pargue. Nicholls recruited volunteers at the Ontario Science Centre ranging in age from four years to adult (16–77 years, mean age 32). The volunteers were shown an opaque cube and asked to make their best drawing of it. For the children, we did not set the cube at a fixed location and stress its orientation, as we suspected that they might not be able to make what they deemed to be a "best" drawing under such conditions. Some drew the cube as though it were transparent or made of wires, like a Necker cube. These were set aside since we could not be sure whether they arose from a failure to understand the task or an inability to eliminate the lines representing the hidden sides of the cube. There remained 789 drawings by 4–15-year-olds (one per person) and 945 from adults (also one per person).

The classification scheme was as follows (fig. 5.3). Five categories were adopted from Willats. The first stage he called "pre–single aspect." The child shows a cube as a closed, roughly circular shape. The principle behind the drawing could be the attempt to replicate extendedness. The second stage is "single-aspect" drawing. A face of the object—here, one square—is shown, following a similarity geometry. Stage 3 is "foldout" drawing, which Willats calls "multiple aspect." Stage 4, "two square," is indicated by two faces shown attached, in which the horizontal or vertical is thought to represent depth. In stage 5, called "near oblique" or "Y and T junctions," a central vertex of the cube is shown by a Y junction and a vertex at the base by a T junction. We distinguished what Willats grouped as a sixth stage into four different kinds of drawings (categories 6–9), two based on parallel projection and two on polar projection. A "square with obliques" was a cube drawn as a frontal square and two sides shown by oblique parallel lines. A "vertex with obliques" was a cube drawn with a vertex or edge to the front, shown by a Y, the faces around it drawn with oblique parallel lines. Two other kinds of drawings were based on the "square with obliques" and the "vertex with obliques" but showed the sides with converging lines rather than parallel lines. A tenth type of drawing was based on a Caron-Pargue category that is not easily reduced to any of the Willat stages. Caron-Pargue noted "dissection" drawings in which the cube is shown by a complete square ("emphasizing" the square aspect, in her terms) inscribed with diagonals, perhaps to denote that the overall object is divided into sections meeting at a vertex. A final category in the initial analysis was "other," meaning drawings that did not fit any of the 10 definite classes.

The sorting of the 1,734 examples was carried out by Carol Flynn. To check on the reliability of the procedure, another judge (Gordon Mack) assessed 25 examples drawn from Flynn's groups, with at least two examples of each category. The second categorization was performed without knowledge of the results of the first. Twenty-three of the drawings were categorized in the same manner by both judges, indicating that the scheme is reliable. The results of Flynn's categorization are presented in table 5.1.

In the children's drawings, the distribution is clearly far from random. Categories 2 (one square), 6 (square with obliques), and 11 (other) account for 67 percent of the children's drawings. Together, categories 3 (foldout), 4 (two squares), and 5 (Y and T junctions) accounted for only 23 percent. Only 2 percent are dissection drawings (category 10). Convergent drawings (categories 8 and 9) occur only four times. There were only two category 1 (pre–single aspect) drawings.

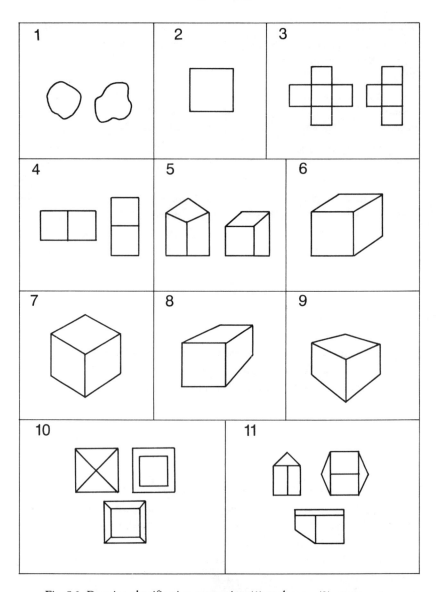

Fig. 5.3. Drawing classification categories: (1) enclosure; (2) one-square; (3) foldout; (4) two-squares; (5) drawings with center-Y and base-T junctions; (6) square with obliques; (7) edge with obliques; (8) square with convergent obliques; (9) edge with convergent obliques; (10) dissection; and (11) other.

TABLE 5.1

Number of subjects producing each drawing type at each age level.
Percentages are in parentheses.

					Drawing Types							
Age	W1	W2	W3	W4	W5	Obl	Edge	Conv Obl	Conv Edge	Diss	11	N
4	2 (13)	11 (73)									2 (13)	15
5		43 (83)	3 (6)								6 (11)	52
6		46 (63)	13 (18)	1 (1)							13 (18)	73
7		31 (43)	11 (15)	7 (10)	3 (4)	1 (1)	2 (3)			4 (6)	13 (18)	71
8		21 (29)	15 (21)	7 (10)	6 (8)	5 (7)	1 (1)			1 (1)	17 (23)	73
9		11 (12)	15 (16)	7 (8)	12 (13)	21 (22)	5 (5)			2 (2)	18 (20)	92
10		12 (14)	6 (7)	2 (2)	13 (15)	25 (30)	5 (6)			2 (3)	19 (23)	84
11		3 (4)	2 (3)	2 (3)	13 (18)	32 (44)	5 (7)	1 (1)	1 (1)	3 (4)	11 (15)	74
12		3 (4)	3 (4)	1 (1)	15 (17)	39 (46)	8 (9)	1 (1)	1 (1)	3 (3)	12 (14)	86
13			1 (2)	1 (2)	8 (16)	26 (52)	8 (16)			1 (2)	5 (10)	50
14		1 (2)			1 (2)	39 (67)	9 (16)			2 (3)	6 (10)	58
15			1 (2)		5 (8)	35 (57)	14 (23)			1 (2)	5 (8)	61
Child Total	2 (0.3)	182 (23)	70 (9)	28 (4)	76 (10)	223 (28)	56 (7)	2 (0.3)	2 (0.3)	19 (2)	127 (16)	789
Adults		15 (1.5)	10 (1)	3 (0.3)	35 (4)	545 (58)	224 (24)	20 (2)	22 (2)	7 (0.7)	64 (7)	945

147

Drawing Development

I shall set aside category 1 drawings since these were confined to two four-year-olds. I shall also combine categories 6 and 8, which contain squares with obliques, since there were very few category 8 drawings. Similarly, I shall combine categories 7 and 9, which contain vertices with obliques. Table 5.2 shows the mean ages of children producing each category of drawing. Categories 2–5, 6 + 8, and 7 + 9, in that order, were highly correlated with age ($r = 0.77$, $N = 640$, $d.f. = 5$, $p < 0.001$).

Three of the categories reveal strong linear trends. In the case of category 2 there is a negative linear correlation with age ($r = -0.90$, $d.f. = 11$, $p < 0.01$). For category 6 + 8 the correlation is positive ($r = +0.96$, $d.f. = 11$, $p < 0.01$). Similarly, category 7 + 9 is positively related to age ($r = +0.95$, $d.f. = 11$, $p < 0.01$).

Peaks for four categories occur in the middle of the age range (categories 3, 4, 5, and 10). But two of these contain comparatively few drawings. Category 4 only contains 5 percent of the children's drawings, and category 10 only 2 percent. Even categories 3 and 5 are never more frequent than 21 percent (age eight, category 3) and 18 percent (age 11, category 5).

The adult data closely match the child data at ages 14 and 15. They differ from the distribution produced by 13-year-olds, $\chi^2(7,995) = 18.17$, $p < 0.05$, and the lower age groups (and an overall Age (Children vs Adults) by Category chi-square test of independence is significant, $\chi^2(7,1732) = 71.57$, $p < 0.001$).

The most frequent kind of drawing from the adults is the frontal square with parallel obliques (58 percent, compared to 57 percent for 15-year-olds), and its nearest rival is the frontal vertex with parallel obliques (24 percent, compared to 23 percent for 15-year-olds). Apart from the unclassified drawings, no other type is more frequent than 4 percent (T and Y vertices).

The impression given by tables 5.1 and 5.2 is of a developmental progression from a single jumping-off spot to a well-defined terminus. The least variety of drawings is produced by the youngest subjects (for ages 4, 5, and 6, two types classify more than 70 percent of the drawings) and the oldest subjects (for ages 13 and above two types classify more than 68 percent of the drawings). Interestingly, among the eight-, nine-, and 10-year-olds no category

TABLE 5.2
Mean ages of children drawing cubes in various categories.

Category Type	1	2	3	4	5	6+8	7+9	10	11
Mean Age	4.0	6.7	8.2	8.6	10.8	12.2	12.3	10.5	9.3

holds more than 30 percent of the drawings. There is a diaspora after age five and a refocusing at ages 12–15. Likewise, the greatest frequency for drawings not captured by the 10 explicitly defined categories is found in the 8–10 age range. The eight-, nine-, and 10-year-olds produce 20 percent or more "other" drawings.

In the main, the categories increase in frequency of use, then decrease, several virtually dropping out of use. The adults do not seem to have progressed beyond the prowess of 15-year-olds, and at least a few adults use each category except the lowest (pre–single aspect). The most emphatic trend is from getting a single face of the object correct following a similarity geometry (more than 60 percent of 4–6-year-olds) to getting three faces present, coordinated around a front face or vertex (more than 70 percent of 12-year-olds and older). What is most variable is how other faces are added to the single face before the use of obliques is apparent.

What do the results indicate to be the chief principles in drawing development? Two children at age four show the use of a rounded form, which suggests the extendedness principle. After that, there appear to be two major stages. One could be described as following similarity geometry, meaning that a form on the page matches an aspect of the object. It is reflected in the single-aspect drawing at around age five (approximately 80 percent of drawings at this age), where the cube is drawn as a single square. The second stage could be described as using vantage point geometry. Obliques are employed to show three faces that face a vantage point, as in the square-with-obliques drawing around age 14 (approximately 70 percent of drawings at this age).

How do children advance from one stage to the other? There is no dominant intermediary category, though there is some indication of rather tenuous stages. Foldout drawings are most common at ages 6–8, two-square drawings at ages 7–8, and drawings with Y and T vertices at ages 10–13. But none of them are more frequent than "other" (category 11) drawings at ages 7–10. It is possible that once single-aspect drawing has been mastered in principle, children make a variety of attempts to show the faces that confront a vantage point. They may try to follow a vantage point geometry in restricting the drawing to the aspects facing a vantage point, though initially they may copy the features of the aspects using a similarity geometry. That is, direction from the vantage point is used to select the faces, but not to establish the angles projected by vertices or the line lengths projected by corners. The result is that first one set of the object's features can be favored, then another, none being satisfactory so far as perception is concerned until obliques are used. Then children may begin to realize that line lengths should be foreshortened, and perhaps later they may realize that many angles should not be projected as 90°.

Older children and adults may be attempting to use not only the faces confronting a vantage point but also the directions from the vantage point that produce obliques. They recognize that drawings of faces do not have to follow a similarity geometry.

With these conjectures in mind, Nicholls and I turned to the unclassified drawings. With Carol Flynn's assistance, we devised a set of possible precursors to the use of three faces with obliques and sorted the unclassified drawings (category 11) with these. If the adult and child drawings were based on quite different principles, this might be evident, we thought, in the unclassified drawings.

The children produced 127 category 11 drawings. The adults produced 65. Nicholls eliminated some from further consideration because the examples contained words, another drawing on top of a first drawing, partial transparency, or lines that could not be deciphered. Types of which there were only one or two examples were also eliminated. There remained 69 drawings by children and 32 from adults—a total of 101.

The difficulty for children, we surmised, resides in adding the third face once two have been drawn. Similarity geometry indicates that the first two faces can be rectangles attached along one side. But how can one show the shape of a third face, and how can it be joined to the first two faces that were drawn? The third face could be a rectangle, a triangle or a rounded form. We categorized the 101 as follows (fig. 5.4). (*a*) Rectangles are added to one or two squares. Seventeen children (mean age 8.2, s.d. 3.5) added thin rectangles to one square. No adults produced this kind of drawing. Eleven children (mean age 8.2, s.d. 1.7) drew two attached squares and then added rectangles. Again, interestingly, none of the adults drew in this manner. (*b*) A rounded top or side was added to two attached squares. Six of the children's drawings took this form, (mean age 9.2, s.d. 1.0). Again, none of the adult drawings took this form. (*c*) Triangles were added to two attached squares. Nineteen of the children's drawings took this form (mean age 10.3, s.d. 2.6) and 8 of the adults'.

The last two categories were concerned with obliques: 16 of the children's drawings (mean age 10.3, s.d. 1.2) and 13 of the adults'. (*d*) The drawings in this category included diverging lines for the obliques as they receded from the frontal square. (*e*) Drawings where two attached squares were each given an oblique top were mostly obtained from adults (six adults and one 11-year-old).

It is striking that in this set of 101 drawings, the adults on the whole create the same types of drawings as the older children (mean age 10). The versions offered by the younger children (mean ages 8 and 9) are not used at all by the

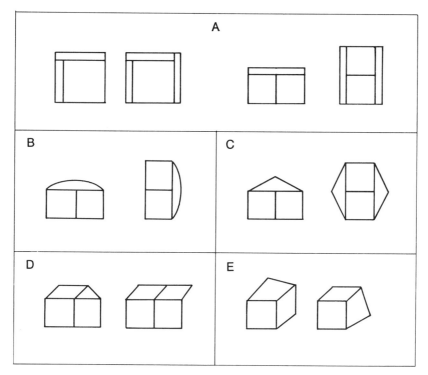

Fig. 5.4. Breakdown of category 11 ("other") drawings: (A) square with rectangles (left) and two-squares with rectangles (right); (B) two-squares with curve; (C) two-squares with triangle; (D) two-squares with obliques; and (E) divergent obliques.

adults. Adult drawings are probably based on different principles from those that govern drawings by younger children. What might these principles be? One promising account starts from the premise that the dilemma is how to add the third face. The eight-year-olds, still in the sway of similarity geometry, try to preserve angles (90° corners of rectangles). The nine-year-olds reject the need to preserve angles but insist on topological connections (their curved line shows that corners are joined). The 10-year-olds and adults consider directions from a vantage point and aim to show that the top of the cube recedes from the observer, employing obliques for the purpose. Their use of obliques, however, is imperfect. For example, the product is often a triangle on top of a line with a T junction. It leaves the impression that the third face has very unequal angles at the vertices, with the one above the T junction appearing to be 180°. In short, the younger children are matching individual features by copying the right angles, and adults and possibly children age 10 and older are attempting to follow a system based on directions by employing obliques.

In summary, this survey of almost two thousand drawings indicates the course of drawing development and suggests the principles involved. The youngest children chiefly draw a single aspect of a figure. Slightly older children add more faces in foldout style. Still older children restrict themselves to faces in front of a vantage point. The governing principles initially seem to be feature matching, by which features of the cube are matched on the picture plane; the number of features being replicated and their relative positions are highly variable. Later principles derive from directions from vantage points, which govern the number of faces to be shown as well as their connections, proportions, and angles. The children, then, are feature-based and the adults direction-based.

METAPHOR

I do not think that drawing development is finished when vantage point principles are solidly in place. Once limits and criteria of depiction are evident to the child, the vantage point stage of drawing development may pave the way for turning errors to good use. In language we can say, "A teacher opens doors for students." The teacher does not literally open doors for students to walk through but makes opportunities available, one of the functions of doors. Superficially, it is an error to describe the teacher as a doorman. The error, however, can make a point. Similarly, in pictures one can distort a shape deliberately to make a point. To show the unfeeling landlord's mean ways, the artist can depict his wallet as made of steel. His hands reaching for the rent may be drawn to look huge and hard. The description of the teacher and the picture of the landlord are both tropes, figurative uses of representations. Some trope pictures convey their meaning metaphorically but so aptly they do not need to be explained. For many people, a picture of a miscreant looking contrite while his shadow is doubled over with glee needs no more explanation than a proposition such as "The jailer had a heart of granite."

Since the vantage point stage of drawing development makes drawing precise, errors become salient. Therefore, once the vantage point system is understood, deliberate errors can be made in drawing with the well-founded expectation that the recipient of the picture is likely to discern the error. With ingenuity, the error can be made apt for a purpose. Three distinct purposes of verbal metaphor are to exaggerate, to contrast, and to make an allusion. All of these are evident in pictures (Kennedy, 1982a). Caricatures exaggerate.

Wolves can be portrayed in sheep's clothing. Advertisements try to associate products with wonderful scenery and movie stars.

In addition, some of the devices used in pictorial tropes may involve comparisons between two dimensions. A building's pillars may be shown S-shaped to suggest their shaking in an earthquake. These devices may be used systematically (Goodnow, 1977, p. 116): the more curves, or the more extreme the curves, the more powerful the earthquake. In a cartoon, the surprise and delight as the prodigal son returns home is greater the more extreme the father's pose: his eyes bug out and his jaw drops to the floor. A dimension of variation in the picture thus stands for the relevant dimension in the referent. The features used by the picture to show the referent may be apt and intuitively obvious, but also at times image and referent can be linked entirely by fiat, as in a graph or chart. Skills with diagrams and charts often need to be taught since they can be based on sophisticated conventions. In a diagram, by fiat, length can represent popularity, number of telephones, or bank balance. There is no way of knowing without consulting the key to the diagram. Unlike apt metaphors, diagrams violate the requirement that a picture use elements that spontaneously evoke features of objects in perception.

Metaphoric pictures rest on deliberate errors. In principle, there can be errors once any restrictive rule is established. Deliberate errors, however, are more likely when the domain of pictures is understood. Until that juncture is reached, children may imagine that a particular goal is not solved because of their own limitations, not the limits of the medium. If children know only a few rules, they might interpret an error as permitted by some rule as yet unknown. Errors become salient only when the set of rules is clear and restrictive. Furthermore, since pictures are a means for people to communicate, making pictorial metaphors makes most sense when the error is likely to be understood as an apt error by others. In a stage when the set of rules is unclear, even if a particular rule violation is evident, the child may feel that the error will be overlooked or misinterpreted by others.

Metaphoric drawing development has a different character from the emerging use of the principles of fiat, extendedness, connections, and directions. Each of these builds on its immediate predecessor. Metaphor can be an adjunct to any one of these principles. It also entails an intuition about others knowing the same rules and deeming something to be a deliberate rule violation. The others have to appreciate the intent behind the drawing. As a basis for metaphor, the vantage point system of drawing is particularly suitable since it is coherent and inclusive, offering rules that are restrictive and consistent. But it only favors the possibility that the child may choose to use errors deliberately, and metaphors could in principle be offered at any time the child imagines that there is a shared rule.

Metaphoric pictures have another specific characteristic. An algorithm or recipe can be given for vantage point drawing so that any object can be drawn, and any two sketches will in essence be identical. No algorithm yet exists for metaphors. Two thousand years of thought about tropes have failed to devise a procedure for finding the set of apt metaphors for a given topic, in part because the set is infinite and in part because the definition of the term *trope* is unsettled. Nevertheless, when a person using a device describes it as an intentional apt violation of a rule, it can be classified as a trope. Without being certain of the foundation for the person's claim, it is still possible to classify the device as a trope, for the definition rests on the *intention* to err aptly.

IMPLICATIONS FOR THE BLIND

The first drawing system the child uses emerges from the will to represent, seen in its purest form in representation by fiat, though in the intermediate stages shapes and their locations with respect to the self become relevant, ultimately moving the basis of representation out of will and into perceptual effects. In the earliest stage of representation, typically a work is made and other people are told what it represents. In the later stages, when metaphors are made, the artist bears in mind how other people will interpret the drawing. In both stages, how other people will understand the image matters to the young picture maker. What is in other people's minds is taken into consideration in both stages.

Will, abstract representation, object shapes, perceptual impressions, communication, metaphor, intent, errors, and other minds are all relevant notions in drawing development. Many of these terms apply as much to the blind as to the sighted. Blind people have will like sighted people and understand abstract representation, communication, metaphor, intention, errors, and other minds as much as sighted people do. The unsettled questions, I suggest, are: Do blind people have the same conception of object shapes as the sighted? Do pictorial elements such as outline fit with their impressions of features of surface layout, as occurs for the sighted? Do they think about the task of rendering three dimensions in two dimensions in much the same way as the sighted? Do they make the same judgments of apt metaphors as the sighted? If so, their drawing development could be much like that of the sighted.

Previous chapters examined recognition tasks and reported some drawing tasks attempted by blind adults. The lesson was that object shape and line depiction made sense in the same way to the blind and the sighted. Here I shall report on drawings by blind children. I have selected for detailed study drawings by the youngest children tested in the three research sites my assistants and I have visited and by three older children from the same areas. The three older children show more advanced drawing skills. And I shall consider Tracy, a blind adult who draws notably well, and compare her skills to those of the children and to those of another blind adult, who contends she has trouble with any task involving shape. My assistant in Haiti was Diane Girard, and in Arizona my assistants were Maryanne Heywood and Jay Campbell.

Cel

The youngest Haitian we tested was Cel, age six, blind as a result of malnutrition. Cel was admitted at age three to the school where Diane Girard and I tested him. At that point he was recorded as totally blind, and we may reasonably conjecture that Cel has had no pictorial experience since going blind and probably had little if any pictorial experience while sighted. He made seven pictures in one interview if we count false starts as well as completed pictures. The five pictures Cel deemed complete are in figure 5.5.

Cel's drawing of a coat hanger has a square enclosure rather than a triangular one, but the hook and the shoulders and straightness of sides around a central region are clear (fig. 5.5a).

After drawing a single closed form to depict a ring, Cel was asked to show the thickness of the ring. He drew two overlapping square-like regions (fig. 5.5b).

He depicted a box with square top and bottom and rectangular sides by four long horizontal lines. He indicated that each line stood for one side of the box. He finished the drawing with two vertical lines, standing for the top and bottom of the box (fig. 5.5c).

He drew a glass as an enclosed area for the open top, four lines for "the sides," and a line across the ends of the four side lines for the bottom. He explained the four vertical lines by touching the glass at four equally spaced intervals around it (Fig. 5.5d).

For a table, he drew an enclosed area ("the top") and put four parallel lines inside the area ("the legs") (fig. 5.5e).

Cel used the shapes of lines for legs, a hook, and the lip of a glass. These features are shown in outline using similarity of shape. Cel also used straight lines for whole flat "sides" of a box. In Willats's (1981) terms, a one-dimensional mark (a line) stands for a two-dimensional referent (a side). The line may show straightness or flatness and extent, not how the side projects to a vantage point. Therefore, this may or may not be the outline style, where a line stands for change in relief at corners and occlusions. Certainly Cel violates

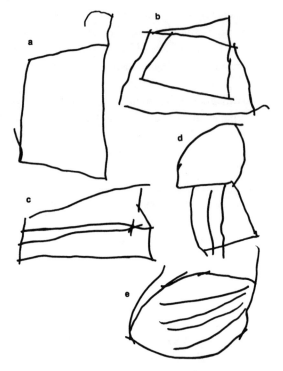

Fig. 5.5. Five pictures by Cel (totally blind at age three):
(a) coat hanger; (b) ring; (c) box; (d) glass; (e) table.

this outline style in using lines for the straight front and back of a glass
showing their extent. Also, the line encircling the region showing the top of
the table probably is not showing the shape of the tabletop. Rather, a region in
the picture surface is representing a region in the world, and they extend
equally in two dimensions. Concern for connections is fickle. The hook is
connected to the shoulders of the coat hanger, but the legs are not connected
to a table perimeter (probably because the line does not depict the perimeter
in the first place). The fact that the legs are part of the table may be shown
topologically by having the legs inside the region representing the tabletop.
But in a feature that follows similarity geometry the fact that they all go in the
same direction in the referent may be reflected in their being parallel in the
picture. Their direction with respect to a vantage point probably is never
considered by Cel. In sum, Cel seemed to make inconsistent use of outline,
similarity, extendedness, connections, and possibly the directions of parts of

the object to one another. In terms of the two main drawing stages, Cel's drawings sometimes achieve the single-aspect stage.

Ros

Ros, 16 years of age, also from Haiti, is early totally blind. The cause of her blindness is well established, a rarity in Haiti. Both of her eyes had to be removed surgically at 18 months following bilateral retinal blastosis. Her experience in making drawings was therefore minimal if any prior to blindness, and after blindness has been none so far as one can ascertain. Further, since the blastosis was inevitably present for some time before the operation, visual experience with pictures must have been slight. During one interview Ros drew 18 pictures (perhaps 16, for two pictures are probably two linked parts). Four are shown in figure 5.6.

Ros began by drawing a bracelet. Of three attempts, Ros, laughing, said the one in figure 5.6a was the best. It was rounder than the others.

Drawing a coat hanger (fig. 5.6b) Ros again laughed, saying, "It's not very good."

Her table (fig. 5.6c) is notable. It is long and thin with two legs at each end,

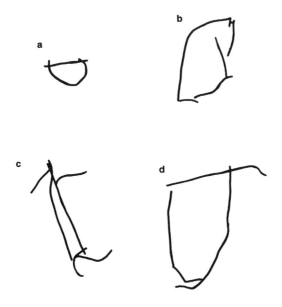

Fig. 5.6. Four pictures by Ros (early, totally blind): (a) bracelet; (b) coat hanger; (c) table; and (d) glass.

the lower ones meeting the lines for the sides of the table at acute angles, the upper ones more normal to the sides.

Her glass (fig. 5.6d) has U-shaped sides, and the mouth is shown by a single straight line at the top of the U.

Ros's drawings are more restricted to outline style than Cel's. The connections of the lines are made frequently, and they appear in suitable locations. Ros never made explicit reference to a vantage point. She herself was discontented with many of her drawings and seemed very defensive. At times she laughed rather than respond directly to questions. In Diane Girard's succinct observation, she was "giddy." We did not push Ros, out of concern for her discomfort, but I should add that the drawings here do seem to me to be her best drawings, and with each fresh start Ros did seem to make a more sophisticated drawing. By way of illustration, figure 5.7 shows Ros's first drawing of a glass. Notice that the length, mouth, and bottom are all shown by separate lines. The length is one set of lines, while the mouth and bottom are each shown by separate lines that happen to cross one another. It is a great leap to the second glass drawing (fig. 5.6d) which uses lines in outline style, with proper shape and connections. The first drawing simply marks lines that Ros then announced to be whatever feature of the glass she considered next on the list of features to be shown. The later drawings use outline in foldout style to depict occluding edges of flat objects and bounds of rounded objects, as well as parallel features such as wires and legs. Ros has clearly made some progress beyond the single-aspect stage. She was not the only blind person we saw

Fig. 5.7. Drawing of a glass by Ros (early, totally blind).

progress remarkably in drawing principles in a matter of minutes and without any instruction from us.

Di

Di, six years old, the youngest child in the Phoenix study, has been totally blind since birth. Di had made raised-line drawings of a face and a spider before commencing our tests, but so far as is known she had not been given pictures prior to our interviews. She made seven pictures for us. Six are in figure 5.8.

Di began by trying to draw a coat hanger. She found it easy to draw a horizontal line for the base of the hanger. But then, when she tried to draw diagonals for the sloping shoulders of the hanger, she found she could not produce the line she wanted. (Most children, as Olson [1988] noted, find diagonals difficult.) She ended up with another horizontal line, parallel to the first, and then would do no more (fig. 5.8a).

Fig. 5.8. Six pictures by Di (early, totally blind): (a) coat hanger; (b) ring; (c) bottom of a box; (d) man; (e) spinning wheel; (f) L-shaped block.

Di next drew a ring (fig. 5.8b) and the square bottom of a box (fig. 5.8c). A hexagonal box was offered to her, but Di refused to attempt to draw it.

Di next drew a man (fig. 5.8d) and a spinning wheel (fig. 5.8e). She identified the parts of the man (eyes, nostrils, mouth, neck, etc.), all of which lie in the proper locations. She accomplished this drawing after somewhat directive questions from us: "Have you drawn the mouth? Where would you put it?" Her drawing, with this kind of supportive questioning, is much like those of sighted $2^1/_2$–3-year-olds (Wolf, 1983; Golomb, 1990) under the same testing conditions.

Di said that she did not know how to draw a running man, and refused our request to try. On the other hand, she drew a series of circles and then straight lines for spokes when asked to draw a spinning wheel. We asked her, "Can you show it's spinning?" She replied, "I did." "How can you tell it's spinning?" "Because I can really tell when it's spinning." "How does the picture show it's spinning?" "Because."

We asked Di to draw an L-shaped solid object. She drew an L made of two straight lines. When we asked her to draw a T-shaped solid object, she drew a figure that does not follow outline style but is nonetheless revealing (fig. 5.8f). Di first drew two separate marks. She indicated that one mark stood for "the block," seemingly the whole object. The second mark, she said, was "the long part" of the block. When asked about the short part of the block, she drew a separate third, circular mark. We asked her if she could put the marks together, the way the parts are together in the block. She said no.

Di's first drawings include aspects of outline. The features she chose fit with outline style (wires and edges of objects). Shape is repeated on the page, emulating the object. Shape that is incorrect was rejected. In the somewhat "dictated" drawing of the man, locations are correct. In the wheel, however, spokes are disconnected from the circles. Movement is understood to be depicted but has no features on the page that can be pointed out. The motion is represented merely because it was intended. In the T-shaped block, one mark stands for the whole, it seems, while other marks stand for parts, and no connections are drawn. As in the drawing of motion, what matters is what the mark is intended to show. Di's drawings sometimes reach the single-aspect stage of drawing, but not always.

Hal

Hal, age 10, from Phoenix, has been totally blind since age $2^1/_2$, when he was blinded by contact with chemicals. Since then he has made some drawings with crayon on paper (leaving tangible tracks) or grains sprinkled on glue, and he has read some of the Expectations series of Braille books that contain illustrations.

Hal made 31 drawings for us, including several attempts at some objects until he felt reasonably satisfied and some drawings he drew at his own behest. Ten of Hal's drawings are in figure 5.9.

Hal drew a ring as a circle and then "went around it on the outsides" to show that the ring was thick (fig. 5.9a). For a rectangular box with square cross section, he drew a rectangle and then "like the circle, I went around it to show its thickness" (fig. 5.9b). But for the hexagonal box, he said "going over it" would show "the sides" and that "would not work." He went on, "The only

Fig. 5.9. Ten drawings by Hal (totally blind since age two and a half years): (a) ring; (b) box; (c) hexagonal container; (d) man; (e) dog; (f) spinning wheel; (g) another spinning wheel; (h) static wheel; (i) L-shaped block; (j) table.

way is to show one side, and another, and another," while he rolled the hexagonal box across the drawing surface. He drew six separate rectangular sides (fig. 5.9c). When we asked him what the lines stood for, he indicated the corners. We asked him if there was any special reason why there are two lines at each corner. He said, "No, that's just the way I drew it." His comment is reminiscent of Willats's three-line corner.

Hal next drew a man (fig. 5.9d). Then he volunteered an elegant stick-figure drawing of a dog (fig. 5.9e).

Hal made three attempts at drawing a static wheel, rejecting two because they were "not good circles." For a spinning wheel, Hal added extra loops around the outside of the wheel (fig. 5.9f) to show movement. In another drawing (fig. 5.9g) he distorted the wheel's shape from circular to oval, and he arranged the spokes in a line to show "one spoke would come right after another." It differs from his static wheel, which was drawn with spokes largely arrayed around the center (fig. 5.9h).

We asked Hal to draw some cubic objects—an L block and a T block. For the L, he drew separate faces, one L-shaped and one rectangular to show the thickness. In another drawing, he also drew the L but then added radiating lines to show the thickness. For the T, he again drew separate faces (one a T, one a rectangle, one a square). He returned to redraw the T, this time adding radiating lines to show the thickness (fig. 5.9i). He said that the radiating lines indicate "the sides that go up" and show that the enclosed space is "the middle."

Included in a set of drawings from a second interview a few days later were stick-figure people in a circle, a glass as a U and then as a circle to show the roundness, and a pair of drawings of a table. Figure 5.9j is a drop-leaf table. It is drawn from the side and has rubber ends on the legs. Beside it he drew a drawing of the "top part" (now round). When asked, "Can you show the legs?" Hal replied, "No, they're down here," pointing below the paper and the surface it was resting on.

Hal draws well and, as Maryanne Heywood put it, within minutes "pictures were improving—neater, straighter lines, more accurate angles." He uses shape similarity and outline style frequently. He connects the parts of objects appropriately in many drawings, but he also draws separate rectangles for an object he is "rolling" in his mind across the picture surface. He departs from outline style to show thickness, to add arcs around a spinning wheel, and to break the arrangement of spokes in a wheel to suggest movement. Hal is aware of the vantage point for his drawing of a table with the legs omitted.

Hal left us with intense respect for the 10-year-old mind's capacity for solving problems of drawing and with virtually no sense that blindness is a bar to use of outline or to pictorial inventiveness. Hal copies the shapes of aspects of objects. He uses foldout style. He shows some aspects of vantage-point style in drawing a table. His departures from outline style are marked at times by his own comments as "somewhat different."

Lu

The youngest child in the Tucson study was Lu (age 5, totally blind since birth). With her mother especially, Lu has made some cutouts, some of which have pictorial aspects, and string designs, some of which are rudimentary pictures. She owned an outline drawing of a hand before our testing program, cut out puzzles of a swan and a dog, and some relief displays of animals.

Lu began with a coat hanger (fig. 5.10), drawing a hook, then some disconnected lines for the neck, then a single line for the bottom and a series of lines, some slanting, some parallel to the bottom line. Her method solves the difficulty in drawing a diagonal by using one long line for the extent of the shoulders of the hanger and shorter ones to show diagonality. Apparently Lu has depicted the two properties separately.

For a ring, Lu first drew a large circle and then said, "Now I have to draw the inside circle" (fig. 5.10b). When we asked her what parts of the ring she had drawn, she indicated the innermost and outermost bounds of the ring.

We gave her a cubic box and a hexagonal box to draw. Her drawing of the cubic box was a series of loops and curved lines, and when asked what part of the box she had drawn, she indicated the edges of some faces. She described her drawing of the hexagonal box (fig. 5.10c) more definitively. She counted six sides of the box and drew the box twice; the second drawing is shown in the figure. Lu first drew six curved lines, counting aloud from one to six. Then below these she drew another curve, saying, "And now the bottom," and above she made another curve, saying, "And now the top." Her second drawing began with a long straight line, to show that the box had long straight sides, she said. Across this line she drew six circular arcs, again counting from one to six. When we asked her what the arcs mean, she replied, "The six sides."

Lu began the interview with outline drawings—lines for wires and boundaries. But the box drawings provide marks that stand for faces of the objects without regard for the shapes of edges. These drawings have marks that refer by fiat, not shape. They do keep the number of facets correct, but features are in a sense shown twice, since the length of the side is shown by a long line separate from the lines that stand for the sides. This is a drawback to the fiat system, which surely is overcome when the child realizes that a copy of the

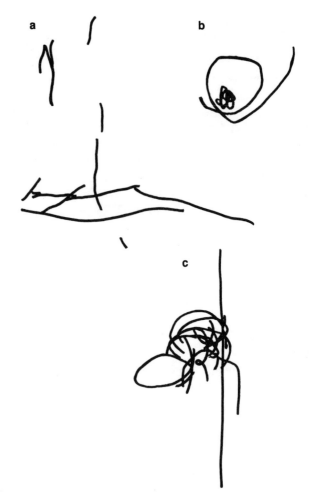

Fig. 5.10. Three drawings by Lu (early, totally blind): (a) coat hanger; (b) ring; (c) hexagonal container.

object shows length, shape, and number all at once. Lu's drawing of a ring is her most advanced, belonging to the single-aspect stage.

Raf

Raf, age 12, has light sensitivity but cannot make out shapes visually. He has a grade five education level but has been attending school only for three years, following his arrival in Tucson from Mexico and with no English-language skills. He is considered extremely bright and is talented musically. He plays guitar in public and now speaks English well. Raf was careful in his drawings, chatty, thoughtful, and good-humored. Before our tests Raf had made some string designs but no pictures. He had been given maps, but not pictures, in school. Raf made 12 pictures in two sittings, including several starts at some objects. Four are in figure 5.11.

Raf began by drawing a coat hanger (fig. 5.11a). Next he drew a ring as a single line. To show the thickness, he said, "You could make it over, I guess— right next to it, around the outside." He added an outer line (fig. 5.11b).

Drawing the cubic and hexagonal boxes, Raf drew faces of the boxes (fig. 5.11c).

To show a man running, Raf drew legs with a kink in them. "It's just

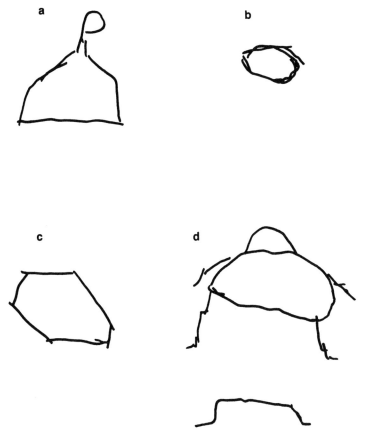

Fig. 5.11. Four drawings by Raf (early blind, with light sensitivity): (a) coat hanger; (b) ring; (c) base of a box; (d) running man, with a bend in the leg, over a hurdle.

showing that his leg is bent. You know, when you run you sort of bend your leg." And he said "you could put one of those things they have to jump over" and he added a hurdle below the man (fig. 5.11d).

Raf used outline for relief features. He also used similarity of shape. He drew single aspects of objects, and he added a hurdle as a context, in outline, to confirm a referent. One cautionary note: Raf did not mention vantage points. Indeed, when we asked him what the lines for his ring meant, he did not indicate, as did Lu, the inner and outer bounds. He traced an area on the ring with his finger somewhat in from the extreme bounds.

Raf's delightful picture of a running man was selected for the cover of the January 1983 issue of *American Scientist*. What a charming eventuality for a boy who came to Tucson at the age of nine with no previous schooling—to have an ability uncovered a few years later, and to have that ability recognized throughout his adopted country.

SUMMARY AND INFORMATION ON GROUPS OF CHILDREN

We have now studied six children in some detail. Each of them uses outline and similarity geometry in some drawing, the youngest children reaching the single-aspect stage of drawing. There are other kinds of drawings, too, including foldout and occasional vantage point drawings from the older children. What can be said about the children as a group? Since the Haitian children fared poorly when asked to examine drawings, we must especially take account of them to demonstrate that drawing is universal.

In Haiti every volunteer made at least one outline drawing with similarity of shape to the referent. The Haitian children were asked to draw a coat hanger, a bracelet, a ring, and a table. Let us consider each in turn.

A drawing of a coat hanger was deemed recognizable when the overall form was present, with the line standing for the hanger wire and a hook connected on the outside to an enclosure. If we include Cel's drawing in this category, then 13 of 15 coat hanger drawings are recognizable.

The bracelet was a single rounded form in 12 of the 13 drawings we obtained. The bracelet's shape was shown and the line stood for a wire forming the bracelet. The thick ring had two concentric circles in 12 of 14 drawings (fig. 5.12, by Ron, age 11, blind before age two).

The table was a closed shape for the tabletop (fig. 5.13, by Ren, age 15, blind before age seven) with four legs in 14 of the 15 drawings. The exception was Man's (age 12, blind before age five), whose tabletop shape is hardly closed (fig. 5.14). She also drew only two legs (the two smaller regions in the figure). Man's drawing is reminiscent of the drawings of coat hangers where

Fig. 5.12. Drawing of a ring, by Ron (age 11, blind before age two).

parts are drawn disconnected. The other 14 drawings are an advance on Man's, adding more legs and appropriate connections.

Now let us consider the coat hanger, ring, and box drawings by the Phoenix and Tucson children.

In Phoenix, five of the children drew the coat hanger recognizably. Another five drew parts—Sean, age 6, only drew the hook, for example—or drew several parts without connecting them, as Di did.

Three of the children drew a ring as a single circle (Di and Sean, both age five, and Rae, age eight). Four drew two concentric circles and three drew "extra lines," that is, redoubled lines, to show the thickness.

For the cubic box, three drew separate lines and indicated that lines stood for sides of the box (not edges) or the "whole front of the box" (Noel, age 12). The other children drew faces of the box. Kim, age eight, said she drew the top and bottom faces, the top with a circle and the bottom as a neat square, with a space in between. We asked her about the front face of the box, and she added some short lines linking the top and bottom, saying that this was the "up and down part." While Kim's box seems to have lines as linkages (which is

Fig. 5.13. Drawing of a table. By Ren (age 15, blind before age seven).

Fig. 5.14. Drawing of a table, by Man (age 12, blind before age five). The drawing shows the tabletop and two legs, the lines not connected.

not outline style) and a circular region standing for a face (which probably shows how the face is extended rather than any similarity of shape), in the form of a square it displays a well-defined use of outline and similarity geometry.

The hexagonal box drawn by six children included indications that the lines stood for edges or corners. Ted, age 14, noted that you could draw a *part* of neighboring sides to show that they "angle off," as he put it (fig. 5.15). In less advanced sketches, four children indicated that the lines they drew stood for sides, not edges or corners; they counted sides and drew one line for each.

Evidently, many of the children tested in Phoenix sometimes used lines standing for edges according to similarity geometry. The most dubious case was Erl (age 13), who was functioning at grade 3 level in mathematics and reading and was receiving special aid. He drew circles for the ring, which seems appropriate, but his coat hanger is merely a series of horizontal lines (which he labeled hook, top, and bottom, in that order). Likewise, the cubic box is a series of vertical lines—left side, bottom, and right side, in his order. His hexagonal box is made up of six lines, which he called six sides. He seemed to note the features in order and draw one line per feature most of the time. This simplicity is not a sign that Erl was uninterested in the task. He volunteered a drawing of a "plastic squeeze ketchup bottle"—a pair of concentric circles for the bottom and some vertical lines as "the front of it," accompanied by a comment that he could not figure out how to draw the nipple.

Among the Tucson children, five drew the coat hanger with its overall form displayed, reaching the single-aspect stage. One disconnected the parts (Lu, age five), and one is a series of lines with no clear description (Lar, age 12).

The ring was drawn as a pair of concentric circles by five children—and perhaps by Lar, who drew several circles, possibly four, and said, "It goes

Fig. 5.15. Hexagonal box, by Ted (age 14, early, totally blind). Short lines "angling off" show the sides at a slant to the front face of the box.

around and around and around." Tim (age 6) drew a circular squiggle, a filled-in patch, and said that it shows the ring "all over."

For the cubic box, five drew a square. Tim drew a squiggle and called it "the box." Lu drew a squiggle and pointed to several sides of the box when asked to explain her drawing.

For the hexagonal box, two drew at least two faces (Jef, age 12, and Ole, age 14). See figure 5.16, by Jef. Two drew a rectangle. Lar drew one line per side, and Lu drew lines for each of several features including length. Tim drew six lines standing not for faces but for corners, as he indicated in response to questions.

For each object, the typical response was in keeping with outline style. Single facets, drawn in shapes governed by laws of similarity, were the chief response. But as usual there are other aspects of the drawings to be accounted for. One line per side is common, and occasionally the drawing represents the object solely by fiat. How can these non-outline aspects of the blind children's drawings be characterized, and how can the prowess with outline be fitted with the rest?

The prime source of drawing is not that marks such as lines can resemble features of the world such as corners, edges, and wires. The will to represent comes before the ability to make resemblances, for the blind as well as the sighted. Nat, a blind adult in his thirties when we tested him in Toronto, remembers wanting to try to draw as a child even though he was told he could not draw because he was blind. Sighted preschool children make marks they call "cars" and "hammers" although shapes similar to the cars and hammers are not apparent in the drawings. Cel drew a cubic box with four straight lines

Fig. 5.16. Hexagonal box, by Jef (age 12, early, totally blind).

for "the sides" of the box, and Lu drew a hexagonal box by means of six curved lines, one for each side, while another line showed the box as long and straight. Displaying will, the children seem to use marks to list the objects or features of interest. On occasion a mark stands for the whole box, "all over." Or it may stand for "a side," or "the front of it," or "the up and down part." It may even be restricted to "the corner" (cf. Tim). Or there may be a line for "the front" and a line for "the back" (Cel's glass). The use of fiat for individual features persists even if the order of the marks on the page may indicate the spatial order of the features on the object—hook, shoulders, and base of the coat hanger (in that order) or the parts of the head, the body, and the limbs (also in order). The marks can be squiggles, individual lines, circles—almost anything, because their shape is not relevant, only their number. Since counting or listing is the basis of this kind of drawing, the marks can be one on top of another, as in Lu's drawing of a hexagonal box.

As in drawings by the sighted, drawings by the blind indicate that the will to represent precedes the ability to depict. This is apparent in choosing any mark to stand for anything. Further, this drawing by fiat is evident even in blind children who are capable of drawing in outline. Lu, for example, accurately drew parts of the coat hanger such as the hook, before drawing sides of the hexagonal box with arbitrarily shaped circular marks. Di reasonably drew a circle for a ring and a square for the box, but in drawing a T shaped block one mark stands for the whole and two other marks stand separately for parts. Kim creditably drew top and bottom faces of a box, the latter using similarity geometry and outline, but added some linking lines arbitrarily for the "up and down part."

Thus the will to represent—to choose, by fiat, to let any mark stand for anything—comes first and persists while other abilities develop in the blind child. This substratum is vital in every stage because it means that the limits in any method of drawing can be overcome. The child can reach the limits of any method and then settle any outstanding needs by asserting that they have been represented by marks chosen at will. The will is still present in adults, of course, as we find in a shorthand list for a trip to a store. Instead of writing out every word longhand, someone might end a list with asterisks and exclamation marks as a reminder to buy thumbtacks and a Frisbee. (If the marks were to be less arbitrary, they might be a swirl as a reminder to buy a Frisbee, dots to mean thumbtacks, stars to mean decorations, and an exclamation mark as a reminder to buy fireworks.) The shorthand list would be an adult employment of the will to represent shown in the "list" drawings of children.

The list drawings of blind children become more sophisticated when the marks are placed in proper order, the one for the hook above the ones for the body of the coat hanger, for example. This presumably enables a major advance on list drawings, to make not just any mark but a mark whose shape is relevant to the shape of the object. Lu's coat hanger has a curve, oriented properly, for the hook, vertical lines for the neck, and so on. But the parts are not connected. Cel's table has an enclosed area ("the top") and four straight, parallel lines ("the legs"), but the lines for the legs are not connected to the top. The objects are drawn piecemeal. Conceivably, each item could be drawn in an arbitrary location, with no special orientation, but I have never seen a drawing like this. Lu used placement, and Cel drew all four "legs" parallel within the enclosed area standing for a tabletop. Hence, placement patterns (Kellogg, 1969) probably precede outlining individual features. Wolf (1983) notes that sighted children ages 3–4 occasionally draw objects in this disconnected fashion for a brief spell, perhaps 2–3 months. It may be fairly common in blind children of an older age, for Lu is five and Cel six. Adults retain the capacity to draw objects piecemeal. We use the system in so-called exploded diagrams, where machines are drawn with their parts separate to make each part clear.

Just as outlined parts are an advance from list drawings because they add relevant shape, so too adding connections is an advance from piecemeal drawings. If the parts are connected, objects like the coat hanger would be drawn with a recognizable overall shape. The boxes would be drawn with each side neighboring another. They would appear as though folded out, in the manner of a cardboard box that has broken down and lain flat on a floor. Hal's box showed "one side, and another, and another" as he rolled the box across the drawing surface. Ros's table is reminiscent of a card table that has had its legs folded out. In this system the front, the back, the top, the bottom, the left sides, and the right sides can all be shown. Each part is drawn in outline style; each part is connected with another; the arrangement of parts on the page follows the order of connections in the object. Willats (1981) notes this kind of drawing in sighted children roughly 7–8 years of age. Table 5.1 shows that it peaks at eight years but is common from six to nine years (where it comprises more than 10 percent of the drawings from sighted children).

As adults we still sometimes draw this way. Car rental firms, for example, provide foldout drawings of their cars—the top in the center, the sides folded out like wings, the back and front folded out like extensions of the center. The rental agencies put on this drawing any scratches or dents on the car they supply to avoid arguments later.

Foldout drawings can be complete drawings of the object, but they fail to show how parts "angle off," as Ted put it. Nor do they show the location of the object. What is to the front, the back, the right, and the left? All the sides are drawn without discriminating their orientations.

An advance on foldout drawings is found in Hal's drop-leaf table. He drew the table once from the side and once from above, showing the location and orientation of parts with respect to a vantage point. The line now shows the arrangement of the tabletop, with one side near and the rest of the tabletop behind the side, hidden. When the table is shown from above, the legs are not drawn because from that vantage point they are behind the tabletop. This drawing surely indicates that Hal was grappling with vantage point issues. Willats (1981) notes this kind of drawing in nine-year-old sighted children, and our study of drawings of cubes suggests that sighted children ages nine and above are struggling with applications of vantage point geometry.

Whereas foldout drawings allow all the parts of an object to be shown, vantage point drawings provide a way of omitting parts systematically. In Hal's table drawings shapes are shown correctly, what connects to what is shown correctly, but also a vantage point is used to eliminate some parts and provide a consistent orientation for the remaining parts.

As with the adult blind subjects, there are few hints of changes of angle and convergent perspective in the children's vantage point drawings. Hal's tables are from above or from the side, not from a three-quarter angle. Perhaps Ted's drawing of a hexagonal box, where wisps of line at the top and bottom of a face indicate how the neighboring sides "angle off," reveals a premonition of convergence. In sum, two drawings indicate clear use of a vantage point.

Although convergence is not demonstrated overtly in the drawings, something else is that may be an important advance beyond single-aspect drawing. Hal initially drew a static wheel as having a circular form with spokes arranged around the center. To draw a spinning wheel, he changed the shape of the wheel and modified the arrangement of the spokes. The wheel was now elongated into an oval, and the spokes were set in a line to show that "one spoke would come right after another." How different this is from the drawings of childlike Di, who "knows" that the wheel is spinning or can only say, "I made it spin" or "It's spinning because I can tell." Hal's distortions suggest he knows that the drawing of a static wheel will not do, and that he has come to the limits of shape and outline.

The shape of an actual wheel does not tell us whether it is spinning or static. Neither does its outline. But the will to represent is broader than the ability to make things resemble their referents. That ability is present before successful resemblance is achieved, and it persists whenever any ability reaches its limits.

The ability to make anything represent anything we want explains part of Hal's drawing of a spinning wheel. But there is more. Hal does not simply make a mark, a squiggle, or a line and declare that it means the wheel is spinning. Rather, he violates a success he has already shown confidently in drawing a static wheel—that is, he modifies. His tactic is not like filling in a space between points because there is something missing (as Kim did to connect "top" to "bottom" parts of a cubic object). Nor is Hal's tactic like drawing the whole object and then, when asked about some parts, adding them as afterthoughts (as Di did to draw a cubic object). Rather, he redrafts the object.

TRACY'S CUBES

At the outset of this chapter, I noted two drawings of a cube by Tracy, a blind woman age 28. The first was a square with four arcs, one per corner. The second was two squares joined along one side, with a curved line connecting the top left and right corners of the squares. To anyone unfamiliar with sighted children's drawings of a cube Tracy's drawings are puzzling. Where, if anywhere, do they fit in normal drawing development?

Tracy's first drawing contains a square. This is her depiction of a cube as a single aspect, the chief method of drawing a cube for sighted children ages 4–8. Tracy's first drawing of a cube places her clearly in a major stage of drawing for sighted children. The drawing also contains four small arcs, which Tracy described as ways of showing "angles." She said that marks like these were drawn at angles in her mathematics classes. Evidently the arcs are a conventional prototype borrowed from a familiar setting.

Tracy's second drawing vaults her abilities beyond single aspect. It shows two squares adjoined, which Willats in his study of sighted children makes his fourth drawing stage. But in addition it contains a curved line joining two outer corners. The age at which we found sighted children drawing like this was nine years. When asked what the curved line stood for, Tracy said it represented a part of the top surface of the cube. She traced along an arc from one top vertex of the cube to another vertex diagonal to it. The arc curved toward the rear corner of the cube but did not touch it. She was asked if the line stood for the rear edges of the top face, and she said that it did not. The line seems to show that there is a connection between the left and right vertices of the cube rather than depicting an edge.

The curve of the line is shallow, but the arc followed by Tracy's finger across the top of the cube was more like a semicircle. This may indicate some fore-shortening, since the top face is horizontal. The conjecture makes sense in the light of a third drawing of a cube by Tracy (fig. 5.17).

Tracy was asked to draw a cube sitting on a table. The drawing contained a square and a rectangle. The rectangle atop the square shows the top surface of the cube above the front face of the cube. The rectangle is much thinner than the square to indicate that it is a face receding from the observer. Thus the drawing uses foreshortening. Her first use of foreshortening in our studies was in drawing a card folded in the middle and set on edge. The card formed two equal rectangles with a rectangle facing Tracy and a rectangle slanting away. Tracy drew this just before the square-and-rectangle drawing of a cube. In sketching the card, she drew the facing rectangle in proportion and the rectangle slanting away as thinner (fig. 5.18). Katz (1946, fig. 14g) reports a similar drawing from a blind student.

In her drawings, Tracy's use of two faces and foreshortening places her solidly in the vantage point stage of drawing development, a stage more advanced than that of many if not most sighted nine-year-olds. Her drawings of a cube seemed to advance rapidly in sophistication with each attempt,

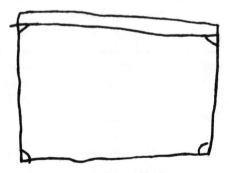

Fig. 5.17. Third drawing of a cube, by Tracy (early, totally blind).

Fig. 5.18. Drawing of a card folded in half, by Tracy (early, totally blind).

moving from a drawing characteristic of five-year-old sighted children to one more typical of 9–10-year-olds.

Tracy drew several figures at my request and volunteered a few drawings of objects of her choosing. One of these may be sufficient to make the point that Tracy drew at least as competently as most sighted 10-year-olds. Figure 5.19 shows a cat. Tracy reported that this was her own cat's favorite posture.

Not all blind adults draw as well as Tracy. Some, like her, have a keen interest in shape and form. Others demur when asked to undertake any project that has to do with shape. They protest that they always have trouble with maps, diagrams, and spatial directions. They report that in school they always felt like failures at spatial problems. They say they try to avoid dealing with form. Like fears some people have about mathematics, computers, or athletics, these fears may be based on initial difficulties but can become self-fulfilling prophecies, preventing the person from advancing in a domain of expertise where they may have appreciable if modest abilities.

Consider Kathy R., age 41, from Ottawa, totally blind at birth. She reports that in school she always avoided tasks that had to do with shape since she felt that she could not succeed in these tasks. She notes that she cannot easily follow spatial directions and she says that she "has to walk it." Even after

Fig. 5.19. Drawings of a bird and a cat, by Tracy (early, totally blind).

walking a route, she finds she cannot easily make the return trip. I wonder if she has set her own standards for success so high that she is bound to fail.

I asked her to draw a cube. Her first drawing was a rounded closed form (fig. 5.20a). She added squiggles and pairs of parallel lines to the closed form to indicate features of the cube such as the top or side faces. She puts some of these marks inside the closed form and some outside. She was not pleased with her drawing and started another. This one had two faces, but they were

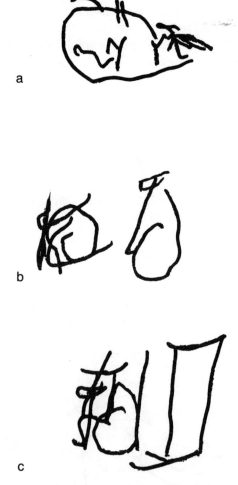

Fig. 5.20. Three successive drawings of a cube by Kathy (early, totally blind). By the third drawing, shapes of faces of the cubes are evidently presented in similarity geometry.

separate and still rounded (fig. 5.20b). A third drawing of a cube also contained two forms, but now both were rectangular and they were connected (fig. 5.20c). A few additional marks and squiggles were meant to show which is the top face.

In a matter of minutes, Kathy moved from a rounded form (the first of Willats's stages) typical of 3–4-year-old sighted children, to two joined rectangular forms typical of a child age 7–8 (Willats's fourth stage). The principles she was grappling with in the third drawing are matters of vantage point geometry, since only the aspects of the cube facing her are drawn. She was also using similarity geometry, showing rectangles by rectangles although they are not well executed. Evidently she has a fairly definite sense of similarity of shape, for she corrected her final attempt at a cube's front face. It was initially drawn as a rectangle about 1 cm by 3.5 cm, and she corrected this to 2 cm by 3.5 cm, noting that this was better but not perfect.

Kathy also drew a man standing and a man lying down (fig. 5.21). The man standing has both legs in the same direction as the body. The man lying down has his legs at right angles to the body. The forms in both drawings show an ability to use similarity geometry, lines for limbs, and rounded patch shapes. The method of drawing the man lying down shows an ability to vary the relative orientation of parts to invent suitable devices.

Kathy's ability was not the equal of Tracy's. Her performance was like a sighted child's of age 3–8, depending on the task and how many previous attempts Kathy had made. Her ability is not negligible, though her remarks indicate that it does not satisfy her. Her drawings, more than her remarks, reveal an ability ready to be tapped, challenged, and refined. Her own problem-solving abilities, unaided, produce refinements. With suitable encouragement she might quickly progress to a basic understanding of as many

Fig. 5.21. Drawings of a man lying down and a man standing,
by Kathy (early, totally blind).

177

problems and principles in drawing as Tracy has. Although Tracy may have a better grasp of edges, proportion, and ways of checking and modifying a drawing, Kathy seems to move swiftly from one key principle to another, more advanced one. A teacher of nine-year-old sighted children once described to me some of the drawings she got from her children as "chicken scratches." Kathy's drawings have this appearance at first, but the underlying principles are not to be gainsaid. When Kathy drew an L-shaped block and a cube, or a folded card, her drawings of these objects were scratchy, but the ideas she was using to guide her drawing were like Tracy's. For example, Kathy said that to show a box set in the middle of the table, as opposed to near the front edge of the table, she should "make it smaller a little bit but not much." To show the box on the far side of the table, "the box would be a lot smaller." To show a folded card, the part receding should be shown with lines that "as they go away from me . . . get thinner," and the part nearer should be "fatter to indicate that it's closer to me." Kathy's ideas are advanced, though her execution often lags behind them.

I conclude that Tracy and Kathy both fit into normal drawing development. Both show major principles of the main stages of normal drawing development, similarity geometry and vantage point geometry. One is extremely interested in shape and has enjoyed self-guided exploration of outline. The other is concerned about her abilities with form to the point of avoiding any tasks having to do with it. Yet both progressed rapidly so far as drawing development is concerned when asked to draw a cube.

Early beginnings are laden with promise. Blind children, like sighted children, make marks and call them objects. They put the marks in proper locations with respect to one another following their relations in the object— top, middle, bottom, left or right. At first, blind children draw with a variety of marks standing for corners, faces, and whole objects. They often draw in outline, choosing lines to stand for wires, rounded bounds of objects, and corners of objects. On occasion, particularly with younger children, the parts are disconnected but distributed in a way that matches their locations in the object. Many blind children draw connected parts in a foldout version of objects. Twice in our studies, a vantage point was used explicitly to govern the selection of parts and their arrangement.

Wolf (1983), Willats (1981), and others have found these same kinds of drawings in sighted children. The set of advances I have described here would be accepted by many students of children's drawings of space and shape. What is salutary is that the drawings presented here come from the blind. Many scholars would have argued that much of children's drawing ability is a product of being taught formulae and being given rules or expectations. For sighted children, there is a great deal of truth to their arguments (Wilson and Wilson, 1982a and 1982b, Wilson, 1985), though even with the sighted it is not the whole story. Yet these arguments are unlikely to explain how blind children come to draw.

Blind children are not taught to draw. They are not given formulae by their teachers (or schoolmates) and do not acquire them as prototypes, like Snoopy in the *Peanuts* strip, as sighted children do. Rather, they seem to be driven by some developing ability that grows and burgeons unknown and unsuspected in all blind children. It only needs tapping to make itself evident.

This talent grows without direct tuition. Tracy and Kathy seemed to advance without guidance. The talent grows even when denied. Nat was told by his teachers that he could not draw and it was not worth his while to try. Yet he drew many pictures in our research program, and one was picked for the May 1980 cover of *New Scientist*. The journal, appropriately enough, gave Nat the cover artist's fee for his drawing. To my knowledge, this makes Nat the first blind man in the history of publishing to be given the cover artist's fee from a magazine—a special moment for publishing, for the psychology of pictures, for the blind, and for Nat.

CHAPTER SIX

Perspective

In drawing familiar objects and interpreting raised-line illustrations, blind volunteers in our studies often mentioned a vantage point. Frequently they commented that an object was drawn from above or the side, for example. A vantage point is a key part of perspective geometry, along with perspective convergence, which arises when parallels recede into depth. To draw in perspective means to consider a vantage point, directions, and distances of the parts of the object from the vantage point and the location of the picture surface. Stimulated by the comments of blind people about the vantage points indicated by drawings, my colleagues and I undertook studies on aspects of perspective in touch and raised-line drawings. Here I shall report the results of these studies, which show how blind people appreciate basic principles of perspective.

PERSPECTIVE AND PERCEPTION

Perspective is an ever-present influence on perception, tactual as well as visual, but how it operates is not always well understood. I should prepare the way for my reports of studies with the blind by giving a brief assessment of the role of perspective in vision.

Vision interprets patterns governed by perspective often rather loosely, but for good reason. Our sense of the direction, proportions, and angles made by parts of an object as it tilts or rotates, approaches or recedes in relation to where we stand, is at times rough. Vision's lax use of perspective criteria may mean that vision and touch have much in common when they cope with problems of perspective.

Perspective

Perception is a result of the interaction of an energy, an object, and an environment for observation. The force can be light and its obverse, shade, or it can be a push and its reciprocal, a pull. Objects have many kinds of characteristic shape and layout affecting the energy. But conditions for observation always entail a vantage point lying in a terrain at a given direction from the object, as well as the source of the energy. Visual perception takes the outcome of the three factors—illumination, shape, and direction—and must solve the outcome as an equation with three roots. For now, let us focus on direction, which is the basis of perspective.

Imagine a cube of width w placed in front of the observer's vantage point. The front face might subtend close to 180°, and the rear face would then subtend about 53°. That is, when the angle between lines joining the top and bottom of the front face and the eye is 180°, the rear makes an angle of 53°. If the cube recedes a distance w equal to its width, the front face would replace the rear face. The rear face would then subtend about 28°. If the cube recedes by w again, the rear face would then subtend 19°. Successive steps of distance w make the rear face 14°, 11.4°, 9.5°, 8.2°, 7.2°, 6.4°, 5.7°, 5.2°, 4.8°, 4.4°, 4.1°, 3.8°, 3.6° . . .

Notice that a move of distance w produces dramatic angular changes when a close object subtends a large angle. The same shift in distance produces very minor angular changes, however, when the object is farther away and subtends a small angle. It follows that when the object subtends a small angle (or is far away) it can change its distance quite a lot before there is a material effect on the angles subtended by the front and rear faces.

The proportion 3.6/3.8 (or 0.95) is close to the proportions 3.8/4.1 (or 0.93), 4.1/4.4 (or 0.93), and 4.4/4.8 (or 0.92). Ergo, a distant cube with a small angular subtense can move a distance equal to several times its width before the projected proportions change appreciably. The proportions 53/180 (or 0.29) and 28/53 (or 0.52) and 19/28 (or 0.68) and 14/19 (or 0.74) are decidedly different. Therefore, a cube subtending a large angle only has to move a short distance before the proportions of the projected angles alter markedly.

These geometrical facts have a major impact on vision's use of perspective. Objects depicted with proportions in keeping with small subtended angles can be viewed at a large range of distances before they look awry. Objects depicted with proportions suitable for large angular subtenses can only be viewed at a small range of distances and still look appropriate.

The application of this principle to pictures is straightforward. Consider an observer who is presented with a drawing of a cube showing the rear making an angle of 3.6° while the front angle is 3.8° (a proportion of 0.95). Imagine that the observer appreciates this as a proper drawing of a cube. Imagine further that the observer judges this drawing to be quite acceptable when it is brought closer, just up to the distance when the front subtends 11.4°. At 11.4° the correct proportions are 9.5/11.4 (or 0.83). This differs from the correct proportions by 0.12 (0.95 − 0.83). This observer is willing to accept as "still proper" proportions within the range 0.95–0.84. (That is, a picture of the cube can be moved from 3.8° to 11.4° without violating this observer's criterion for a proper cube.) The observer has a tolerance for deviation from correct proportions of about 10 percent. This suggests that if the picture of the cube is moved away from the observer so that the angles subtended by the cube shrink from 3.6° and 3.8° to smaller and smaller angles, the picture will always appear to show a proper cube to this observer. As its angular subtense shrinks, the cube picture will never project proportions that move outside the range 0.95 ± 10 percent.

This geometrical analysis of distance, angle, and criteria for judgments indicates that visual perspective can involve considerable tolerance for change of angle and distance, deeming objects to be depicted correctly provided that the proportions are correct for an object subtending a small angle. The central principle psychologically is a criterion for correct proportion. Added to the psychological principle is a physical ally: the proportions projected by an object such as a cube vary little, for a movement of distance w, when the object subtends an angle of about 7°.

The psychological principle and the physical ally are logically independent, but they are closely related in practice. A moment's thought about the rotation and foreshortening of objects explains why. If a cube is set at a fixed distance and rotated, the angles projected by each face as it rotates vary considerably. The front face foreshortens as it rotates to become a side face. This may encourage an observer to set wide criteria when trying to judge correct proportions. In contrast, a rotating sphere has no faces to foreshorten; it always projects a symmetrical cone of light to the vantage point. Consequently, observers have no call to set wide criteria for correct proportions when viewing a picture of a sphere.

Let us check some of these theoretical observations in a demonstration. Consider the cube pictured in figure 6.1. Three of the faces are shown. Since the top of the cube is visible, it is drawn from above. The correct place to view the picture is with the central line of the drawing straight ahead and slightly below the line joining the observer to the nearest point of the page. The two side faces of the cube are shown meeting at the front edge. They are represented by symmetrical foreshortened forms in the drawing. The amount of foreshortening is the proportion between the short line showing the far edge of each face and the long line showing the near edge. The foreshortening ratio

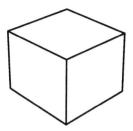

Fig. 6.1. Drawing of a cube in perspective, which looks correct subtending 15°.

is an exact function of the angle subtended by the cube at the correct vantage point for the drawing. If the cube had subtended a larger angle, there would have been more foreshortening, and a smaller angle would have produced less. If the cube had subtended a tiny angle, there would have been virtually no foreshortening.

Vision is sensitive to the relationship between the angle subtended by a cube and the proper amount of foreshortening. To demonstrate this, try increasing the angle subtended by fig. 6.1 by moving it close to the eye. The figure will begin to look distorted, and the distortion will increase as the angle subtended gets larger. The far edge of the cube appears to expand to look larger than the front edge. This shows that if the drawing is to continue to look like a cube, the amount of foreshortening needs to be increased to compensate for the apparent expansion as the figure subtends a larger angle. Evidently there is a correct amount of foreshortening for a given angle subtended. This follows from the geometry of real cubes and the angles they subtend at vantage points (Kubovy, 1986; Veltman, 1991).

Figure 6.1 also shows that vision is only roughly sensitive to the relationship between the amount of foreshortening and the angle subtended. The figure looks quite satisfactory as a cube over quite a range of angles subtended. Strictly speaking, it is only correct at 15°. But it looks undistorted from a range of distances—reading distance, arm's length, two meters, or even ten meters. This range of distances involves changing the angle subtended from much less than 1° to angles 30 or more times larger. (The angle subtended by the moon, the sun, or the thumbnail at arm's length is about half-a-degree.) Since figure 6.1 changes very little over a wide range of angles, it can be called "robust" (Kubovy, 1986).

Figure 6.2 is a cube drawn in parallel oblique perspective. Its sides are parallel, and the line representing the far edge of a side face is not foreshortened in comparison to the line representing the near edge. It could only be accurate at close to zero angular subtense—zero in the limit, strictly

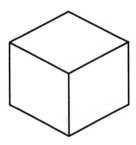

Fig. 6.2. Drawing of a cube in parallel oblique perspective.

speaking. Visually, however, it is quite acceptable as a picture of a cube at angular subtenses ranging up to about 20° (Nicholls and Kennedy, 1991). It hardly changes in appearance over the range 20° to less than 1°. It too shows that vision is tolerant of some discrepancy between foreshortening and sub-tended angle. It is not that vision fails to apply projective criteria to the figure: if it is brought close to the eye and made to subtend angles such as 30° or 40°, the figure will look distorted, with the back edges too large as projective geometry requires. Indeed, it will look considerably more distorted than figure 6.1 at these large angular subtenses.

The alter ego of figures 6.1 and 6.2 is figure 6.3. Whereas figures 6.1 and 6.2 look distorted at a wide angular subtense and are robust at smaller angles, figure 6.3 only looks well proportioned when close to the eye (36° is its correct subtense), and its far edges seem too short otherwise. Figure 6.3 is fragile when it drops much below its correct subtense. Figure 6.1 is the most robust over the range 36° to less than 1°, presumably because its correct subtense (15°) falls in the middle of the range.

It is clear that vision allows drawings of cubes with proportions in keeping

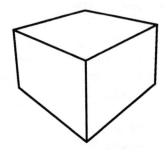

Fig. 6.3. Drawing of a cube in strong perspective, which
looks correct subtending 36°.

with a real cube at a small angular subtense to be robust. Robustness demonstrates that visual perception links projective factors, such as subtended angle and foreshortening, with room for some play between them. The relationship between the two does not have to be precise to a single degree of angular subtense. This freedom permits parallel projection to be visually acceptable and allows observers to examine pictures from a wide range of vantage points without noticing distortions (Nicholls and Kennedy, 1991). The projective angle and foreshortening criteria are being used (if only approximately), and the relationship between the two is appropriate, as the demonstrations show. Figures 6.1 and 6.2 look to have far edges that are too long when their angular subtense is magnified sufficiently, and figure 6.3 looks to have far edges that are too short when its angular subtense is minified. Vision has some rough sense of the correct proportions of the angles subtended by parts of an object.

How can these projective criteria arise in touch? Consider a cube set in front of a blind person. The front face has one edge to the left and one to the right of straight ahead. Now rotate the cube 45° horizontally relative to the observer. One edge is straight ahead, and the other has moved closer to it in direction. Now rotate the cube further until the edges are aligned. The angle between them and the observer has gone to zero. I imagine that the blind observer can be quite aware of the changing directions of the edges as the cube rotates. There is no reason why the blind person cannot realize via touch that, for example, the left edge of a frontal face rotates to become the right edge of that face when it is on the back of the cube. Touch can certainly reveal to the blind person that a side face has its edges aligned with him and the front face has left and right edges widely separated in direction. It can also discover that when the cube has an edge to the front, the two faces on either side of the front edge are symmetrically placed, one to the left of the front edge and the other reaching out exactly as much to the right.

Clearly, information about the direction of edges and the extent to which one edge is located to the left or right of another is a matter of direction from a vantage point, foreshortening, and proportions between angles. This information is pertinent to touch as well as vision. Experiments in touch and vision may reveal the same principles of perspective at work in both senses and may well tap a source common to both senses (E. J. Gibson, 1969, p. 23; Spelke, 1987, p. 238–240).

I am not arguing that visual imagery permeates touch or that vision is crucial for providing the quality of spatiality to tactual representation (Katz, 1925; 1989, p. 229, commentary by Krueger, p. 3). I am pointing out, rather, that dealing with direction requires similar abilities in vision and touch (Millar, 1986) and that the two may access a common spatial process in

Perspective

perceptual analysis—a common spatial sense. Further, pictorial displays may be based on some matters of direction and be intelligible to the blind in much the same way they are to the sighted.

DRAWINGS AND DEPTH

Solid objects have parts at different distances from the observer. A picture, on the other hand, is a surface; it has no depth and cannot replicate these changes in distance. How can solid objects be drawn by blind people? Steinberg (discussed in Katz, 1989) argued that the congenitally blind perceive the shapes of three-dimensional objects, within broad as well as narrow confines of tactual space, much as the sighted do in the sense that the structure of the object is adequately perceived (p. 144). How can this three-dimensional shape be portrayed, and can the picture indicate something about the location of the observer?

In a study undertaken with Maryanne Heywood, 13 adult volunteers from BOOST in Toronto (table 6.1) drew some objects made of cubic blocks. One of the tasks was to draw an L-shaped block. Seven of our volunteers drew an L— the distinctive face of the object—and left it at that. Three drew the L and then, to show that the object had depth, added other lines that echoed the L shape. Nat and Jay (both early, totally blind) and Roy (late, totally blind) made the extra lines parallel to sides of the L. Jay said that this was "to make it solid." Nat said "because I couldn't go through the page, I showed the depth with four or five lines. If it were only slightly thick, I would have used just one or two lines." He described this technique as "expanding sideways" in proportion to the depth. Caron-Pargue (1985, p. 118) identified this device in drawings by sighted six-year-old schoolchildren. It might be termed a thickening or build-up technique. It is a rather simplified version of the foldout style, where the shape of all the edges of the side face are drawn following the rules of

TABLE 6.1
Volunteers from BOOST who drew objects made of blocks.

Onset of Blindness and Degree of Loss	Participants
Early (0–2 years)	Cal, Dee, Jay, Lys, May, Nat, Pat, Pau
Early, light perception	Jim, Nip
Late, totally blind	Mo, Ray, Roy

Fig. 6.4. Drawing of an L-shaped block in a foldout style,
by Dee (early, totally blind).

similarity geometry. It shows there is a side face and gives an indication of its width, but it does not show the shape of the far edge. Three of the volunteers drew two or more faces of the L in foldout style: Dee, early, totally blind; Pau, early, totally blind; and Ray, late, totally blind (figs. 6.4 and 6.5).

Similar results were obtained with a T-shaped block. We then asked the volunteers to draw two objects in which the limbs project in the three spatial dimensions. Held at certain angles, one of these has a Y-shaped silhouette (fig. 6.6) and the other a V-shaped silhouette (fig. 6.7). Twelve of our informants undertook this part of the study.

The Y-shaped block can be considered to be three cubes forming an L shape with an additional cube on top of the vertex. To draw the Y-shaped block, one of the volunteers (Lys, early, totally blind) drew three squares. She said she could not think of a way to show the fourth block, the one that is in the third spatial dimension. Two drew separate units, using the separation on the

Fig. 6.5. Drawing of an L-shaped block in a foldout style.
By Pau (early, totally blind).

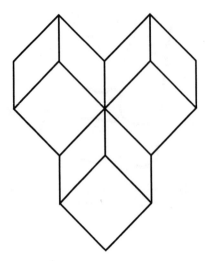

Fig. 6.6. Block object with limbs projecting in three dimensions.
The object has a **Y**-shaped silhouette.

page to indicate that the referents were separate in depth (Dee, early, totally blind; Pau, early, totally blind). Three used a build-up technique. Eight used some variant of the foldout technique, in which the sides around a central square were shown. Interestingly, two used slanted or oblique lines to show depth. Pau (early, totally blind) said that he "added a slanted line to indicate

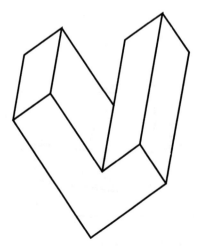

Fig. 6.7. Block object with **V**-shaped silhouette.

they're on a slant to each other—one's pointing one way and one's pointing the other." Cal (early, totally blind) used an oblique line, saying, "We get into three dimensions. In 3-D graphs they put in another axis at 45° to represent the third dimension. Maybe I could do the same." Pat (early, totally blind), who used a foldout technique, was also able to employ a vantage point. She drew a form standing for a limb of the Y and indicated this showed "the top one." She said, "It's drawn as if I were looking at it from *this* angle." The direction indicated was above the object. She added a small circle positioned at a 45° oblique to the form depicting "the top one" to indicate her vantage point (fig. 6.8). (Willats says that the use of an oblique is the sighted child's advance in drawing development from the foldout system. It may indeed be an advance, though, alas, our drawing study with Andrea Nicholls found no one path of development toward the use of a vantage point.)

Similar results were obtained in the task where the volunteers drew the V shape of an object with two limbs, one bar (or parallelepiped) lying beside an upright bar attached to its side. The majority used a foldout technique (fig. 6.9, by Ray, late, totally blind). Obliques and comments on the vantage point appeared infrequently. In one instance, Jim (early, light perception) said of one object, "Looking at it from here, I think this [limb] would be longer than this [other limb]."

To introduce the vantage point explicitly, we asked our informants to draw the objects at a certain orientation with some parts near and some far. Seven volunteered for this study: Cal, Dee, Nat, and Pau (early, totally blind), Ray and Roy (late, totally blind), and Nip (early, light perception).

Many of the drawings used foldout and build-up techniques, and several used conventions such as arrows or printed words such as UP. Four of the volunteers, though, introduced devices using change of width, a kind of convergence, to show depth. Roy drew the nearer limb of an L-shaped block as wide and the farther limb as narrow. Nat drew lines that got thinner to show increasing distance. He said, "The line gets thinner as it gets farther." Ray

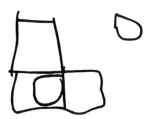

Fig. 6.8. Drawing by Pat (early, totally blind) of the object shown in figure 6.6.

Fig. 6.9. Drawing by Ray (late, totally blind) of the object shown in figure 6.6.

drew the shape of part of the blocks progressively narrowing to show that it recedes into the distance. Cal was interviewed on two occasions. In both he used lines that were thick at one end and thin at the other to show change in distance. His use changed in a notable way, however. In the first interview he used thick for far and thin for near, and in the second he changed his mind and gave reasons. He said on the second occasion that he had drawn the near parts with "heavier" lines and the far lines as lighter or faded because the heavier lines gave "more of a presence" and thereby suggested proximity. There is an important hint here of perceptual effects in touch akin to perspective effects in vision.

Interestingly, none of the informants in this study used oblique lines to show orientation with respect to a vantage point. It may be that the progressive change of width is enough to show the referent. If so, obliques are unnecessary. In the development of drawing in the sighted, the use of convergent shapes to show parallels receding may be more advanced than the use of parallel obliques, though I confess I do not know of a single study that gives this idea a thorough test.

Perspective

It is evident from studies on drawing that the blind commonly draw objects where a shape of a part of the object is depicted by a line form with a similar shape. Blind people also have a clear sense of top, bottom, and sides. They realize, as Ray put it, that "you could make a point of view by drawing only certain parts of the object." Knowledge of the vantage point for a picture is shown by comments that a picture is drawn from the side, front, or top. In trying to show the depth inherent in a solid object, the blind use foldout and other techniques including occasional obliques. Asked to make the orientation of an object evident, so as to show which parts are near and which far, blind subjects make use of convergence. On occasion, the lines themselves are drawn thick and thin. On a very rare occasion, the shape of the outlined region is transformed. The result is a shape that has two functions: to show the shape of a part of the object and to show the orientation of the parts. In a word, it shows the *direction* of parts of the object from a vantage point.

The ideas about the relation between the observer and the object are at times quite advanced in these comments from the blind. But one key idea seems to be missing: the role of the picture surface. A set of directions is a far cry from the set of actual shapes of the faces of the object. In a directional system, a given shape can produce a variable set of directions. The directions of two corners of a table may be wide apart while the directions of the other two corners, farther away, may be close together. Any attempt to depict this fact is quite unlike thinking of the shape on the picture surface as a kind of imprint made by a face of the object. The set of directions of a face of an object has to be carefully related to the plane or orientation of the picture surface, so the move from an imprint system to a directional system requires two new ideas. The first is the shift from shapes of faces to directions of faces. The second is the shift from an imprint system, where the picture surface can be wholly in contact with the object's face, to the directional system, where the picture surface cannot wholly contact the face. Since many theories of pictures and vantage points have foundered when debating matters that arise from the location of the picture surface, I should explain the relation more precisely.

When we consider an imprint system, the orientation of the picture surface to the object is set, fixed, and obvious. On my younger son's door, for example, there is a picture he made in elementary school of a fish on a cloth. To make it, a fish was covered with paint. It was then left on top of a cloth sheet and pushed firmly. The result is an imprint picture of a fish. The picture plane is the side of the fish.

In my older son's room there is a pencil drawing he made when he was in junior high school of a room full of desks. Each of the shapes standing for a rectangular desk top is a trapezoid. The picture plane for the drawing of the desks is not in contact with the surface of the desks. We might imagine it to have been a window at the front of the classroom.

When blind volunteers drew square and rectangular faces of cubes as lines forming squares and rectangles, they were clear about the shapes on the paper standing for similar shapes on the object, and they were often clear about the vantage points suitable for viewing these shapes. But even though they occasionally introduced obliques and narrowing lines or shapes, they never explained how both a vantage point and the plane of the picture have to be controlled simultaneously for the system to be complete. A vantage point and a picture plane that produces trapezoids from rectangles was never mentioned. Comments on the picture plane's effect on projected shape were never made spontaneously by any of our volunteers in a drawing task.

Although the orientation of a picture plane was never mentioned, the comments by the blind volunteers on the drawings do suggest that a vantage point is familiar to the blind. If so, there should be ways of showing skill in dealing with changes in direction to fit with changes of vantage point. Understanding of the vantage point can be tested when no picture plane or drawing is entailed. To examine these skills, Jay Campbell (in Arizona and Toronto) and Diane Girard (in Haiti) and I gave some tasks to blind children and adults requiring pointing as directions change.

POINTING TASKS

We asked volunteers to point to objects from different locations. This task involves a sense of direction, which is the basis of perspective. Understanding the direction of objects guides locomotion for the blind as well as the sighted exploring near and distant spaces (Humphrey, Dodwell, Muir, and Humphrey, 1988). It is a principle of perspective that an object subtends a smaller angle when it is far away than it does when it is near. The decrease in angle with distance is familiar to sighted people, but there is an unfortunate tendency to think of the decrease as purely visual. It is, in fact, not restricted to vision. If two people are having a conversation, one on either side of the observer, one voice comes to the observer from the left and one from the right. If the two people walk away from the observer, the directions of the two voices gradually approach one another. If someone is standing midway between two rose bushes, to smell one he turns 90° to the left; to smell the other he turns back 180° to the right. But let the person step back just two paces. Now to smell the roses, he leans forward and only turns a little to the left or right.

Further, imagine someone standing in the middle of a wide avenue pointing to two trees, one on either side. The pointing arms are 180° apart, one arm a straight extension of the other, with a straight line from one fingertip through both arms to the other fingertip. Let there be another two trees 10 meters down the road. To point to them, the pointing arms must converge to form a V. They are no longer 180° apart. To point to two more trees 10 meters farther down the road, the V between the arms would become narrower. And for two more trees another 10 meters down the road, the V between the arms would become narrower still. For a distant pair of trees, the arms should be practically parallel. The pair of trees in the distance subtends a very small angle, whereas the trees on either side of the observer subtend 180°. It is in the nature of direction and perspective that the principle of convergence is not restricted to vision. Rather, it is a general principle that governs hearing, smell, and vision—any perceptual system that encounters objects and locations. Since pain has a location, even pain reveals its directions and perspective to the observer. A child's pain can be in her hand, which she might hold in front of her body at waist height. The child can change the direction of the pain vis-à-vis her head by bringing the injured hand to her mouth. It is now in front of the head rather than below it, above the waist rather than at waist height.

As we walk past a post we are aware that the post is ahead of us, then to the side, then gradually falls more and more directly behind us (Loomis and DaSilva, 1989). Surely blind people become aware of these changing directions by means of several sensory avenues. If so, they should appreciate that as things go into the distance, they subtend smaller angles. Landau and Gleitman (1985) found an ability to deal with change of direction in a blind two-year-old. Likewise, Diane Girard and I asked children in Haiti to point to the corners of a wall from close up and far away. We asked them to point with outstretched arms and measured the distance between their fingertips. If the children have a sense of perspective, they should point with a smaller distance between their fingertips when they are farther away from the wall.

We thought that it might be difficult to measure the angle formed by the arms. It is hard to be sure where the vertex for the angle is. Is it exactly midway between the shoulders? Is one shoulder favored as the base? Or is the vertex in an imaginary locus on an extension of the arms, behind the body? For our purposes, it is not necessary to find the answer. Whether the vertex is behind the shoulders or nearer one shoulder than the other, in our task the distance between the fingertips should shorten if the person understands how direction works.

Eight blind Haitian children ranging in age from nine to 18 years, mean age 13.1 years, participated in the study (table 6.2). They were led by the arm alongside a wall from the middle of the wall to one corner, then to the other corner, then back to the center of the wall while lightly brushing it with their

TABLE 6.2

Haitian children pointing at the corners of a wall from near (1 m away) and far (3.5 m away): Distance between fingertips is measured in centimeters.

	Jan	Mim	Jea	Yur	Ron	Jag	Ros	Jac
Age	9	10	11	11	14	16	16	18
Onset of Blindness								
Before Age	5	6	11	2	13	1½	16	15
1 m Away	119	112	112	147	130	165	145	117
3.5 m Away	84	102	102	97	84	107	109	91
Decrease with Distance	Yes	Yes	Yes	Yes	Yes	Yes	Yes	Yes

Note: All the children are totally blind except Jan, who has light perception. Onset of blindness is assessed conservatively, from the date of admission to their residential school or the date of an eye operation. Other medical records are scanty or absent.

fingertips. The wall was about 4.5 m long. The children were asked to step backward from the center of the wall until they were standing about 1 m from the wall. From there, the children pointed to the corners, left arm outstretched to the left corner and right arm outstretched to the right corner. The distance between the left and right fingertips was measured. Then the children were walked backward to a point 3.5 m from the wall, and they pointed again to the corners with both arms outstretched.

The results were that all the children decreased the distance between their fingertips when pointing from the farther distance ($p < 0.01$ on a sign test). There were no exceptions. Variability was quite striking, ranging from a decrease of 10 cm from 112 cm (9 percent) to a decrease of 58 cm from 165 cm (35 percent).

The age of onset of the children's blindness, an important factor in evaluating the test results, is hard to assess given the lack of standard medical records in Haiti and the children's own hazy recollections. We have usually used the school's date of admission as a conservative estimate of the onset of blindness. Occasionally we have had available a medical record of an eye operation. Malnutrition is the most common medical explanation for the children's blindness. Deprivation often had had several other ill-effects including general difficulties with attention and comprehension. Furthermore, the education of the children had not been steady or comprehensive by any means.

None of our volunteers had gone beyond the fifth grade, and several were still below grade 2. Despite the intellectual deficits of the children, their performance was consistent. The implication is that the vantage point test appears to be understood by people who are poorly educated and "unlikely to be test-wise"—that is, unsophisticated in following complex instructions and appreciating rather artificial testing procedures and their intentions.

To confirm this finding, however, it is necessary to try the test with children for whom we have more precise knowledge of age of onset of blindness. The Tucson children we tested in drawing studies, the records indicate, are congenitally blind. For our pointing studies, we tested nine of them—eight who had participated in our pictorial tests and one other, a girl age 12 who has extremely low vision (table 6.3).

All of the Tucson subjects decreased the distance between their fingertips when pointing from afar ($p < 0.01$ on a sign test). Even if the most extreme convergence is taken from the set of results (it was from the child with low vision and she may have too much vision to be counted as blind for this task), the results remain significant. The results from Haiti and Tucson were always collected using a test procedure where the "near" measure was taken first and the "far" measure second. The reason was to preserve as "natural" a test procedure as possible. To control for the order in which the measures were taken, we modified the procedure in Phoenix, with four blind volunteers, Di (age eight, early, totally blind), Ram (age 10, early, totally blind), Gale (age 15, early, light perception), and Jel(age 22, totally blind, but low vision from birth to age 7–8). I asked the Phoenix subjects to point from afar first. In this study we used two vertical rods (supported by bases on the floor) joined by a string instead of two corners of a room with a common wall. The string was 4.5 m long and 73 cm high at midpoint. The subjects were asked to point to the rods, left arm to the leftmost rod and right arm to the rightmost rod. All four

TABLE 6.3

Tucson children, congenitally blind, pointing at the corners of a wall from near (1 m away) and far (3.5 m away).

	Distance between fingertips (cm)								
1 m Away	140	145	145	137	91*	102	142	102	97
3.5 m Away	112	86	140	94	20	48	56	56	46
Decrease with Distance	Yes	Yes	Yes	Yes	Yes	Yes	Yes	Yes	Yes

*This subject may have too much vision to be counted as blind.

volunteers diverged when pointing from the nearer distance. The results suggest that convergence arises on the more distant measure, rather than on any measure near or far that happens to be taken second.

The success on this vantage point task encourages some further questions. Is convergence appreciated by the blind on smaller scales than the 1–4 m scales used in our tasks? Meters are a scale on which most of domestic life is lived. But some of the objects we use everyday, such as cups, are a mere few centimeters in size, graspable and manipulable by one hand. Is there an intuitive sense of perspective when the scale is so reduced that one can feel the whole object at once and the distinction between the front and the back is unclear? Barber and Lederman (1988) call this scale "manipulatory space."

Further, we can ask about the vertical scale. People in our pointing tasks are using the horizontal—the location of objects to left and right. Is vertical perspective (up and down) also well defined? Sighted people know that as they walk away from a building, the top is at first directly above them, but later it is at 45°, and as they walk still farther away, the roof eventually may be only a few degrees above the horizontal. Do blind people appreciate the principle? To find out, Jay Campbell and I tested eight congenitally blind adults in Toronto on small-scale tasks and vertical tasks as well as larger scales and horizontal arrays.

The Domestic Horizontal test involved pointing to poles linked by string and set 2.5 m apart. The volunteers pointed from 60 cm back from the center of the string (which was removed while pointing was being tested) and from 2.5 m back. A plumb line was dropped to the floor from the extended fingertip and the location of the plumb line on the floor was noted, allowing the left and right positions of the subject's pointing finger to be recorded.

The Domestic Vertical test called for pointing to the top and bottom of a 188 cm stand from the same near and far distances as in the horizontal conditions. Subjects felt the stand, stood back, and then pointed to where the top and bottom of the stand had been. (The stand was removed while pointing occurred, otherwise some subjects when nearby might have brushed against it.)

The Manipulative Horizontal and Vertical tests involved pointing by moving a wrist rather than the whole arm from the shoulder. The subject put a wrist on a block of wood and swiveled the hand left and right, or up and down, pointing with the index finger. The subjects were seated at a table, on which the block rested. The two stands for the horizontal condition were only 13 cm tall and were connected by a 30 cm string. The vertical condition used a 30 cm pole. The distance from the pole or the center of the string to the edge of the block was 13 cm or 30 cm.

The four tasks—Domestic Horizontal and Vertical, Manipulative Horizontal and Vertical—were undertaken in random order. There is considerable variability in the size of the movements the subjects made in responding, especially on the Domestic scale. Accordingly, I shall report the direction of change—convergence or divergence.

On the Domestic Horizontal scale, all the subjects converged with distance. The other three conditions usually resulted in convergence, but there were occasional ties or divergent results. On the Domestic Vertical scale, six subjects converged, one diverged and one did not change. On the Manipulative Horizontal scale, six subjects converged with distance, two diverged. On the Manipulative Vertical scale, five converged with distance, two diverged, one did not change. The subjects clearly grasped the principle involved, though their performance was uneven. Overall, the change is in the direction of convergence on all four conditions for four subjects and shows more convergence than divergence for three subjects. With the exception of one subject, for whom the number of converging results equaled the number of diverging results, seven out of eight subjects offered a majority of converging results ($p < 0.05$ on a sign test).

The variability between conditions is considerable, including seven convergence changes greater than 40 percent, though convergence with distance is evident overall. The mean convergence is 24 percent. The mean divergence is only 11 percent. The Manipulative Vertical conditions appear to be the least well defined, though the differences between conditions are dwarfed by the individual variability. In sum, on two functionally different haptic spaces—the space of manipulation and the space of domestic movement (the space for walking in a room)—convergence is evident with distance.

Following the Domestic and Manipulative tests, we asked the subjects about pointing to tops of tall buildings from near and far, like from across the street and from miles away. Every person we interviewed indicated that to point to the edge of a roof it is necessary to point straight up when standing at the front door of a building, at an acute angle when on the other side of the street, and at lesser and lesser angles when farther away.

In pointing to the corners of an extended object, some blind people try to use the full extent of the arms to show the actual *length* of the desk, while swiveling only the fingers and hand to show the *directions* of the corners. Two systems are competing here. One shows unchanging length, the other changing direction. The direction of one corner is indicated by swiveling the left hand using the left wrist as the vertex, whereas the other corner is indicated by the right hand using a different vertex, the right wrist.

Thus, pointing tasks run across the same difficulty that arises on occasion in drawing, namely, the mixing of direction with some other property of spatial relations. When we point, length mixes with direction if we try to show extent and angle at the same time. In drawing, we might try to draw the shape of the object at the same time as we show the direction of its edges. This creates no problem if the vantage point is directly above or to the side of, say, a rectangular table. A drawing of such a table from above represents it as a rectangle. But a three-quarter view—that is, from a vantage point intermediate between the top and the side—requires us to draw a trapezoid, not a rectangle. At once a clash between criteria of direction and similar shape arises.

The pointing studies indicate that blind people, young and old, educated and uneducated, have a strong sense of the convergence principle crucial to perspective. Hence it is not because they lack an appreciation of convergence that they rarely employ three-quarter views in their drawings. More likely, it is because a novice does not consider direction-based criteria when drawing. A specific task and explicit instructions can draw attention to the criteria; sighted children, for example, will then use depicted occlusion (Cox and Martin, 1988) and height in the picture plane (Ingram and Butterworth, 1989). Often, direction criteria can produce a conflict with similar-shape criteria. When they do, the directional system is rejected by many people. When directional criteria are used to note what will be to the front and what will be behind, to organize the set of features to be shown and the set of features to be omitted, there is no clash with similar-shape criteria. It is only when the vantage point is intermediate between the front and the side that the clash with similar-shape criteria arises.

JUDGMENT TASKS

Evidently, blind people as young as five or six years old understand that an object subtends a smaller angle as it recedes from a vantage point. This knowledge, however, is not revealed in many drawings of objects. There is no evidence of vantage point geometry in the foldout drawings common in sketches from many blind adults as well as sighted children. But occasionally vantage points are mentioned spontaneously. To what extent do blind people realize that vantage point geometry is an advance on foldout geometry? To study this question, we had blind volunteers compare different kinds of drawings of objects.

Paul Gabias and I designed tasks that compared foldout geometry to perspective (vantage point) geometry. The first task involved comparing two different drawings of a table, one in perspective. The second task required only one drawing of a table, with two different rationales or descriptions, one using the notion of a vantage point. The tasks were undertaken by 15 blind volunteers, adults recruited from colleges in New York City.

Our drawings were raised-line drawings on 20 × 30 cm plastic sheets. We told the volunteers that we had prepared these drawings ourselves on the basis of sketches made by blind people. We said that our drawings were tidied-up versions of the sketches, to remove any differences in line quality or skill in execution that might give away the age of the sketcher. One pair of drawings showed tables, one table in foldout style and one in vantage point style (fig. 6.10). The foldout drawing shows the parts of the table as though they were splayed out on a flat surface. Two of the legs go up the page from the central square, two go down. The vantage point table is shown as though from the side—a central, slim rectangle and two legs coming down. The blind volunteers were given the pictures accompanied by instructions explaining which lines stood for the top of the table and which stood for the legs. They were told that one drawing showed the table and all four legs, and the other showed the table from the side, with only the front legs drawn.

If a judgement about the drawings were based on complexity, measured in terms of number of features shown, then the foldout table would be deemed better, as it shows all four legs. But the drawing from the side considers not only the features of the object but also the relation between the observer and the object, thereby introducing a principle over and above the arrangement of features in the object. The drawing from the side is *observer-centered* whereas the foldout drawing is *object-centered*.

Another drawing showed a table depicted as a rectangle with four lines for

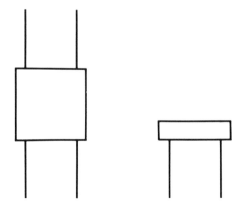

Fig. 6.10. Drawings showing tables, one done in foldout style and one using a vantage point.

the legs radiating from the corners (fig. 6.11). This "star" table was accompanied by two descriptions, one in foldout style and the other in vantage point. The volunteers were told that two people had drawn the same design. One had explained that in drawing the star table he had shown the shape of the tabletop, the juncture of all four legs at the corners, and the symmetry of the table. The other person had made exactly the same drawing while explaining that the only place from which all four legs and the top of the table were in front of the observer is underneath the table, so he had shown the table from underneath. If a judgment about the systems is to be based on showing not only the features of the table but also its relation to the observer's vantage point, then the second rationale would be deemed superior. The volunteers were told the two rationales and then asked which drawing came from an older person.

Of the 15 blind volunteers for these tests, four were totally blind from birth, two had some light sensitivity for a time and are now totally blind, two once had some ability to detect gross objects and are now totally blind, five have had light sensitivity since birth, one has light sensitivity now but until the age of 12 could distinguish shadows from objects, and one still can detect gross objects in bright light.

The results for the first pair of tables were as follows: 11 out of 15 subjects judged the vantage point table as more likely to have been drawn by an older person. The results for the star table were similar: 11 out of 15 subjects judged the vantage point description as more likely to have come from an older person. Only one person described both the vantage point conditions as likely to have been drawn by a younger person. (The results are significantly differ-

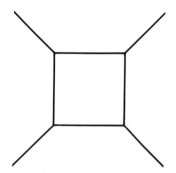

Fig. 6.11. Star-like drawing of a table, which could be
a foldout or a vantage-point drawing.

ent from chance at the 0.01 level, $\chi^2 = 11.2$, 1 d.f. Eight blind subjects judged both vantage point drawings as "older," and only one judged both as "younger," $p < 0.05$, binomial test.)

The one person who judged both vantage point versions of the table as younger was totally blind from birth. He felt that the vantage point description of the star table indicated that the "artist" failed to understand that the same shape could be produced from above. And he considered that the foldout table with two legs up and two legs down was superior because no matter what the orientation of the page, the table is still drawn appropriately.

The results are enlightening. They indicate that these blind subjects deem a perspective drawing to be more sophisticated than a nonperspective drawing, even when the nonperspective drawing shows more of the parts of the object. But several intermediary steps are possible between foldout and perspective drawings. Accordingly, a more strenuous test of the ability of blind people to assess vantage point effects can be devised. A series of drawings of an object—say a cube—can run the gamut from foldout to perspective convergence. In our next study, volunteers were asked to compare such drawings of a cube with drawings of another object, a table, and then match drawings made according to similar systems.

The procedure in the test hinged once again on the star table, with two different descriptions or explanations. The star table was to be compared with four different drawings of a box or cube (fig. 6.12). Again, our volunteers were told that our figures were tidied-up versions of sketches by blind people.

One drawing of the cubic box presented five squares arranged in a cross—a central square with four squares attached one per side. The subjects were told that the person who drew this version of the box said he had shown the

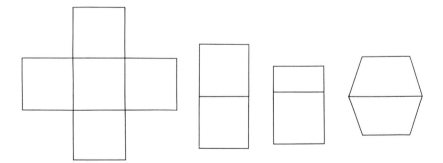

Fig. 6.12. Drawings of a box, in four different projections.

front face in the middle, and that the top and bottom squares show the top and bottom sides of the box. The squares on either side of the middle square were said to show the faces of the box to the left and right of the front face.

An alternative drawing of the box showed two squares attached at the top side. The person who drew the box this way, we informed our volunteers, said he had shown the front face and top of the box. He said you should not show any other faces because they are facing away from the observer and are hidden behind the parts he had shown.

The third version of the box was one square with a rectangle half the size of the square attached along the top side of the square. The person who drew this version, it was reported, said that the front face should be shown as a square and the top face as narrower—as a rectangle—because it does not face directly toward the observer.

The last version of the box was two symmetrical trapezoids joined along their longest side. We reported that the person who drew the box in this way said that the nearest corner of the box has to be shown longer than the others, and that the front face and top have to be shown on an angle if both are drawn. Besides the four versions of the cubic box, the volunteers were also given the star table and the two different descriptions.

After the descriptions of all the drawings were given, the subjects had to repeat them back in their essentials. If someone displayed a misunderstanding of a rationale, the description was given again until it could be repeated by the volunteer.

The volunteers were 24 congenitally blind adults, four recruited from colleges in New York City and 20 recruited at a convention for the blind in Philadelphia. Fourteen of the subjects were totally blind, nine had light perception, and one could detect gross objects. Five were totally blind from birth and one from six months of age; five others had gone blind by age three years. Three had had light perception for a period, but by age 13 two were totally blind and the remaining person could see no light by age 2. Eight of the volunteers said that they had never been exposed to haptic pictures, and 16 admitted some very limited exposure to them. Eight of these 16 said that they found the particular pictures they had come across in the past helpful or clear; eight indicated that the pictures they had encountered were unhelpful.

The star table versions and the cubic box drawings were compared. Volunteers were asked to consider one of the two descriptions of the star table—say, the vantage point description. Then they were asked to pick the most compatible version of the cube. That is, volunteers had to predict which version of the cube was most likely drawn by the person who drew the table using the

vantage point system. Then the other three versions of the cube had to be
ranked in order of likelihood. Once all the selections had been made for one
description of the star table, it was time to turn to the other description, and
the process was repeated. A rank of 1 was given to the most likely version and
4 to the least likely version. The average rank for a drawing, combining the
judgments of all 24 subjects, is given in table 6.4.

When the vantage point table was the basis for judgment, the most likely
version of the cubic box was said to be the two trapezoids (mean rank 1.75).
The next most likely was deemed the square and rectangle (2.42), then the two
squares (2.83). The least likely version was said to be the foldout drawing of
five squares(3.0).

In complete contrast, when the foldout (no-vantage-point) table was the
basis for judgment, the most probable drawing of the cubic box was deemed
to be the foldout five squares (mean rank 1.63). The next most likely was
judged the two squares (2.29), third was the square and rectangle (2.79), and
the least probable drawing was said to be the two trapezoids (3.29).

There was considerable agreement among the volunteers, and one set of
judgments is exactly the reverse of the others. The blind volunteers seemed to
have a coherent assessment of the role of vantage points in the drawings. As
aspects of vantage point geometry were introduced, the fit to the table drawings was made in an orderly and appropriate fashion. In the first drawing, all
the sides were present and folded out; in the next, some sides were omitted in
keeping with a vantage point; in the third drawing, not only were sides
omitted but the picture used compression of shape relevant to facing away
rather than toward the observer; and in the final drawing, angles were used
that vary from the 90° in the actual object, with a side shown elongated

TABLE 6.4

Mean ranks (1–4) assigned to drawings of a cube when the basis for judgment is
a comparison to a vantage point rationale for a drawing and when the rationale
omits a vantage point.

| | Drawing of Cube | | | |
Rationale	Foldout	Two Squares	Square and Rectangle	Two Trapezoids
Vantage point	3.0	2.83	2.42	1.75
No vantage point	1.63	2.29	2.79	3.29

because it was near the observer. Overall, the order from all sides being shown to a drawing with angles changed from 90° was properly assessed by the blind.

The consistency of the judgments is well shown in detail in table 6.5, which notes the number of subjects putting a table in a particular rank. The most favored rank usually dwarfs the other ranks. The eight favored ranks have a mean of 14.4. The remaining ranks have a mean of 3.4. The steps from first rank to second are often large: 17 to 3, 12 to 4, 16 to 3, 11 to 6, 15 to 4, 13 to 9, 15 to 4, and 16 to 5. The concordance in the judgments is statistically significant (W, no vantage point = 0.304, $p < 0.001$, W, vantage point = 0.186, $p < 0.01$).

Twelve of the 24 subjects ranked the foldout cube drawing first, the two-squares version second, the square-and-rectangle version third, and the two-trapezoid version last when fitting the cube drawings to the no-vantage-point version of the star table. The probability of any one order of ranking being assigned to the set of four cubes is one in 24, so to have half of the volunteers concur is unlikely to be due to chance ($p < 0.001$). Furthermore, the order

TABLE 6.5

Frequency of judgments of versions of the cubic box, when the basis for judgments is a vantage point rationale for the star table and when the basis is a no-vantage-point rationale.

	Rank			
	1	2	3	4
Foldout Cube				
No Vantage Point	17	2	2	3
Vantage Point	4	4	4	12
Two Squares				
No Vantage Point	2	16	3	3
Vantage Point	3	4	11	6
Square and Rectangle				
No Vantage Point	2	4	15	3
Vantage Point	1	13	9	1
Two Trapezoids				
No Vantage Point	3	2	4	15
Vantage Point	16	3	0	5

that these volunteers chose is exactly the one we would expect if the judgments were based on an understanding of perspective.

Nine of the 24 subjects produced the sequence that ranks the two trapezoids first, the square and rectangle second, the two squares third, and five squares last when the judgments were based on the vantage point description of the table. Again, this number of subjects concurring on an order is unlikely to occur by chance ($p < 0.01$) when the possibility of a given ordering is one in 24. And again the order on which they concurred suggests that judgments were based on the appreciation of some perspective system.

The results imply that the blind generally concur on some impressions of perspective in drawings. They concur on what is developmentally more sophisticated, and they concur in ranking drawing systems that approximate convergent perspective.

Morton Heller and I continued this investigation of blind people's understanding of perspective by studying the ability to deal with several pictorial vantage points around a fixed scene. The volunteers were given a scene with three objects in it. They made drawings from their own vantage point and from others. In addition, they were offered drawings and had to identify the vantage point suggested by the drawing.

The objects in the scene were a wooden cube (9 cm³), a wooden cone (9 cm diameter at the base by 8 cm high) and a wooden ball (9 cm diameter). Figure 6.13 shows a plan view of the objects mounted on a rectangular base 30 cm by 42 cm and an elevation. The cube was to the observer's left; in depth it was at the middle of a narrow side of the rectangle. The cone was centered at the far side of the rectangle, midway along a long side of the rectangle. The ball was to the observer's right, at a near corner of the rectangle. The objects were inside the rectangular perimeter, close to the edges but not overlapping them. The volunteers, blind or sighted, first drew the individual objects from above and the side, then identified drawings that we had made of each object from above and the side and presented in a random order. The drawings of the objects from the side contained a line standing for the edge of the table from the side. Feedback was given to ensure that the volunteers knew what each drawing we had made represented.

Next the observers drew the objects arranged on the rectangular base. Initially they were asked to draw the scene life-size, from above, then they were asked to draw it on a reduced scale. Next the observers drew the array from their own vantage point, the front side. Then it was drawn from a vantage point 90° to the side, as though for someone sitting near a short side of the rectangle. Next it was drawn for someone sitting on the far side of the rect-

Fig. 6.13. Pictures of an array of three objects (a cube, a cone, and a sphere) made from various vantage points.

angle 180° away, and finally for someone at 270°, the remaining short side of the rectangle. After the drawing part of the study, the volunteers attempted to identify pictures suggesting various vantage points (fig. 6.13). Five pictures were presented, one for each of the vantage points used in the drawing part of the study.

The participants were 18 blind adults recruited from workshops for the blind in North Carolina. In addition, there were nine sighted adult volunteers recruited from a college campus in Winston-Salem and 11 sighted adult volunteers from Toronto. The blind adults included nine early blind and nine late blind. Of the early blind subjects, seven were congenitally blind and two had lost sight before age three months. None of the early or late blind individuals had more than minimal light perception. None could see form or hand movements. The characteristics of the blind volunteers are shown in table 6.6.

On the drawing task, the volunteers were assigned a score from 0 to 5. In each side-view drawing, the objects had to be arranged in the correct order to be scored as correct. One point was given for drawing both of the top views correctly—that is, for putting the cube in the left center, the cone in the rear center, and the ball in the right foreground. The mean number of correct drawings out of five was 3.4 (s.d. = 1.5) for the early blind, 4.2 (s.d. = 1.1) for

TABLE 6.6

Blind volunteers from North Carolina in the Heller and Kennedy study on perspective taking.

Early blind*		Late blind		
Age (Years)	Light Perception	Age (Years)	Light Perception	Age at Onset of Blindness (Years)
26	Yes	32	Yes	15
34	Yes	38	Yes	21
35	Yes	41	Yes	18
36	Yes	49	Yes	11
52	Yes	24	No	13
33	No	35	No	30
50	No	42	No	8
51	No	49	No	31
52	No	53	No	32

*Onset of blindness for early blind volunteers was before age 3 months.

the late blind, and 3.9 (s.d. = 1.4) for the sighted adults who undertook the task blindfolded (F < 1, not significantly different from chance).

On the identification task, the participants could score up to 10, since there were five drawings to recognize and each was administered twice. The number of correct identifications was 6.7 (s.d. 2.4) for the early blind, 8.3 (s.d. 1.8) for the late blind and 7.4 (s.d. 2.7) for the sighted. The differences between the groups are not significantly different from chance [F (2,24) = 1.2, $p < 0.05$].

In Toronto, we tested 11 sighted adults (mean age 45 years), who undertook the tasks visually. They were recruited from among visitors to the Ontario Science Centre. The objects were shown to the participants visually, and they responded by making paper-and-pencil drawings. They also looked at black-line versions of the raised-line drawings in the identification tasks. To keep the visual conditions of the tasks somewhat comparable in procedure to the tactual ones, we arranged screens so the participants could not look at the array while drawing or making the identification. A vertical screen hid the objects while volunteers responded. But if during the trial observers wanted to check back with the array of objects, the drawing they were making or trying to identify was covered by a horizontal screen before the array was unscreened. When participants wished, the array was screened again and then the drawing they were considering was uncovered. In this way, the visual exposure was successive, rather like the tactual condition in which the blind observers could first explore the array tactually and later examine the raised-line drawing, then return to the array if they wished and turn back to the drawing.

The mean score of the sighted adults on the drawing task was 3.4, identical to the score of the early blind. Their mean score on the identification task was 7.5, midway between the scores of the early blind and late blind, and not significantly different from either.

We have tried these vantage point tasks on 15 children ages 6–14 years. Five ages 13–14 were recruited at the Ontario Science Centre and 10 ages 6–12 from a summer camp. The mean number of correct drawings was 2.6 (and the mean number from both of the groups was also 2.6). The early and late blind adult subjects scored higher, at 3.4 for the early blind and 4.2 for the late blind.

The lesson of the vantage point study is that blind people have the same ability as sighted people to envisage the pictorial role of a vantage point on a simple scene. The task, which Heller and I adapted from a task called the three-mountains test by Jean Piaget, reveals that blind people are no more spatially egocentric than sighted people in their drawings of the three objects.

CODING AND MODELS

Recent investigations have tried to assess the basis on which blind people represent their knowledge of space internally and the way they manipulate their knowledge. One possibility is that the direction and distance of spatial matters are encoded verbally. There is no dispute that blind and sighted people can recall that, say, after passing the post office you turn right to get home. Some blind people do try to remember sets of directions in a predominantly verbal manner, recalling a route as "first left, second right, then first right again and then go to the fourth house." This can be particularly helpful in a bewildering building or a housing development where the roads have bends at odd places. A careful study of the anatomy of an object we want to draw can involve studious description and explicit labeling of the parts and their order, as in "the leg bone's connected to the hip bone." Another mode of representation involves "spatial" or "map-like" or "iconic" understanding. In this, the angles between directions and the proportions of distances are prominent. Klatzky et al. (1990) find early and late blind observers to be equivalent to the sighted on map-like tasks involving walking a triangular route (similar results come from Haber et al., 1988).

These two kinds of representation are not easy to distinguish, for several reasons, and various theories take radically different positions about their status in vision, touch, and cognition. Touch is sometimes thought to lead readily to verbal coding and only poorly to map-like apprehension of space. Dodds, Howarth, and Carter (1982) found that four 11-year-old congenitally blind children learned to navigate an S route successfully after only one trial, but in several tests the children did not show "spatial understanding" of a map-like kind. The tests used to indicate map-like apprehension were pointing tasks and map drawing. The children seemed to learn a pattern of self-referential changes in direction, such as left, then left again, then right, and so on. Their drawings of the route were idiosyncratic (according to the authors) in three cases and map-like in only one case. I notice that the "maps" may actually be lists of indicators of left and right turns in the three cases (KC, CC, and JE) shown by the authors. Each seems to contain seven or eight forms (or bends), and the forms are arranged in linear order. This way of portraying a route is used by sighted eight-year-olds (Goodnow, 1977, p. 49). Regrettably, the authors do not seem to have questioned the children on the meaning of the forms and bends.

Millar (1979) and others have pointed out that many blind children will try to remember the locations and directions of objects with respect to the self. I do not doubt it. There seems no reason to quarrel with the idea that the blind can use egocentric directions from a fixed location and lists of bodily turns to left or right in a route without regard to overall directions (north, east, south, west). Yet it is quite a leap from the idea that some people use egocentric direction as a mnemonic for spatial arrangements to the idea that "congenitally blind individuals cannot represent spatial layout" and are "locked into egocentric spatial coding" (Dodds et al., 1982, p.11). Over the telephone I often give people directions to my house that are just sequences of left and right turns, but I expect that my visitors could use a map if I sent one to them by fax. Presumably, congenitally blind people might be able to follow a map too (Berla, 1982) with a raised-line fax.

A more sophisticated argument about touch and space is made by Barber and Lederman (1988). They argue that simple quantitative comparisons reveal little about the qualitative differences between vision and touch as they create their own distinctive representations of spatial arrangements. They insist that attention needs to be paid to heuristics for processing and representing space in each modality. The stamp of the input heuristic will be found on the resulting representation, they think, and they contend that cognitive factors are hallmarks of tactile representations of space. Cognitive heuristics assist touch especially in the apprehension of space, supplementing its more direct perception: "The result of a heuristic rule is combined with the information derived from other sources to achieve a composite representation of space" (p. 100).

Barber and Lederman attempt to use a distinction made by Rieser, Guth, and Hill (1986) and Rieser, Lockman, and Pick (1980). The information acquired during action can allow knowledge of the layout around the observer to be continuously "updated" perceptually (Gibson, 1979). Or, we can use an item of information obtained "cognitively" to change what both Rieser and Lederman call a cognitive map, a "higher-level construction that unifies the sensory input obtained temporally" (Barber and Lederman, p. 100). Logically, it is possible for perceptual information given by a spatial layout to be encoded cognitively (for example, in words), and this in turn could change the cognitive map. Hence in this theory perceptual information could be used directly (perceptual updating) or indirectly (cognitive mapping). Evidently, the fact that the input is perceptual cannot dictate how it is used. The same ambiguity arises with cognitive (such as verbal) input. Our intuitions about east and west directions may have become turned around as we walk around in a subway, but a word from the wise can help put our impressions to rights. Note that in an ambiguous situation, even a slight hint can tilt the balance between one percept and another.

Is it possible to discern what "internal representation" is the basis for perceptual intuitions about space? There is a devilishly difficult logical problem facing any possible indicator of the basis. Space can be expressed in many different ways. It can be described verbally or shown by a map or by coordinates from a given point, or as geographic directions, a picture, or a flow chart, and so on. Further, any descriptive system has its subordinate systems. Maps can be flat or spherical. They can be created by Mercator projections (on cylinders), perspective projections, equal-area projections, or projections that allow the north (and south) poles to be shown by several points and the east and west extremities of the area to be represented twice each in a kind of wraparound. The center of a map's projection can be a particular spot (for purposes of tourism or navigation), or there may be no central spot (the map can be laid out as an endless belt). Once someone knows a physical medium of representation *he or she can imagine using it.* Most people use many means of representation, both physically and in imagination. It would be inappropriate to ask someone which system he or she always uses, for certain systems match certain purposes. People select the system to suit the needs of the moment. A friend of mine is likely to give directions to her house with a mixture of norths and souths, landmarks, turns to left and right, and useful hints about speed and time.

Not only can space be represented in different ways; each way can be translated into another. A square route can be translated into "ahead one mile, turn left and go a mile, turn left again and go a mile, turn left again and go a mile. You are now back where you started from." A square form can also be described in coordinates from two axes or drawn as a picture. It can be sequential or simultaneous. Understanding the form means knowing how to translate from one system to another, especially from perception to cognition to action. Johnson-Laird (1989) notes that we use general logical skills as well as ones sensitive to context.

In principle, there is no single test that can tell what representational system is being used by someone who knows how to translate from one system to another. As a result, investigators attempt in various ways to supplement tests such as pointing, which is often thought to favor perceptual understanding, and verbal description, which is often thought to favor more cognitive matters. They ask their subjects questions about strategy, or they time the response lags. Researchers who are interested in map-like understanding and in pointing tasks may attempt to distinguish perception-based maps from cognitive maps by showing that responses are swift to pointing tasks and slow to verbal ones. It is possible, however, that the splitting of knowledge into subtypes can be taken even further. Lederman, Klatzky, and Barber (1985) argue that perceptual and cognitive maps in vision are not quite like those in touch, and Barber and Lederman conjecture that maps of the near space of manipulation could be different from those of ambulatory-scale space. Alas, there is no reason in principle to stop the subcategorizing at this point.

Nothing is settled by the studies on the basis of mental representation because there is nothing that prevents a person from coding in one way and decoding to answer the test. The logical problems arise in principle in tests of mental imagery in the sighted as well as the blind. Often sighted subjects are asked to undertake a task that involves a continuous transformation of imagery. Close correlations between the time needed to solve a spatial problem in imagination and orderly transformations such as steady rotation are taken as evidence that imagery involves rotation as well as motion to and from an object. But where this evidence is particularly unconvincing is on the issue of the "basic" mode of representation (Millar, 1986). It is always possible to argue that the method of representation is being chosen by the individual being tested from a set of methods, much like choosing one or another projection for making a map. Furthermore, the orderly transformation being used has to be *understood* as it proceeds, unlike thinking in abstractions, where new combinations of symbols can be decoded later. Visual imagery rarely uses colors, for example, unless we expressly want it to, and when colors are used they often follow the laws we know, not the sensory laws per se. Similarly, chiaroscuro—the illumination laws—is rarely involved in imagery, and usually only when expressly willed. Imagery can be independent of the sensory laws of form, especially the subtleties of perspective that are not consciously known by the observer but are vitally present in vision proper. Thus the sensory bases of perspective, laws of form, color, and chiaroscuro are only partially reflected in imagery, which has more to do with general awareness of form than input-gathering machinery and the laws it incorporates. Hence blind people behave on spatial-imagery tasks much as sighted people do (Kerr, 1983; Finke, 1989).

The general principle that "touch, the major spatial modality for blind people, is different from vision in the way it extracts information from the environment, and in the emphasis it gives to different types of information" (Hollins, 1989, p. 62) does not lead clearly to the supposition that there are major cognitive differences in the ideas of space used by the sighted and the blind. Likewise, the fact that near space is explored by reaching and more distal space by walking does not lead straightforwardly to the idea that the two spaces have major differences in arrangement so far as perception and cognition are concerned. It is dangerous to conclude that each operation used to explore a resource is highly independent. Science, as well as general knowledge, is threatened by this kind of operationism. Common sense tells us that walking along a grassy path and a gravel road have pretty much the same outcome. Science, similarly, rests on the principle that two different operations can measure the same thing.

It is reasonable that the blind could use two different representational schemes and be unable to transfer knowledge instantly from one to the other. Sighted people asked to describe a block letter T as a series of left and right turns, starting at the bottom left vertex, cannot do so without considerable effort. I have encountered blind people who could recall spatial directions I was giving despite the sudden interruption of a telephone call, and others who report that they have enormous trouble understanding spatial tasks. The safe conclusion is that there is nothing about touch as a method of perception that prevents spatial understanding being based on it. Appreciation of each of the major principles of spatial layout can be achieved either through vision or through touch. Whether this is "spatial perception," "cognitive mapping," "perceptual-information-based cognitive mapping," or any combination of sensory-perceptual systems one can devise is in principle virtually unanswerable in the general case.

For any system that allows translation between schemes, the task and the observer's estimation of the best way of solving the task are deeply influential. The observer can be given a task that is about space and perspective. But although the method chosen to solve the task may be useful for the spatial problem, it can alter the task quite a lot. It is crucial of course that the person realizes that the method of solution is relevant to space and knows the meaning of each part of the method so far as space is concerned. One might, for example, reverse A-B-C-D to D-C-B-A because we realize that this is a good way to figure out the order of things left to right for someone sitting opposite. Verbal reversal, we know, is relevant to a 180° turn. The understanding is spatial though the method involves words.

One way to discover the mixtures of spatial understanding and nonspatial labels in a representational scheme used by the blind is to ask them point-blank what heuristics or problem-solving strategies they use in a spatial task. Barber and Lederman (1988) found, in a group of congenitally blind observers undertaking a spatial task, that four imagined an analog clock face with the numerals on the periphery as targets, one imagined a spoked wheel with targets at the ends of the spokes, one imagined a hand presumably with targets on the fingers and thumb, four kept track of a "start" position, and two specifically mentioned a mental "map." Only one did not describe a method. Adventitiously blind observers relied on what they called a visual map in eight cases and the image of a clock or a hand in four others. Barber and Lederman's volunteers apparently had good spatial skills. They appreciated which features of the task were spatial, how they were arranged, and how they could be represented spatially in a slightly different fashion (such as by a clock face). The volunteers use spatial models to solve spatial problems.

Rieser, Guth, and Hill (1986) asked their blind observers to walk around a spatial arrangement and then to point out the directions of locations. They contended that the observers "perceptually updated" their understanding of space continuously. That is, they were aware of the changes in direction that occurred during walking (Klatzky et al., 1990), and did not imagine clocks, hands, or other devices. Similarly, Bailes and Lambert (1986) found that blind adults understand a spatial arrangement of straight line segments as a pattern without reporting any need to recode and decode.

I discern no contradiction between studies where spatial apprehension is reported as merely an intuition or percept about an arrangement and studies like Barber and Lederman's where a model is used to solve a task. It takes spatial understanding of the task to know which spatial properties are relevant. The same kind of understanding underlies the model. Any manipulation of the model has to be followed and interpreted by spatial skills. It would be self-contradictory to argue that the blind do not have immediate, direct apprehension of spatial arrangements *because* they use spatial models to solve imagery tasks. I therefore conclude that Barber and Lederman's results show that spatial understanding by the blind is often advanced enough to be employed as models in imagination, in addition to its use in apprehending spatial arrangements physically present to the observer. The basis on which blind people represent knowledge of space is sensitivity to the relevant spatial variations around them, followed by selection of appropriate models which contain those variations, albeit labeled in familiar forms like numerals on a clock or names for fingers. These forms mark the spatial variations but do not precede them.

Thus, blind and sighted people organize spatial information along similar dimensions and therefore image in similar ways (O'Donohue, 1991). Kerr (1983) argues this case, noting one minor exception. She found that blind adults were somewhat slower than the sighted to image an array, verify statements about the imaged array, and recall and describe the array. Differences in time to respond, however, are not differences in spatial principles, just as $e = mc^2$ said slowly or quickly entails the same principles.

Hollins (1989) concludes that the blind have coherent spatial imagery but adds that blind people may often imagine "in the round" rather than "just like a picture." He devised an interesting test of his conjecture, comparing mental "pictures" to mental "statues." Hollins asked blind subjects to image a flat checkerboard with 8 by 8 squares. He then dictated which squares were filled in. The result was an image of a dog. Hollins also asked subjects to image a large cube made up of 4 by 4 by 4 smaller cubes. The image of the cube uses three dimensions, like a statue, and the checkerboard uses two, like a picture. Hollins dictated which of the small cubes should be filled in. The result took the form of an armchair. Hollins found that the longer a person had been blind the better he or she was able to form and recognize the mental "statue" in comparison to the mental "picture."

Haber, Haber, Levin, and Gramata (1988) tested blind adults who were highly proficient at navigating within their environments. They were asked about a familiar space involving several rooms with more than a dozen objects located therein. Each volunteer was asked to judge distances to the objects from where he or she was seated. The procedure also involved estimating the distance between each pair of objects. A highly accurate map of all the locations, with a slightly reduced scale, could be drawn on the basis of the judgments from any one of the subjects, whether congenitally blind or adventitiously blind. Judgments from the observer's location were about as accurate as judgments of distances between pairs of objects. This important study shows that spatial understanding in a blind person who is reasonably skilled at using the environment reflects proportional distances and good understanding of the vantage point, as well as distances between two objects away from the vantage point.

Problems in perspective entail consideration of the direction of parts of the object from a vantage point, as well as convergence of the directions of the parts as the object recedes into the distance. The blind appreciate vantage point principles, relevant directions, and convergence. This is not to say that they can solve any and all perspective problems. There are many unsolved riddles in the relations between perception, perspective, and depiction, and it is hardly likely that blind people can explain them all any more than sighted people can. Rather, the conclusion is a more modest one. Key principles that create perspective effects are understood by the blind because perspective is a science of direction, and direction is as relevant to touch as it is to vision.

CHAPTER SEVEN

Metaphor

A political cartoon shows a politician and a lobbyist fishing. They have cast their lines so wildly that they have hooked each other and got hopelessly tangled in fishing line. In their rivalrous efforts to reel something in they have pulled each other off balance. Nobody is likely to mistake this cartoon for reality, as the truth is not in the shapes of the objects depicted. Rather, we are expected to notice what is in common between entangled fishermen and ambitious politicians and lobbyists undone by their own overzealous efforts. The political cartoonist borrows from familiar perceptible situations like fishing, playing cards, and parenting to put the objects of caricature into poses and situations we can readily recognize. If the cartoonist succeeds, the intended message is clear.

Political caricaturing is an art with a long history. In the 1940s, David Low's "Baby like to play with nice ball?" showed a gaunt scientist handing over a round atomic bomb to infant humanity. In the late nineteenth century, *Punch* portrayed Bismarck's loss of power to the kaiser as "Dropping the pilot." The ship of state, heading out to sea and hence to its destiny, was shown passing beyond the shoals where the skills of a harbor pilot were necessary. Bismarck was pictured as leaving the ship to the captain, the kaiser. Both Bismarck and the kaiser appreciated the portrayal. Philipon in 1834 got into trouble for pillorying the king of France as "une poire," a fathead. He drew a series of pictures demonstrating just how easy it was to transform the king's head into a pear (Gombrich, 1960). Baldinucci, in 1681, in a dictionary of artistic terms, pointed out that although a good caricature aims at "the greatest resemblance," for social purposes such as fun and mockery components are changed, proportions altered, and effects emphasized (Gombrich, 1960, p. 344). Caricaturists combine likeness and purposeful distortion.

The goal of this chapter is to show that blind children and adults deliberately introduce distortions into drawings of objects. That is, blind children and adults who can produce and understand good resemblance intentionally eschew it to show referents that are difficult to draw by copying the form of the object.

METAPHORS ARE THOUGHTS

Let us return to drawings by Lu and Hal from chapter 5. To depict a hexagonal box, Lu drew marks that showed features individually and separately. One line meant "long and straight," while others, quite separately, show the sides—the very things that are "long and straight." Lu drew arcs to stand for the sides. Lu seemed unable to draw a rectangle to depict the sides of the box. One of Hal's drawings of a wheel spinning showed the wheel as an oval in which he said he arranged the spokes one after another. He said about the oval shape, "I put it long so one spoke would come right after another." Hal seems to have deliberately replaced the proper shape with another shape, an unrealistic one, not in keeping with the true shape of the wheel or the locations of the spokes in the wheel.

Hal's tactic has its parallels in language. In "She's unemotional—indifferent to others' needs" we make a claim and add an explanation. We could replace the proper description and remove the added explanation saying metaphorically, "She's got a heart of stone." Children, the uninitiated, or the unwary might be puzzled by the phrase *a heart of stone*. They might wonder if it is a mistake or an indication of a lack of linguistic skill. In fact, it indicates that for a moment, for a restricted purpose, normal language is being modified by the speaker. The speaker has a set of standard meanings for words and phrases as well as rules for changing the meaning of the words temporarily. The rules for changing meanings for special purposes include using a term to mean its opposite (saying "really bad" and meaning "really good"), its subordinate (saying "Norway" and meaning "the Norwegian king"), its superordinate (saying "Ottawa" and meaning "Canada"), and its analog in another context (saying "the hawk" and meaning "the fighter pilot"). In addition, an associate can be used ("barbell" to mean "strong man"), a part can stand for the whole ("hardtop" to refer to "car"), the whole for a part ("lobster" to refer to "claw"), the more extreme for the less extreme ("giant" to mean "tall man"), and the less extreme for the more extreme ("cheerful" to mean "drunk"). Where a relationship, feature, or dimension can classify an object, it can be used in a metaphor. Purcell (1990) noted that familiar concepts can be pursued "in a new light" and have innumerable functions (p. 52).

Every kind of relationship offers the basis for a kind of trope. What they all have in common is that the use is changed to emphasize some aspect of the referent, and the expression involves an error that is deliberate. In each case the category defined by the term being used is incorrect for the referent. But the listener knows what is meant by the incorrect term and knows that the term was deliberately used incorrectly—for effect, emphasis, or explanation. These rules allow special-purpose meanings, which do not replace the standard, literal meanings. The new meanings can be adopted without changing the standard meanings and often can be understood immediately. We know what it means to say a heart of granite, of reinforced concrete, of solid shale, or of gray slate. Of course, the metaphor is not always apt. That is, it may follow the rules for language modification ineptly. We cannot change the use of words in just any way: "He has a heart of orange" is more mystifying than clear. "He has a heart of boulders" is a poor version of "He has a heart of stone." In these cases the categories invoked by the words whose use is being modified are not effective or explanatory (Kennedy, 1990).

A good metaphor violates normality but does so in a way that makes sense, presenting violations that introduce relevant ideas. The unyielding quality of a rock, granite, and concrete is crucial to our conception of these objects. Boulders on the other hand are things that rumble down hills in a landslide and hence do not convey the necessary sense of being unyielding. Just so, a good pictorial metaphor should introduce relevant shape where it does not actually belong in the physical object. We could draw a realistic wake behind a swimming bird, and then put the wake in the sky behind a flying bird. A wake is relevant, being intrinsic to movement.

The history of recorded thought on metaphor, reaching back to Ancient Greece, has not produced a satisfactory definition of metaphor. Aristotle's analysis in the *Poetics* emphasized the transference of a name from species to genus, genus to species, or species to species, and the use of analogy. His account (like Cicero's, which stressed similarity) was restricted to verbal metaphor (Purcell, 1990). Only recently has an attempt been made to apply all types of figurative language to pictures (Kennedy, 1982a), though the idea that pictures can be metaphors has been proclaimed many times (Arnheim, 1974; Gombrich, 1960; Goodnow, 1977). The major problem at the core of any definition of figurative communication is the distinction between literal and metaphoric expression. Is there a clear way to define one without the other? Figurative language departs from ordinary language in a graceful manner, an unknown Roman scholar wrote in the first century B.C. (Purcell, 1990). Others described the figures or tropes as artistic alterations or alien names (Aristotle), or a word applying to one thing being applied to another. Alas for these definitions, we can speak formally to depart from ordinary language in a graceful manner, or alter someone's name artistically to get a pet name, and in neither case is the result a metaphor. Similarly, we can call John by the Irish "Sean" to get an alien name. And we constantly learn the meaning of words in one context (cars in streets) and apply them in other contexts (cars in wreckers' yards) without speaking one whit metaphorically.

Tropes may be expressed in language but fundamentally be matters of thought. "Surgeons are butchers" is an invitation to make one thing a sub-category of another. But what sets a trope apart from literal expression is that the claim being made is not open to all the principles of categorization. As John Vervaeke pointed out to me, we may agree that all surgeons are butchers and that all butchers are shopkeepers, but it does not follow that "all surgeons are shopkeepers." The deduction is not a relevant one, hence it does not falsify the original metaphor. The deduction would be relevant if the original claim about surgeons as butchers were literal. Thus, tropes are ways of categorizing that do not employ the full set of principles of categorization. Only a deduction that happens to be relevant is allowed. So it matters to the aptness of the original metaphor that butchers accept payment. One can conclude that the kind of surgeons to which the metaphor applies will accept payment. Butchers are not heroes. No more are surgeons, the metaphor implies. Metaphors are open to the principles of categorization and deductions from category membership. The use of the laws of category membership gives them enormous power to guide thought, but they are not bound by the full set of principles since deductions can be dismissed if they are irrelevant.

The advantage given to tropes by principles of classification is that the invitation to put a group of objects into a new class and check what is relevant opens up thinking about the objects in a host of ways. There is always an infinite set of ways of thinking about anything: someone might think what this book might suffer if it were dropped in a volcano or a bowl of soup or Jupiter's red spot. A metaphor determines what is relevant for thinking about an object. It brings many previously unexamined matters to the fore. Tropes are powerful because they involve categorization and influence what is relevant.

What forms of expression can trigger categorization and sway considerations of relevance? I suggest that the heart of a trope is nuance. The maker of the trope has in mind standard ways to indicate the referent and substitutes another way which is thought to be apt but also is known to be in error. The definition rests on intention, not on common parlance. The new term can then be in a method of representation which is gestural or pictorial, not just verbal. It can be a nuance in any mode of intentional communication. Furthermore, if a dimension for classifying an object can be used in several sensory modes, then it enables a trope to be based on each of the sensory modalities. Matters like length, curvature, and motion are examples. They are detectable by more than one modality. They allow the sighted and the blind to refer to tall people as skyscrapers (hyperbole), a curved road as a hairpin (following Cicero's contention that a name can be transferred to another thing because of similarity) and agitated nervous motion as being in a stew (for in the realm of cooking, a bubbling stew is a species of particularly vigorous activity, as Aristotle would have it).

The blind and the sighted alike can be aware of a standard use of a term and decide to make an apt but erroneous substitution. On occasion, there is nothing inherent in the new term that marks it overtly as an error. A good example is "Jake is our priest," when Jake is the barman to whom we confess our troubles. The maker of a trope can think of the new term as an apt error, and that alone defines the communication as a trope. Ergo, to have a pictorial trope the only essential matter is that some part of the drawing be an intentional apt error. It is not necessary that an expression violate a widespread convention for it to be a trope.

There was an interesting phase in the history of depiction when objects were given symbolic, conventional significance, such as goats for evil, rays of sunlight for divine influence, and ribbons for rhetoric. This practice blossomed in the sixteenth and seventeenth centuries with the widespread production of emblems (Vicari, 1991). These were pictures with a text, including a brief motto, intended as a lesson in morals. Emblems began as aristocratic pastimes. Later, pictorial dictionaries were devised in which abstract concepts such as justice and glory were represented by arcane symbols in bourgeois manuals of instruction. The list of representations and abstract ideas grew long as images proliferated. The exercise, which started as a way to make a picture represent relationships between important ideas, lost favor when it became too difficult to keep track of the hordes of images and their conventional meanings. The movement was known as *emblematica,* a term coined by Andrea Alciati in 1531 to refer to a "mosaic" of pictures, text, and ideas. It largely disappeared, though a few hackneyed favorites such as an overspilling cornucopia for riches and the hourglass and scythe for death remained popular.

One reason why emblematica is no longer a mainstream interest in illustration is that it is not necessary to designate a symbol for an abstract idea, make it conventional, and teach people its meaning. We are quite capable of seeing a new pictorial vehicle for an abstract idea and appreciating its significance without explanation. We do not have to be taught why the mayor is portrayed as a shark with sharp teeth or why a pile of money is shown burning as it pours over a dam that was never completed. A child can be shown as flying from school like a bird as the schoolbell rings and the calendar shows the end of June. The scene is easily interpreted, and it metaphorically deals with the idea of freedom. Many pictures reward us with meaning if we study them, but study is not inevitably needed for a picture to convey an abstract idea (Gombrich, 1982).

All that a picture needs to make a metaphor is a deliberate, apt distortion of a familiar shape. This connects metaphors to proverbs. A proverb, like "too many cooks spoil the broth," is a statement of advice. It is usually recited in a situation where its terms do not literally apply. We mention cooks, but the room is full of, say, computer programmers. The metaphor in the proverb is "the programmers are cooks ruining a dish." The concrete situations involve different occupations, but the common thread is that the efforts of one expert are being undone by another. Similarly, a picture might show a child following a path through thick woods. One can take this as a metaphor for life. The situation is part of the struggle of inexperienced people to find their way. A proverbial picture might show a kitten stranded up a tree while the owner tries to tempt it back to a nearby window with a saucer of milk. The feeling suggested by the style of the picture could emphasize the caring shown by the owner. If this picture were to appear on the editorial page of a newspaper, we might have to read it as a parallel to some newsworthy event where a novice minister had made some rash proposal (had gone out on a limb) and the powers-that-be were trying to coax him back to a safe position. Since nothing in the picture concretely refers to the minister, the picture functions like a proverb. It has nothing overtly erroneous about its contents, and only its location calls for an explanation. Its siting violates Grice's conversational maxim: Be relevant. It has to be interpreted like a proverb in order to become relevant.

In sum, a metaphor is not just decoration in language, like speaking sweetly or in a colorful accent. Metaphors convey meaning; they give the audience notions about the referent. Metaphors involve manipulation of classes, not just phrases (Glucksberg and Keysar, 1990; Kennedy, 1990). The category of a referent is in question when a metaphor is used. When we say, "Painters are magicians," we imply that painters are part of the group of people who practice magic, and that not all magicians are painters. Metaphors can be defined formally as expressions that borrow the apparatus of class inclusion and make class-inclusion statements, but not all the class-inclusion mechanisms are valid for any particular metaphor. If a statement is literal, then all the implications of class inclusion are relevant to the expression. If metaphors are products of thinking, then what a blind person needs to understand metaphor is the same as what a sighted person needs. Hence if metaphors can be found in pictures for the sighted, they should be useful to the blind too.

My concern is with the kind of metaphoric pictures in which there are overt errors, intentional distortions of shape. Two questions arise. First, when are shape distortions introduced into drawings deliberately? Such distortions could be intended as metaphors. That intention alone, however, does not make them apt. To be apt is to be relevant as well as to be intended. Thus, the second question is, Can some distortions be shown to be apt for both blind and sighted people? To answer this question it is necessary to show several devices to many people and ask them what those devices mean.

DRAWINGS OF MOTION BY BLIND ADULTS

Our first studies of pictorial metaphor and the blind sprang from the drawing volunteered by Pat, an early blind adult from Toronto. She drew a fairy-tale princess at a spinning wheel. The wheel was an oval with a single arc inside. We determined to ask others to try drawing motion—a wheel spinning and a man walking and running. The purpose of the study was to discover what devices the blind would use for these referents and what they would say about the devices.

In Toronto, 13 blind adults volunteered for a movement study (table 7.1). Eight were totally blind early in life (five from birth and three from age two), two could sense light at birth (early, light perceivers) and three went blind later in life (late, totally blind).

We asked the adults to draw a man standing, then a man walking, and last a man running. Then the participants drew a wheel spinning or rolling, and a car going fast.

TABLE 7.1

Volunteers from BOOST in a study on drawing movement of people and a wheel.

Onset of Blindness and Degree of Loss	Participants
Early (0–2 years)	Cal, Dee, Jay, Lys, May, Nat, Pat, Pau
Early, light perception	Jim, Nip
Late, totally blind	Mo, Ray, Roy

We can divide the devices used by the Toronto adults to show a man moving into three kinds: *modified shape or posture, context, and added graphics*. The postural devices were the most common. For the walking man, the ratio of postural devices to context devices to added-graphics devices was 10:1:2, and for the running man it was 11:5:3 (table 7.2).

The postural devices generally concerned legs and feet. Typically, the standing man was drawn from the front, with arms and legs symmetrical and feet pointed out like Charlie Chaplin. The moving man, by contrast, often was facing front but had both feet pointing in the same direction, left or right (fig. 7.1). Ives and Rovet (1979) note that this "Egyptian" pose is a common indicator of movement in children's drawings in Canada and the Caribbean. It is an "invented" device since it does not appear in children's comics or photographs—invented by the blind as well as the sighted. The pose may arise from drawing the person while following a foldout principle common in drawing development. It may not be metaphoric but merely a consequence of drawing the person's limbs in a foldout style. In our study it was not accompanied by comments that the pose is an error.

The moving man often had both legs and arms bent, or one arm bent more than the other, as in figure 7.2. The arms and legs were sometimes spread apart more than in the standing-man drawing. Again, these are not metaphoric devices. Walking entails these postures and standing need not. Moreover, the accentuation of the dimensions does not mean the devices are diagrammatic, related to their referent by fiat only. Carello, Rosenblum, and Grosofsky (1986) note that static postural devices can specify many kinds of actions by the body and that sighted children recognize the motions specified by the postures. The devices present in the walking-man drawing would typically be accentuated in the running-man drawing to indicate greater speed—legs and arms further apart and bent more. These devices mean motion to sighted preschoolers, Friedman and Stevenson (1980) found and

TABLE 7.2
Frequency of devices used by BOOST volunteers to show a person moving.

	Type of Device		
Referent	Posture	Context	Added Graphics
Man walking	10	1	2
Man running	11	5	3

Fig. 7.1. Drawing of a man walking, by Scot (age 13, totally blind, some form perception in infancy), and a man running, by Pau (late, totally blind).

Carello, Rosenblum, and Grosofsky confirmed. In short, the blind invent what the sighted have deemed appropriate.

The context devices used by the blind adults were as follows: drawing a person on a road, or with dust "kicked up" behind him (fig. 7.2), or at one end of a path, or by a stream with much of the stream to the back of the figure. The

Fig. 7.2. Drawing of a man walking, by Jim (early, light perception). One arm is bent more than the other, and the man is kicking up dust behind him as he comes toward the observer.

Metaphor

end of the path and the stream in back were said to suggest that the person had traversed the path or walked along the stream. One distinctive device from Pat (early, totally blind) was her use of a fence, which "decreases in size suddenly instead of gradually [and this] shows he's running" (fig. 7.3). The decrease-in-size device cannot be described as literal or realistic. It is not only imaginative; it is also imaginary, involving a deliberate error in depicting a shape. Hence it is metaphoric. The fence device is imaginary because it uses an unrealistically sudden decrease in size. The device uses the context of the object—the fence near it—to show the object's movement. Therefore, figure 7.3 is best classified as both a metaphor and a context device. Thus, besides pictorial metaphors involving the shape of the object, as in Hal's wheel, there are pictorial context metaphors.

Hal not only changed the shape of a spinning wheel and the location of its spokes. He also, in another drawing, added extra arcs around the perimeter. These can be called *added graphics*. They are pictorial runes. In writing, runes are simple versions of graphics that convey an entire alphabetic character. For convenience, a few brief marks substitute for the full depiction. Similarly, in pictures a few added graphics can substitute for multiple views of a vibrating wheel or a running man (Kennedy, 1982b; Newton, 1985). Some added-

Fig. 7.3. Drawing of a man running, by Pat (early, totally blind). The fence, which "decreases in size suddenly," provides metaphoric context.

225

graphics devices were invented by the adults. Pau (early, totally blind) added horizontal lines at neck level as a sign of the direction of movement. Lys (early, totally blind) added small circles, each standing for a foot, to indicate "steps he's taking—as if walking towards me" (fig. 7.4). In drawing the man running, she packed swirls beneath the man's feet quite densely. She said the man's speed—"very quick, as if his feet were moving"—was indicated by the very dense swirls. Pau also added circles for footsteps when he drew the running man. Nat (early, totally blind) put a curved line behind one foot "which shows how fast he's running" (fig. 7.5).

It is curious that Lys and Pau display intended footprints instead of completed strides. Pau said, "I make marks that are supposed to be strides that he's taking. He started here [behind the foot] and now he has to go to here [the mark he made ahead of the foot] to take this stride next." When we asked him if these stride marks are like footprints, he answered yes. Lys said that her lines indicate the "steps that he's taking—it's as if he was walking towards the end of the table towards me." She indicated the motion down the page with her fingers, starting at the feet she had drawn and then moving onto the marks she had made for the steps. Ergo, they are indeed intended steps to come, not past steps.

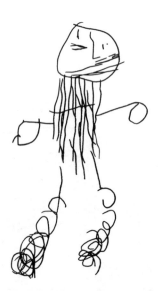

Fig. 7.4. Drawing of a man walking, by Lys (early, totally blind). The small circles represent feet and show "steps he's taking."

Fig. 7.5. Drawing of a man running, by Nat (early, totally blind). A curved
line from one foot "shows how fast he's running." The horizontal line
from the other foot is the ground.

Nat's line of movement of a foot is an indication of what is past. He pointed
to the line and said, "If you followed it around [he traced it along to the foot
and then continued the arc beyond the foot] his right foot would land here,
and he'd be further ahead." Sighted people would draw lines like Nat, lines of
past movement. Graphics for intended movement are rare in sighted people's
drawings (though I have come across them in narrative Mexican murals of the
nineteenth century, courtesy of Jack Child). For the sighted, what has already
been done often leaves impressive visual traces. The sweeping movements of a
blackboard eraser, the trail of footprints on a dusty floor, and the muddy
finger marks on a bar of soap are all clear records of past actions. By contrast,
for the blind, what they are about to do, where they are going to move, and the
path they hope to traverse are often at least as vivid in their consciousness as
the route that brought them to the present moment. Many of the traces we
leave are unavailable to normal touch even though they stand out boldly to
vision. We cannot feel a fingerprint on a smooth surface; we can only inspect it
visually. It would be unwise, however, to describe the differences between
records of the past for the blind and the sighted as absolute. Rutted tracks are
perfectly evident to touch and indicate the passage of wheels in the past.

Metaphor

PICTORIAL METAPHOR

If we borrow a wake created by a duck swimming on a lake and put it behind the duck flying in the sky, that is a pictorial metaphor without a doubt. If Nat borrows his line of movement from things like tracks left on a soft path by moving objects and puts it in air behind the foot, that too is metaphoric. Are the feet shown by Lys and Pau metaphoric? It is hard to decide without more evidence. If the "extra feet" of Lys—"one foot in front of the other, moving"—and the future footprints of Pau are imaginary, then they too are metaphoric. At the stage in our research that this study was conducted we were not sure how to question the volunteers about their intentions, so the notion that the drawings were metaphoric must remain somewhat tentative.

Changes of posture can be quite literal when one is drawing people. But to distinguish a spinning wheel from a static wheel we cannot just freeze an instant in the movement. More needs to be done, and if the shape of the object is depicted as changed, a metaphor may be involved. The devices for showing a spinning wheel can be divided into the same three categories as we used for a walking person: modified shape, context, and added graphics. Modified-shape devices appeared six times, context devices once, and added-graphics devices three times.

Shape modifications included curving the spokes. This device was used by three people (Pat, early, totally blind; May and Ray, both late, totally blind). Nat (early, totally blind) put the hub off center, and Jim (early, totally blind) drew the spokes crossing one another (fig. 7.6), more "mixed up," as he put it.

The context device was Roy's (late, totally blind). He drew a wheel held by a bicycle fork and being pushed along by a boy.

The added graphics included extra circles or circumferences inside or outside the main circle for the wheel. These were drawn by Pau, Dee, and Lys

Fig. 7.6. Drawing of a wheel spinning, by Jim (early, light perception). The spinning is shown by having the spokes "mixed up."

(all early, totally blind). Pau also drew a dense spiral around the wheel (fig. 7.7).

To show the wheel rolling, on five occasions shape was changed, context was used seven times, and extra graphics appeared four times (table 7.3).

The shape modifications were curving the spokes (Dee, Pat, May, and Ray) and making the spokes longer in the direction the wheel is rolling (Nat).

In six people's drawings, a context was shown in the form of a ground line. Three times the wheel was shown touching the ground on a hill slope (Jay and Cal, both early, totally blind; Nip, early, light perceiver). Roy and May had a line of anticipated movement from the wheel connected to the ground "ahead" to show where it was rolling to. Ray put in grass bent down by the wheel and springing up again. He also put in a fender partway around the wheel, which he thought helped show the direction of movement. He noted that the motion would be away from the fender.

Graphic devices included straight trailing lines (Nat) and a series of arcs behind the rolling wheel (Jim, Pau, and Lys).

In drawing a car in motion, the same difficulty arises as in depicting a rotating wheel. Wheels and cars do not change their pictorial shape when they move. Hence the solutions to depicting moving cars were similar to those offered in picturing a rotating wheel. The shape of the car was modified five times, context was drawn six times, and graphics were added twice.

Dee drew a foldout version of the car showing all four wheels and the top. This layout can be counted as following the rules of a foldout drawing system and as intended to show attachment relationships realistically. In her drawing of the wheels, Dee used what may be counted as a pictorial trope: the spokes of the wheels are curved to indicate the wheel's motion. Jim and Pat drew the

Fig. 7.7. Drawing of a wheel spinning, by Pau (early, totally blind).
The spinning is shown by the line spiraling around the wheel.

TABLE 7.3
Frequency of devices used by BOOST volunteers to show a wheel in motion.

Referent	Type of Device		
	Shape	Context	Added Graphics
Wheel spinning	6	1	3
Wheel rolling	5	7	4

car with larger front wheels than back, which again is best counted as a metaphor. Roy left the wheel behind its axle. Confirming that this is a trope, he said "the car doesn't actually [do this], that's just stretching the imagination." By contrast, Cal uses a literal device: he has the car's aerial bent to indicate the motion.

Context was provided by a dog chasing the car (Cal), gravel kicked up by the car (May and Ray), and lines meant to show smoke or light coming from the car (Jim, Pat, and Cal). Using hyperbole, Nat drew the ground so that it "barely touches the back wheels and the front wheels are off the ground."

The graphic additions were from Lys, who drew lines trailing after the car, and Nat, who put a line of intended motion from the driver's seat to the road to indicate that "he wants to get there fast."

In sum, the motion tasks resulted in context devices, often showing quite realistic context but sometimes stretching into hyperbole, and devices pertaining to the object itself, sometimes showing quite appropriate realistic poses and sometimes distorting the shape of the object in imaginary ways. Furthermore, trailing lines, extra circumferences, and lines of intended motion were volunteered.

DRAWINGS OF MOTION BY BLIND CHILDREN

To continue the investigation of drawings of motion and blind people's use of metaphor, the same tasks were given to blind children. The children we had tested with pictures of static objects in Phoenix and Tucson were asked to draw static and spinning wheels and a running man.

The wheel devices used by children in Phoenix included seven cases where the shape was modified, one where context was used, and six where graphic additions appeared. Shape modifications included modifications to the spokes (Hal, Ray, Noel, Erl, Sean, and Gale), which were more scattered, more curved, or closer together than in the original sketch of a static wheel, or were even absent or parallel. Noel (age 12), for example, drew a static wheel with spokes as a circle with straight lines in it. His spinning wheel was a mass of circles. Asked if he could add the spokes he drew a separate picture, again with a mass of circles, to show the spokes "going round and round." Hal (age 10) made the wheel "long" to show it moving, and he has the spokes drawn parallel to show that they came one after another. Hal, along with Gale (age 14), added extra arcs as graphic indicators of movement. Gale further added a ground line as context.

To show the wheel spinning, the Tucson children used context and added graphic indicators. Tip (age six), Amy (age seven), and Ole (age 14) added an axle to the spinning wheel, probably because when we explained the tasks we demonstrated a wheel spinning on an axle. Furthermore, Jef (age 12) drew concentric rings (rather than a circle with spokes and a hub as in his static version), and Amy drew circles in a row, with a central row of dots standing for the hub (fig. 7.8). When Amy was asked if she could think of another way of

Fig. 7.8. Drawing of a wheel spinning, by Amy (age 7, early, totally blind). Dots show the hub.

drawing a wheel spinning she drew a series of concentric circles, again with an axle (fig. 7.9).

The drawings of a running man done by the Phoenix children involved posture devices (twice) and what may be metaphoric modifications of the body. To show running, Kit (age eight) said, "I made his knees go up," which is a literal device. Gale had the man's arms bent, his right foot forward, and his left foot "getting ready," which also is literal. But Ray (age eight) had the front foot bigger to show it as "more powerful," he said. And Sean (age six) made the front legs "real long," the arms "real long" too, and even the ears "real long," saying this was "to show he's running—it makes him be real strong and he's running very fast!"

In Sean's delightful humor there is the essence of metaphor. This seems to show that tropes can be used as early as age six. Sean's metaphor is humorous rather than precise and apt, as there is nothing about long ears that suggests speed. It is a connection between two dimensions made by fiat, albeit humorously.

Three of the Tucson children used devices to suggest the movement of a running man. Raf (age 12) added context in the form of a hurdle and modified posture by drawing bent legs (fig. 7.10). Jef (age 12) and Amy added extra legs (Amy's drawing has ten!). Since the extra legs are unrealistic, it seems appropriate to classify these pictures as metaphoric.

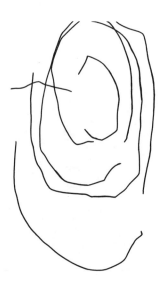

Fig. 7.9. Second drawing of a wheel spinning, by Amy. There is a central axle and concentric circles.

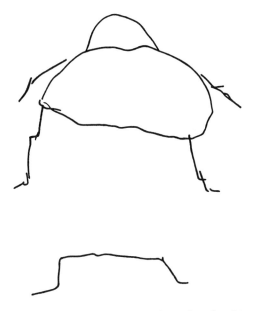

Fig. 7.10. Drawing of a man running, shown by a bend in the leg
and a hurdle, by Raf (age 12, early, light perception).

In sum, both children and adults used postural, contextual, and graphic
indications of movement and employed metaphor in their drawings.

METAPHORIC, LITERAL, AND DIAGRAMMATIC DEVICES

Many matters besides motion can be represented in pictures for the
sighted. Radiating lines are used to show pain, a collision, or someone puffing.
Wavy lines above an object show heat or scent or tingle. I have never come
across any books for the blind containing illustrations using these devices. It is
important to note that many of the referents are tangible. Logically, it is
possible that the blind might find outline entirely appropriate for depicting
the perimeter of a hot spot, the warm air rising from a heating vent, the
boundary of a pain, or the shock of a sudden blow. Alternatively, they may
spontaneously comment that lines stand best for shapes of solid substances
and that any other use of outline is anomalous. They may even say that one
cannot picture a pain except indirectly in an agonized expression or pose; that
is, they may use a context that tells us about the pain. If they have a grasp of
pictorial metaphor, they may comment that although pain cannot really be
drawn and outline is not suitable for the boundary of a pain, only for edges of

surfaces, they nevertheless are going to violate standard usage and borrow from drawings of edges to outline the perimeter of a pain as though it were a surface.

Another alternative would be to draw some conventional or diagrammatic symbol, like an exclamation mark or a graph line, and assert that for the moment this symbol will stand for pain, heat, or whatever the topic. A conventional mark, too, can be treated metaphorically. An exclamation mark or graph line could be tied in a knot to show the frustration of a nagging pain. I have never had any blind person make such a metaphoric diagram, however, so we may put aside this last option for the moment.

It seems possible that blind people may deem a referent suitable for depiction and draw it realistically, metaphorically, or diagrammatically. Or they may feel it necessary to show the context and draw that realistically, metaphorically, or diagrammatically. Each person volunteering a device may make an idiosyncratic decision about that device. Someone may think that a line for the boundary of a pain is as sensible as a line for the boundary of a ball. Someone may contend that outline shows pain readily but does not show surface edges. Conceivably, someone might think that a person can be blown over literally by the vehemence of a shout or actually have his head split open by a headache. Others may take these to be purely metaphoric. The intent behind the device must be discovered before we can classify the device as literal or metaphoric. It is important, then, to delve into what the volunteer says as he offers a device. What do the comments indicate about his or her intentions?

Ramona Domander and I asked BOOST volunteers and other blind volunteers recruited in Toronto to draw some referents that we, as sighted people, took to be unsuitable for outline drawings. We wondered if the blind would feel the same way about the suggested referents. We requested drawings of the wind, a hand in pain, a person shouting, smelly garbage, and a hammer hitting a table and making a loud noise.

We tested 15 volunteers (table 7.4), all of whom had participated in our previous studies on haptic pictures. Six were congenitally blind, five were early blind, and four were late blind. The congenitally blind ranged in age from 23 to 32 years. Five were totally blind from birth and one had some light sensitivity since birth. Four of the early blind subjects ranged in age from 26 to 34, and one was 13. The early blind volunteers were diverse. The 13-year-old has been totally blind since age 12 and at best had 2 percent vision in one eye. He has never been able to see a picture, he said, and this assertion was supported by his mother and teachers. Another has had minimal light sensitivity since age six months. One has been totally blind since four years of age,

TABLE 7.4
Toronto volunteers for a study on drawing pain, wind, noise, and smell.

Congenitally blind	Boi	Totally blind since birth
	Dec	Light sensitivity since birth
	Jay	Totally blind since birth
	Lys	Totally blind since birth
	May	Totally blind since birth
	Nat	Totally blind since birth
Early blind (before age 3)	Dem	Minimal light sensitivity since age 6 months
	Jae	Totally blind since age 1 year
	Joi	Totally blind since age 4 years; decline in sight since age 6 months
	Pau	Totally blind since age 6 years; rapid decline since age 6 months
	Scot	Totally blind since age 12 years; 2 percent vision in best eye since birth
Later blind	Ann	Totally blind since age 10 years; low vision since birth
	Dot	Low vision since birth
	Mo	Totally blind since age 7 years
	Ray	Totally blind since age 14 years; very low vision since birth

following a decline since he was six months old. The last (Pau) has had a decline in vision from age six months and has been totally blind since age six. He is on the borderline between early blind and late blind (in Kennedy and Domander [1986] we treated him as late blind). The late blind range in age from 26 to 29 years. They include one person who has had low vision since birth: she is unable to make out headlines. Two had reasonable or normal vision until ages 7 and 10 years respectively. One (Ray) has had very low vision since birth and became totally blind at age 14 (in Kennedy and Domander [1986] we treated him as early blind).

The late blind include three who probably had exposure to a wide range of pictures. All of the volunteers told us that they had never tried before to draw a hand in pain, the wind, a person yelling, a hammer hitting a table, or smelly garbage.

The procedure involved, as usual, asking for an explanation of the drawing as it was made, and the experimenter, Ramona Domander, prodded with nondirective questions like, "Can you think of a way to draw X?" The volunteers often made comments like, "This line is imaginary. I guess anyone [examining it] will have to realize that." These comments indicate that the topics were taken by the blind to lack suitability for line drawings since, by contrast, no one drawing a table ever describes their lines as imaginary. The comments were written down and formed the basis for our attempts to classify the blind person's intention for each device.

Domander wrote down each person's comments and, where needed, a brief description (here in brackets) of each device on cards (one card for each device). Examples are SHOUT: "The little lines [inside the mouth] suggest the yell," and PAIN: "That the fingers are apart and straight out suggests that the hand is painful." Then she and an independent judge, William Simpson, classified the devices according to the intentions of the person inventing the device.

Domander and Simpson sorted the devices into six categories. The devices could deal with the *object* literally, metaphorically, or diagrammatically, or they could deal with its *context* literally, metaphorically, or diagrammatically. Literal devices are ones said by the subject to stand for perceived edges of the object or its context. An example of a literal object device would be one said to show the tangible edge of a stream of air coming swiftly through a narrow opening or the apparent bounds of a clearly circumscribed pain. Metaphoric devices are those said by the volunteer to be anomalous, unreal, abstract, or imaginary; a comment may indicate that the depicted edges do not exist or that the use of line in a picture is in some regard inappropriate and unlike the use of other lines standing for edges of surfaces. An example of a metaphoric device would be a line described as an imaginary "aura" of pain around the hand. Diagrammatic devices are writing, axes of graphs, arrowheads, and other conventional graphic symbols.

A total of 185 devices were discerned by Domander. She and Simpson classified the devices independently and then found that they had classified 175 similarly (95 percent). They discussed the remainder and resolved their disputes. The final classification is in table 7.5.

The 10 disputed cases included seven having to do with the wind. In these drawings, Simpson took wind lines with no arrowheads to be diagrammatic, whereas Domander took them to be like imaginary tracks and hence metaphoric. After discussing the matter, they concluded that the blind meant them to be metaphoric. The point is moot, I think. The comments from the blind do not allow the decision to be unequivocal. Apart from these cases, the diagram category was unambiguous. Two clear examples for noise are the words BANG! BANG! BANG! written near the hammer, and dots offered as "symbols

TABLE 7.5

Devices intended as literal (L), metaphoric (M), or diagrammatic (D)
ways to show pain, wind, noise, and smell.

	Name	Depiction of Referent			Depiction of Context			Total
		L	M	D	L	M	D	
Congenitally	Lys		2		3			5
blind	May				10			10
	Jay		1	1	2			4
	Nat		5	1	2	3		11
	Boi		1	2	12	1		16
	Dec		8	3	7	2		20
Subtotal			17	7	36	6		66
Early blind	Dem		3	3	9	1		16
	Jae		5	1	8			14
	Joi		4		7	2		13
	Scot				10			10
	Pau				10	1		11
Subtotal			12	4	44	4		64
Late blind	Dot		3	1	14			18
	Ray		1		7			11
	Mo		3		8			11
	Ann	1	4		12	1		18
Subtotal		1	11	1	41	1		55
Total		1	40	12	121	11		185

representing the force of gravity on the hammer." Two clear examples for the
wind are "You could draw an X and Y axis" and "an arrow to show the wind's
direction."

Most of the devices (132 out of 185) pertained to the object's context. This
indicates that the blind feel that the referents cannot be depicted directly in
outline drawings. Without this result, there would be no reason to think that
the blind consider the referents to lie beyond the scope of outline drawing.

When subjects depicted the referent itself (53 cases) rather than its context, they most often (40 cases) used what were intended to be metaphoric devices (fig. 7.11). The figure shows fingers with an "imaginary aura of pain around," by Jan (early, totally blind), a hammer hitting a table and making a loud noise, indicated by the lines emerging from the collision and bouncing around the room (by Joan, early, light perception), and smelly garbage with lines indicating the smells wafting up from the garbage (by Jay, early, totally blind). Most of the remaining devices for the referent were diagrammatic (12 cases). Only one was judged as intended to be literal. The literal device was a

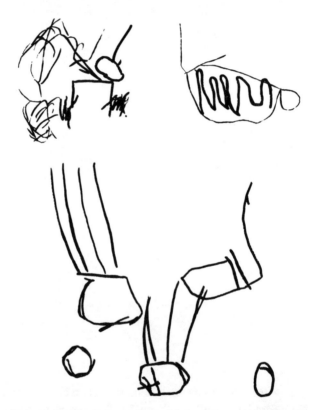

Fig. 7.11. Drawings using devices intended as metaphors: (top right) fingers with an "imaginary aura of pain around," by Jan (early, totally blind); (top left) a hammer hitting a table and making a loud noise, indicated by the lines emerging from the collision area and "bouncing" around the room, by Joan (early, light perception); (bottom) smelly garbage, with lines indicating the smells wafting up from the garbage, by Jay (early, totally blind).

drawing of the wind as a tornado, with arcs showing wind-borne dust in the air.

When our volunteers chose to depict the referent's context (132 cases) they used what they intended as literal devices most often (121 cases). Again, the result is as it should be. The reason that people turn to the context is presumably because the context can be drawn literally and the object cannot. Examples of literal context devices are PAIN: "Fingers are apart to suggest they're stiff and sore," or "Thumb is swollen." The contrast between context and object devices is striking. Of 132 context devices, 121 were literal. Of 53 object devices, 52 were nonliteral ($\chi^2 = 136$, 1 d.f., $p < 0.0001$). Of the 11 nonliteral context devices, all were metaphoric (for example, WIND: A "wavy line suggests that it gives you the shivers").

Only two subjects did not produce any metaphoric or diagrammatic devices: May, congenitally blind, and Scot, early blind. At age 13, Scot is also the youngest subject (by 10 years). Like May's, all of Scot's 10 devices were literal and context-related, for example, NOISE: "A knife and spoon bouncing off the edge of the table"; WIND: "Some leaves blowing around in the air"; SMELL: The garbage is "away from the house. That indicates it's smelly"; PAIN: The wrist is "swollen."

Of the 185 devices, 66 were obtained from the congenitally blind (mean of 11.0 per person), 64 from the early blind (mean of 12.8 per person) and 55 from the late blind (mean of 13.7 per person). The means for the three groups are similar. The lowest number for any individual is four (Jay, congenitally blind) and the highest is 20 (Dec, congenitally blind).

Of the 53 devices pertaining to the object, 24 were from the congenitally blind (4.0 per person). The early blind volunteered 16 object devices (3.2 per person), and 13 were from the late blind (3.2 per person). Again, the means appear similar.

Forty of the object devices were classified as intended to be metaphoric: 17 from the congenitally blind (2.8 per person, range from zero to eight), 12 were from the early blind (2.4 per person, range zero to four), and 11 were from the late blind (2.7 per person, range zero to four). Again the differences between the groups are not significant.

Only 12 devices were diagrammatic, and all of these pertained to the object. Seven were from the congenitally blind, four from the early blind, and one from a late blind person. The totals are too few to be analyzed with any confidence, but if anything they suggest that diagrammatic devices are obtained more frequently from the congenitally blind than from the adventitiously blind. Perhaps the late blind have a wider experience of objects in more detailed contexts and think more readily about context devices, and the early blind, for whom diagrams may be an especially prominent part of their educational experience, turn to more abstract forms of representation. The ratio of 40 metaphoric devices to 12 diagrammatic devices is unlikely to be due merely to chance ($p < 0.001$, binomial test, two-tailed). Even if the seven wind-track devices are reclassified as diagrammatic, the frequencies would be 33 to 19, a difference that is still unlikely to be due to chance ($p < 0.01$, binomial test, two-tailed).

A primary aim of this investigation was to check whether the blind would find it necessary to produce indirect solutions to pictorial problems. By contrast, if someone were asked to draw a chair, we would be dumbfounded if the only way that she could think of doing it was to draw the context in which one would find a chair. The primary goal of the exercise was achieved since the referents were almost always depicted by indirect means. Only once did a volunteer produce a device and intend it to be a literal drawing of the object. Rather, the volunteers turned away from the object in various ways, mainly by offering telltale contexts, but also quite often by attempting a metaphoric rendering. Occasionally a diagrammatic device was offered.

It is important that pictorial metaphors were obtained from the early blind and congenitally blind as well as from the late blind. If metaphors were learned tricks passed on informally by exposure to inventions from older generations, then only the late blind would have produced them. Instead, the three groups produced pictorial metaphors at about the same rate. Apparently, all three groups recognize what can and cannot be deemed suitable for outline drawing, making similar distinctions between acceptable and outré uses of outline. The comments from all three groups indicate that as a last resort one can muster outline to show shapes and locations of pain, wind, smell, yells, and sounds of hammer blows, but there is something anomalous about this compared to drawing edges of objects.

DETERMINING INTENTION

What underlies the sense that some referents fall within the scope of outline and others do not? What is the nature of the violation of standard outline drawing in metaphor? To assess the nature of metaphor further, we asked three of the blind volunteers directive questions about devices we deemed metaphoric. Normally, our questions to the volunteers were non-directive, but we decided to take the risk of putting some of our own notions forward in directive questions. We asked three adults, Pat, Nat, and Ray, a set of questions that spiraled in closer and closer to our own suppositions about metaphor.

We asked them to draw a spinning wheel and then we began the check on their devices. We asked:

1. Do spinning wheels really have [here we indicated the device being used]?
2. Which lines in your drawing might have to be explained to other people, and which ones would they be likely to understand without any explanation?
3. Which lines would children—including blind children—find easy to understand, and which ones would they find hard?
4. Which lines are realistic, and which ones are imaginary?
5. Which lines are literal, and which ones are metaphoric?

Two of the volunteers drew a wheel with curved spokes and one (Nat) drew a wheel with an extra, enlarged circumference and spokes extended to meet the surrounding circle. All three reported the devices to be unreal and said that they might have to be explained, would be hard for children to understand, were imaginary, and were metaphoric. By contrast, lines standing for hubs, spokes, or circumferences were said to be real, not in need of explanation, easy for children to follow, realistic, and literal.

As part of the interview Nat mentioned an interest in sailing, so he was asked to draw a sailboat (fig. 7.12). He drew a horizontal wavy line or sine curve under the boat and a somewhat irregular horizontal wavy line at the top of the mast. In response to our questions, Nat said that the mast, sail, and

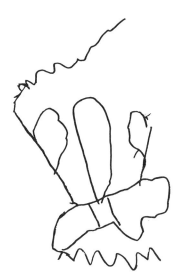

Fig. 7.12. Drawing of a sailboat, by Nat (early, totally blind).

body of the boat were real, did not have to be explained, were easy for children to comprehend, were realistic, and were literal. The lines for the wave and the wind, however, he said were unreal, in need of explanation, hard for children to grasp, imaginary, and metaphoric.

The judgments of curved spokes, the extra circumference, and the wind line all fit with a sighted person's conceptions of what lies beyond the scope of outline drawing and is fit for metaphor. But Nat's classification of the line showing the wave is anomalous. A wave is a shape of a surface. It is perfectly visible, of course, which may explain why a line shape can show edges of a surface and stand for a wave in pictures for the sighted. But perhaps a wave is hardly tangible. Its shape may be hard to feel. To touch, water waves seem to go up and down; the water does not seem to move forward with the wave. Indeed, it may be that Nat relied on science *diagrams* for his wave, as our questioning did not distinguish metaphors from diagrams. But Nat himself was fickle in his classification of the wave. In a second interview, over a year later, he was asked to draw a sailboat again. He drew a similar picture, but in this instance he classified the line showing the wave as literal, along with the outlined hull, mast, and sails. Only the wind line was said to be metaphoric.

Our probing, directive questions zoomed in on the odd, anomalous, false side of metaphor. In expressions and depictions, this is the side that puzzles the naive person if he hears, "Joe's a real winner!" when Joe, he knows, is something of a loser. The other side to metaphor is its aptness. Because of aptness, the listener can concur that fighter pilots are hawks, not albatrosses. It is proper to say, "Jeanne is neat!" when we mean Jeanne has a lot of charm, and it hardly makes sense to say "Jeanne is careful!" for the same purpose. Aptness is not just a matter of familiarity. "The counselor had the ethics of a wastepaper basket" is apt and can be appreciated at first hearing without having to be repeated, even if we disagree with the speaker. Like agreement, repetition and familiarity have no bearing on aptness. Novelty, surprise, familiarity, conventionality, and boringness form a dimension largely orthogonal to aptness. Therefore, we can test a new pictorial metaphor by showing it to people to whom it is quite unfamiliar to discover whether it is apt. A good metaphor can engender wide agreement without needing to be explained. People should concur and should not have to become familiar with the metaphor over a long stretch of time before realizing its significance. So far as pictorial metaphor is concerned, the metaphor can be based on the shapes of objects known to vision and touch. If the metaphor is based on appropriate grounds, then it should make sense to the blind as well as to the sighted.

Metaphor

Paul Gabias and I devised a series of studies to show how pictorial metaphors can be judged similarly by the blind and the sighted. We explored one
metaphor that had been offered by some of the blind volunteers: several times
they used curvature to show spin. We presented a picture of a wheel showing
movement by curved spokes with pictures of four other wheels having quite
differently shaped spokes, and asked our informants to discern which set of
spokes best suggested a spinning wheel.

We gave sighted subjects printed copies of the five wheels, and the blind we
gave raised-line drawings of the wheels. The five wheels are shown in figure
7.13. One wheel has curved spokes, another has bent spokes, a third has wavy
spokes, a fourth has dashed spokes, and a fifth has straight spokes extending
beyond the circumference. The task we gave was to discern which picture was

Fig. 7.13. Five metaphoric pictures of wheels, with spokes curved,
bent, wavy, dashed, and extended.

best for showing a spinning wheel, then which one was worst, then which was second best, and then which was second worst. The outcome was that the volunteers ordered the pictures from best to worst.

We tested sighted children, teenagers, and adults, and blind adults. The children, 28 Toronto public school students ages 10–12, were tested in their classroom. They were given the five wheels all on one page; there were five different arrangements, and no two neighboring children got pages with the same arrangement. The blind subjects were given large versions of the wheels (16 cm by 16 cm), one raised-line drawing per page. The sighted teenagers and adults were given photocopy versions of the raised-line drawings.

Eleven sighted adults and teenagers and 15 blind volunteers were recruited from colleges in New York City. The 15 blind volunteers ranged in age from 18 to 25. Four were totally blind from birth, two had had some light sensitivity at one time and now are totally blind, two once had some ability to detect gross objects and now are totally blind, five have had some light sensitivity since birth, one has some light sensitivity now although until age 12 he could distinguish shadows from objects, and one can still detect gross objects in bright light.

All the blind volunteers were unfamiliar with research on pictures for the blind and indicated that they were taken aback by the idea that pictures made by blind people could be recognized by the sighted and other blind people. None of the blind recalled ever using raised-line drawings depicting motion. The blind recruits and the sighted adults were tested individually. All the subjects were reminded, once they had indicated they had finished, that the object was to show a wheel spinning. They were permitted to change their minds from their first attempt, prior to the reminder, to a final attempt, after the reminder. The blind often took as much as 20 minutes to explore the drawings and come to a decision, so a reminder of the wording of the original instructions seemed a sensible idea. Several changed their rankings of the wheels after the reminder. I shall report both their initial and their final rankings.

Best at suggesting spin was given a rank of 1 and worst a rank of 5 (table 7.6). I shall call the kinds of spokes Curved, Bent, Dashed, Wavy, and Extended. The 28 sighted children rated the curved spokes best (mean rank 1.29, near perfect agreement). The other ratings were Bent (2.93), Dashed (3.3), Wavy (3.57), and Extended (3.93). A measure of the amount of agreement among the children—Kendall's coefficient of concordance, W—is highly significant ($W = 0.42$, with four degrees of freedom, $p < 0.01$).

The results from 11 blind subjects who did not change their minds following the reminder are: Curved (1.27), Bent (2.18), Wavy (2.72), Dashed (4.27),

TABLE 7.6

Rankings of wheel drawings from best to worst (1–5) at showing spin.

Volunteers	Type of Spokes				
	Curved	Bent	Wavy	Dashed	Extended
Blind	1.2	2.27	2.67	4.2	4.67
Sighted adults and teenagers	1.28	2.36	3.09	3.27	4.81
Sighted children ages 10–12	1.29	2.93	3.57	3.3	3.93

and Extended (4.5). W is again significant ($W = 0.77$, with 4 d.f., $p < 0.001$). If the four who changed their minds are included, using their final ranking the results are: Curved (1.2), Bent (2.27), Wavy (2.67), Dashed (4.2), and Extended (4.67). W is again significant ($W = 0.81$, with 4 d.f., $p < 0.001$).

The four who changed their responses following a reminder cross all the categories of blindness status: one was totally blind from birth, one had some light sensitivity since birth, one had light sensitivity until age seven and now is totally blind, and one can detect gross objects in bright light.

All three groups strongly agree on the best and worst devices for suggesting movement: curved spokes are best, extended spokes are worst, and bent spokes are judged second-best by all three groups. It is only on the relative merits of wavy and dashed spokes that there is any dispute. The sighted children favor dashed over wavy spokes. The other groups—both sighted and blind—favor wavy spokes, and within each group there is a strong measure of accord.

These results show that although the blind are pictorially inexperienced, they agree with the sighted on the meaning of pictorial devices that violate nature. They rank the devices' power to suggest spin as do the sighted. The measures of accord in the blind are as clear-cut as in the sighted.

Gabias and I felt encouraged to push the case further. Would each of the devices mean the same to the blind and to the sighted? Often our subjects told us that a device that was poor for suggesting spin would be appropriate for suggesting another kind of movement, perhaps wobbly or jerky. Gabias and I took these suggestions to heart and devised a second study using several kinds of motion. We gave a new set of blind and sighted volunteers a list of five kinds of motion and drawings of the five wheels. We asked the participants to pair the motions with the wheels. The kinds of motion were Spinning, Jerky, Wobbly, Too Fast, and Brakes On. The list of kinds of motion was read twice to the volunteers, in different orders for each person, and then the volunteers paired up the wheels with the kinds of motion. The motions were read a third time in a different order when reminders were given.

The sighted subjects were 18 undergraduates from the University of Toronto. The blind subjects were 18 blind adults recruited by advertisement at a conference for the blind. None of these volunteers knew of research on depiction and the blind. All said that they found it surprising that blind people could make pictures intelligible to other blind people and to the sighted. Four of the blind people were totally blind from birth. One was totally blind at age six months. Four were totally blind before they were three years old. Two had light perception for a period. Five have some light sensitivity. One can detect gross objects but never had detail vision. One went blind at age seven months, could detect gross objects until age 15 years, and now has light perception.

The results for both the blind and the sighted are in table 7.7. One of the blind volunteers insisted on using the bent-spokes drawing for suggesting two kinds of motion, and he omitted use of the extended-spokes device entirely. His decisions are included, but excluding him would not affect the analysis. The options preferred by the blind are the options preferred by the sighted in every case ($p < 0.01$).

Sighted subjects made their decisions about kinds of motion relatively quickly, so we asked them to do an additional task. They were asked to rate the success of each type of pictorial device in depicting each type of motion, that is, to do for Jerky, Wobbly, Too Fast, and Brakes On what was done for Spinning in the previous study. The measure of concordance W for the sighted is significant ($W = 0.4$, with four degrees of freedom, $p < 0.001$). There is considerable agreement on the relative orders of each of the devices for each of the kinds of motion.

The blind and sighted volunteers picked curved lines as best representing spin in both studies. Both blind and sighted said that bent lines showed the wheel jerking to and fro, wavy lines meant wobbling, dashed lines meant that the wheel was spinning too fast to make out the spokes, and extended lines meant that the brakes were on. Generally the top-ranked drawing was chosen two-to-one over the second-ranked drawing. All of the devices had at least nine of the 18 subjects in each group (blind or sighted) agreeing on their meaning. If the data from the two groups are pooled, the strongest second preference still had a low rate of agreement: eight out of 36 subjects took extended lines to mean spin. The mean level of agreement for the five most

TABLE 7.7

Judgments of devices indicating different kinds of motion.

Spoke shapes	Motion suggested				
	Spin	Jerky	Wobbly	Too Fast	Brakes On
Curved					
Blind	10	3	2	1	1
Sighted	12	0	3	3	0
Bent					
Blind	0	12	3	0	4
Sighted	2	12	0	0	3
Wavy					
Blind	1	2	11	2	2
Sighted	0	3	14	0	1
Dashed					
Blind	2	1	1	13	1
Sighted	1	1	1	13	2
Extended					
Blind	5	0	1	2	9
Sighted	3	2	0	2	12

preferred options is 23.6 out of 36 subjects. The mean of the remaining 20 options is a mere 3.1.

There seems no doubt that the blind and the sighted match a given metaphoric shape to the same referent. Neither I nor Gabias, with several decades of experience between us in schools and libraries for the blind, have ever come across these devices being used to convey motion to the blind. Nor do we know of anyone who teaches the meaning of these devices to the blind. Evidently, the blind volunteers figured out the significance of these devices individually and independently. The sighted probably do likewise, in childhood, as I know of no custom of instruction in these devices. Like the blind volunteers, the sighted subjects may have encountered some of the devices for the first time during the testing session. Whereas wavy lines for unsteady motion and dashed lines for speedy motion are reasonably common in comic books, the three others are not. A sample of three comic books from Britain (*Hotspur, Beano,* and *Buster*) and three from the the United States (*Conan, Spiderman,* and *Green Lantern*) contained the following devices for motion:

trailing lines, blur, obscured background, clouds behind a moving character, vibration lines as arcs around a silhouette, posture and location devices, change of background color (blackness of a space becoming white behind a moving object), incomplete outline, and multiple postures of the limbs attached to the figure. The curved-, bent-, and extended-line devices were absent.

Actually, I can well recall my first encounter as a child with a special kind of motion device, a long trail of *c*'s behind a spaceship. The ship was the *Black Cat* in "Dan Dare," the feature story in the first issues of *The Eagle,* a British comic book. I felt that the *ccccccc* trail was unlike the swooping ribbon of speed lines behind Dan Dare's spacecraft. The trail of arcs indicated to me that the *Black Cat* (driven by the despicable Mekon) putted along, albeit silently and somewhat unpleasantly. It had an entirely different principle of propulsion than Dan Dare's craft. I imagine that the blind volunteers in our study were having a somewhat similar experience. Perhaps they felt surprised, as I had in childhood, that these quirky devices often suggested a kind of movement. There can be something curiously apt about these odd deviations from realistic outline drawings.

What kind of comprehension of these devices would arise spontaneously? To understand a verbal metaphor like "The jailer was stony," the listener examines the two parts for something in common and realizes that stone and the jailer are unyielding, the one to physical pressure and the other to entreaty. Presumably, if the graphic devices are metaphors, a device and its referent share a crucial feature, though in the picture it is in the wrong place. The curved lines representing spokes were a useful device for showing spin. In a smooth spin, points on the wheel move in arcs of constant curvature. In reality the arcs are across time; in the device they are across space. Thus something appropriate is shown, albeit in the wrong place. A switch between a temporal path and a spatial path has occurred. Also, a point on the wheel moves in a circle around the hub. An arc of this circle has been used as the shape of a spoke, although a spoke radiates straight from the hub. The shape is actually put out of place.

The bent-line device showed a jerky to-and-fro motion. This kind of motion involves an abrupt change in direction. A bent line has an abrupt change in direction too. Here a switch between a time-based change and a spatial change has occurred. A similar analysis fits the wavy-line device. Wobbly motion is a sinusoid in time, and its equivalent in a static picture is a wavy line.

The dashed-line device may work differently. Here an obvious common feature between the device and its referent is an inability to perceive the whole. Parts are missing to perception—in the picture through not being drawn, in the referent by moving too fast for the visual or haptic perceptual system to register them. Gombrich (1960) points out that the great Spanish painter Velásquez is credited with using the absence of spokes in a picture to show a wheel spinning; in the early nineteenth century Berwick, an illustrator from northern England, used partially drawn spokes for the same purpose. Absence of parts is now a common device for showing motion in comics, having become widespread by the beginning of the twentieth century.

The extended-line device had two popular referents. The most favored one was Brakes On. Brakes can be applied to the exterior of the rim of a wheel. The exterior projections of the extended-line device may be taken as mechanical parts touching the wheel to retard its motion. The second-most popular referent for this picture was Spinning. Some subjects mentioned that the wheel was like a sailor's capstan or a ship's wheel that is easily turned because of its projecting knobs. If brakes and knobs have indeed been the basis for the interpretations, then the interpretation is based on context or associations, not the path of the motion. There is no translation here from space to time, no use of an abstract equivalence. Rather, the shapes and locations of adjuncts to the motion—components causing the motion—are being considered by the blind for the extensions from the wheel.

The knobs and brakes are shapes that are easy to bring to mind when seeing the extended-line device. Blind people actually volunteered such reasons for their choices in this instance. But it would be misleading to suggest that explicit, clear arguments can be given by our subjects for each of their choices. Their comments were usually vague or circular. When a volunteer was asked why a shape was picked for a certain kind of motion, the response usually was simply something like, "Well, it reminds me of that movement." The fit appears to be perceptual or intuitive rather than thought-out in a manner easy to make explicit. The fit is found or noticed; it is not something arising from conventions or formal argument. One might say that the pairing of picture and motion depends on formal or design criteria. I am tempted to say that the devices work perceptually and not through a process of association (with the possible exception of the Brakes On/Extended device, which is associated with a ship's wheel). The devices genuinely suggest a kind of motion to me, and each device is in keeping with some kinds of motion and not others. Once the usefulness of a device becomes evident, I may try to work out why the device works as it does. Whatever the process may be, the lesson of the experiments is that blind people and sighted people come to similar resolutions when matching devices to referents. It seems reasonable to suppose that the intuitions and percepts of shape that underlie the resolutions are also similar.

Metaphor

BREAKING RULES FOR GOOD REASONS

In the Genesis myth, man loses his place in an orderly universe (the Garden of Eden) by breaking a rule. The transgression brings disorder and dismay. The undercurrent to this chapter is a different myth, where deliberate rule breaking has a special, honored place. What the studies on metaphor reveal is that we can go beyond the limits of our domain. We can expand beyond the rules because people are not rule followers but rule users. Once we know the rules we know their limits, and once we know the limits we can react to them. We can do something uncalled-for, not just to be in error, but to communicate with others who appreciate the rules and their limits as we do. I must stress that the rules are not modified or thrown away, but are subservient to the will to go beyond them. The limits are intelligible, and we do not go beyond them for no reason. The breach of the rules must be in a sensible place, and the actual violation must be apt. Otherwise the violation is random and can only be understood if someone explains it.

Some rule violations occur out of ignorance; others are deliberate devilment. Some are meant just to test the limits of authority. All of these violations, however, are specious in the sense that they are not motivated by a genuine attempt to incorporate territory that lies beyond the limits of our regulations. Metaphors are rule violations that are based on pertinent knowledge. They are aimed at communication and affirm the rule they violate. In depiction, the target declared to be out of reach of the line elements and configurations of literal outline drawing is something that can be indicated indirectly once metaphors can be countenanced. The rule violation capitalizes on prior rules. It allows a target that is otherwise hard to draw to be shown by something that can be imaged, something that has an essential property in common with the target. One way to do this is to substitute a spatial pattern for a temporal pattern. Another is to borrow what is proper and informative in one context and apply it where it does not literally belong.

There are many ways of making a picture metaphoric. A shadow or a reflection of the central object may show the protagonist's eventual fate to the viewer, much as prolepsis does in language. The use of knobs on a ship's wheel to suggest spin is a kind of synecdoche. Hyperbole appears in caricatures daily. Fig leaves covering sex organs are euphemisms. Pictures can minify and so understate a tragedy, with the meiosis serving to deepen our feelings. Pictures can show ancillaries and so put us in mind of the intended referents—a trope called metonymy. Evidently every kind of metaphor found in language can be used in pictures (Kennedy, 1982a; Kennedy and Simpson, 1982).

Metaphor

Pictures can display particulars such as people fishing to raise general ideas such as vain striving. Of course, trying to achieve a goal is both more general and more specific than going fishing. Not all fishers or politicians are in search of something, and not all seekers are fishers or politicians. Consequently, to understand metaphors we have to use some method of comprehension that takes a particular picture or saying and tries to find the right level of generality (Arnheim, 1974). In looking at a pictorial trope, we often have to ask what *more general* idea or *more abstract* notion the particular shapes may be meant to stand for. We have to ask what is the particular object or motion suggested by a device that indicates the referent. To find the particular referent at the right level of generality is not always easy, and it often involves good general knowledge of a culture and its roles and artifacts (Gombrich, 1974, 1982).

If we have to take people fishing in a cartoon as betokening politicians, the fact that there is a cartoonist who means to convey something about affairs of state has to come to mind or the picture will lose its point. Similarly, the blind have to consider the person behind a metaphoric picture of motion. They must ask what is intended, not just what is similar to the shape. Anomalous lines have to be more than error. If they are meant, then to be apt they should capitalize on important features of what is meant. The practiced sighted person looking for what a cartoonist means and the unpracticed blind person feeling for an apt device are guided by the same kind of comprehension. Metaphor in a communication system arises because we know that other people often intend meanings beyond the limits of any particular word or picture. Surely humans have a great deal of knowledge in common about the shapes of objects. We also realize that much of our knowledge is held in common. Further, we realize that our peers can often anticipate that we are relying on shared knowledge to communicate indirectly. Therefore, we both, the blind and the sighted, can offer devices we intend as metaphors, and since we do have much in common, we can often succeed in communicating with one another by means of them.

251

CHAPTER EIGHT

Impressions
and Universals

Picture perception is part of the general problem of information and representation. How a thinking, sensitive creature can deal with representations is no small mystery. My task here has chiefly been to examine properties of physical displays and to show how these can serve us as representations without our needing to be trained in recognizing specific conventions for the properties. The lesson is that pictorial representation is intelligible in this way whether the property being tested is a matter of a line or pattern or metaphor. Picture perception involves all three of these and so it is not just one enigma but several. Outlines form configurations, and the configurations make good sense when they copy what scenes do and, at times, when they transgress the proper order of things.

Outline, shape, and metaphor certainly span a wide range of issues. But more topics need to be covered if pictorial representation is ever to be fully and deeply understood. Any investigation of depiction can only do a reasonably thorough job on a few issues, of course. But it may be wise here to survey some of the lines of inquiry that have been initiated but not yet pursued at length.

The purpose of this chapter is not to take up a single problem but to recognize several promising leads and the ideas and quandaries they raise. What does it mean to get a perceptual impression from a representation? What is an axis? What can a picture show? How may outline pictures have originated? What can be amodal? What can a line picture reveal about a psychological state or a property of a surface other than shape? How can pictorial style be captured in nonvisual media? None of these topics have attracted diligent investigations. None of them can stand on their own as convincing experiments. But they map the stimulating ideological terrain that lies around the problems of line, form, and communication in graphic images. On occasion, they show us that the basic theoretical tools we need to undertake their further inquiry are not available at present. Consequently, the studies provide empirical stepping stones—an impressive path to as-yet unknown theories.

FIGURE-GROUND AND PERCEPTUAL IMPRESSIONS

The shape seen in an outline drawing can be the shape of a surface bounded by a line so that the shape acts like a profile, or it can be the shape of a line itself acting like a wire or crack or ridge. In this chapter I shall report studies on recognition of both these kinds of shapes in outline drawings.

An outline drawing can use lines to show a foreground surface ending at an occluding edge or boundary, with the foreground surface being to one side of the line and the background being on the other side. This is what Rubin (1915) called figure-ground perception. Rubin noted that the appearance given by the outline drawing can change remarkably if vision reverses its use of the line so that what was taken to be foreground becomes background and what was background becomes foreground. The picture remains physically constant during the perceptual reversal. What changes is the impression the perceiver has of the spatial layout depicted. The outcome is that one physical pattern gives rise to two different spatial impressions. This depicted space can change while the physical picture remains constant (Peterson, Harvey, and Weidenbacher, 1991).

In describing their reactions to pictures, blind adults from BOOST in Toronto have sometimes hinted at an impression of a spatial layout in addition to the flat surface of the depiction itself. Nat drew a balloon on a string as a circle and a line. Then he wanted to show that the circle was a mound or protuberance rather than a hollow, so he criss-crossed the circle with straight lines from rim to rim (fig. 8.1). The pattern would give the right impression, he said, if one felt the lines as a group instead of individually: "If you feel like with your hand—I can't explain it any other way—but if you feel—just get the general idea, you know, without caring so much about each line, you know, but just get the general feel of it—it should give you the idea of a three-dimensional thing almost."

Pat mentioned something similar as she drew a jar as two straight vertical

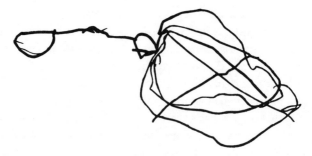

Fig. 8.1. Drawing of a balloon on a string, by Nat (early, totally blind). The interior lines give an impression of "a three-dimensional thing almost."

lines joined by a curve at the bottom (fig. 8.2): "I think from the bottom lines . . . it would give the illusion of roundness as opposed to a definite concrete . . . it would give an image of . . . to me I think it would represent an image of roundness as opposed to a firm, firm factual kind of thing. I think it's more of an illusion of roundness."

Another blind adult, Cal, drew the jar with central lines thick in the middle and thinning out toward the periphery (fig. 8.3). He explained this device: "Well, it just seemed to me that if you were concentrating—you know, if you were to put your hand on a jar just on one spot and you can tell just by putting your hand on that one spot that it does have that curved shape—it gives me the impression that the parts that are curving away from you on either side are lighter whereas the part that's right closest towards you would be heavier."

Nat, Pat, and Cal all may be saying that the feel of the picture can involve

Fig. 8.2. Drawing of a jar, by Pat (early, totally blind).

Fig. 8.3. Drawing of a jar, by Cal (early, totally blind).

some kind of experience of three-dimensionality, roundness, or a surface receding into depth. Their language, however, is not conclusive on this point. Nat's mention of an "idea" of an object is vague, and Pat's "illusion" of roundness, like Cal's "impression," concerns the object as much as the device. It is hard to be sure which comments pertain to the percept, which to the device, and which to the referent. These difficult notions are worth pursuing because the basis of depiction is the fact that pictures allow us the *perception* of an object. A squiggle can change its appearance from time to time if we take it to depict a mountain range at first and then later take it to depict paint dripping down the side of a can. That the appearance of the line changes has been demonstrated in experiments on recognition. Rubin (1915) showed that if one side of a line or contour is seen as foreground on one occasion and the other side is taken to be foreground on a later occasion, often the display will not be recognized on that second appearance. That is, the foreground change can seriously impair recognition. Hence, the foreground and background relations seen in the display control the observer's attempts to identify whether the display has been seen before or not.

Rubin's experiment can be extended to the blind to show that the pictorial effects arising from haptic pictures are sufficient to affect recognition. Consider figure 8.4. It can look like a profile facing to the left or like a profile facing to the right. Notice that the depicted faces are quite different, although the line of course remains unchanged physically as the display alternates perceptually from one face to another. Ramona Domander and I presented raised-line drawings of profiles like figure 8.4 to blind volunteers and asked them to describe, say, the left-looking face; then a few seconds later the same display was given them with instructions to describe the right-looking face.

Fig. 8.4. Drawing of a profile facing right, or a profile facing left.

The volunteers were asked if the first display and the second display were physically the same or different.

In our first version of the experiment, we planned a set of such trials to discover how long it would take a blind person to realize what we were doing. We initially expected that it would take at most a few trials before Scot (age 13, early, totally blind), the test subject, would notice that in each trial he was given the same display twice and that only the instructions changed. The alternative hypothesis was that a pictorial change in the referent controls recognition quite strongly in touch, and that Scot would not readily notice that an unchanging display was being described differently on each of its presentations.

The exact procedure was as follows. Scot was given a picture with a line running irregularly down the page. He was asked to imagine that there was an eye to one side—say, the left—at a particular location indicated by our placing his finger there. Then he was asked to feel the line, running his hand from top to bottom, slowly, and tell us where the facial features were—hair, brow, nose, mouth, and so on. The line was about 13 cm long. The maximum peak-to-trough height—the swing of the line from the tip of the "nose" to the recesses of the "mouth"—was about 3 cm. Then Scot was given a second picture, also said to be a profile, and he was asked to imagine the eye again, this time on the opposite side. Again, Scot felt his way along the line, identifying the features.

Next, Scot was given the test display. His task was to determine whether this display was "old," that is, one of the first two sheets of paper, or "new" if it was a different sheet. In the trials we presented "old" and "new" test displays in random order. The "new" displays, like the "old," had a wavy line with a dot that could be taken as a profile and eye. If the test stimulus was one of the "old" pictures, then it could be presented to Scot as either of the two profiles it depicted. Scot undertook 32 trials. In 16 the test display was "old," eight of these using the first profile he had been shown and eight using the foreground-background reversed condition. In 16 trials the test display was "new," half with a leftward-looking profile and half the reverse.

Scot scored 15 correct out of 24 in the "new" and "old" trials combined (nine out of 16 "old," and six out of eight "new"). In the foreground-background reversed condition only one correct response (an "old" display) was obtained in the eight trials ($p < 0.01$, if p correct is 15 out of 24).

Scot called the displays "new" when they were foreground-background reversed. We asked him explicitly about this. He said that the displays seemed to him to be new sheets, new displays, not the same displays with the assignment of the eyes switched from one side to another.

Scot's results on the "new" and "old" combined are not terribly accurate—nine errors in 24 trials. And we were concerned that asking questions of Scot after the test, rather than giving him unambiguous instructions before the test, left some room for equivocation. We determined to test more subjects, with displays containing clearer differences and more elaborate instructions. Displays with clearer differences would increase accuracy on the "new" and "old" trials, and the more detailed instructions would emphasize that anytime a display reappeared it was to be called "old," even if the accompanying description had changed. To make the displays easier to distinguish, the features on some were drawn in a more exaggerated fashion: noses were enlarged, chins lengthened, brows drawn with more sweeping curves. The peak-to-trough height was about 6 cm. Both the displays from the previous experiment and the new enhanced displays were used in the present experiment. They were divided into three groups: the 16 most enhanced displays, the 16 least exaggerated displays (those with peak-to-trough height less than 2 cm), and the middle 16. Every trial used at least two of the three degrees of exaggeration.

To clarify the instructions, the subjects were familiarized with a display and expressly shown how an eye imagined to be first on the left and then on the right side of a line gives rise to two different faces. It was stressed that the same display—the same sheet—could come up in a test trial with the location of the eye changed but still be the same physical display. It was said that this display should be called "old" rather than "new." Next came two practice trials, one "old" and one "new." A third practice trial ("new") was given to two subjects whose judgment had been incorrect on a practice trial.

In total, there were eight experimental trials; four were "old," two were "new," and two were "foreground-background reversed," with the order randomized. Again, half the presentation pairs had the imaginary eye on the left and half had it on the right.

The subjects were three girls and two boys, ages 8–14, tested in Calgary. Two were totally blind from birth, one had a pinpoint of vision, one could make out large print, and one had good vision until total loss of vision at age five. With the exception of the early-sighted child, neither the parents of the children nor the children themselves reported training with haptic pictures. The children's schools did not make pictures a part of the curriculum. The children were taught in regular schools, not segregated in a special school for the blind, so there would have been many opportunities to overhear discussions of pictures. But art classes did not seem to include picture making for the blind. As one parent put it after seeing some drawings made by her child on completion of this study, "Now our child can have her drawings up on the wall like everyone else." (One child, who appeared surprised at her own abilities with the displays, came back to me after I had tested her, knocked on the door of the testing room while I was working with another child, and politely asked if she could have some of the pictures she'd made to take home to show her parents that she could draw. On a cold Canadian winter day it warmed my heart to see her interest and surprise.)

In the six "old" and "new" conditions combined, three of the children scored six correct responses, and the other two made one error each. In the "foreground-background reversed" trials, all the subjects reported that all the stimuli were new ($p < 0.01$, since p of an inaccurate response is 1/6 per subject, estimating conservatively from the two subjects who made errors, and there are five subjects).

The first study, with Scot, was conducted cautiously. Scot was not told about foreground-background reversal. Our supposition was that if we told him about reversal and demonstrated it to him, he might try reversing the stimuli frequently and thereby frustrate the experiment. No warmup trials were given and everything hinged on Scot following our instructions properly. Surely, we thought, at some point in the 32 trials, which lasted about an hour, Scot would twig what was going on and the study would come to a halt. How long would it take? we wondered. Scot is an assertive boy, a competitive swimmer, free-spoken and confident. He commented quite openly on many aspects of our work with him. He would discern the manipulation after a few minutes at most, we thought. In fact, Scot apparently never discovered the trick. Discussions with him afterward included asking him point-blank if he thought we had ever given him an eye-reversed display in the test condition. He said no. When we explained that we had, he was amused and intrigued, and the displays seemed to become all the more interesting to him.

It is curious indeed that a display Scot saw once could feel to him like a new display a few seconds later on its second appearance. Motivated by Scot's results, the second phase of the study used stimuli that were much more differentiated and began by demonstrating that reversal could occur, using the demonstration to remove any question about the meaning of the instructions. Both parts of the study—one part using a long sequence of trials with no demonstration of reversal, the other using a demonstration of reversal to clarify instructions but few trials—suggest that pictorial foreground-background reversal can impair recognition by the blind.

As we visually inspect figure 8.4, we find that its "looks" change if we switch foreground and background. It is not like a graph line that remains the same whether we call it "mean monthly rainfall" or "median yearly income." To change the name of the line does not change its looks. Surely the change in looks, not any change in names, is responsible for the decrease in recognition that research has found with the sighted (Rubin, 1915; Zusne, 1970). The impression given by the foreground face seen after reversal can be quite different from the impression given by the face seen before the reversal. Our study found a change in haptic recognition when foreground and background were reversed. If the logic of the visual case holds, something analogous to the looks of the display may have changed. We might say that the feel or impression given by the display has changed.

What is the perceptual impression that may have changed? In vision, when we take a line to show foreground to one side, it results in one side looking far and the other near, the far side going behind the near, and in the case of profiles the foreground appears rounded rather than just flat. The referent of the line *appears* in perception; it is not just *understood* to be meant.

It is a rare sketch that puts in enough detail for anyone to be able to calculate the proper sizes, depths, and orientations of the objects in the array. So drawing relies on elements like line for its effects. It does not rest on patterns that are specific to calculable depths and slants. A drawing often presents just enough of a familiar object to tell us what kind of object it is, what species it belongs to. It may also be accompanied by a label or caption from the person who presents us with the drawing. Taking the caption along with the drawing, we know where the foreground and background are meant to be. If the elements in the drawing are suitable, foreground and background are seen, not just meant, and the line can be viewed in terms of certain foreground-background relationships. The relations are *seen as* an edge without fooling us into thinking an edge is actually present.

The foreground-background relationships can be a flat object against a flat background or an empty space, or a rounded object against either background, or two surfaces coming together, both foregrounded, at a corner or crack. Or the line itself can be a foreground object like a wire or stick with background on both sides. What the study with Scot and the children shows is that mere squiggles can be taken to be foreground-background arrangements by the blind, and when the blind take the line this way, perceptual impressions arise in sufficient strength to control recognition. The effects are intense enough to impair recognition of a physically unchanging display returning for inspection after a mere few seconds' absence. These strong impressions arise without the line being so detailed that it could be nothing but a face. I doubt whether many of our squiggles would be taken to be faces if we did not make the suggestion. Accordingly, lines seem to give impressions of edges of foreground objects to the blind without need of unambiguous, informative, perceptible detail.

An ability to take a line as a representation of a feature of relief, notably a foreground-background arrangement, is surely the crucial factor that enables sketches of objects to be effective in touch. It confers undoubted advantages. First, tangible edges and corners are the boundaries of the haptic world. The shape of the object is given not so much by heat, cold, texture, and surface qualities like oiliness but purely by the beginnings and ends of surfaces. If a line is not only readily taken to show an edge but also gives the feel of an edge, it can represent the basic shapes of the furniture of the tactile world in a perceptibly impressive way. Second, even a child can make a line be active perceptually in a drawing if the sketch does not have to be unambiguous. If the only ingredients needed for a picture are a squiggly line and an attempt to take it as depicting an edge, then a child can feel or draw an imperfect, simplified version of part of the object and successfully will it to be depicting a foreground-background arrangement.

The will to depict is evident in a blind child's list drawings, where by fiat a mark stands for an individual feature of an object. A perceptual experience of depiction probably follows hard on the heels of list drawings, for quite young blind children use outline for individual features of objects. It makes sense that first would come the will to depict and the use of fiat, then the use of outline. But on the limited evidence available at present it is by no means certain yet which comes first, fiat or perceptual experience of depiction, and some five-year-old blind children making drawings switch from one to another and back again within a few minutes.

STICK FIGURES

Once the blind recognize that the line gives suitable impressions, this can provide a base for further development of drawing skill. Some of the development of drawing concerns the scope of outline. Relief foreground-background arrangements work well, but some other referents do not. Pain, noise, and smell, for example, are judged by the blind to be unsuitable for line depiction. Presumably, the reason is that line gives definite impressions of the edges of surfaces of objects, but when the will to depict tries to mold an experience of pain, noise, or smell around the tangible line, no suitable impression arises.

In searching for uses of line, a moment may come when the adult or child realizes: I have reached the limits not of myself but of the line. The person may test in his or her own perceptual experience and find one use of line appropriate and another inappropriate. A line cannot depict the boundary of a pain in a finger or a tingle of excitement in the hands and feet or a knot of anxiety if it does not create a perceptual impression that simulates pain or anxiety. But outline drawing has an additional component besides the line itself, and that is the pattern. What cannot be achieved as a perceptual impression let loose by the line can sometimes be indicated by the pattern. Patterns can suggest not only affect but also complex attitudes and relationships. Kathy N. (early, totally blind), for example, volunteered to draw a raised-line picture of marriage (fig. 8.5). She drew linked pairs of small circles. The pairs are sometimes close, sometimes apart. Sometimes the links have dots on them representing children. The pairs are surrounded by a corral with a gate. The gate's handle or lock is on the inside; the implication is that marriage is a voluntary bond.

Outline drawings can show states and relations by depicting scenes of various kinds. The line in each part of the scene can stand for a feature of surface layout, and the layout can be arranged to indicate a psychological state. Sighted people see pictures suggesting states such as sadness or pride, or roles such as mother or father, or relations such as someone leaving someone else. If blind people are to make effective use of pictures, the psychological states, roles, and relations that pictures can express to the sighted need to be conveyed to the blind as well. One highly economical device for doing so is the stick figure. A scene containing a few people drawn as stick figures and depicted in various postures can convey moods and passions to the sighted

Fig. 8.5. Drawing of marriage, by Kathy N. (early, totally blind).

person. Accordingly, Ramona Domander and I presented stick figures to blind and sighted volunteers. Would they mean the same to both groups?

Emotions like sadness are mental states. They can be shown by postures although the state is not quite the same as the posture: an actor can strike a sad pose without actually feeling sad. And we often feel emotions like sadness without revealing them to anyone but our intimates. In a word, our postures can be poses. Hence while the postures are to some extent universal, they are also conventional (Gombrich, 1972). It may be that the conventionality is not quite as reinforced for the blind as the sighted, who regularly see conventional melodramatic pictures. The meaning of a representation is largely independent of its frequency, however, so the meanings could be clear to both groups even if one group has had more frequent use of such pictures than has the other.

We asked the volunteers to examine raised-line drawings of simple postures and to choose their meanings from among a few alternatives that we presented to them. In this task the primary referent was the significance of the human posture. The representation was a few schematic marks on paper showing poses of people in various relations to one another.

The 15 blind volunteers, again mostly from BOOST, were tested in Toronto. They included six congenitally blind (five totally blind since birth, one with light sensitivity since birth). Others had a variety of conditions, six being effectively blind at age three. One was totally blind since age four (a decline in sight from age six months), one was totally blind since age one year, one had mere light sensitivity since age six months, one had 2 percent vision since birth and by age 12 had lost all vision, one had very low vision since birth and had lost all vision by age 14, one had a rapid loss since age six months and had lost all vision by age six. There were also three late blind volunteers (one had low vision since birth and two had total vision loss at seven and 10 years of age, respectively). The early blind subject with total vision loss at age 12 was Scot, from Calgary, tested at age 13. The remaining blind subjects ranged in age from 23 to 31. All had participated in at least one previous study of ours. We also included 13 sighted children, ages 7–11, at a public school, testing each of the sighted children individually with inkprint versions of the figures. Sixteen sighted undergraduates at the University of Toronto also participated in the study.

The figures were highly abbreviated line drawings, so schematic that we decided to call them "twig figs" since they are even more stripped down than most stick figures. Being schematic, they have the advantage that they are easy to explore in touch within a few moments. They comprise a small oval for the head, then a long line for the body and then a short horizontal line for the feet.

We told our volunteers that the twig figs stood for people, in pairs, engaged in various actions. The twig figs were arranged in contrasting pairs. We said, in each trial, "Here are two pictures. In each picture there are two people. One pair of people is doing X. One pair is doing Y. Which is which?" So for each set of figures, subjects were given labels and asked to judge which label best fit which pair of twig figs.

There were six pairs of pictures, each picture containing two people (fig. 8.6). The pairs were given in different orders. Every twig fig was always paired with the same partner. The labels were:

1. A pair of people talking vs. angry people
2. Two old people vs. two sad people
3. Two proud people vs. two polite people
4. One person walking past another vs. one person walking behind another
5. Someone who has just seen a pretty girl vs. someone leaving another person
6. Mother and child vs. father and child

We were somewhat concerned about the option "someone who has just seen a pretty girl." But in the first place the verb *see* is used as common currency by the blind. "I'll see you around," they might say, and "I'll see" or "I see" to mean "perhaps" or "I understand" (Landau and Gleitman, 1985; Bigelow, 1990). We also thought the reference to "a pretty girl" was a tad sexist. We decided to use this form instead of a phrase like "someone who has just taken an interest in someone of the opposite sex," which has the disadvantage of sounding clumsy. The short form seemed acceptable. None of the volunteers objected. In hindsight, however, I would prefer a less politically loaded option such as "someone who had just noticed someone interesting."

Agreement on the assignment of the labels was high (table 8.1). Agreement

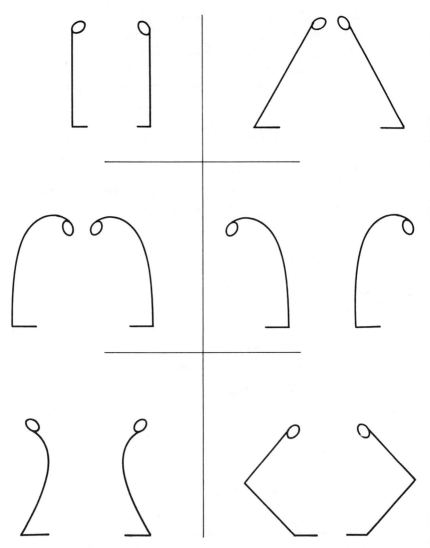

Fig. 8.6. "Twig figs"—highly abbreviated stick figures.

among the children was 95 percent, with three pairs of pictures reaching 100 percent agreement. The sighted adults agreed with the majority opinion among the children 85 percent of the time, with two pairs of pictures reaching 100 percent agreement. The blind agreed with the majority reactions by the sighted 77 percent of the time (early blind 76 percent, late blind 79 percent). Only for walking past/walking behind was there 100 percent agreement

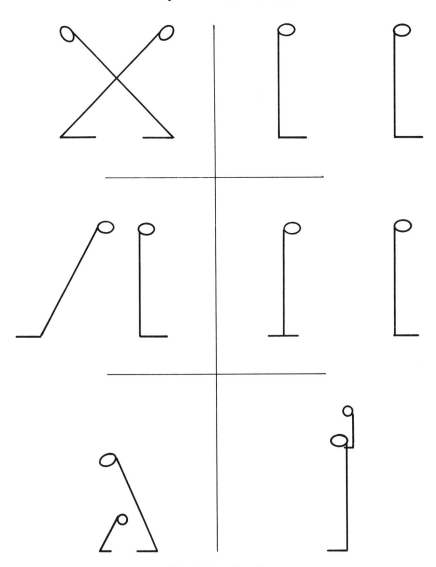

Fig. 8.6 (continued).

by the blind. For another three of the judgments (old/sad, polite/proud, leaving/seen a pretty girl) there was agreement by 13 of the 15 blind respondents.

On one judgment the blind generally concurred with the sighted but with caveats. The angry/talking pair was ambiguous, several said. They noted that the people leaning together could be intense and angry, or could be very

TABLE 8.1

Identifications of "twig figs." The percentage given
is the agreement with the majority decision by the children.

Pairs of Pictures	Sighted Children	Blind Adults and Teenagers
Angry or talking	100	73
Old or sad	92	87
Polite or proud	92	87
Walking past or behind	100	100
Leaving or seen a pretty girl	100	87
Mother and child or father and child	85	27

friendly, indeed deeply interested in one another. Their alternative response
to the figure makes visual sense, I would judge. The alternative pair can seem
coldly hostile, as though standing erect stiffly.

On only one of the six figures did the responses of the blind depart
noticeably from those of the sighted: father-child/mother-child. The blind
said that the father-child figure was hard to make out, and it was often
interpreted as a small-headed adult holding a baby with a large head, at chest
height—that is, at the breast. The adult's head was taken to be the child's and
vice versa. With this tactual impression in mind, we tested eight blindfolded
sighted undergraduates, giving them the tactual pictures under the same
conditions as the blind. Seven of the eight made the same assignments of the
father-child/mother-child figures as had the blind, that is, the opposite judgment to that of the sighted children and adults in the tests based on vision.

Overall the agreement among the blindfolded students with the majority
opinion of the sighted children and adults was 69 percent. The blind rate of
concurrence (77 percent) with majority opinion is midway between that for
the blindfolded (69 percent) and that for the sighted adults (85 percent) and
children (95 percent). This result is good evidence that the basis for these
judgments is as available to the blind as to the sighted.

In sum, the blind and the sighted agree substantially on the interpretation
of twig figs. The one exception is due to faulty discrimination of shapes, which
could be rectified presumably by enlarging the figure.

The schematic figures here show events, relations between people, moods
such as sadness, and traits such as pride. Evidently touch is an appropriate
sense for depicting a range of scenes with psychological significance.

The blind are as interested in moods, relations, and dispositions as the sighted are. If there is any universality to the poses used to express feelings and intentions, it should be possible for the blind to interpret schematic postures much as the sighted do. This means that these ideas can be depicted and not just enacted when discussing them, for instance, with children. It is important and useful that these postures can be drawn in brief, bare figures that communicate to the blind as they communicate to the sighted.

UNIVERSALS OR CONVENTIONS

The twentieth century has produced a store of critical thought about how pictures function, how pictorial skills developed through the ages, and what constraints pictures operate within. In Gombrich's (1974) words, it is important to clarify the potential of the image in communication, to ask what it can and cannot do. Pictures not only show us objects; they also allow us to transform ideas and metaphors into useful images. Previous chapters have explored the line standing for relief edges, organizational principles of spatial representation, and the deployment of deliberate errors. Here I shall examine the thesis that many aspects of pictures are conventions, varying from society to society, rather than universals.

Fundamentally, there are two conceptions of pictures. One idea is that pictures are based on social conventions. The other is that they are governed by universals of perception and cognition. Of course, fashions in pictures come and go—that is not in dispute. The argument is rather about picturing per se.

In one conception, pictures are products of social forces that are more profound than the tides of fashion. The convention thesis is that technology, education, and popular culture work together to modify the beholder's reaction to pictures. Together, these influences are thought to control much more than the beholder's preference for one genre or style of pictures. In theory, they control the beholder's ability to recognize what any picture depicts. The convention theory is supported by comments from European travelers in regions with little contact with technology, who offer rather ethnocentric reports such as "Take a picture in black and white and the natives cannot see it. You may tell the natives: 'This is a picture of an ox and a dog,' and the people will look at it and look at you and the look says that they consider you a liar" (Laws, quoted in Deregowski, 1989). Marshall Holmes, an educator in Ethiopia in the 1920s, interviewed in 1980, reported to me that he found that rural Ethiopian villagers could not recognize highly detailed realistic black-and-white drawings of local flora and fauna on first examination of the pictures.

Deregowski (1989) noted that the pictures that were initially abstruse to people from nonpictorial cultures often became recognizable after a few minutes' inspection. Tutoring was not necessary. Holmes made the same observation to me. The villagers, he observed, would recognize the pictures spontaneously after a while. Hence the convention thesis is untenable. If it were taken to the extreme—a transport that some scholars have in fact advocated—the convention thesis would hold that every aspect of pictures rests on a learned convention, and spontaneous recognition would be impossible.

Goodman (1968) is often alleged to hold an extreme convention thesis. He argues that realistic representation depends "not upon imitation or illusion or information but upon inculcation" (p. 38). He qualifies his position to a degree, saying that "almost any picture may represent almost anything" (p. 38), with some hedging by the term *almost*. He also notes that "judgements of similarity in selected and familiar respects are . . . as objective and categorical as any that are made in describing the world" (p. 39). But despite these cautions, he is an enthusiastic conventioneer in asserting "just as a red light says 'stop' on the highway and 'port' at sea, so the same stimulus gives rise to different experiences under different conditions" (p. 14); and so far as depiction is concerned, "the behaviour of light sanctions neither our usual nor any other way of rendering space" (p. 19). Related arguments are made by Herskovits (1948) and Steinberg (1953), and there is a consistent line of allied arguments from Wartofsky (1977, 1980), who asserts emphatically that pictures are seen as convention dictates and in turn pictures help shape our perception of the world.

When we consider a simple line drawing and see a foreground object set against a background, this is due to some convention we have learned in childhood, the extreme convention theory holds. The thesis is that physically lines are not found at the edges of objects, hence to identify one with the other is learned. When observers examine a picture and see depth represented systematically, following a perspective system, a convention theory tells us that we are obeying just one of many possible systems, all equally valid (Goodman, 1968), and this one system we have adopted merely out of social consensus. Kubovy (1986) points out that artists often use a projective system that contains compromises, departures from exact perspective. Goodman notes that this could be used as support for the convention thesis. An alternative explanation is that the compromises indicate strong biases in vision, limits to the extent that untutored vision can follow the laws of perspective (Olmer, 1943; Pirenne, 1970; Nicholls and Kennedy, 1991).

The convention thesis can go beyond the analysis of line elements and perspective systems. When we take a concrete picture to symbolize an abstract idea, the convention thesis can continue to argue that this is as much a convention as the adoption of a logo, emblem, or mascot. Further, when a picture shows a quality such as hard or soft, or a mood such as anger, this would be interpreted by the extreme thesis as due to education in a convention, much as white symbolizes simplicity in some cultures and mourning in others.

I have argued in the preceding chapters that the evidence from the blind supports a diametrically opposed conception of pictures. In this radically different theory, pictures are products of capacities of the human mind that are not specifically taught. In the use of outline, vantage point, and metaphor the blind reveal abilities that are not conventions taught to them prior to their use.

Brian Molyneux (1980) of the Royal Ontario Museum, following the work of Selwyn Dewdney (1970), an early student of Canadian Indian petroglyphs or rock-face paintings, noted the universality of recognizable pictures in the rocks and caves of prehistory. He observed to me that on every site he had inspected there were always some pictures he recognized. No matter whether it is located in Europe or Africa or America or Australia, early "parietal" art (art found on rock faces) is often recognizable by untrained contemporary observers (Kennedy and Silvers, 1974). The modern eye can often tell what the lines and contours stand for without instruction or prompts. There are sites on every continent where the flora and fauna of the cave artist's time are plainly identifiable. The cave artist's language would be uninterpretable to the uninitiated, but the daubs use a means of communication that is universal.

It seems unlikely that picture making could have been invented in one place as a set of graphic conventions and then spread throughout the prehistoric world, all the while retaining the system of conventions. More likely, cave artists in separate antipodal communities discovered the laws of visual representation independently. The same laws of perception and cognition were discovered at each site. The prehistoric artists found that tracings in the earth could look like a disparate referent. Their companions were shown the discovery, not taught what it meant.

Evolution has produced a species that uniquely can make and interpret outline pictures. Evolution achieved this end even though there was no evolutionary pressure to make pictures. Interestingly, the making of pictures was not initially inept, only improving very slightly, gradually, with each succeeding age. There is no fossil record of pictures gradually improving in likeness across aeons. The making of pictures did not confer an advantage that selected one species over another. Rather, the capacity to understand depiction is an evolutionary spin-off. It is an example of a complex skill universally present in contemporary humanity that has had no role in evolutionary selection. Its latent presence for vision was discovered more than 20,000 years ago, but its latent presence for touch is being discovered only today. Deregowski (1989) notes that nonpictorial peoples such as the Tallensi of Africa are able to draw at first attempt. He provides appropriate illustrations of a man, a woman, a horse and rider, and a crocodile, all in stick-like form, from the Tallensi. Likewise, I have reported here that the blind are capable of making similar kinds of drawings on request or at their own initiative.

Evolution is capable, the evidence indicates, of producing talents that are not honed over millions of years, as there is no trace of their evolution before modern man. These abilities have not given an advantage in evolution, though components of the ability may have been subject to evolutionary pressure and gradual improvement. In addition, the ability from which a talent has emerged as a spin-off may have undergone gradual evolution. But a functioning ability can emerge fully fledged without a gradual process of improvement and selection, as a result of a good fit of previously independent components, or a spin-off that is latent in an ability with its own particular function.

The sudden emergence in evolution of an ability such as depiction is not likely to be an isolated instance. Other species may show confluences of abilities that produce new, coherent, useful capabilities with no evolutionary history of use. In humans, we developed a clear intuition of infinity long before the idea could be put to practical use in physics. The intuition itself cannot have come into being by gradually counting larger and larger numbers, as it would take forever to count to infinity. It is appreciated by realizing that in principle counting has no preset limit. Most children realize this without explicit tuition. At about age 6–8 years many children observe phenomena such as pairs of mirrors reflecting each other, or pictures containing pictures of pictures, and understand without any prompting that this sequence continues forever.

Whether it is a spin-off or the result of a confluence in evolution, outline perception piggybacked on a perceptual activity that presumably did have an obvious advantage in evolution. That activity cannot be color perception, since outlines work well in black and white. It cannot be motion perception, since static pictures work well, or binocular vision, since monocular displays are also easily recognized. It is unlikely to be object recognition, since schematic and novel objects can be shown in outline, and outline functions control object recognition in Rubin's foreground-background experiments. It must be a perceptual system that deals with edges, corners, and wire-like objects. Clues to the relevant faculty may be found in the characteristics of axes. One hint is provided by axes that do not conform to the contours of outlines. Axes can be asymmetrically positioned between contours, figure 8.7 shows.

In figure 8.7, a convex corner is perceived lying close to one of its flanking contours and considerably farther from the other flank. The cube depicted in the figure appears to have been painted at that corner, with a thin stripe on the top surface of the cube and a wider stripe on the vertical surface. The axis divides the narrow stripe from the wide stripe. The two contours flanking the axis help to show the location of the axis. The axis is also defined by the lines indicating the other corners and edges of the cube. If the two contours come closer and closer together, eventually they will simply form a thin line or outline. The appearance of a stripe painted on a surface becomes just an impression of a corner, and the contours are seen but not used as borders in themselves. The principles of axis formation may, however, be essentially the same for a thin line and the wide line of figure 8.7.

What figure 8.7 suggests is that contours are used to define perceptual features lying between them. The features can be axes, which can be perceived as corners or occlusions. But moreover, in wide lines the contours define surfaces and characteristics of surfaces stretching between the contours.

Contours can often determine the shape that is perceived between them. A black circle can be seen as depicting a shiny sphere if the circle contains a small white patch functioning as a highlight. A silhouette can indicate the shapes of the surface within the border of the silhouette (fig. 8.8). Vision can extrapolate the locations of surfaces and corners from context and flanking contours. So too can touch. If the fingertips rest on a surface of a table, that surface is only contacted at a few locations, but it is perceived as a flat,

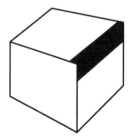

Fig. 8.7. Drawing of a cube with a convex corner indicated by a thick line. The perceptual axis that marks the change in apparent slant at that corner is not in the center of the thick line. The information for the corner is contained in the set of lines that indicate the rest of the cube and the thick line's contours.

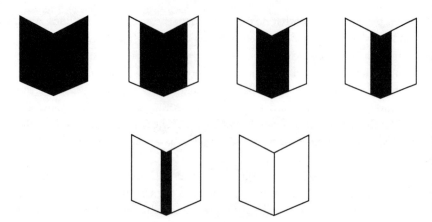

Fig. 8.8. Folded cards. The central fold is most evident in
the silhouette and the line figure.

continuous surface stretching between the contacts. If the fingertips are
rubbed along the horizontal top surface of a desk and the thumb is rubbed
along the vertical front surface, the impression of a corner is obtained. The
fingers never have to run along the actual bend where the front meets the top
surface for the bend to be located perceptually.

These observations suggest that lines invoke a perceptual process that
detects corners and other features of surface relief lying between contours. An
inspection of figures 8.7 and 8.8, however, reveals that the corners are easiest
to see when the line is thin. Moreover, when the line is thin it does not look like
the surface is painted. Evidently outline perception is not identical to the use
of silhouettes or painted areas, though it may be related. As a result, alas, there
is no certainty about the origins in evolution of outline perception. Silhouettes
and marks on surfaces that indicate painted areas are the kinds of phenomena
to consider, but neither has all the properties of outline.

OCTAVES FOR THE DEAF IN VIBRATORY TOUCH

It is quite possible that many aspects of language, logic, music, and visual
esthetics have appeared abruptly in human history as the rough spin-offs of a
confluence of independent abilities. Only for depiction, however, is there a
physical record of the sudden appearance of the facility in prehistoric rocks.
Further, there is no clear evidence about these abilities that parallels the
evidence from the blind—that is, evidence from people today who are im-
mersed in contemporary culture and blocked for some reason in their exercise

of these abilities. If the evidence from the blind is a good guide, then these abilities should be dormant but available via routes that bypass the blocks.

One case in point is music for the deaf. "Pictures for the blind" seems superficially like an oxymoron, and so does "music for the deaf." But it is a matter of everyday observation that rhythm, an important aspect of music, is available to touch. For some time, schools for the deaf have commonly included rhythmic exercises in their pedagogy. I have recently met an elderly Toronto engineer who designed a floor almost six decades ago for use in a school for the deaf. The floor transmitted rhythmic drumbeats and other tangible percussive events.

Music consists of rhythm and tonal events based on the octave. The octave is a relation between vibrations. A tone of x cycles per second (c/s or Hz) has as its octave a tone of $2x$ Hz and higher octaves at $3x$, $4x$, and so on. Touch can discriminate vibrations as well as rhythm. Hence, there may be an octave relationship that is significant in vibratory touch. In audition, each note and its octave form a pair with a noticeable affinity. Hearing an octave has an effect on untutored children and even animals (Blackwell and Schlosberg, 1943; Winner, 1982). The relationship can best be described as one of affinity, not just similarity, since if the two notes are played one after the other, the change in the note is evident. If the relationship were merely one of similarity the change would be hard to discern, like playing 100 Hz and then 101 Hz, a change of only 1 percent. Rather, the octave relationship can be described as an affinity, in which the two tones are grouped as a related pair. They may perhaps be described as easy to compare or as having similar functions.

Since the two tones in an octave pair are related but different, the octave has properties like outline and abrupt changes in relief. In each case, there are striking perceptual affinities without the members of the pair appearing identical. Since outline-relief pairing is present without tutoring in both vision and touch, it is reasonable to suspect that the octave relationship might be present without tutoring in both audition and touch. Just as touch can discern relief and raised lines, it can discern vibrations in surfaces.

Touch is capable of detecting vibrations from about 10 Hz to about 1000 Hz, with greatest sensitivity around 250 Hz (Sherrick and Craig, 1982). In monkeys, three nerve fibers have been found that favor different frequencies (Loomis and Lederman, 1986). A slowly adapting fiber roughly favors 20 Hz, a rapidly adapting fiber centers on 40 Hz, and the Pacinian fiber is likely most sensitive to 250 Hz vibrations. Discrimination between different vibratory rates or haptic tones is not well understood, especially in the handicapped (Warren, 1984, pp. 50–51), but certainly it is possible to make some distinctions between tones within the range of sensitivity. Tones much below 10 Hz probably are perceived as individual pulses, and tones above 1000 Hz are most likely discerned as onsets, quiet durations, and cessations rather than continuous tones.

Many of the notes in the lower half of the piano make a clear impression in touch, as one can check informally by placing a hand on the piano. Middle C is about 261 Hz, and the lowest note on the piano (an A) is 27.5 Hz. Thus, much of the range within which music is played is significant for touch. To test whether the octave is relevant to haptics, notes within the mid and lower ranges of the piano can be used. A vibration of 60 Hz can be compared to its octave, 120 Hz, and to notes straddling the octave, near 120 Hz. Comparisons between two tactile vibrations might be governed by their closeness in frequency. If so, 60 Hz would appear virtually identical to 70 Hz, close to 80 Hz, fairly distinct from 120 Hz, and quite different from 160 Hz. Alternatively, it might be that along with differences in frequency, tactile perception is affected by octave relations. If so, comparisons between 60 Hz and 120 Hz would be facilitated, as against comparisons between 60 Hz and notes around 120 Hz, such as 103 Hz and 137 Hz. These differ from 120 Hz by 17 Hz, a prime number which does not evenly divide into 60 Hz, and thus they are incommensurate with the simple octave relationship.

Ruth Schuler and I devised a test for use with the deaf to determine whether the octave relationship had a special significance in vibratory touch. Six profoundly deaf and four hearing-impaired volunteers were tested (table 8.2). The volunteers were recruited through a center for deaf adults in Toronto where Schuler was a staff member. Her communication with the profoundly deaf was chiefly by sign language and written cards, although occasional use was made of speechreading ("lipreading") and, in the case of the hearing-impaired who used hearing aids, spoken language.

Four of the profoundly deaf were congenitally deaf with no known hearing. One became deaf at three weeks as a result of measles and the other at three years as a result of meningitis. All of the profoundly deaf communicated by sign language. One (George, age 73) has had some instruction on a musical instrument, a piano. None of the profoundly deaf used hearing aids. They had no known auditory capabilities. All of the profoundly deaf had had seven or more years of schooling. None had any college-level education.

All of the hearing-impaired volunteers normally used hearing aids, but for the purposes of this test these were set aside and industrial hearing protectors were worn to further block out any extraneous sound from the tone generator. Each of the hearing-impaired had had a minimum of four years education and one had had three years of education beyond high school as a nurse. None had had formal training in music, though Rose (age 82) had played piano without

A study on the ability of the deaf to differentiate tones as tactual vibrations.
Errors on same/different tests given pairs of tones.

| | | | Pairs of Tones (Hz) | | | | | | |
| | | | Different Tones (max 12 trials) | | | Same Tones (max 5 trials) | | | |
Participants	Age	Onset*	60/103	60/120	60/137	60/60	103/103	120/120	137/137
Profoundly Deaf									
Winifred	69	birth	1	0	1	2	1	3	3
Florence	60	3	0	0	1	2	1	2	1
George	73	1	4	3	2	0	1	2	2
Ruth	61	birth	3	0	1	1	1	0	0
Lee	73	birth	3	1	2	4	4	3	2
Mabel	66	birth	8	1	4	0	2	1	0
Hearing Impaired									
Ford	83	40	5	1	4	2	2	0	1
Cora	77	67	4	1	5	1	1	0	0
Rose	82	?	6	1	11	1	1	1	1
Total			34	8	31	13	14	12	10

			60/90	60/120	60/150	60/60	90/90	120/120	150/150
Roley	61	?	7	3	6	0	0	1	0
Total with Roley				11		13		13	

*Age at diagnosis as severely handicapped.

taking lessons. Audiograms were available on Ford (age 83), whose best speech reception threshold was 55 dB (right ear), and on Roley (age 61), whose speech reception threshold was 60 dB (right ear). Roley had no response to sound in the left ear. Pure tone tests at 250 Hz showed thresholds at the same levels as speech in the right ear.

An 80 watt Sony speaker diaphragm (range 20–20,000 Hz) was mounted in a wooden speaker box 27 cm by 27 cm by 35 cm. Pure sine wave tones, recorded on a cassette tape, were played through this speaker. The box was held with the 35 cm by 27 cm base resting on the seated volunteer's thighs and the hands placed on the sides of the box with the forearms touching its sides. The diaphragm faced away from the volunteer, that is, it was out of sight, and the rear of the box was in contact with the volunteer's abdomen.

Each trial involved a comparison between a pair of tones presented successively. The tones lasted five seconds each, and there was a 10-second blank interval between the two tones. The volunteers judged whether the two tones were the same or different. To clarify the procedure, the volunteers were given six pretrials. The first pretrial involved a 120 Hz tone followed by another 120 Hz tone, which the volunteer was told were the same. Then a 60 Hz tone and a 250 Hz tone (which the volunteer was told were different) were presented. There followed four more pairs: 90/90 Hz (same), 60/137 Hz (different), 150/150 Hz (same), and 60/103 Hz (different). The pretrials were used to adjust the vibration intensity levels to a level where the volunteer indicated the tones could be felt but, in the case of the hearing impaired, not heard.

The experimental trials included 36 "different" pairs (12 trials each at 60/103, 60/120, and 60/137 Hz). On half, the 60 Hz tone was presented first and on half it was presented second. There were 20 "same" trials (five each at 60/60, 103/103, 120/120, and 137/137 Hz). The distribution of the pairs was random. One subject, Roley (hearing-impaired), was given 90 Hz and 150 Hz tones instead of 103 Hz and 137 Hz before we realized it would be better to depart from the octave at 120 Hz by a prime number such as 17 Hz. For completeness, the data from Roley were reported in table 8.2.

The volunteers were in error on 49 of their 180 "same" trials (with a range of 22 percent error on 137/137 Hz pairs to 31 percent error on 103/103 Hz pairs). Evidently there is nothing distinctive about 60/60 Hz pairs (28 percent errors) and 120/120 Hz pairs (26 percent errors). Roley made only one error on a "same" pair, and that was on the 120/120 Hz pair.

Only 8 errors (7 percent) were made on 60/120 Hz pairs in 108 trials (11 errors out of 120 trials, Roley's data included). By contrast, there were 34 errors (31 percent) on 60/103 Hz pairs and 31 errors (28 percent) on the 60/137 Hz pairs. All but one volunteer with tied scores made more errors on

60/103 Hz pairs than on 60/120 Hz pairs ($p < 0.01$, binomial, one-tailed). All but one volunteer made more errors on 60/137 Hz pairs than on 60/120 Hz pairs ($p < 0.05$, binomial, one-tailed). The 60/120 Hz scores are less than the mean of the 60/103 Hz pairs and the 60/137 Hz pairs for all of the volunteers except one, whose data are a tie ($p < 0.01$, binomial, one-tailed). Roley's data fit the pattern.

The results show that the octave holds a special position in vibratory touch. Judgments of the octave pair are more accurate than judgments of tones straddling the octave. Judgments of the octave pair (60/120 Hz) are more accurate than those of tones that are less distant in terms of frequency (60/103 Hz) or more distant in frequency (60/137 Hz). Further, accuracy in judging identical tones to be the same in the range 60–137 Hz is less than accuracy in judging 60/120 Hz to be different. Schuler noticed that the deaf described the judgments of the 60/120 Hz pairs as comparatively easy. The deaf described themselves as especially confident about their judgments of these pairs, and they responded more quickly to these than any of the other pairs. Schuler observed that the facial expressions and body gestures of the volunteers indicated confidence with the 60/120 Hz pairs and uneasiness with the others. The volunteers often described their judgments on the nonoctave pairs as guesses.

One might describe the 60/120 Hz pair as easily grasped for purposes of comparison. The relation between the tones in the pair is quickly evident to touch. Given a time interval of only ten seconds, the relation between the vibrations allows accurate judgments of the tones. An implication of the results is that the affinity between the members of the octave pair could produce quite different results if the interstimulus interval were lengthened. There might eventually be a kind of auditory deception, a *trompe l'oreille*. That is, if the interstimulus interval were lengthened to, say, 60 seconds, the affinity might be taken as similarity. In that case, judgments of octave pairs should result in more errors than judgments of nonoctave pairs.

Descriptions of the deaf participating in music programs, learning to play musical instruments, and enjoying dancing are now available in articles and texts from educators (Birkenshaw, 1965). The unique contribution of the present study is its implication that the octave may be present in vibratory touch. There are important analogies between this result and the use of outline by the blind. It is possible to build significant patterns with outlines, meaningful to untutored observers, blind and sighted. So too it may be possible to create significant patterns with octave relations which are equally appropriate for untutored auditory or tactile listeners. In vibratory media the patterns would be chords, if they are simultaneous, and melodies, if they are sequential. The deaf, using vibratory touch, may be able to distinguish between coherent chords and random assortments of notes. They may be able to tell simple melodies from random sequences of notes. They may even be able to distinguish combinations of sound that express cheerfulness and those that express sadness, emotions often associated with major and minor keys. They may be able to distinguish complete from incomplete melodies. If so, they may be able to distinguish increasing tension as melodic lines depart from a home key, and release of tension as the lines return home.

All of these relations built on octaves offer the promise of being universals in music, and they may be available to a central vibratory sense that is accessible through touch as well as audition. I should add, as a cautionary note, that data from the hearing-impaired cannot distinguish between vibratory touch serving as a channel for bone conduction to the ear and vibratory touch per se working independently of the auditory nerve. My hypothesis is that there is an octave in both kinds of vibratory touch. It is more radical to suggest that there is an octave in vibratory touch per se, but the data are equivocal on this point. The data from the congenitally deaf indicate that the octave's special status arises without any need for instruction.

The analogy between the octave and the outline's affinity for features of relief is interesting and provocative. Each is the basis for perception of structures. The octave is the basis for harmonic structures (Winner, 1982, p. 230). The outline's affinity for relief is the basis for depiction of structures made of surfaces. The analogy has clear limits because the rules for combining the elements are different for vibrations and surfaces. The structures for vibrations are "harmonious" if they consist of vibrations with ratios 1:2 (the octave itself), 1:3, 1:4, etc. (the overtones or higher octaves). The structures for surface relief are not ratios. The structures of surfaces are possible or appropriate if they consist of conjunctions that follow the laws of the physics of surfaces (Kennedy, 1974a). At no region along its length can a wire (space on both sides of a thin cylinder) turn into a crack (empty space between surfaces). The wire must have a termination. The surfaces on either side of the crack must have edges. But an occluding boundary of a mountain's rounded surface can become at any region along its length an occluding edge of a flat surface such as a cliff. In short, surface features have types that can and cannot adjoin. The combinatorial rules for vibrations use ratios and for surfaces use types.

Vision does use ratios—in fractals and in judgments of proportions. The vibration sense does use rules for combinations of sounds, especially in perception of speech. It also can give an impression of impossible combinations, just as drawings of surfaces can show impossible combinations, for a set of pitches can seem to increase in frequency ad infinitum. This may be as effective in touch as in audition. But the perception of representations of surfaces as possible and the perception of notes as harmonious use different bases for judgment.

There is an important logical difference between perception of harmony and perception of acceptable surface combinations, in addition to the mathematics defining the structures of the elements. Any combination of vibrations can be presented to the perceiver. Inharmonious selections are as physically possible as harmonious ones, but only some combinations of surfaces are physically possible. Therefore, the distinction between harmony and discord is a psychological one at heart. The distinctions between combinations of surfaces is a physical one that allows no compromises.

PERCEPTUAL STATES

The difference between a psychological base and a physical one has great force when the study of depiction attempts to encompass matters of metaphor, expression, and style. In examining drawings showing a terrain, physics provides an objective check on what is correct and incorrect, and the mathematics of perspective defines correct arrangements and proportions. In some metaphors, the domains being depicted involve translations between physically measurable dimensions such as space, time, and distance or physical features such as shape and location. But some metaphors involve crossing into perceptual domains where it is impossible or unclear how an experimenter could measure dimensions independently of the volunteer's own perceptions.

Metaphors of pain or numb feelings are a case in point. Morton Heller, Paul Gabias, and I have tested blind adult volunteers on drawings (fig. 8.9) suggesting motion, pain, and numbness. The drawings consist of four sketches of a hand in outline, with the lines for the fingers and the side of the hand standing for the occluding bounds of rounded surfaces. The thumb varies from drawing to drawing. In one, the outline of the thumb consists of dashes. In the other three, the outline of the thumb is complete, but extra lines are added as graphic devices to suggest various states. In one, five short straight lines radiate from the thumb. In the second, five short arcs surround the thumb. In the third, five short arcs cut across the thumb.

Volunteers in this study were asked to decide which drawing showed a hand with a thumb in pain, numb, moving in a circle (like twiddling one's thumb), and moving back and forth (like someone flexing the thumb, in the same plane as the palm and the fingers).

Twelve sighted undergraduates, from the University of Toronto, ages 19–24, tested independently, identified the drawings by sight. To 11 of them, the

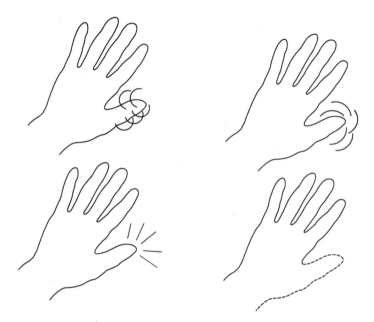

Fig. 8.9. Drawings of hands, with devices suggesting that the thumb is in
pain (bottom left), numb (bottom right), moving in a circle (top left),
or moving to and fro (top right).

dashes meant numb, the radiants meant pain, the arcs across meant movement
in a circle, and the arcs surrounding meant back-and-forth movement.

The 17 blind volunteers who participated in this study were adults recruited in North Carolina, New York City, Baltimore, and Ottawa. They were
given tactual versions of the figures examined by the sighted volunteers. Nine
were congenitally blind (one had low vision and the others were totally blind)
and eight were later blind (one had light perception and the others were
totally blind). All had participated in at least one previous study on depiction.
None, however, had dealt with pictures showing pain or numbness with these
devices. Four had made or explored pictures showing motion, but they had
not dealt with pictures showing motion in the plane versus motion out of the
plane of the picture.

The majority decisions by the blind were as follows (table 8.3). Nine said
that the radiating straight lines showed pain. Ten took the dashes to show
numbness. Nine deemed the surrounding arcs as suggesting motion in a
circle. Seven thought that the arcs across were for motion back and forth. On
four occasions, across three of the devices, no referent was selected. For two

TABLE 8.3

Blind adults' judgments of devices indicating states of the hand. On four
occasions the subject did not select one of the options offered.

| | | | Possible Referents | |
| | Pain | Numb | Thumb Circling | Thumb Back and Forth |
Devices				
Radiating lines	9	2	1	3
Dashed outline	1	10	3	3
Arcs surrounding the outline	1	2	9	4
Arcs cutting across the outline	4	4	2	7

volunteers, the same referent was said to be shown by two devices. Six of the
volunteers concurred entirely with the majority decisions (two of the congenitally blind, four of the later blind).

In identifying which figure showed pain and which showed numbness the
majority of the blind concurred with the sighted. The blind also concurred
with the sighted in judging that the two drawings with arcs show motion, but
they attributed opposite meanings. The blind often took the arcs around but
not crossing the thumb as indicating a complete circle, and understood the
arcs across the outline as indicating motion of the thumb only along the length
of the arc. The sighted (and some of the blind) took the arcs surrounding the
outline as indicating partial silhouettes of the thumb in various locations
distributed to the left and right of the outline in the plane of the picture and
the palm. The arcs across, some of the sighted supposed, indicate breaking
out of the plane by a line of motion breaking the outline. Thus, there are
equivocal procedures for relating the device to the referent, and for reasons
that are as yet unclear the blind may select a different procedure from that
chosen by the sighted.

The evidence in previous chapters suggests that the disagreement with the
sighted is not likely to be in understanding shape or motion or how to use an
outline of the thumb itself. Hayley Naor and I tested 20 blindfolded sighted
subjects ages 8–58 (mean age 27, s.d. 14.1) at the Ontario Science Centre,
asking them to examine the displays by touch. The majority (12 of 20) said
that pain is best shown by the radiants and numbness by the dashed outline
(13 of 20). On the thumb-circling referent they were split between arcs cutting
across (eight votes) and the arcs surrounding (nine votes), with three selecting other options. There was a similar split concerning which figure showed

back-and-forth motion. It seems that the judgments of the blind are comparable to those of the blindfolded volunteers, and on the motion referents both groups depart from sighted subjects taking the test visually.

On the pain and numbness devices, the graphic additions to the outline form of the thumb are interpreted alike by the sighted and the blind. Investigation of this correspondence, however, is more difficult than is the case with depiction of relief edges in outline, and even more difficult than explanation of the use of graphic devices for motion. There is a clear set of physical rules for surfaces and motion. Although pain and numbness indicate physiological states, they are percepts whose description or phenomenology is obscure, and the physiological underpinnings are hardly better understood. As a result, whereas the explanation of a correspondence between a pictorial device and its referent in the case of surfaces is a projection from one set of physical features to another, with perception in the middle, in the case of pain or numbness the correspondence is between a pictorial device and a referent that cannot be readily measured, with perception of the device in the middle. At present, all one can do is attempt to clarify which features of the device seem most closely related to the referent, as far as the perceiver is concerned, and which features the referent has, again so far as the perceiver is concerned. In the long run, there is likely to be a theory of pain perception as mathematical as the theory of harmony, and it will be allied to a theory of painful stimuli as objective as the theory of physical vibration. At present, the referent for devices suggesting pain and numbness is a little-understood percept.

A device in a representation can be ambiguous. If so, there is no objective criterion favoring one judgment over another. At best, one can anticipate that one group's judgments can be predicted from another's—the blind by the sighted or the reverse. Just such a case is reported by Kennedy, Gabias, and Pierantoni (1990), who tested devices for showing motion. The pictures contained a circle described as a rolling ball. Behind the ball was a trail of arcs. One trail had dense, evenly spaced arcs; another had widely separated (sparse), evenly spaced arcs. In a third, the arcs were denser the closer they approached the ball. In the fourth, the arcs were more widely separated the closer they came to the ball.

Subjects were asked to judge which picture showed a ball going fast, which showed a ball going slowly, which showed a ball speeding-up, and which showed a ball slowing down. There are two modes of responding. In a "stroboscopic" mode, the wider the spacing, the faster the ball. In this judgment, spacing shows the distance traveled per unit time. In a "density" mode, the more closely packed the arcs, the faster the ball. Sighted subjects ($n = 176$)

responded chiefly in the density mode (55 percent) and about half as frequently in the stroboscopic mode (24 percent). The remaining subjects were inconsistent. Some (14 percent) gave a density judgment on the evenly spaced ball (the denser the faster) and a stroboscopic judgment on the decelerating ball (dense near the ball meant slower). A few (7 percent) offered the reverse—a stroboscopic judgment on the evenly spaced ball (the denser the slower) and a density judgment on the decelerating ball (widely spaced arcs near the ball meant that it was slowing down).

Kennedy, Gabias, and Pierantoni (1990) tested 14 blind subjects. Five had never used pictures. Six had made occasional use of raised-line pictures. Three had made frequent use of pictures. No one had used the device in question—a trail of arcs to indicate motion. Like the sighted, the blind favored a density response. Thirteen of the blind subjects were consistent: 10 consistently used density judgments and three used stroboscopic judgments. The inconsistent person gave a stroboscopic judgment to the evenly spaced stimuli but said that the dense arcs near the ball show acceleration. He mentioned that he "could make a real good case" for either kind of judgment: "If you take a picture—say the ball is here—and you take another picture, and it moved to there, you'd say 'wow, it moved that far!' [But also] you could say that the ball obviously has got twice as many marks here, so it could have traveled twice as fast. Like a fan blade, as it gets faster it kind of blurs together."

A repetition of the experiment by Gatti (1991), in an undergraduate thesis under Pierantoni's supervision, involved a large group of adult blind subjects, 86 in all. The results were very close to the responses from the sighted subjects. Consistent density judgments were made by 54 percent of the subjects and consistent stroboscopic judgments by 28 percent. Inconsistent judgments were 15 percent using density judgments for even displays and stroboscopic judgments for deceleration displays, and 3 percent stroboscopic for even and density for deceleration.

The judgments by the blind and the sighted are good news for any theory contending that the blind and the sighted have similar amodal perceptions of space and motion through space. But in any task where there are two logical alternatives, both having appropriate physical bases, there is no a priori way to predict how the blind and the sighted will behave. There is some deciding factor, but in the absence of any clear physical problem with one alternative, the rationale for a bias toward one alternative rather than another is elusive. There is some psychological factor at work, but what it is remains unclear.

DEPICTING A PROPERTY OF A SURFACE

Theories of expression and notions about art styles are in much the same quandaries as theories of pain or numbness perception. Emotion is as psychological as pain, and its physiological underpinning, like its basis in stimulus information, is not well understood. Gibson (1979) argues that the environment has physical affordances, offering physical comfort, threats to life and limb, succor, and privation. His ecological theory of psychological universals holds that these affordances are the basis for expression and emotion. Gestalt theory (Arnheim, 1974) considers expression to be based on formal properties of design and contends that these properties are not easily explained as affordances. Symmetry, balance, and proportion are formal properties that can make a display seem orderly, intended, and calm. To explain these effects as affordances, Gestaltists contend, is too vague to be useful. They suggest that perception has more degrees of freedom than the physical world of natural objects and their affordances. Convention theory holds that expression and emotion are a social construct. Its theorists propose that in a society with no established roles for anger, hope, or sadness, these emotions would not be felt, nor would displays be seen as expressing them. They also assert that devices for expressing emotions or affordances in representational displays are effective as a result of social rules, not universals of perception.

Research on expression is difficult because there is no clear physical theory of affordances, and it is doubly difficult since Gestalt theory and convention theory dispute the possibility of such a theory. Gestalt theory wishes to anchor expression in perception, and convention theory in social customs. The problems can be examined with a case in mind. Gabias and Kennedy (1984) studied a depiction of a property of a surface rather than an outline depiction of the edges of the surface. Figure 8.10 was shown to blind and sighted volunteers. The figure has a square crossed by wavy lines and a square crossed by zigzag lines. The volunteers were asked which picture showed a hard, unyielding surface and which showed a soft, yielding surface. The blind and the sighted agreed that the wavy lines suggested a soft surface and the zigzag lines a hard surface.

The simplicity of the study and the coherence of the results conceal theoretical puzzles. Why should waves suggest softness and zigzags hardness? Certainly the waves could be like fur or rolling hills and the zigzags like metallic blades or rocky outcrops. Each of these suggest an ecology and appropriate hard or soft affordances. But it is easy to think of counterexamples. Rounded stones are hard; zigzag outlines of leaves are soft. Wavy pat-

Fig. 8.10. Drawings of textures where one surface is hard and the other is soft.

terns in marble are hard; zigzag tips of feathers are soft. Perhaps the basis for the comparisons between these static patterns lies in kinetic events. When something melts, it loses sharp edges. When it freezes again, it can acquire sharp angular forms like icicles. This explanation is post hoc and has little in the way of independent evidence to support it. The Gestalt theory that formal properties are used by the perceiver independent of an ecological referent has as much validity at present. Gestaltists note that some made-up words like *takete* are unfamiliar but possess abrupt changes, sound "hard," and are associated with angular forms with straight lines, whereas *maluma* sounds soft and is associated with rounded forms. These cross-sensory links, Gestaltists argue, occur without tutoring. Convention theorists could argue, too, that the adult perceiver may have heard that curves express softness and sharp angles express hardness, and that this is a social convention. Convention theorists note that *takete* and *maluma* are not readily connected with rounded and soft or angular and hard forms by some non-Western peoples (Kennedy, 1982a). It will take many converging lines of investigation to uncover the truth here, as cross-cultural and developmental evidence needs to be brought to bear. The enterprise can only be successful when an explicit theory of affordances is available so that one can show either that expression occurs independently of affordances but universally, as Gestalt theory has it, or independently of affordances but only after being taught a culture's customs, as convention theory asserts. At present, it seems that all three theses can explain some of the evidence, and the evidence is merely the agreement in judgments by various kinds of adults at some times but not others.

STYLE

Elizabeth Saltzhauer-Axel (1989), of the Whitney Museum in New York, teaches about art styles to the blind. She has tackled cave art and cubism, and she is creating allied programs on Egyptian art and the Renaissance. Her aims are complementary to the thesis of this book, and deserve to be compared and contrasted to the universals of perception and depiction described here.

Saltzhauer-Axel and her colleagues in Art Education for the Blind, a New York organization she founded in 1987, make tactile versions of celebrated works of art and explain them to the blind, accompanying their tuition with sound tapes. Marcel Duchamp's *Nude Descending a Staircase,* for example, has been simulated as a wooden statuette. The original painting has many heads, bodies, legs, and arms forming a single figure on a staircase looking rather like a Marey stroboscopic, multiple-image photograph of an angular but elegant robot descending stairs. Similarly, the statuette offers figures on a staircase, and the figures form a single mass with several legs, arms, bodies, and heads. Each part of the body is represented by pieces of wood, usually with a rectangular cross-section and a profile that has several straight edges and some shallow arcs. The effect of both the picture and the statuette is mechanical, and yet both represent a human body in continuous motion simultaneously at several phases of the motion. A living entity, a single body, and a continuous motion are shown by something that appears mechanical, multiple, and discontinuous. The statuette is accompanied in Saltzhauer-Axel's lesson by an auditory tape that reproduces the sounds of someone running up and down wooden stairs. The continuous rushing motion of the person on the stairs is signaled by a series of abrupt, brief footfalls. Once again, the continuous and the living are evoked by a sequence of discontinuous events. At the end of the tape the footsteps blend into a clacking mechanical sound fading away as though into the distance. It helps draw attention to the clockwork quality of the sounds of the feet on the wooden staircase. In addition, the repetitive clacks, like the footfalls, resemble echoes, multiple auditory images of a single event.

Saltzhauer-Axel's commentary points out that cubism, the style in the *Nude Descending,* was concerned with repetition, successive and simultaneous events, and the exploration of the effects of using multiple vantage points in making a single image. As Parsons (1987) pointed out in an examination of art styles and their comprehension, an art style is a series of elements and ways of combining them, and it is also a technique that is used at particular times for particular purposes. Cubism, for example, is a means for presenting bodies as sums of parts, often as geometrical parts such as rectangles, circles, cubes, cones, and ovoids. By reducing bodies, whether animate or inanimate, to sums of similar parts, cubism can be a tool for exploring the rather desperate intuition that life is no more than matter, no more than the sum of physical, electrical, and mechanical activities. In exploring the breakdown of the distinction between the living and the dead, cubism is also a tool for exploring opposites, like successive and simultaneous states, the whole and the broken. Cubism is visually exciting because it defies many standard distinctions. It shows in one moment what can only be seen across time or from several vantage points. It allows the viewer to try to see what is familiar in a radically new and often superficially violent guise, for things look as though they have been broken into many parts. *Nude Descending* allows the perceiver to try to make out the nude despite the transformations from single to multiple, from successive to simultaneous. Further, cubist representations make the perceiver wonder whether this picture could even be taken as realistic if the style became familiar enough. It makes one question the boundaries of perceptual learning.

Audiences of blind and sighted people react very favorably to Saltzhauer-Axel's statuettes, tapes, and discussions. The blind people I have observed in her audiences seem intrigued by her interpretations of particular pieces and by the idea that art styles are ways of exploring issues. They seem to be interested in the reproductions and to find the tapes valuable, not only in themselves as appealing sounds that catch the imagination, but also as vehicles by which to approach the reproductions. The audiences have been composed of adults so far, but I believe that this program holds promise for work with children.

Saltzhauer-Axel's sculptors and sound artists have to deploy considerable skill if their versions of aspects of an original work are to reproduce the target aspects effectively. A fragile version of *Nude Descending*—say, made of balsa wood—would betray the steely robot that comes down Duchamp's stairs quite elegantly. If the sound tape had creaky or slippery stairs, or the footfalls were hesitant or slithery, that would also violate the Duchamp's impression.

I believe that much thought could be put into devising sound tapes that have metaphoric qualities, in Saltzhauer-Axel's program. The footfalls on the stairs could be engineered to have reverberation, which might work well as an auditory analogue to the repetition in Duchamp's drawings of multiple legs. Sounds that are continuous like a sled on rough packed snow could be presented in staccato bursts to simulate the contrasts between simultaneous and successive. The multiple arms, legs, and heads of a single person could be evoked by a voice on tape that apparently says several phrases simultaneously. The analogy between an echo and a recording could be used to emphasize differences between a natural repetition and a mechanical reproduction. Echoes, for example, always get quieter, whereas sound recordings can get louder on each repetition. Differences like this one could be used to draw attention to an event as mechanical, not natural, part of the study of the event and not the event itself.

Style has elements and combinational rules, but it also has meaning and purpose. Some styles probably lend themselves to delicacy and others to massive weight, suiting certain moods as well as challenging everyday perception. Some uses of style, it seems, can readily be applied to evoke contradictions, ironies, hyperbole, and litotes (Kennedy, 1982a). Abstract ideas about value and human significance on the scale of the universe or history can be embodied in particular works. The vantage point chosen can suggest that we are comparatively small or elevated (Kubovy, 1986; Kennedy, 1988c). Further, the embodiment reminds one of the occasion in which it was made and its place—whether derivative or original—in the traffic of its time. Duchamp's painting has a good deal to do with the influence of multiple-image still photography and the study of motion in early twentieth-century France. Cave art reveals the flora and fauna of its age and gives rise to unanswered questions about the culture that originally surrounded it. Convention theorists point out correctly that Duchamp's purposes cannot be read unambiguously from the appearance of the work, and the more that is known about the era, the better the piece can be recognized.

A cautionary note is sounded by deconstructionists, who emphasize our limits in establishing the visual impression the work was designed to create for its contemporaries. They note that the limits to our appreciation that are so blatantly obvious when it comes to cave art are still in force when we try to recapture any meaning or intended impression even of a recent work. What is undoubtedly true is that education adds considerably to the reaction that a depiction can reliably instigate, and many aspects of style will go unnoticed, or remain as unresolved ambiguities, without a program of instruction such as Saltzhauer-Axel's.

In principle, if an art style lends itself to a certain purpose for the sighted, it can also serve that purpose for the blind. A good guide can enable the blind or sighted person to envisage that purpose and to test whether the style and a particular graphic work fits it. Without the guide, finding the relevant purpose to consider would be almost an impossible task—the purposes to which a picture can be put are too many. Depictions have served quite serious purposes, communicating about matters as profound as religion, politics, science, and economics, so it is worth the effort to build on what is natively endowed, universally, and to explore the cultural settings of pictures. There is also reward in pictures in a lighter vein that act as pastimes in comic strips. Pictures can be humorous, quizzical, even at times bizarre illustrations of the day's mores and imagination. They can allow us, as Parsons (1987) points out, to discover the limits of our perception, to find out individually what our own perception can and cannot do, where in matters of motivation we have become jaded, unfortunately, and where our appetites are still fresh.

Parsons's reminder of the powers and limits of perception is a valuable part of the theme of this chapter: the boundaries of what can reasonably be expected of perception and of pictures given the evidence about universals and perceptual effects from quarters such as the blind. In this chapter I have argued that there are universals of perception and representation, and that it is important to determine what can be built from the universal elements and what rules are spontaneously followed by those who have not been taught them. Pictures can have a style, but many of the more profound uses of style should be described along with the illustration, for they will escape the casual perceiver, blind or sighted. At the same time styles, like the basic elements of depiction, can surely suit their intended referents, and if so the fit should be equally apparent to the blind and the sighted.

CHAPTER NINE

Drawing
Conclusions

How people perceive and represent space is a matter that has been warmly debated for several centuries. Contributions from touch and action have often been compared to the donations from vision, and many experiments and theories pit one against the other. I have passed over this tug-of-war. Instead of favoring one modality or the other, I have emphasized how both vision and haptics can discover arrangements of surfaces and their directions from the observer. My special focus has been the human ability to use axes to represent the three-dimensional layout of the environment. In this final chapter, I shall summarize the main achievements of the work to date while being mindful of some of the limits of the theory of perceptual axes and some of the courses that need to be followed to respect and challenge today's research achievements.

GOALS

Arnheim (1990) has listed some of the goals of the study of perception, pictures, and touch. First of all, the haptic world needs to be understood in its own terms. What is found by touch has to be described. Haptic experience comes about by cooperation between kinesthesis and touch, or action and cutaneous sensitivity. What is revealed when touch, across time, goes beyond the presence of objects within bodily reach? How does haptics locate the self in the outer world?

Second, it is crucial to understand how the world can be represented. The world can be shown via displays that transform it and yet in some fashion repeat it. In particular, outline drawings are not copies of line-like shapes found in nature. In some way they are graphic equivalents of features of the world such as boundaries and elongated shapes. The question around which most of this book has circled is, How can people understand the meaning of lines as axes without the help of vision?

Perception of shape involves appreciating the distribution of tangible and visible surfaces—the arrangements of flat and curved surfaces that compose individual objects. Can the blind recognize and reproduce objects in line drawings, much as the sighted do, since they have a ready access via touch to combinations of surfaces? Reaching out from a fixed position in space is governed by the principles of direction that permit visual projection. Can the blind capitalize on their appreciation of directions from a vantage point and apply this intuitive understanding of the role of the observer's location in an ambient world to the devices used in pictorial displays to show the orientation of objects? It is, as Arnheim writes, a far cry from someone successfully pointing to the sides of an extended object in space as the object recedes to someone successfully appreciating a line drawing of the sides of the object in perspective.

Being rational animals, we are suited for the use of reason, Arnheim notes following Kant. Hence transformations of form should often be detected as deliberate, as motivated by a purpose other than just copying the shape of an object. This recognition should provide an avenue for pictorial tropes, meta-phoric devices used to communicate without replicating the referent. Touch goes to and from the mind, hence tactile pictures should be suitable vehicles for tropes.

In Arnheim's view, realistic representation is only one among many equally valid styles. Like Arnheim, I have taken the view that it is not my task to teach the blind the pictorial standards of the majority. Rather, I have tried to provide tasks and displays to which the blind can react. Their reactions indicate what they deem to be appropriate within the limits set by the tasks and displays.

Arnheim's discussion of the aims of the study of picture perception and haptics stems from a Gestalt theory of perception, which is somewhat at variance with the positions I have taken here. Notably, he thinks of perception as "dynamic" and regards haptic perception in particular as concerned with the dynamic properties of pushing and pulling. The result must be, he con-cludes, impressions of effort and relaxation "in a purely abstract, that is, shapeless fashion." I argue instead that the mechanism of haptics is triggered by variations in resistance, but the percept that arises is one of shape, not just force. According to this theory, the dynamic properties discussed by Arnheim could underlie expressive properties perceived in displays that suggest tension, bending, balance, and shifting weights. Ultimately, a coherent theory of perception will, I think, include these dynamic properties and show how they can be represented in a picture. At the moment, the only approach to dynamic properties here is via expressive stick figures, and there is still much to be done to create an articulate theory of expression and form.

DIDEROT'S CONCLUSIONS

If I were to reach back into history to select an early, clear precursor of the present framework for ideas about form depiction, the list of distinguished contributors eligible for praise would be impressive. The question of the relationship between touch, vision, and form was first brought to prominence by William Molyneux in a letter to John Locke, and vigorous responses to Locke came from Reed, Berkeley, Condillac, Lotz, and Kant. But it was Denis Diderot in the late eighteenth century who put forward the most prescient assessment, in practical terms, of many of the main findings of today.

Diderot wrote that touch excels at giving the blind person the idea of three-dimensional objects. He quoted a blind man to this effect: "When I place my hand between your eyes and an object, you see my hand and not the object, and the same thing happens to me when I look for an object with my stick and find another instead" (Diderot, in Morgan, 1977). The blind, Diderot wrote, readily realize that objects interpose in three dimensions between the observer and the object. Thus, touch has some sense of perspective. "The blind man of Puiseaux," Diderot observed, "judges the nearness of fire by the degree of heat, the fullness of containers by the noise of the decanting liquid, and the nearness of bodies by the action of air on the face." "How does the blind person form ideas of space?" Diderot asked. His answer: by "the movements of his body, the successive existence of his hand in different places, and by the continuous sensations given to him by an object that slides through his fingers." In touch, a taut thread is a straight line and a sagging wire a curve. The blind person has no difficulty combining these sensations or points into shapes. A curve is a surface of a concave or convex solid object in touch. The blind can even mentally expand or contract a shape. "By these means," Diderot vouchsafed, "the congenitally blind person can construct points, surfaces and solids; he could even have a conception of a globe as large as the Earth." He even reported that a blind person "with a bit of practice . . . was able to recognize a friend from a drawing made on his hand." A succession of pencil strokes on the skin constituted a picture.

Diderot's anticipation of results of studies on haptic pictures with the blind not only anticipates the work I have reported here; it also is a precursor of interesting experiments using the skin as a kind of canvas. Studies with pictures taken with a television camera and turned into pictorial arrays of points on the skin, some vibrating and some quiet, have been undertaken for more than two decades (Bach-y-rita, 1972; White, Saunders, Scadden, Bach-y-rita, and Collins, 1970; Epstein, Hughes, Schneider, and Bach-y-rita, 1989). It is difficult to make a patch of skin (which has low acuity) act as a retina (which has high acuity) responding to small images of squares, circles, and triangles of vibrating points. But it is not impossible. Motion seems to make the detection of shape slightly easier. I think that there is more promise for raised haptic pictures to be explored via touch than for images impressed on the skin, judging by the difficulty in attaining significant comprehension of patterns on these "television sensory substitution" devices. But new tactics are being devised for these devices, and there is every reason to hope for a breakthrough.

Diderot did not offer a theory of pictures or a list of the features of an object that would be suitable for outline drawing. He argued that we are endowed with sensations, which we can combine in perception, but he was at times unclear about how sensations could lead to perceptions. He rather vaguely concluded that we compare sensations with their occasioning causes without indicating how anyone could know about the occasioning objects independently of the sensations he supposed to be the sole basis of perception. I have tried to offer a theory of tactual knowledge which verifies Diderot's observations, extending them into a broad examination of depiction. I have avoided any theory of sensations which avers that they are separate from perceptions and much more limited than perceptions. Once sensations are broken off from perceptions and claimed to be the sole givens in sensitivity, it is impossible to establish a coherent basis for perception. When such a basis is given for perception, it must be rich in variety if it is to provide specific information about the furniture of the world around the observer (Gibson, 1979).

THE ISSUES AT THE CENTER

My task in this work has been to understand space, depiction, direction, and communication—especially tactual space, outline, perspective, and metaphor. I think we need a theory that uses force and resistance but produces shape, and the theory should indeed provide a base for perception; but that base should be a world and a medium and an informative set of variations, not a set of sensations. The theory needs, however, to include a special factor. In some way, elements should be able to act as surrogates of spatial features spontaneously. They should create impressions of edges, axes, and shapes of certain types. The elements do not trigger sensations in the sense of a meaningless patchwork of areas. Rather, they capitalize on perceptual machinery that detects forms in depth in dealing with the real world. They stimulate perceptions of the edges and axes of these forms while simultaneously evoking perceptions of the flat patchwork they form on the display's surface.

The research findings and theoretical discussions over the past eight chapters have attempted to satisfy many of the requirements of a theory of haptics and depiction. I have also entertained speculations on the edge of established fact. The issues at the very center of the discussion, however, can be demonstrated unequivocally by a few well-chosen figures.

Figure 9.1 shows an object in a special way. The contours that reveal the

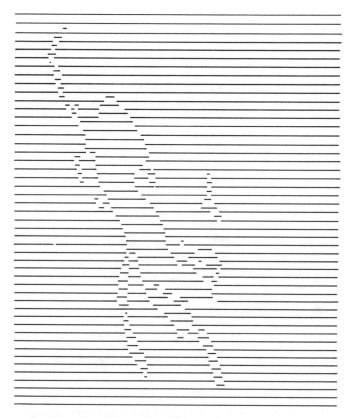

Fig. 9.1. Subjective contour version of figure 2.4, a man's face.

object are subjective, joining the termini of lines. The shape on which the subjective contours are based is a man's face. It is exactly the same shape found in figure 2.4—a man's face in strongly directional illumination. The shape of the subjective contours is a chiaroscuro (shape-from-shadow) form. The face is perfectly easy to see in the original, positive, patchwork display, which shows a face with deep shadows on the right side. In figure 9.1 the areas on either side of the subjective contours are filled with horizontal lines, with the same density and spacing on both sides of the contours. Overall, there is no brightness difference between the two sides of the contours. As figure 9.1 reveals, the result is that vision cannot perform shape-from-shadow analysis to recover the shape of the face. Subjective contours cannot stimulate shape-from-shadow perception of the face.

Subjective contours are single contours. Figure 9.1 shows that the single contour with no brightness difference cannot support chiaroscuro analysis of the relief and illumination structure copied by the contour. Outlines also function as single divisions with no brightness differences in vision. Neither do they permit vision to analyze their chiaroscuro structure when they follow the laws of shape-from-shadow form. What outlines do well is copy the structure of tangible form. Figure 9.2 is a drawing of a man (by Pat; early, totally blind). Figure 9.2 shows that outline drawing is intelligible to touch

Fig. 9.2. Drawing of a man, by Pat (early, totally blind).

unaided by vision. The lines show well the features that vision finds make sense in line drawings. The overall form of the depicted object is intelligible, as well as the features depicted by individual lines.

The overall shape of an object is perceived by an observer coping with the vagaries of vantage points and distances from an array of objects. This is true of touch as well as vision. Hence, perspective is an issue for touch just as it is for vision. Figure 9.3 is another picture by Pat. It shows railroad tracks receding into the distance,where they converge. The observer is shown by a mark in the center of the picture. Interestingly, the tracks converge ahead of the observer and, in a curious turn, behind the observer as well. Pat noted that this shows far distances ahead of and behind the observer at the same time.

Diderot's observations on how blind people reach out with a stick or decipher pencil strokes on their hands contain the same lessons as figures 9.1, 9.2, and 9.3. The attempt to learn those lessons here has spanned eight chapters. Let me bring the key points forward for review.

To consider touch as proximal is to set its confines too narrowly. Touch is distal as well as proximal in its everyday use. It uses many of the features of central concern to vision, allowing perception of relief, including surface layout, with occlusion, corners, and vantage points. It ascertains how features of surface layout are arranged in scenes and in individual objects. It involves

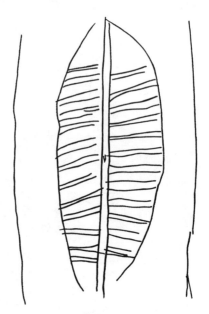

Fig. 9.3. Drawing of railroad tracks with convergence in two directions, by Pat.

use of tactile media, as well as contact with actual objects. It takes in information across time to detect objects arrayed simultaneously. The geometry of the objects that are found by touch is in principle the same as the geometry found by vision, so far as matters of direction and distance are concerned. Touch deals with energy, including vibratory energy as well as continuous pressure. It also deals with patterns. It gains information about a world through these patterns, and it is reasonable to expect that representational patterns, as well as patterns constituted by the objects themselves, could make sense to an observer using touch. These patterns can reveal intention, at times by contradicting reality, and observers who entertain intentions may be expected to consider the intended use or aim of a tactile representation.

Limits to touch include the amount of time touch needs to explore a scene. A survey of a scene is made more quickly by vision than by touch. This has led to the mistaken idea that vision is instantaneous. It is not: vision also takes time, and many samples, before it can survey a scene. The fact that touch takes time has also led to the mistaken idea that touch cannot yield an impression of an array of objects in space. Not so: touch yields an impression of a scene just as unequivocally as vision. Both senses take time to gain information about a spatial layout. The principle is clear, but much could be learned about how skillful deployment of touch is developed, how much of this development is spontaneous, and when it is best to offer training in mobility to the blind (Warren, 1984).

A key observation about vision is that lines in outline drawings depict features that are tangible. Outline does not trigger shape-from-shading or chiaroscuro processing. Most likely, outline processing occurs after chiaroscuro analysis. It may trigger axes and be governed by a general, amodal sense of space. Little, however, is understood about the physiological channels that allow its visual effects.

Blind children and adults recognize haptic pictures. Like nonpictorial peoples inspecting pictures for the first time (discussed in Deregowski, 1989), blind people are slow to recognize outline drawings on first exposure but do succeed handsomely after some moments, unaided. How much faster they may become with practice is as yet unknown. Given that touch is slow at some tasks compared to vision but faster and more accurate at others (Heller, 1989, 1991), there is reason to hope that they would become considerably faster. One should certainly not assert that first-time performance indicates the eventual limits on visual or tactile recognition of pictures, or that pictures are unsuitable for touch simply because first-time users have a laborious time.

Blind adults draw using lines in outline style, employing them for occluding boundaries and corners and as stick-figure versions of cylindrical forms.

The evidence indicates two barriers to drawing by the blind—low-rise barriers, one might call them, for they are not insurmountable. The first is the coordination of three factors, each of which is well understood in its own right, namely vantage points (and associated directions), object shapes (and facets facing a vantage point), and the picture surface (and its location between the vantage point and the object). Blind people do not usually comment spontaneously on how the shape on the picture surface can vary from a shape similar to the referent's (or an edge-on version of the referent), to a projective transformation, if a suitable vantage point is chosen. The second barrier is the drawing of familiar shapes of referents such as dogs, which, unlike utensils and furniture, involve silhouettes where curves vary systematically along the length of the curve. I have described this as the problem of distinguishing one species from another and providing distinctive information. Sighted people also meet these barriers to drawing development, and there is much to do to define the barriers properly, to show why they are so awkward and what routes lead past them.

The hallmarks of drawing development in the sighted can be discerned in drawings by blind children. The kinds of drawings blind children produce are indeed recognizable as drawings that would be produced by sighted children. The examples were obtained by asking blind children of various ages to make drawings. The hypothesis that blind children develop drawing skills along the same developmental course as sighted children could be supported further by following some individual blind children for, say, five years and noting how their drawing skills mature.

Blind people, children as well as adults, have a sense of the vantage point, but the use of the vantage point in drawing develops through several stages. Evidence from pointing tasks indicates that blind children do use the principle of convergence in pointing to an array of objects from close-up and far away. Evidence from tasks with drawings indicates that blind adults judge drawings using vantage points as developmentally later than drawings that do not involve vantage points. Also, drawings of objects using vantage point geometries are compared and ranked appropriately by blind adults.

Metaphor uses class inclusion and a violation of a rule to create an apt change, to communicate a referent, not simply to break the rules. Whereas young blind children make any mark stand for any referent at will, drawings by older children and adults use outline for relief features and follow configurational principles. These rules can be broken, but they are deemed to be rule violations by the person making the sketch. Reasons for introducing a rule violation include the belief that the referent lies outside the boundaries of outline drawing. At their best, the rule violations are not only motivated but also apt, that is, the shape being used is an appropriate one for the referent. It may borrow from another context, like a wake behind a flying bird, or another dimension, like a motion trajectory across time being drawn as a spatial line present at one moment and offered metaphorically as the shape of a wheel's spoke. Evidence from a study on motion indicators showed that blind and sighted people understood these motion indicators in much the same way.

Young blind children will use lines for any referent, but older blind people use the lines selectively, so that some of the uses evident in sketches from children appear in the drawings from their older colleagues only in the guise of metaphors. Thus, knowing about the sketch and the intended referent is not sufficient to establish whether the line is intended literally or meta-phorically. The same problem arises in language: "A man is a machine" is not a metaphor if the speaker is a determined determinist. It is a metaphor if the speaker is an athlete who emphasizes that the body needs regular exercise. The proper classification of the vehicle of communication depends on inten-tion.

Metaphor in pictures arises with intentional violation understood as a violation. Some contend that the blind mistakenly lump together both literal and metaphoric forms of depiction, claiming that blind people treat these equally. In chapter 7, however, I argued that the blind distinguish the two means of representation and resort to the metaphoric when literal depiction is understood to be unable to show a referent. I oppose the argument that literal and metaphoric pictures are on an equal footing for the blind—that they use drawings to convey ideas but not as a way of duplicating objects. Blind people, after an early stage where anything depicts anything, seek ways of drawing objects by shapes similar to the objects—indeed, many blind people have trouble drawing from a vantage point that entails a projective shape not similar to the object's shape. Correspondingly, metaphoric variations on shapes are often understood as violations of similarity.

Occlusion depiction gives rise to problems in recognition when the direc-tion of occlusion is taken by the perceiver first one way, then the opposite way. These effects, known as figure-ground reversal (Rubin, 1915), were present for blind volunteers examining profiles depicted by lines. The implication is that haptic lines are not just taken by the blind as indicators of relief features, but rather they give rise to perceptual effects on which recognition can be based. Stick figures are also understood by the blind as they are by the sighted, in most respects, when allowance is made for vision's ability to decipher more detail in the stick figures. These studies are at present rather isolated experi-ments, and the range of application of the principles deserves attention. Figure-ground depiction is not the sole function of outline, for outline depiction includes corners, wires, and cracks. The extent to which the Rubin findings (that outline gives rise to perceptual effects that control recognition) can be applied to all the outline functions is not known, but I suggest that each and every depiction function can influence recognition, and that each function effecting recognition in vision can also influence recognition in touch.

Chapter 8 also considered some directions that seem promising given the weight of evidence on outline pictures of objects and their significance for the blind. I argue that the ability to recognize outline drawing is universal. An octave relationship may have a status in vibratory touch like the outline's affinity for relief features. Art style may be taught to the blind with as much value as it has for the sighted.

Touch allows us to understand outline drawing without our having to be taught how to use it. Therefore pictures could help the blind to communicate. Outline pictures rest on the ability of a line to depict features of relief, an ability that comes late in the analytic pathways of vision, after purely visual matters such as shape-from-shading. Perception involves elements that generate experiences, and elements are restricted in their powers to evoke experiences. The perspective geometry of the world that can be used to make outline pictures is largely the same for touch and vision, including matters of convergence, vantage point, and occlusion. Consequently, drawing development occurs in a similar way in the blind and the sighted. Metaphor can be used in pictures since it rests on class-inclusion principles that can be invoked by any system of communication. Pictures with tropes make sense to the blind since blind people appreciate that a picture can contain an intentional rule violation. These are claims about properties of the human mind—the experience in perception created by outlines, the different geometries chosen to configure the outlines, and the appreciation of class inclusion and intention. All people share these universal properties of the human mind. They experience, represent, know, and intend.

References

Appelle, S. 1991. Haptic perception of form: Activity and stimulus attributes. In M. Heller and W. Schiff, eds., *Touch perception*. Hillsdale, N.J.: Erlbaum.

Arnheim, R. 1974. *Art and visual perception: The new version*. Berkeley and Los Angeles: University of California Press.

————. 1990. Perceptual aspects of art for the blind. *Journal of Aesthetic Education* 24:57–65.

Attneave, F., and B. Benson. 1969. Spatial coding of tactual stimulation. *Journal of Experimental Psychology* 81:216–222.

Bach-y-rita, P. 1972. *Brain mechanisms in sensory substitution*. New York: Academic Press.

Bailes, S. M., and R. M. Lambert. 1986. Cognitive aspects of haptic form recognition by blind and sighted subjects. *British Journal of Psychology* 77:451–458.

Barber, P. O., and S. J. Lederman. 1988. Encoding direction in manipulatory space and the role of visual experience. *Journal of Visual Impairment and Blindness* 82:99–106.

Berbaum, K., T. Bever, and C. S. Chung. 1984. Extending the perception of shape from known to unknown shading. *Perception* 13:5–20.

Berla, E. P. 1982. Haptic perception of tangible graphic displays. In W. Schiff and E. Foulke, eds., *Tactual perception: A sourcebook*, 364–386. Cambridge: Cambridge University Press.

Biederman, I. 1987. Recognition by components: A theory of human image understanding. *Psychological Review* 94:115–145.

Bigelow, A. E. 1990. Blind and sighted children's ability to infer what others see when others look at them. Paper presented at the Canadian Psychological Association Conference, Ottawa, May 31–June 2.

Birkenshaw, L. 1965. Teaching music to deaf children. *Volta Review,* May, 352–361.

References

Blackwell, H., and H. Schlosberg. 1943. Octave generalization, pitch discrimination, and loudness thresholds in the white rat. *Journal of Experimental Psychology* 33:407–419.

Carello, C., L. Rosenblum, and A. Grosofsky. 1986. Static depiction of movement. *Perception* 15:41–58.

Caron-Pargue, J. 1979. Etudes sur les représentations du cube chez les enfants de 3 à 11 ans. Doctoral diss., University of Paris V.

———. 1985. *Le dessin du cube chez l'enfant.* Bern: Peter Lang.

Cavanagh, P. 1987. Reconstructing the third dimension: Interactions between color, texture, motion, binocular disparity and shape. *Computer Vision, Graphics and Image Processing* 37:111–195.

Cavanagh, P., and Y. G. Leclerc. 1989. Shape from shadows. *Journal of Experimental Psychology: Human Perception and Performance* 15:3–27.

Clifford, W. K. 1946. *The common sense of the exact sciences.* New York: Knopf.

Clowes, M. B. 1971. On seeing things. *Artificial Intelligence* 2:79–116.

Costall, A. 1991. Are "stage theories" of depiction *really* stage theories? Paper presented at the Sixth International Conference on Event Perception and Action, August 25–30, Free University, Amsterdam.

Costall, A., and D. Vedeler. 1992. David Katz: On touch, pictures and pictures to touch. Paper presented at American Psychological Association Conference, Washington, August 14–18.

Cox, M. V., and A. Martin. 1988. Young children's viewer-centred representations: Drawings of a cube placed inside or behind a transparent or opaque beaker. *International Journal of Behavioural Development* 11:233–245.

Critchley, M. 1953. Tactile thought with special reference to the blind. *Brain* 76:19–35.

DeLoache, J., M. Strauss, and J. Maynard. 1979. Picture perception in infancy. *Infant Behaviour and Development* 2:77–89.

DeYoe, E. A., and D. C. Van Essen. 1985. Segregation of efferent connections and receptive field properties in visual area V2 of the Macaque. *Nature* 317:58–61.

Deregowski, J. B. 1989. Real space and represented space: Cross-cultural perspectives. *Behavioral and Brain Sciences* 12:51–120.

Descartes, R. 1637. *Discourse on method, optics, geometry and meteorology.* Translated by P. J. Olscamp. Indianapolis: Bobbs-Merrill, 1965.

Dewdney, S. 1970. *Dating rock art in the Canadian Shield region.* Toronto: Royal Ontario Museum.

Dodds, A. G., C. I. Howarth, and D. C. Carter. 1982. Mental maps of the blind: The role of previous visual experience. *Journal of Visual Impairment and Blindness* 76:5–12.

Dunlea, A. 1989. *Vision and the emergence of meaning.* Cambridge: Cambridge University Press.

Epstein, W., B. Hughes, S. L. Schneider, and P. Bach-y-rita. 1989. Perceptual learning from an unfamiliar modality. *Journal of Experimental Psychology: Human Perception and Performance* 15:28–44.

Finke, R. 1989. *Principles of mental imagery.* Cambridge, Mass.: MIT Press.

References

Fraiberg, S. 1977. *Insights from the blind*. New York: Basic Books.

Freeman, N. 1980. *Strategies of representation in young children*. London: Academic Press.

Friedman, S. L., and M. B. Stevenson. 1980. Perception of movement in pictures. In M. A. Hagen, ed., *The perception of pictures*, vol. 1. New York: Academic Press.

Fussell, D., and A. Haaland. 1976. *Communicating with pictures in Nepal*. Kathmandu, Nepal: Unicef.

Gabias, P. 1987. Drawing systems: Blind and sighted adults judge developmental priority. Ph.D. diss., New York University.

Gabias, P., and J. M. Kennedy. 1984. Blind people identifying textures as representations of hard and soft surfaces. Paper presented at the Eastern Psychological Association Conference, New York, April.

Gatti, A. 1991. Studio per un codice iconico per non vedenti. Baccalaureate thesis, Milan Polytechnique, Department of Architecture.

Gibson, E. J. 1969. *Principles of perceptual learning and development*. New York: Appleton-Century-Crofts.

Gibson, J. J. 1962. Observations on active touch. *Psychological Review* 69:477–491.

———. 1966. *The senses considered as perceptual systems*. Boston: Houghton-Mifflin.

———. 1979. *The ecological approach to visual perception*. Boston: Houghton-Mifflin.

Gibson, J. J., and P. M. Yonas. 1968. A new theory of scribbling and drawing in children. In H. Levin, E. J. Gibson, and J. J. Gibson, eds., *The analysis of reading skill*. Washington, D.C.: U.S. Department of Health, Education, and Welfare, Office of Education.

Glucksberg, S., and B. Keysar. 1990. Understanding metaphorical comparisons: Beyond similarity. *Psychological Review* 97:3–18.

Golomb, C. 1981. Representation and reality: The origins and determinants of young children's drawings. *Review of Research in Visual Arts Education* 14:36–48.

———. 1990. *The child's creation of a pictorial world*. Berkeley and Los Angeles: University of California Press.

Gombrich, E. H. 1960. *Art and illusion*. Princeton: Princeton University Press.

———. 1972. The mask and the face: The perception of physiognomic likeness in life and in art. In E. H. Gombrich, J. Hochberg, and M. Black, *Art, Perception and Reality*. Baltimore: The Johns Hopkins University Press.

———. 1974. The visual image. In D. Olson, ed., *Media and symbols: The forms of expression, communication and education*. Chicago: National Society for the Study of Education.

———. 1982. *The image and the eye*. Ithaca, N.Y.: Cornell University Press.

Goodman, N. 1968. *Languages of art*. Indianapolis: Bobbs-Merrill.

Goodnow, J. 1977. *Children drawing*. Cambridge, Mass.: Harvard University Press.

Gordon, G., ed. 1978. *Active touch: The mechanism of recognition of objects by manipulation: A multidisciplinary approach*. Oxford: Pergamon Press.

Guzman, A. 1968. *Computer recognition of three-dimensional objects in a scene*. Cambridge, Mass.: MIT Technical Report MAC-TR-59.

Haber, R. N., L. R. Haber, C. A. Levin, and J. Gramata. 1988. Comparison of spatial layout knowledge in sighted and blind. Paper presented at the Psychonomic Society Conference, Chicago, November 10–12.

Halverson, J. 1992. The first pictures: Perceptual foundations of Paleolithic art. *Perception* 21:389–404.

Hayes, A. 1988. Identification of two-tone images: Some implications for high and low spatial frequency processes in human vision. *Perception* 17:429–436.

Hayes, A., and J. Ross. 1988. The visual properties of lines in line drawings. Paper presented at the 11th European Conference on Visual Perception, Bristol, August 31–September 3.

Heller, M. A. 1989. Picture and pattern perception in the sighted and blind: The advantage of the late blind. *Perception* 18:379–389.

————. 1991. Psychology of the blind. In M. A. Heller and W. Schiff, eds., *Touch perception*. Hillsdale, N.J.: Erlbaum.

Heller, M. A., and J. M. Kennedy. 1990. Perspective taking, pictures and the blind. *Perception and Psychophysics* 48:459–466.

Heller, M. A., K. D. Nesbitt, and D. K. Scrofano. 1991. Influence of writing style and categorical information on identification of tactile numbers and letters. *Bulletin of the Psychonomic Society* 29:365–367.

Herskovits, M. J. 1948. *Man and his works*. New York: Knopf.

Hochberg, J. E. 1962. The psychophysics of pictorial perception. *Audio-Visual Communication Review* 10:22–54.

Hochberg, J. E., and V. Brooks. 1962. Pictorial recognition as an unlearned ability. *American Journal of Psychology* 75:624–628.

Hollins, M. 1989. *Understanding blindness*. Hillsdale, N.J.: Erlbaum.

Hubel, D. H., and M. S. Livingstone. 1987. Segregation of form, colour and stereopsis in primate area 18. *Journal of Neuroscience* 7:3378–3415.

Huffman, D. A. 1971. Impossible objects as nonsense sentences. *Machine Intelligence* 6:295–323.

Humphrey, G. K., P. C. Dodwell, D. W. Muir, and D. E. Humphrey. 1988. Can blind infants and children use sonar sensory aids? *Canadian Journal of Psychology* 42:94–119.

Ingram, N., and G. Butterworth. 1989. The young child's representation of depth in drawing: Process and product. *Journal of Experimental Child Psychology* 47:356–369.

Ives, W., and J. Rovet. 1979. The role of graphic orientation in children's drawings of familiar and novel objects at rest and in motion. *Merrill-Palmer Quarterly* 25:281–292.

Jansson, G. 1988. What are the problems with pictures for the blind, and what can be done to solve them? In C. W. M. Magnée, F. J. M. Vlaskamp, M. Soede, and G. Butcher, eds., *Man-machine interfaces, graphics and practical applications*. London: Royal National Institute for the Blind.

Jennison, R. C. 1972. The basic science of the art of line drawing. *Perception* 1:363–364.

References

Johannson, G., and E. Borjesson. 1989. Toward a new theory of vision: Studies in wide angle space perception. *Ecological Psychology* 1:301–332.

Johansen, M. 1954. *An introductory study of voluminal form perception.* Nordisk Psykologiske Monografserie, 5.

———. 1959. *Voluminalfigurale faenomener.* Copenhagen: Munksgaard.

Johnson-Laird, P. 1989. *The computer and the mind.* Cambridge, Mass.: Harvard University Press.

Kanizsa, G. 1968. Percezione attuale, esperienza passata e "l'esperimento impossibile." In G. Kanizsa and G. Vicario, eds., *Ricerche sperimentali sulla percezione.* Trieste: Trieste University Press.

———. 1988. *Communicare per immagini: problema di lettura percettiva.* Rome: Multigrafica Editrice.

Katz, D. 1925. Der Aufbau der Tastwelt. *Zeitschrift fur Psychologie* 11.

———. 1936. A sense of touch: The technique of percussion, palpation and massage. *British Journal of Physical Medicine* 11:146–148.

———. 1946. Hur technar blinda? *Nya psykologiska stroevtag.* Stockholm: Kooperativa foerbundets bokfoerlag. Translated by D. Vedeler and A. Costall as, How do blind people draw? Unpublished manuscript. 1991.

———. 1989. *The world of touch.* Edited and translated by L. E. Krueger. Hillsdale, N.J.: Erlbaum.

Kellogg, R. 1969. *Analyzing children's art.* Palo Alto, Calif.: National Press.

Kennedy, J. M. 1974a. *A psychology of picture perception.* San Francisco: Jossey-Bass.

———. 1974b. Perception, pictures and the etcetera principle. In R. B. MacLeod and H. L. Pick, eds., *Perception: Essays in honor of J. J. Gibson.* Ithaca, N.Y.: Cornell University Press.

———. 1980. Blind people recognizing and making haptic pictures. In M. A. Hagen, ed., *The perception of pictures,* vol. 2, pp. 263–304. New York: Academic Press.

———. 1982a. Metaphor in pictures. *Perception* 11:589–605.

———. 1982b. Haptic pictures. In W. Schiff and E. Foulke, eds., *Tactual perception,* pp. 305–333. Cambridge: Cambridge University Press.

———. 1983. What can we learn about pictures from the blind? *American Scientist* 71:19–26.

———. 1988a. Outline and shape from shading: The little lines that can't. Paper presented at the Psychonomics Society Conference, Chicago, November 10–12.

———. 1988b. Line endings and subjective contours. *Spatial Vision* 3:151–158.

———. 1988c. Perspective and vantage points. Review of Kubovy, *The psychology of perspective and Renaissance art,* 1986. *Contemporary Psychology* 33:336–337.

———. 1989. Pictures to see and pictures to touch. Invited address to the American Psychological Association, divisions 1, 3, and 10. New Orleans, August 11–15.

———. 1990. Metaphor—its intellectual basis. *Journal of Metaphor and Symbolic Activity* 5:115–123.

Kennedy, J. M., and R. Domander. 1986. Blind people depicting states and events in metaphoric line drawings. *Metaphor and Symbolic Activity* 1:109–126.

References

Kennedy, J. M., and N. Fox. 1977. Pictures to see and pictures to touch. In D. Perkins and B. Leondar, eds., *The arts and cognition,* pp. 118–135. Baltimore: The Johns Hopkins University Press.

Kennedy, J. M., N. Fox, and K. O'Grady. 1972. Can "haptic pictures" help the blind see? *Harvard Graduate School of Education Bulletin* 16:22–23.

Kennedy, J. M., P. Gabias, and M. A. Heller. 1992. Space, haptics and the blind. *Geoforum* 23:175–189.

Kennedy, J. M., P. Gabias, and A. Nicholls. 1991. Tactile pictures. In M. Heller and W. Schiff, eds., *Touch perception.* Hillsdale, N.J.: Erlbaum.

Kennedy, J. M., P. Gabias, and R. Pierantoni. 1990. In K. Landwehr, ed., *Ecological perception research, visual communication and aesthetics.* New York: Springer-Verlag.

Kennedy, J. M., and A. S. Ross. 1975. Outline picture perception by the Songe of Papua. *Perception* 4:391–406.

Kennedy, J. M., and J. Silvers. 1974. The surrogate functions of lines in visual perception: Evidence from antipodal rock and cave artwork sources. *Perception* 3:313–322.

Kennedy, J. M., and W. Simpson. 1982. For each kind of figure of speech there is a pictorial metaphor: A figure of depiction. *Visual Arts Research* 16:1–11.

Kerr, N. 1983. The role of vision in visual imagery experiments: Evidence from the congenitally blind. *Journal of Experimental Psychology: General* 112:265–277.

Klatzky, R., S. Lederman, and V. Metzger. 1985. Identifying objects by touch: An "expert system." *Perception and Psychophysics* 37:299–302.

Klatzky, R. L., J. Loomis, R. Golledge, N. Fujeta, and J. W. Pellegrino. 1990. Navigation without vision by blind and sighted. Paper presented at the Psychonomic Society Conference, New Orleans, November 16–18.

Koffka, K. 1935. *Principles of gestalt psychology.* New York: Liveright.

Krueger, L. E. 1982. Tactual perception in historical perspective: David Katz's world of touch. In W. Schiff and E. Foulke, eds., *Tactual perception: A source book.* Cambridge: Cambridge University Press.

Kubovy, M. 1986. *The psychology of perspective and Renaissance art.* Cambridge: Cambridge University Press.

Landau, B., and L. R. Gleitman. 1985. *Language and experience: Evidence from the blind child.* Cambridge, Mass.: Harvard University Press.

Lederman, S. J., and R. L. Klatzky. 1987. Hand movements: A window into haptic object recognition. *Cognitive Psychology* 19:342–368.

Lederman, S. J., R. L. Klatzky, and P. Barber. 1985. Spatial and movement-based heuristics for encoding pattern information through touch. *Journal of Experimental Psychology: General* 114:33–49.

Lederman, S. J., R. L. Klatzky, C. Chataway, and C. Summers. 1990. Visual mediation and the haptic recognition of two-dimensional pictures of common objects. *Perception and Psychophysics* 47:54–64.

References

Lee, M., and G. Bremner. 1987. The representation of depth in children's drawings of a table. *Quarterly Journal of Experimental Psychology* 39A:479–496.

Livingstone, M. S., and D. H. Hubel. 1987. Psychophysics of separate visual channels. *Journal of Neuroscience* 7:3416–3468.

Loomis, J. M., and J. A. DaSilva. 1989. Accurate blind pointing to previewed targets while walking. Paper presented to the Psychonomic Society Conference, Atlanta, November 17–19.

Loomis, J. M., R. L. Klatzky, and S. J. Lederman. 1988. Similarity of tactual and visual picture recognition with limited field of view. Paper presented at a pre-conference meeting of the Psychonomics Society, Chicago, November 9.

Loomis, J. M., and S. S. Lederman. 1986. *Tactual perception*. In K. Boff, L. Kaufman, and J. Thomas, eds., *Handbook of perception and human performance*, vol. 2. New York: Wiley.

Lowenfeld, V., and W. Brittain. 1970. *Creative and mental growth*. 5th ed. New York: Macmillan.

Luquet, G. H. 1927. *Le dessin enfantin*. Paris: Delachaux et Niestle.

McCloskey, D. I., and S. C. Gandevia. 1978. Role of inputs from skin, joints and muscles and of corollary discharges, in human discrimination tasks. In G. Gordon, ed., *Active touch*. Oxford: Pergamon Press.

Magee, L., and J. M. Kennedy. 1980. Exploring pictures tactually. *Nature* 283 (5744):287–288.

Malik, J. 1987. Interpreting line drawings of curved objects. *International Journal of Computer Vision* 1:73–103.

Marr, D. 1982. *Vision: A computational investigation into the human representation and processing of visual information*. San Francisco: Freeman.

Merry, F. 1932. A further investigation to determine the value of embossed pictures for blind children. *Teachers Forum* 4:96–99.

Merry, R. 1930. To what extent can blind children recognize, tactually, simple embossed pictures? *Teachers Forum* 3:2–5.

Merry, R., and F. Merry. 1933. Tactual recognition of embossed pictures by blind children. *Journal of Applied Psychology* 17:148–163.

Millar, S. 1975. Visual experience or translation rules? Drawing the human figure by blind and sighted children. *Perception* 4:363–371.

———. 1979. The utilization of external and movement cues in simple spatial tasks by blind and sighted children. *Perception* 8:11–20.

———. 1986. Drawing as representation and image in blind children. In D. G. Russell, D. F. Marks, and J. T. E. Richardson, eds., *Imagery* 2. Human Peformance Associates, Dunedin N.Z.

———. 1991. A reverse lag in the recognition and production of tactual drawings: Theoretical implications for tactual coding. In M. A. Heller and W. Schiff, eds., *Touch perception*. Hillsdale, N.J.: Erlbaum.

Molyneux, B. 1980. Cave art. Videotaped interview. Scarborough College, University of Toronto.

307

References

Molyneux, W. 1692. *A treatise on dioptricks*. Dublin.

Mooney, C. M. 1957. Age in the development of closure ability in children. *Canadian Journal of Psychology* 11:219–226.

Moore, V. 1986. The use of a colouring task to elucidate children's drawings of a solid cube. *British Journal of Developmental Psychology* 4:335–340.

Morgan, M. J. 1977. *Molyneux's question*. Cambridge: Cambridge University Press.

Nalwa, V. S. 1988. Line drawing interpretation: A mathematical framework. *International Journal of Computer Vision* 2:103–124.

Newton, D. P. 1985. Children's perception of pictorial metaphor. *Educational Psychology* 5:179–185.

Nicholls, A. L., and J. M. Kennedy. 1990. Drawing development: From similarity to direction. Paper presented at the Canadian Psychological Association Conference, Ottawa, May 31–June 2.

———. 1991. Perception of polar and parallel projections of cubes. Paper presented at the Sixth International Conference on Event Perception and Action, August 25–30, Free University, Amsterdam.

———. 1992. Drawing development: From similarity of features to direction. *Child Development* 63:227–241.

O'Donohue, N. 1991. Blind and sighted children's reasoning in transformational geometry: Modality specific and non-specific influences. Ph.D. diss., City University of New York.

Olmer, P. 1943. *Perspective artistique*. Vol. 1. Principes et methodes. Paris: Plon.

———. 1949. *Perspective artistique*. Vol. 2. Traces pratiques. Paris: Plon.

Olson, D. R. 1988. Or what's a metaphor for? *Metaphor and Symbolic Activity* 3:215–222.

Ostad, S. A. 1989. *Mathematics through the fingertips*. Oslo: Norwegian Institute of Special Education.

Parsons, M. J. 1987. *How we understand art: A cognitive developmental account of aesthetic experience*. Cambridge: Cambridge University Press.

Perkins, D. 1972. Visual discrimination between rectangular and non-rectangular parallelepipeds. *Perception and Psychophysics* 12:396–400.

Peterson, M. A., E. M. Harvey, and H. J. Weidenbacher. 1991. Shape recognition contributions to figure-ground reversal: Which route counts? *Journal of Experimental Psychology: Human Perception and Performance* 17:1075–1089.

Petter, G. 1956. Nuove ricerche sperimentali sulla totalizzazione percettiva. *Rivista di Psicologia* 50:213–27.

Piaget, J., and B. Inhelder. 1956. *The child's conception of space*. London: Routledge and Kegan Paul.

Pirenne, M. H. 1970. *Optics, painting and photography*. Cambridge: Cambridge University Press.

Pring, L. 1987. Picture processing by the blind. *British Journal of Educational Psychology* 57:38–44.

———. 1989. Getting in touch with pictures and words: Educational strategies for the blind. *International Journal of Rehabilitation Research* 12:57–65.

References

———. In press. More than meets the eye. In R. Campbell, ed., *Mental lives*. Oxford: Blackwell.

Pring, L., and J. Rusted. 1985. Pictures for the blind: An investigation of the influence of pictures on recall of text by blind children. *British Journal of Developmental Psychology* 3:41–45.

Purcell, W. M. 1990. Tropes, transsumptio, assumptio and the redirection of studies in metaphor. *Metaphor and Symbolic Activity* 5:35–54.

Ramachandran, V. S. 1987. Visual perception of surfaces: A biological theory. In S. Petry and G. E. Meyer, eds., *The perception of illusory contours*. Berlin: Springer-Verlag.

Ratliff, F. 1971. Contour and contrast. *Proceedings of the American Philosophical Society* 115:150–163.

Revesz, G. 1950. *Psychology and art of the blind*. Translated by H. A. Wolff. London: Longmans, Green.

Rieser, J. J., D. A. Guth, and E. W. Hill. 1986. Sensitivity to perspective structure while walking without vision. *Perception* 15:173–188.

Rieser, J. J., J. J. Lockman, and H. L. Pick. 1980. The role of visual experience in knowledge of spatial layout. *Perception and Psychophysics* 28:185–190.

Rose, S. A., A. W. Gottfried, and W. H. Bridger. 1983. Infants' cross-modal transfer from solid objects to their graphic representations. *Child Development* 54:686–694.

Rubin, E. 1915. *Synsoplevede figurer*. Copenhagen: Gyldendals.

Saltzhauer-Axel, E. 1989. Teaching art styles to the blind. Paper presented at a conference on pictures and the blind, National Federation of the Blind Headquarters, Baltimore, June 9.

Sherrick, C. E., and J. C. Craig. 1982. The psychophysics of touch. In W. Schiff and E. Foulke, eds., *Tactual perception: A sourcebook*. Cambridge: Cambridge University Press.

Spelke, E. 1987. The development of intermodal perception. *Handbook of infant perception*, vol. 2, pp. 233–273. New York: Academic Press.

Stein, J. 1978. Effects of parietal lobe cooling on manipulative behaviour in the conscious monkey. In G. Gordon, ed., *Active touch*. Oxford: Pergamon Press.

Steinberg, S. 1953. The eye is a part of the mind. *Partisan Review* 20:194–212.

Street, R. F. 1935. *Gestalt completion test*. Teachers College [New York] Contributions to Education, 481.

Strelow, E. R. 1985. What is needed for a theory of mobility: Direction perception and cognitive maps—lessons from the blind. *Psychological Review* 92:226–248.

Strommen, E. 1988. A century of children drawing: The evolution of theory and research concerning the drawings of children. *Visual Arts Research* 14:13–24.

Todd, J. T., and E. Mingolla. 1983. Perception of surface curvature and direction of illumination from patterns of shading. *Journal of Experimental Psychology: Human Perception and Performance* 9:583–595.

Tulving, E. 1983. *Elements in episodic memory*. Oxford: Clarendon Press.

Van Essen, D. C. 1985. Functional organization of primate visual cortex. In A. Peters and E. G. Jones, eds., *Cerebral cortex*, vol. 3. New York: Plenum.

References

Van Sommers, P. 1984. *Drawing and cognition.* Cambridge: Cambridge University Press.

Veltman, K. H. 1986. Literature on perspective. *Marburger Jahrbuch für Kunstwissenschaft* 21:185–208.

———. 1991. *The sources of perspective.* New York: Caratzas Press.

Vicari, P. 1991. Renaissance emblematica. Paper presented at the Symposium on Visual Rhetoric, Scarborough College, University of Toronto, April 26.

Von der Heydt, R., and E. Peterhans. 1989. Mechanisms of contour perception in monkey visual cortex. 1. Lines of pattern discontinuity. *Journal of Neuroscience* 9:1731–1748.

Von Senden, M. 1960. *Space and sight.* Translated by P. Heath. Glencoe, Ill.: Free Press.

Wally, G. B. 1976. *Drawings and paintings by the blind in perspective.* La Barra, P.R.: First Museum of Blind Arts and Sciences.

Warren, D. H. 1984. *Blindness and early childhood development.* New York: American Foundation for the Blind.

Wartofsky, M. W. 1972. Pictures, representation and the understanding. In R. Rudner and I. Schiffler, eds., *Logic and art: Essays in honor of Nelson Goodman.* Indianapolis: Bobbs-Merrill.

———. 1977. Pictures and nature. Address given at Swarthmore College, Symposium on Pictures and Psychology, November.

———. 1980. Visual scenarios: The role of representation in visual perception. In M. Hagen, ed., *The perception of pictures,* vol. 2. New York: Academic Press.

White, B. W., F. A. Saunders, L. Scadden, P. Bach-y-rita, and L. L. Collins. 1970. Seeing with the skin. *Perception and Psychophysics* 7:23–27.

Whitney, H. 1955. Singularities of mappings of Euclidean spaces I: Mappings of the plane into the plane. *Annuals of Mathematics* 62:374–410.

Willats, J. 1981. What do the marks in the picture stand for? The child's acquisition of systems of transformation and denotation. *Visual Arts Research* 13:18–33.

———. 1989. What is the matter with Mary Jane's drawing? Paper presented at the National Society of Educators in the Arts, London, March.

Wilson, B. 1985. The artistic Tower of Babel: Inextricable links between culture and graphic development. *Visual Arts Research* 11:90–104.

Wilson, B., and Wilson, M. 1982a. The persistence of the perpendicular principle: Why, when and where innate factors determine the nature of drawings. *Review of Research in Visual Arts Education* 15:1–18.

———. 1982b. The case of the disappearing two-eyed profile: Or how little children influence the drawings of little children. *Review of Research in Visual Arts Education* 15:19–32.

Winner, E. 1982. *Invented worlds: The psychology of the arts.* Cambridge, Mass.: Harvard University Press.

Wolf, D. 1983. Is there graphic representation before picturing? Children's drawings between one and three years. Paper presented at the British Psychology Association Conference on Psychology and the Arts, Cardiff, September 5–9.

Zusne, L. 1970. *Visual perception of form.* New York: Academic Press.

Index

Abstract types of form, 48

Accidental discovery and drawing, 131–32

Accretion and deletion, 26

Active and passive perception, 13–15, 124

Added graphics, 223–33

African drawings (Tallensi), 270

Ambiguity: of bas-reliefs, 73, 75; of contrasts, 26; in figure-ground, 260; of motion devices, 282; and occlusion, 97; in tactile pictures, 70; and top-down input, 50; and types of form, 48

Amodal properties, 16, 18, 278

Announcing: and construction tasks, 123; in early drawing development, 134–35

Anstis, S., 30

Aristotle and metaphor, 218–20

Assembly task, 123

Australian aboriginal art, 97

Axes: of junctions, 39–43; of lines, 21–22; midway between contours, 48; off-center, 271; and physiological channels, 50–55; and shape-from-shadow, 35–38; and tactile lines, 90–91

Baldinucci, Filippo, 216

Bas-reliefs, 73–77

Bewick, Thomas, 249

Betty, blind volunteer, 61–62, 96

Bilevel pictures, 46

Blindness status, comparisons: by Heller, 67–69; by Klatzky et al., 16; by Lederman et al., 70–71

BOOST defined, 62

Brunelleschi, Filippo, 141

Categorization and metaphor, 219–20

Cave art, 32, 269–70

Cel, youngest Haitian volunteer, 155–57

Chiaroscuro: defined, 25. *See also* shape-from-shadow

Child, Jack, 227

Clifford, W. K., 10

Coding space, 209–15

Collinear contours, 41

Color change, 44

Comic books, 247–48

Communication principles, 3, 19, 153, 250–51
Composite pictures, 62
Compromise pictures, 105
Computer vision and outline, 24
Connections used in drawings by children, 138–40, 156, 158, 171, 174
Context and identification tasks: categories, 67, 83; list, 68; picture, 67; story, 62–66, 84–85
Contour: defined, 25
Contrast: defined, 25

Da Vinci, Leonardo, 25
Deafness and octaves, 272–79
Deletion and accretion, 26
Di, youngest Phoenix volunteer, 159–60
Diagrams, 153, 233–42
Dictated drawings, 135–36
Diderot, Denis: observations on the blind, 292–93
Dimensions: Lederman et al.'s classification, 71; of variation, 106–7
Disintegration: defined by Caron-Pargue, 103
Direction from a vantage point, 104, 117, 143–52, 156, 191
Dissection category of drawings, 145–47
Distal senses, 1–9
Drawing studies with the blind: cubic objects, 127–28, 173–77, 186–92; hand, 96–98; children, 155–73; glass, 99–106; moving objects, 222–33; pain, noise, wind, and smell, 233–40; volunteer's choice, 112–17; wind and wheel, 240–42
Drawing study on the sighted and a cube, 144–52
Drawing traces, 134
Duchamp, Marcel, 286

Early grouping stage, 37
Early blind defined, 63
Emblems, 220–21
Encoding specificity, 17–18, 212–13
Extension, 105, 136–37
Expression theories, 284
Errors in identification as near-misses, 59–60
Errors as intended in metaphors, 152–54, 222
Ethiopian subjects, 75, 267
Euclid, 10

Familiarity, 26, 42, 70, 124–25
Feedback, 38, 49
Fiat, 135, 153, 169
Foldout drawings: cubes and cylinders, 139; cubic objects, 186–91; disadvantages, 140; by Hal, Phoenix, 163; by Katz's subjects, 121–22; by Ros, Haiti, 158; table, 109–12
Foreground-background change, 255
Form, abstract types, 48
Fourier analysis, 46
Fractals, 27

Grice's maxim, 221

Haiti: older child, 157–59; pointing study, 193–95; recognition study, 87–89; summary of drawing study, 166–67; youngest child, 87–89
Haptics: and chain of perception, 8–15; definition, 8; and dynamics, 290–91; exploratory procedures, 14–15; and pointing, 192–98; and sensation-centered representation, 72–73; skill assessed, 14; and vibration, 13, 272–79
Harvard students, 57–60
Haut-reliefs, 73–77

Index

Impressions, local: 30, 130–31, 144, 253–61; and figure-ground, 259
Imprints, 57–61, 73–74, 103, 191
Infants, 55
Intention: and early representation, 130–32; made explicit, 240–42; and tropes, 217–22; and early representation, 130–32
Interlaminar–Thin Stripes (ITS) channel, 52
Interpolation, 53

Junctions, 22–24, 39–41, 69–70, 97–98, 106, 112, 145–52

Kathy N., 261
Kathy R., 175–78

Lu, youngest Tucson child, 163–64

Magnocellular-Thickstripe-Medial Temporal channel, 52
Manipulatory space, 196
Maplike coding, 209–15
Marking and non-marking pens, 134
Metaphor: and categorization, 219; events, 19; and humor, 232; and meaning change, 217–18; and nuance, 219–20; and pain, noise, and smell, 233–40; and pain, numbness, and motion, 279–82; in pictures, 6, 19, 152–54, 172–73; and spokes, 243–50; and style, 280; types, 217–18, 250
Motion and drawing studies: person, 222–27; wheel, 228–33; 243–49
Motion line: first example from a blind person, 115
Motion and shape-from-shadow, 29–30
Motor consequences of tracing, 134

Negatives and positives, 28–32
Nepal, 32
Norwegian subjects, 73–78

Object-centered, 199
Observer-centered, 199
Octaves, 272–79
Optic array: defined, 25
Orientation, 78–80, 141, 172, 191–92
Outline: and axis as contour, 39–40; and axis as median, 48; and axis off-center, 271–72; chiaroscuro figures, 28–30; computer vision, 24; constancy, 36; and contours, 25; and contrasts, 28; convenience of, 1–2; and emotion, 262; and evolution, 269–72; processing and axes, 35–38; and scission, 39–42, 50–53; and silhouettes, 271–72; style violations, 102–3, 117, 137–38, 155–56, 158, 160, 168; and subjective contours, 33–34, 294–95. *See also* Junctions; Perspective; Metaphor

Parietal area, 49
Parvocellular-Interblob-Pale stripes (PIP) channel, 52
Passive and active, 13–15
Pathways in vision, 34–35, 50–54
Pattern perception, 18–19, 27, 181
Perception: as ambulatory, 11–12; amodal, 16; chain of events, 8; using a medium, 11–13; and space, 16; and time, 9
Perspective: and Cal's glass, 7, 255; convergence, 5, 181–85; and cubic objects study, 186–92; and Diderot's observations, 292; drawing development theory, 140–44; drawing development study, 144–52; foreshortening, 122, 174; Hal's table, 161–72; judgment

Perspective (*continued*)
tasks, 198–205; Kathy R's cubes, 176–77; and obliques, 111–12; and parallels, 27, 117; and Pat's railroad, 296; in Piaget's three-objects task, 205–8; pointing tasks, 192–98; and Ray's glass, 100–101; and Ray's table, 109; subtense change, 181, 192–98; teaching and drawing, 122; in touch for a cube, 185; and Tracy's cubes, 127–28, 173–75; in vision fragile, 184; in vision informal, 27; in vision robust, 183

Petroglyphs, 22, 32, 67

Picture identification by touch: children from Arizona, 80–86; children from Haiti, 87–89; and figure-ground reversal, 253–26; Heller on effect of a list of referents, and advantages of the late blind, 67–70; illustrations in stories, 62–67; imprints vs. projections, 57–62; Katz on the blind identifying pictures by the blind, 71–72; Lederman et al. and Loomis et al. on two-dimensional and three-dimensional referents, 70–71; motion devices, 243–50, 279–83; orientation of the picture surface, 78–80; Ostad on training, 73–78; perceptual states, 279–82; Pring on general hints, 71; scene, 67–68; surface properties, 284–285; twig figs, 261–67

Pinhole camera, 142

Pointing tasks, 192–98, 209, 214

Polarity, 34–37

Positives and negatives, 28–32

Postural devices, 165–66, 223–40

Processing order, 34–38, 49

Profile, 61, 118–20, 129

Projections, 57–61, 71, 191–92. *See also* Perspective

Prototypes, 119, 129–30

Proverbs, 221

Proximal senses, 1, 3–5, 8

Psychophysics, 18

Puerto Rican students of Wally, 122–23

Raf, older Tucson child, 164–66

Ridges, 45

Ros, older Haitian child, 157–59

Runes, 225

Sally, studied by L. Pring, 71, 120

Scale, 17, 70, 73–76, 215

Schematic patterns, 42–45, 49. *See also* Stereotypes in drawing

Schuler, R., 274, 277

Scission, 34, 39–41, 49–55 passim

Separate-and-distinct analysis, 35

Shadow lettering, 52

Shape-from-shadow analysis 28–38, 42, 294–95

Silhouettes, 271

Skills in exploratory touch: examples, 12–14, 185; theory, 15–16, 185–85, 209–15; studies 4, 14, 15, 209, 214–15

Songe of Papua New-Guinea, 23, 32

Spatial awareness: coding 209–15; and sensory channels, 16. *See also* Perspective

Spatial frequency, 46–48

Specificity, 24, 42–45, 55, 132, 259–60, 266–67

Star table, 108–9, 200–205

Stereotypes in drawing, 119, 122, 126, 129–32

Stick figures, 96–97, 101, 115, 120–21, 162, 261–67, 270

Stories with illustrations: "Guitar"

and "Tricycle", 91–94; and study on recognition, 62–66
Street figures, 30–31
Style, 286–89. *See also* Outline
Subjective contours, 33–34, 49, 294–95
Surface: as basis of perception, 9; geometry, 2, 3, 9–11, 37; of the picture and its orientation, 78–80, 141, 191–92
Swedish subjects studied by Katz, 71–72, 120–22

Tacit knowledge, 114
Tallensi, 270
Topology, 27, 140, 156
Terminations, 23, 33–34
Texture defined, 25
Thermoforms, 73
Thickness-of-line device, 7, 100, 189–90
Three-objects (perspective-taking) Piagetian task, 205–8
Top-down processing, 48. *See also* Feedback
Touch as dynamic, 291. *See also* Haptics

Tracy's drawings, 117–19, 127–28, 173–75
Training effects: Ostad's study, 73–78, Wally's exercises, 122–23
Transduction, 37
Twig figs, 263–67

Undifferentiated activity, 134
Universals and conventions, 267–70
Updating in perception, 210–11

Vanishing points, 141
Vantage points, 11–12, 26, 100–101, 104, 106, 108–11, 126, 137, 140
Velasquez, 249
Vervaeke, John 219
Vibratory touch, 273–79

Wide-angle pictures, 27, 142
Will, 135, 154, 169–73. *See also* Fiat

X-ray style, 97

Zero-crossing, 25